MILLER'S

PREFERABLE ACCOUNTING PRINCIPLES

A COMPREHENSIVE RESTATEMENT OF THE "PREFERABLE
ACCOUNTING PRINCIPLES" CREATED BY FASB STATEMENT 32

MARTIN A. MILLER, C.P.A.

Harcourt Brace Jovanovich, Inc.
New York   Chicago   San Francisco   Atlanta   Dallas

This publication is designed to provide accurate and authoritative information in regard to the subject matter covered. It is sold with the understanding that the publisher is not engaged in rendering legal, accounting or other professional service.

The publisher has not sought nor obtained approval of this publication from any other organization, profit or non-profit, and is solely responsible for its contents.

Miller's Preferable Accounting Principles
is a trademark of Harcourt Brace Jovanovich, Inc.

Table of Contents

NONPROFIT ORGANIZATIONS

MISCELLANEOUS

Introduction

There is a presumption that once adopted, an accounting principle should not be changed in accounting for events or for transactions of a similar nature. This presumption is based on the pervasive accounting principle of consistency, which significantly contributes to the comparability of financial information.

A change in accounting principle is the result of changing from one acceptable accounting principle to another. However, a change in practice or in the method of applying an accounting principle, or practice is also considered a change in accounting principle.

FASB-32 which became effective on October 31, 1979, has created a whole new body of preferable accounting principles (PAP). Simply stated, FASB-32 specifies that the specialized accounting and reporting principles which appear in certain AICPA Statements of Position and Guides on accounting and auditing matters are *preferable accounting principles* for the purposes of justifying a change in accounting principle under APB-20 (Accounting Changes).

The following Industry Audit Guides and one Statement of Position (SOP) were expressly excluded from FASB-32 because they, in the opinion of the FASB, do not contain any specialized accounting and/or reporting principles:

1. SOP 75-4, Presentation and Disclosure of Financial Forecasts
2. The Auditor's Study and Evaluation of Internal Control in EDP Systems
3. Audits of Service-Center-Produced Records
4. Computer Assisted Audit Techniques
5. Medicare Audit Guide

In addition, FASB-32 also excludes the Industry Audit Guide entitled "Audits of State and Local Governmental Units", and SOP 75-3 (Accruals of Revenues and Expenditures by State and Local Governmental Units). The reason for the exclusion of these specific publications from FASB-32 was that the FASB decided to defer action on exercising responsibilities for specialized accounting principles and reporting practices for state and local governments. The FASB recognized the fact that the National Council on Governmental Accounting (NCGA) and the AICPA were presently setting accounting standards and practices for governmental units.

FASB-32 also states that future Statements of Position and Guides on accounting and auditing matters, if acceptable to the

FASB and after appropriate due process, may become additional preferable accounting principles (PAP).

A clear understanding of PAP is absolutely necessary. Some PAP are merely the application of existing GAAP to specialized circumstances. However, many PAP are clearly new principles that are apparently equivalent to promulgated GAAP. The latter category of PAP are probably the most difficult to comprehend. Included in this last category are the PAP which violate or contradict existing GAAP. A good example of this latter category is the practice of commercial banks to capitalize only the par value of a stock dividend while existing GAAP require that the fair value be capitalized. The PAP on commercial banks allow the capitalization of the par value of the stock dividend!

Unfortunately, most of the publications in which this new body of principles appear, were primarily developed and prepared for other purposes. Thus, several of these publications have few, or no PAP at all. The result is that this new body of principles is widely disbursed throughout these various publications and is difficult, at best, to locate.

With the advent of FASB-32, an enterprise making a change in an accounting principle, must now have to determine whether an alternative preferable principle exists in any of these many different publications. This seemed to me to be an arduous, if not impossible task, and I decided that a great deal of utility would result from a publication which contained a compilation of all of these newly created accounting principles, grouped together by topic, and restated in plain everyday language. Thus, evolved this book . . .

Each publication covered by FASB-32 has been carefully reviewed to extract this new body of PAP into one meaningful document. The utmost care has been exercised in restating these principles, so that they can be easily comprehended. Illustrations are used generously to demonstrate the applicability of specific concepts and observation paragraphs are utilized to stress important information.

Most of the publications covered by FASB-32 have not been recently updated and apparent errors are brought to the reader's attention in observation paragraphs.

Several innovative indexes have been provided to increase the utility of this book and to assist the reader in locating specific information.

Martin A. Miller

Cross-Reference

ORIGINAL PRONOUNCEMENTS TO PREFERABLE
ACCOUNTING PRINCIPLES (PAP) CHAPTERS

The accounting standards division and the auditing standards division of the AICPA issue Statements of Position (SOP), Industry Accounting Guides, and Industry Audit Guides, in an attempt to influence, clarify and recommend changes in accounting standards. The publications listed below were specifically enumerated in FASB Statement-32 as containing preferable accounting principles (PAP).

This locator provides instant cross-reference between an original AICPA publication that contains preferable accounting principles and the chapter(s) in this publication where such pronouncement appears. Original pronouncements are listed chronologically by classification on the left and the chapter(s) in which the pronouncement appears in this publication on the right.

STATEMENTS OF POSITION

ORIGINAL PRONOUNCEMENT	PAP CHAPTER REFERENCE
SOP 74-6	
Recognition of Profit on Sales of Receivables with Recourse	Sales of Receivables with Recourse,p. 19
SOP 74-8	
Financial Accounting and Reporting by Colleges and Universities	Colleges and Universities, p.375
SOP 74-11	
Financial Accounting and Reporting by Face Amount Certificate Companies	Investment Companies, p. 191
SOP 74-12	
Accounting practices in the Mortgage Banking Industry	Mortgage Banking Industry, p. 165
SOP 75-1	
Revenue Recognition When Right of Return Exists	Recognizing Revenue When Right of Return exists, p. 11

SOP 75-2

Accounting Practices of Real Estate Investment Trusts

Real Estate Investment Trusts, p. 65

SOP 75-5

Accounting Practices in the Broadcasting Industry

Broadcasting Industry, p. 293

SOP 75-6

Questions Concerning Profit Recognition on Sales of Real Estate

Profit Recognition on Real Estate Transactions, p. 37

SOP 76-1

Accounting Practices in the Record and Music Industry

Record and Music Companies, p. 333

SOP 76-2

Accounting for Origination Costs and Loan and Commitment Fees in the Mortgage Banking Industry

Mortgage Banking Industry, p. 165

SOP 76-3

Accounting Practices for Certain Employee Stock Ownership Plans

Employee Stock Ownership Plans, p. 501

SOP 77-1

Financial Accounting and Reporting by Investment Companies

Investment Companies, p. 191

SOP 78-1

Accounting by Hospitals for Certain Marketable Equity Securities

Hospitals, p. 403

SOP 78-2

Accounting Practices of Real Estate Investment Trusts

Real Estate Investment Trusts, p. 65

SOP 78-3

Accounting for Costs to Sell and Rent, and Initial Rental Operations of Real Estate Projects

Costs to Sell and Rent Real Estate Projects, p. 53

SOP 78-4

Application of the Deposit, Installment, and Cost Recovery Methods in Accounting for Sales of Real Estate

Profit Recognition on Real Estate Transactions, p. **37**

SOP 78-5

Accounting for Advance Refunding of Tax-Exempt Debt

Advance Refundings of Tax-Exempt Debt, p. **25**

SOP 78-6

Accounting for Property and Liability Insurance Companies

Property and Liability Insurance Companies, p. **211**

SOP 78-7

Financial Accounting and Reporting by Hospitals Operated by a Government Unit

Hospitals, p. **403**

SOP 78-8

Accounting for Product Financing Arrangements

Product Financing Arrangements, p. **17**

SOP 78-9

Accounting for Investments in Real Estate Ventures

Investments in Real Estate Ventures, p. **57**

SOP 78-10

Accounting Principles and Reporting Practices for Certain Non-Profit Organizations

Certain Nonprofit Organizations, p. **439**

SOP 79-1

Accounting for Municipal Bond Funds

Investment Companies, p. **191**

SOP 79-2

Accounting for Cable Television Companies

Cable Television Companies, p. **275**

SOP 79-3

Accounting for Investments of Stock Life Insurance Companies

Stock Life Insurance Companies, p. **227**

SOP 79-4

Accounting for Motion Picture Films   Motion Picture Films, p. 311

SOP 80-1

Accounting for Title Insurance Companies   Title Insurance Companies, p. 259

INDUSTRY ACCOUNTING GUIDES

ORIGINAL PRONOUNCEMENTS	PAP CHAPTER REFERENCE
Accounting for Franchise Fee Revenue (1973)	Franchise Fee Revenue, p. 13
Accounting for Motion Picture Films (1973)	Motion Picture Films, p. 311
Accounting for Profit Recognition on Sales of Real Estate (1973)	Profit Recognition on Real Estate Transactions, p. 37
Accounting for Retail Land Sales (1973)	Retail Land Sales, p. 71

INDUSTRY AUDIT GUIDES

ORIGINAL PRONOUNCEMENTS	PAP CHAPTER REFERENCE
Audits of Banks (1969)	Commercial Banks, p. 87
Audits of Brokers and Dealers in Securities (1973)	Securities Brokers and Dealers, p. 451
Audits of Colleges and Universities (1973)	Colleges and Universities, p. 375
Audits of Construction Contractors (1965)	Construction Contractors, p. 341
Audits of Employee Health and Welfare Benefit Funds (1972)	Employee Health and Welfare Benefit Funds, p. 493
Audits of Finance Companies (1973)	Finance Companies, p. 137
Audits of Fire and Casualty Insurance Companies (1966)	Property and Liability Insurance Companies, p. 211
Audits of Government Contractors (1975)	Government Contractors, p. 365
Audits of Investment Companies (1973)	Investment Companies, p. 191
Audits of Personal Financial Statements (1973)	Personal Financial Statements, p. 485

Audits of Stock Life Insurance Companies (1972)	Stock Life Insurance Companies, p. **227**
Audits of Voluntary Health and Welfare Organizations (1974)	Voluntary Health and Welfare Organizations, p. **421**
Hospital Audit Guide (1972)	Hospitals, p. **403**

AUDIT AND ACCOUNTING GUIDES

ORIGINAL PRONOUNCEMENT	PAP CHAPTER REFERENCE
Savings and Loan Associations	Savings and Loan Associations, p. **103**

PREFERABLE ACCOUNTING PRINCIPLES

APPLICABLE TO ALL INDUSTRIES

RECOGNIZING REVENUE WHEN RIGHT OF RETURN EXISTS

Overview

Statement of Position 75-1 (SOP 75-1) contains the preferable accounting principles that should be followed in recognizing revenue in certain sales transactions in which the buyer has the right to return previously purchased property to the seller. SOP 75-1 applies to those situations in which personal property may be returned because of existing industry practice, or as a result of contractual agreement. SOP 75-1 does not cover real estate or lease transactions and is silent on its coverage of regulated industries. However, in accordance with the Addendum to APB-2, companies in regulated industries should comply with SOP 75-1.

Background

The realization principle requires that revenue be earned before it is recognized. Revenue is usually recognized when the earning process is complete and an exchange has taken place (APB Statement-4). The earning process is not complete until collection of the sales price is reasonably assured (APB-10).

It is common practice in some industries for dealers and distributors of personal property to have the right to return unsold merchandise. The right to return merchandise is usually an industry practice but also occurs as a result of a contractual agreement. The return period can last for a few days, as in the perishable food industry, or can last for several years, which is not infrequent for some types of publishers. The rate of return of some publishers may be as high as 60%, while in other industries such as perishable foods, the rate of return may be insignificant.

As long as a right to return exists and the returns can be significant, the seller is exposed to reacquiring the ownership of the

✦ property. In other words, the risks and rewards of ownership are not, in substance, passed on to the buyer.

Since the earning process is not complete until collection of the sales price is reasonably assured, certain accounting problems arise in recognizing revenue when the right to return exists.

Revenue Recognition for Returnable Merchandise

SOP 75-1 contains the preferable accounting principles for recognizing revenue when the right of return exists. However, all of the ordinary tests for recognizing a sale under GAAP must be met before applying the preferable accounting principles.

In order to recognize a sale with a right of return, all of the following provisions must be met:

1. The price between the seller and the buyer is substantially fixed, or determinable.
2. The seller has received full payment, or the buyer is indebted to the seller and payment is not in anyway excused until the merchandise is resold.
3. Physical destruction, damage, or theft of the merchandise would not change the buyer's obligation to the seller.
4. The buyer has economic substance, and is not a front, straw party, or conduit, existing for the benefit of the seller.
5. No significant obligations exist for the seller to help the buyer resell the merchandise.
6. A reasonable prediction can be made on the amount of future returns.

All of the above provisions must be met before revenue is recognized when a right of return exists. Also, a provision must be made for any costs or losses which may occur in connection with the return of any merchandise.

After the return privilege has substantially expired, the seller may recognize as revenue any remaining balance which was initially set aside for future returns.

Where merchandise returns are significant, financial statements should disclose the amount of gross sales and the accounting policies covering merchandise returns.

FRANCHISE FEE REVENUE

Overview

The industry accounting guide entitled "Accounting for Franchise Fee Revenue", (hereinafter referred to as Franchise Fee Guide), is devoted solely to the accounting problems of the party granting the franchise (franchisor).

In brief, a franchise agreement usually transfers certain rights (the franchise), which are owned by the franchisor, to a franchisee. The rights transferred for a specified period may include the use of patents, secret processes, trade-marks and trade names. Payment for the franchise rights may include an initial franchise fee and/or continuing fees or royalties. The agreement should also provide for any continuing services which are to be rendered by the franchisor, and any inventory or purchases which may be required of the franchisee. In addition, the franchise agreement should clearly set forth the procedure for cancellation, resale, or reacquisition of the franchise by the franchisor.

Conventional accounting practices and methods, including existing promulgated GAAP should be used in accounting for franchise revenue. However, the timing and classification of franchise revenues and the association of franchise costs to related franchise revenues, may create unique accounting problems which are discussed in this chapter.

Revenue Recognition of Initial Franchise Fees

The two major accounting problems in revenue recognition of initial franchise fees are (1) the time the fee is properly regarded as earned, and (2) the assurance of collectibility of any receivable resulting from unpaid portions of the initial fee.

> *OBSERVATION: These accounting problems are not unique to franchise accounting and merely represent a rehash of the basic realization of revenue principle. The realization principle requires that revenue be earned before it is recorded. GAAP*

require that the realization of revenue be recognized in the accounting period in which the earning process is substantially completed and an exchange has taken place (APB Statement 4). In addition, revenue is usually recognized at the amount established by the parties to the exchange except for transactions in which collection of the receivable is not reasonably assured (APB Statement 4). In the event that collection of the receivable is not reasonably assured, the installment method or cost recovery method may be used (APB-10).

The Franchise Fee Guide continues with the following statement:
"The usual sale of a franchise is linked to certain conditions, such as performance of certain services, which affect the consummation of the transaction in much the same way as delivery, installation, or meeting certain qualitative specifications affect the consummation of a conventional sale of equipment".

The concluding recommendation of the Franchise Fee Guide, as to the timing of revenue recognition on initial franchise fees, is that revenue should be recognized on the consummation of the transaction, which occurs when all material conditions of the sale have been substantially performed. Substantial performance by the franchisor occurs when the following conditions are met:

1. The franchisor is not obligated in any way (trade practice, law, intent, or agreement) to excuse payment of any unpaid notes or to refund any cash already received.
2. The initial services required of the franchisor by contract or otherwise, have been substantially performed.
3. All other conditions have been met which affect the consummation of the sale.

The other accounting problem which the Franchise Fee Guide raises in connection with revenue recognition of initial franchise fees is the collectibility of any receivable resulting from unpaid portions of the initial fee. Several specific circumstances are cited which could make the determination of collectibility a difficult matter. The circumstances are as follows:

1. Payment of unpaid franchise notes by the franchisee may depend upon future events or the capitalization of the franchise.

2. The credit standing of the franchisee may be affected by its business inexperience.
3. Legal council may be required to interpret uncertainties in franchise agreements which could affect collectibility of any unpaid balances.
4. Investigation of the credit standing of guarantors or others may be necessary.

The final determination of collectibility is a matter of using reasonable estimates and judgment.

In the event that the continuing franchise fees appear to be insufficient to cover the costs and normal profit of the franchisor for the continuing services required by the franchise agreement, a portion of the initial franchise fee, if any, should be deferred as appropriate, and amortized over the period in which continuing services will be provided by the franchisor.

If the collection of unpaid amounts of the initial franchise fee is not reasonably assured of collectibility, the installment method, or the cost recovery method, should be used to recognize revenue.

OBSERVATION: In essence, the Franchise Fee Guide concludes that the recognition of revenue from initial franchise fees should be accounted for under existing GAAP.

Other Matters

The balance of the Franchise Fee Guide is devoted to specific problems, all of which are to be accounted for under existing GAAP. Thus, no new *preferable accounting principles* are established. The specific problems covered in the remainder of the Franchise Fee Guide are:

1. Related party transactions and intercompany eliminations may arise in a franchise transaction.
2. Noninterest bearing notes which require the application of APB-21 (Interest on Receivables and Payables) may arise in a franchise transaction.
3. Commingled revenues
4. Continuing franchise fees
5. Continuing product sales
6. Agency sales

7. Matching of costs and revenue
8. Cancellation of the original franchise sale.
9. Franchise acquired in a business combination to be accounted for under APB-16 (Business Combinations).
10. Disclosure of pertinent franchise information.

PRODUCT FINANCING ARRANGEMENTS

Overview

Statement of Position 78-8 (SOP 78-8) deals with product financing arrangements. Product financing arrangements usually provide for one entity to obtain inventory or product for another entity (the sponser), which agrees to purchase the inventory or product at specific prices over a specific period. The agreed upon prices to be paid for the inventory or product, by the sponser, usually includes financing and holding costs. The following are a few of the more common types of product financing arrangements:

1. A sponsor sells inventory or product to another entity and in a related arrangement agrees to buy the inventory or product back.
2. Another entity agrees to purchase a product or inventory for a sponsor who in a related arrangement agrees to buy the product or inventory from the other entity.
3. A sponsor by arrangement controls the product or inventory purchased or held by another entity.

In all of the above arrangements the sponser agrees to purchase, over a specified period, the product or inventory from the other entity at prearranged prices. The substance of a product financing arrangement, regardless of its legal form, reflects a financing arrangement and not a sale or purchase by the sponsor. Thus, the substance of these type arrangements must be carefully examined to determine the appropriate accounting recognition. SOP 78-8 contains the preferable accounting principles for product financing arrangements and similar agreements.

SOP 78-8 expressly covers nonprofit organizations which present financial statements in accordance with GAAP, and does not alter any of the provisions of SOP 75-1 (Revenue Recognition when a Right to Return Exists).

Preferable Accounting Principles

An arrangement that, in substance, contains the characteristics of a product financing arrangement, shall be accounted for by the sponser of such an arrangement, as follows:

1. If another entity buys a product from a sponser and in a related arrangement agrees to sell the product, or a processed product containing the original product, back to the sponser, no sale should be recorded and the product should remain as an asset on the sponser's books. Also, the sponser should record a liability in the amount of the proceeds received from the other entity under the provisions of the product financing arrangement.

   Product financing arrangements are in substance a method of financing a product and should not be recorded as a sale and repurchase by the sponser.

2. If another entity buys a product for a sponser's benefit and the sponser agrees, in a related arrangement, to buy the product, or a processed product containing the original product, back from the other entity, an asset and the related liability should be recorded by the sponser at the time the other entity acquires the product.

Excluding processing costs, the difference between the regular product cost which the sponser would have paid if there was no product financing arrangement, and the cost that the sponser actually pays under the terms of the product financing arrangement, should be accounted for by the sponser as financing and holding costs. These financing and holding costs should be recorded on the books of the sponser in accordance with its regular accounting policies for such costs, even though the costs are incurred and paid directly by the other entity.

SALES OF RECEIVABLES WITH RECOURSE

Overview

SOP 74-6 covers the *preferable accounting principles* on the recognition of profit on sales of receivables with recourse. This SOP expressly applies to financial statements which present financial position, changes in financial position, and results of operations, in conformity with GAAP. Both unregulated companies and regulated companies must comply with SOP 74-6.

Receivables are frequently sold to financial institutions by business enterprises to raise cash. When receivables are sold on a recourse basis, the purchaser usually has a contractual right to demand payment from the seller in the event of default by the debtor. Upon receipt of payment for the defaulted receivable, the purchaser returns the defaulted receivable to the seller.

There are many different types of arrangements that are employed in the sale of receivables. Factoring is a process by which a company can convert its receivables into cash by assigning them to a factor either with or without recourse. "With recourse" means that the assignee can return the receivable to the company and get back the funds paid if the receivable turns out to be uncollectible. "Without recourse" means that the assignee assumes the risk of any losses on collections. Under factoring arrangements, the customer may or may not be notified. Pledging is the process whereby the company uses existing accounts receivable as collateral for a loan. The company retains title to the receivables but pledges that it will use the proceeds from the receivables to pay the loan.

One type of recourse arrangement for the sale of receivables provides for the purchaser to retain a percentage of the total amount paid for the receivables. These safety cushions retained by the purchaser until the receivables are collected are called "hold backs" or "dealers' reserves". The agreement for the sale of receivables may contain a provision for the purchaser to automatically charge defaulted receivables to the "reserve" account. Any amount remaining in the reserve account after all, or a specified percentage, of the receivables have been collected, is then remitted to the seller.

The actual collection and dunning function to collect all of the receivables is called "servicing". The sale agreement for the receivables should specify whether the seller will continue servicing the receivables or whether the purchaser will assume the servicing function. A "servicing fee" for either the seller or purchaser may be stipulated in the agreement. If a servicing fee is not included in the agreement of sale, the ultimate price paid for the receivables will, no doubt, provide for the additional costs involved in servicing the receivables.

The face amount of a receivable may include amounts for unperformed portions of executory contracts, such as a contract to repair and maintain the property purchased. For example, a $600 receivable for a washing and drying machine may include a $100 contract to provide maintenance of the appliance for a specified period. Unused portions of executory contracts are frequently refundable to the buyer in the event of cancellation, or default. Thus, the purchaser of receivables will take executory contracts into consideration when determining the amount that is paid for the related receivable.

Differential

When a receivable is sold, there is almost always a difference between the total amount of the receivable and the amount for which the receivable is sold. This difference represents the gross profit that the purchaser will make on the receivable, assuming entire receivable is collected. SOP 74-6 refers to this difference as the "differential", which is illustrated in the following example.

Original sale price of property	$2,500
Insurance premiums for 3 years	75
Maintenance contract for 3 years	150
Total	$2,725
Less: Down payment	725
Balance to be financed over 3 years	$2,000
Add: Finance charges @ 15% per year	900
Total amount of receivable (payable at $80.55 per month for 35 mos. plus one payment at $80.56)	$2,900
Receivable sold to yield 12% to purchaser (PV of $2,900 @ 12% for 36 mos.)	$2,027
Computation of Differential:	
Total amount to be collected	$2,900
Less: Amount paid for receivable	2,027
Total	$ 873
Less: Executory contracts	225
Differential	$ 648

The differential is always equal to the total amount to be collected on the receivable, less the amount paid for the receivable by the purchaser, and less any amounts included in the receivable for executory contracts. The reason why amounts for executory costs are deducted to arrive at the "differential" is that they have already been paid, or will be paid, by the seller. The "differential" is computed to determine the cost to the seller for selling the receivable. Thus, it is equal to the total amount that will be collected from the debtor, less the amount paid for the receivable, by the purchaser.

The "differential" represents a cost to the seller, and a gross profit to the purchaser.

Recognition of Profit

Sales of receivables with recourse do not relieve the seller of the continuing risk that the debtor will default and the seller will have to pay the purchaser of the receivable, as called for by the recourse provision of the contract. In terms of GAAP, the earning process is not completed in a sale of receivables with recourse.

> *OBSERVATION:* The *"realization"* principle requires that revenue be earned before it is recorded. GAAP require that the realization of revenue be recognized in the accounting period in which the earning process is substantially completed and an exchange has taken place (APB Statement 4). In addition, revenue is usually recognized at the amount established by the parties to the exchange except for transactions in which collection of the receivable is not reasonably assured (APB Statement 4). In the event that collection of the receivable is not reasonably assured, the installment method or cost recovery method may be used (APB-10).

SOP 74-6 states a preference for the "delayed recognition method" for recognizing profit on the sale of receivables with recourse. The delayed recognition method requires that the "differential" be broken down into its two elements; interest expense and interest income. The interest income element is the interest charged the debtor on the financed balance. The interest expense element is the interest charged by the purchaser of the receivable. The difference between the interest income element and the interest expense element is the "differential".

The interest expense element should be charged to expense by the use of a constant rate of interest applied to the outstanding balance of all recourse receivables at the beginning of each period. This method is usually referred to as the "interest method".

The amortization of the interest income element should take into consideration the costs and diminishing risks of the seller. Again, the "interest method" may produce the desired results. SOP 74-6 permits the use of the "interest method" for amortizing the interest income element and also permits the use of three other methods commonly used by finance companies and financial institutions. The three other methods are (1) the effective yield method (also known as "Rule of 78's" or "sum-of digits method"), (2) the pro-rata collection method on a straight-line basis (also known as the "liquidation method"), and (3) the fixed percentage method.

Effective Yield Method amortizes the interest income in declining amounts in relation to receivable collections. The sum-of-digits method is used, but costs incurred equally over the amortization period are not matched with the declining amounts of interest income.

Pro-Rata Collection Method amortizes the interest income on a straight-line basis, in relation to the amount of collections received.

Fixed Percentage Method amortizes the interest income each month to a set percentage of the related receivable balances. This method does not match costs and related revenue, unless the set percentage is adjusted at frequent intervals.

> ***OBSERVATION:*** *The above methods are described more fully in the Chapter on Finance Companies.*

The "delayed recognition method" of recognizing the "differential" emphasizes the financing aspects of a sale of receivables with recourse, rather than recognizing an outright sale. Thus, the "differential" is taken into income in a systematic manner over the period of the receivables sold. Any allowance account for uncollectibles, remains on the books of the seller after the receivables are sold with recourse. During the collection period of the receivables, the allowance for uncollectibles is charged with defaulted accounts and after all of the receivables are fully collected, the allowance account is removed from the seller's books.

A negative "differential" will occur when receivables are sold at a higher interest rate than is being charged on the receivables. SOP 74-6 states that the rationale for the "delayed recognition method" still prevails in accounting for negative "differentials".

> ***OBSERVATION:*** *SOP 74-6 is silent on providing for losses in the case of negative "differentials". It seems unwise to amortize a net loss to income over the period that the receivables will be collected. Thus, the loss should probably be accounted for under the provisions of FASB-5 (Contingencies).*

SOP 74-6 recognizes that practical problems will be encountered where the "delayed recognition method" is applied to those situations where recourse to the seller is limited to a specific maximum, such as a dealer's reserve. Thus, if it is not practical to breakdown the "differential" into the interest expense element and the interest income element, the "differential" may be amortized to income as the risks of the seller are diminished.

Direct costs related to the sale of receivables with recourse may be deferred and amortized on a basis which will match such costs with their related revenue.

Disclosure

Sales of receivables with recourse should be disclosed as contingencies (FASB-5), and the nature and amount of the receivables sold with recourse during the period should be disclosed along with all other pertinent facts. In addition, the amount of "dealer reserves" and its related provisions should also be disclosed.

SOP 74-6 also expressly requires that the company's disclosure of accounting policies include a statement setting forth the treatment of sales of receivables with recourse.

ADVANCE REFUNDING OF TAX-EXEMPT DEBT

Overview

There are several reasons why an issuer may want to refund tax-exempt debt. First of all, an issuer may want to consolidate several small bond issues into one larger issue. Another reason for refunding of tax-exempt debt is an increase in the credit rating of the issuer. However, the most important reason for refundings of tax-exempt debt is lower interest rates.

Tax-exempt debt is repaid from different financial sources ranging from very secure (revenue bonds) to completely unsecured (general obligations bonds). The more secure that the revenue stream is for the repayment of debt, the lower the risk is to an investor.

In a direct refunding, the proceeds from the new debt are immediately applied to retiring the old debt and only the new debt remains outstanding. The revenue stream for repayment of the old debt, if any, becomes the revenue stream for the repayment of the new debt. A refunding is all made possible by the "call provision" in the old debt, which enables the issuer to retire the old debt before its initial maturity date. However, in most cases, the issuer must pay a "call premium" to retire the old debt prior to its maturity date. The rating of the bonds in a refunding is not usually changed, unless the financial condition of the issuer has improved to warrant a rating upgrade.

A defeasance provision in a bond allows the issuer to legally satisfy the debt and obtain a release of lien without necessarily retiring the debt. Most of the recent tax-exempt bond issues contain defeasance provisions.

When a refunding is desired because of lower interest rates or some other reason, the old debt may not be callable for several years. This is the usual circumstance for an advance refunding. In an advance refunding, a new debt issue is sold to replace the old debt issue that cannot be called. The proceeds from the sale of the new debt are used to purchase high grade investments which are placed in an escrow account. The earnings from the investments in the escrow account are used to pay any interest and/or principal payments up to the date that the old debt can be called. On the call date of the old debt, whatever is left in the escrow account is used to pay the call premium, if any, and all remaining principal and interest due on the old debt. While waiting for the call date to arrive, the new debt takes the place of the old debt.

Section 103 of the Internal Revenue Code (arbitrage rules) limits the amount of yield that can be realized on the proceeds of the new tax-exempt debt to the actual yield of the new debt. In other words, if the new tax-exempt debt has a yield of 6%, the earnings on the proceeds from the sale of the new debt cannot exceed 6%. The consequence is the interest on the new tax-exempt debt loses its tax-exempt status and becomes fully taxable to the holder. To avoid this status, most issuers invest the proceeds from the new tax-exempt debt in U. S. Treasury obligations that yield an interest rate not in excess of that of the new tax-exempt debt.

The three methods used for advance refunding of tax-exempt debt are (1) net advance refunding (standard defeasance), (2) full cash advance refunding (full cash defeasance), and (3) crossover advance refunding (crossover method).

In a net advance refunding, enough funds are made available at the call date to pay the call premium, if any, and all interest and principal on the old debt. The available funds may consist of the proceeds from the new debt and additional cash deposited by the issuer, plus the income earned on the proceeds and additional cash. The following illustrates the mechanics of a net advance refunding:

```
┌─────────────────────────┐        ┌─────────────────────────────┐
│ CURRENT PROJECT REVENUES,│        │                             │
│   TAX COLLECTIONS, OR    │───────▶│  ADVANCE REFUNDING BONDS    │
│  LEASE RENTAL PAYMENTS   │        │                             │
└─────────────────────────┘        └─────────────────────────────┘
                                                  │
                                            Proceeds
                                           Invested in
        THE OLD BONDS                            │
   ┌──────────────────────┐        ┌─────────────┴───────────────┐
   │       SERIAL         │        │                             │
   │      PRINCIPAL       │        │        ESCROWED             │
   │    REQUIREMENTS       │        │       SECURITIES            │
   │      BEFORE          │        │         WITH                │
   │     CALL DATE        │◀───────│        CORRE-               │
   │   PRINCIPAL AT       │        │       SPONDING              │
   │   CALL DATE AND      │        │       PRINCIPAL             │
   │   CALL PREMIUMS      │        │       MATURITIES            │
   └──────────────────────┘        └─────────────────────────────┘
   ┌──────────────────────┐        ┌─────────────────────────────┐
   │     INTEREST         │        │                             │
   │   REQUIREMENTS       │◀───────│        INTEREST             │
   │  (Before Call Date)  │        │         EARNED              │
   └──────────────────────┘        └─────────────────────────────┘
```

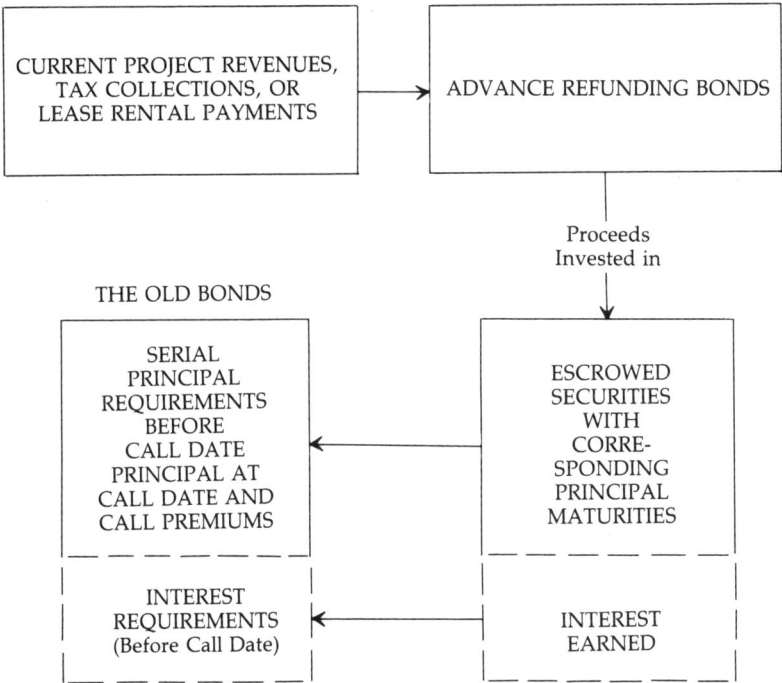

In a full cash advance refunding, enough funds are made available at the call date to pay the call premium, if any, and all interest and principal on the old debt. The available funds usually consist of the net proceeds of both revenue and special obligation bonds, plus additional cash deposited by the issuer, if required. The revenue bonds and special obligation bonds are issued concurrently. The special obligation bonds are issued with a shorter maturity date than the revenue bonds and generally bear a lower rate of interest. The proceeds from the revenue bonds, special obligation bonds, and additional cash deposited by the issuer, if required, are placed in trust to retire the old debt at the call date. However, the income realized from the proceeds placed in trust is used to service and retire the special obligation bonds. Thus, the proceeds must earn a sufficient amount to pay the periodic interest on the special obligation bonds and to eventually pay the principal balance at maturity. The following illustrates a full cash advance refunding:

```
┌──────────────────────────────┐   ┌────────────┐ ┌────────────┐
│  CURRENT PROJECT REVENUES,    │   │  ADVANCE   │ │  SPECIAL   │
│  TAX COLLECTIONS, OR          │──▶│  REFUNDING │ │ OBLIGATION │
│  LEASE RENTAL PAYMENTS        │   │   BONDS    │ │   BONDS    │
└──────────────────────────────┘   └────────────┘ └────────────┘
```

Proceeds
Invested in

THE OLD BONDS

```
┌──────────────────────┐          ┌──────────────────────┐
│  SERIAL PRINCIPAL     │          │                      │
│  REQUIREMENTS         │          │                      │
│  AND PRINCIPAL AT     │          │     ESCROWED         │
│  CALL DATE WITH       │◀─────────│  SECURITIES WITH     │
│  CALL PREMIUMS        │          │  CORRESPONDING       │
│                       │          │    PRINCIPAL         │
│ ─ ─ ─ ─ ─ ─ ─ ─ ─     │          │   MATURITIES         │
│                       │          │                      │
│     INTEREST          │          │                      │
│   REQUIREMENTS        │          │                      │
│  (Before Call Date)   │          │ ─ ─ ─ ─ ─ ─ ─ ─ ─    │
│                       │          │                      │
└ ─ ─ ─ ─ ─ ─ ─ ─ ─ ─ ─           │   INTEREST EARNED    │
                                   └ ─ ─ ─ ─ ─ ─ ─ ─ ─ ─ ─
```

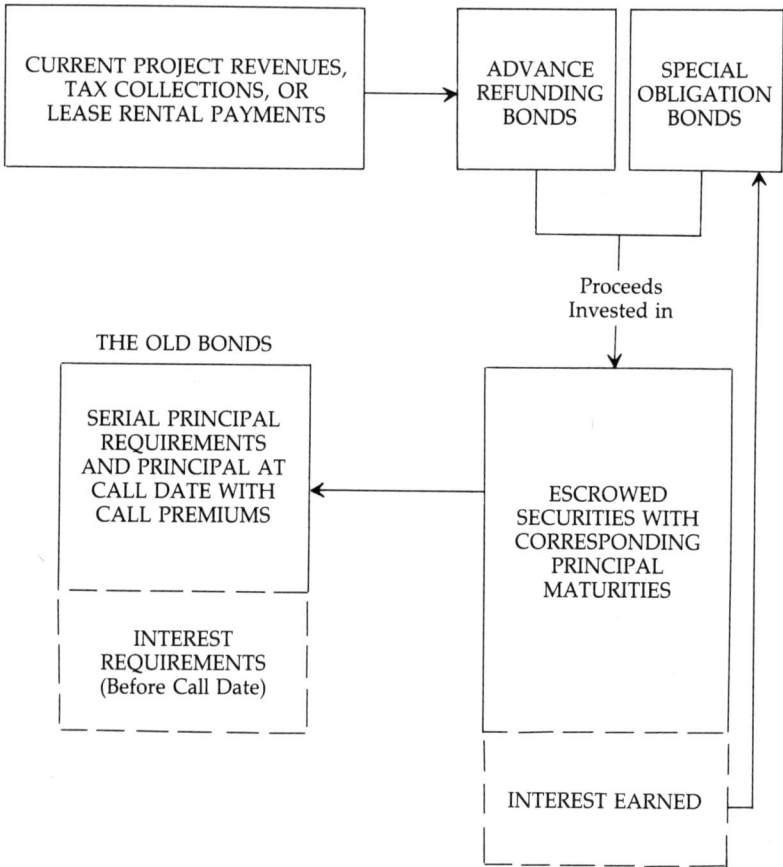

In a crossover advance refunding enough funds are made available at the crossover date to pay the call premium, if any, and all interest and principal on the old debt. The available funds may consist of the same type and sources as that for a net advance refunding. However, prior to the crossover date, the proceeds from the new debt represents collateral for the new debt, and the issuer services the old debt until the crossover date, at which time, the proceeds from the new debt are then used to retire the old debt. After the crossover, the issuer services the new debt. At the time of the crossover advance refunding the old debt is never defeased. The following illustrates a crossover advance refunding:

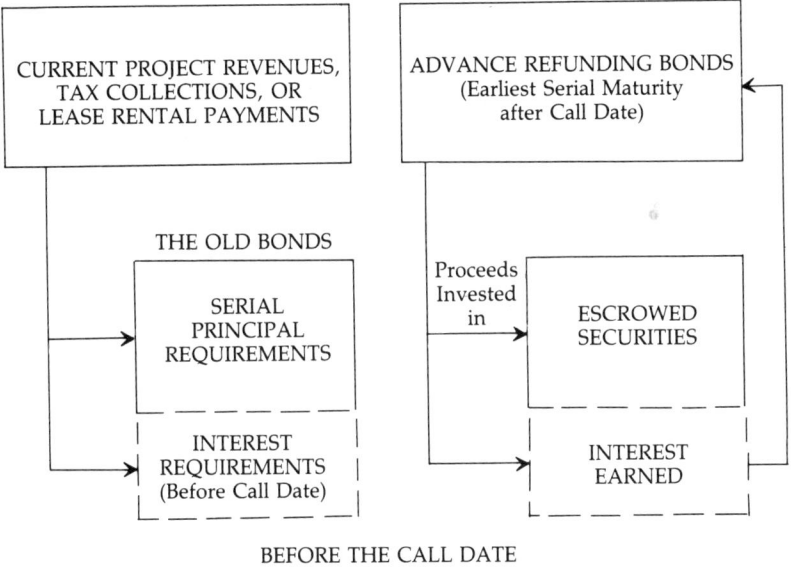

BEFORE THE CALL DATE

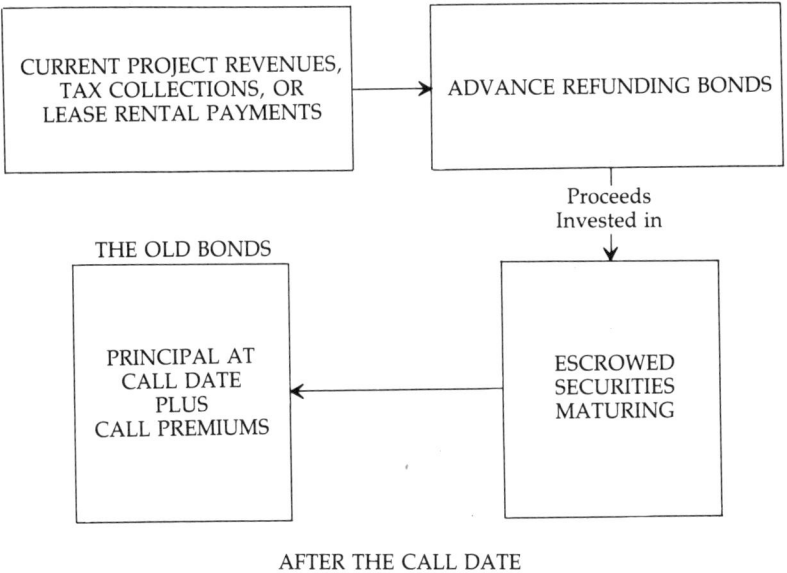

AFTER THE CALL DATE

Preferable Accounting Principles

The preferable accounting principles for accounting and reporting of tax-exempt debt appear in Statement of Position 78-5 (Accounting for Advance Refunding of Tax-Exempt Debt). SOP 78-5 differentiates between advance refundings for state and local governmental units and advance refundings for all other types of entities. Accounting and reporting for advance refundings of tax-exempt debt is based on whether the transaction is defeased or nondefeased. The following is applicable to enterprise funds and all other entities, except state and local governmental units:

Defeasance transactions The old debt is legally satisfied resulting in the culmination of the earning process. Thus, gain or loss from the early extinguishment of debt (APB-26) should be recognized as an extraordinary item (FASB-4).

The old debt should no longer appear on the financial statements of the issuer because it is no longer a liability. However, the new debt should appear on the financial statements as a liability. If the interest and principal on special obligation bonds are to be paid from a trust fund they should not appear as a liability on the financial statements of the issuer, because they represent a liability of the trustee.

Nondefeasance transactions If the following conditions exist a nondefeasance transaction should be accounted for as a defeasance transaction because the old debt, in substance, is being satisfied:

1. There is an irrevocable commitment by the issuer to refund the old debt.
2. The funds for the advance refunding are placed in an irrevocable trust with a reputable trustee with the intentions of satisfying the old debt at a specified future date.
3. The trustee invests the funds for the advance refunding in qualifying investments with maturity dates coinciding with the debt service requirements of the trust.
4. The funds held by the trustee to accomplish the advance refunding are not subject to any liens other than those related to the advance refunding transaction.

In the event that a nondefeasance transaction does not meet the above criteria there is no satisfaction of the old debt and no culmination of the earning process. Thus, no gain or loss should be recognized on the nondefeasance transaction. However, if the retirement date of the old debt has been determined, an adjustment of the cost of borrowing the old debt must be made, as follows:

1. Income on the proceeds for the advance refunding should be included in income of the period in which earned.
2. Interest expense on both the old and the new debt should be charged to income of the period in which incurred.
3. The call premium, unamortized bond premium or discount, and any unamortized initial issuance costs should be amortized over the remaining new life of the old debt as determined by the new retirement date.

In a nondefeasance transaction, the financial statements should reflect the old and new debt as a liability at the same time and the proceeds from the sale of the new debt should be reported as an asset.

In the event that an advance refunding qualifies partially as a defeasance transaction and partly as a nondefeasance transaction, it should be accounted for proportionately as both. The portion of the old debt that qualifies as a defeasance transaction should be accounted and reported as such. The portion is determined by relating the cash provided by the portion that qualifies for a defeasance transaction to the total amount of cash necessary to redeem the entire old debt.

Crossovers Until the date of crossover the proceeds of the new debt serve as collateral for the new debt and the old debt continues to be serviced by the issuer. The old debt is retired at the crossover date and the issuer is then obligated to service the new debt. Neither actual defeasance, nor defeasance in substance, occurs in a crossover advance refunding. Thus, crossovers are always accounted for, and reported as, nondefeasance transactions.

Hospital reimbursements by third parties A hospital should report a loss on an advance refunding, net of any third party reimbursement. However, the third party reimbursement must be reasonably assured of collectibility. Reimbursable costs that cannot be claimed in the current year should be accounted for as deferred charges.

State and Local Governmental Units

SOP 78-5 has a separate section for accounting and reporting on advance refundings of tax-exempt debt for state and local governmental units, except enterprise funds, which are accounted for in the same manner as other entities. Actually, there is no difference in the accounting and reporting procedures except for compliance with governmental accounting practices, such as bond proceeds are recorded as revenue and bond issue costs are recorded as expenditures. The following are the procedures to use for advance refundings of tax-exempt debt of state and local governmental units, except enterprise funds:

Defeasance transactions Accounted for in the same manner as other entities, except the proceeds of the new debt are considered revenue of the appropriate fund and all amounts spent to retire the old debt are considered expenditures. The expenditures should be appropriately broken down into those for retirement of the principal of the old debt, and those which are included in the gain or loss on the advance refunding.

Nondefeasance transactions Accounted for in the same manner as for other entities, except that the proceeds of the new debt are considered revenue and issue costs of the new debt are considered expenditures.

Crossovers Accounted for in the same manner as for other entities.

Deferred Income Taxes

Interperiod income tax allocation should be applied to advance refundings of tax-exempt debt in accordance with existing GAAP (APB-11).

Lease Transactions

Advance refundings of tax-exempt debt which involves a lease should be accounted for in accordance with existing GAAP on leases (FASB-22).

Financial Statement Disclosure

All of the disclosures required in an early extinguishment of debt are applicable to advance refundings of tax-exempt debt, as follows:

1. A description of the advance refunding transaction.
2. Amount of gain or loss.
3. Related tax effects.

Comprehensive Illustration

The following example illustrates a net advance refunding of tax-exempt debt with defeasance:

Information on Old Debt:

Principal	$10,000,000
Term	20 years
Rate of interest	12% annually
Call premium	$ 200,000
Original issuance costs	$ 300,000
Original discount	$ 1,000,000
Earliest call date	10th year
Date of advance refunding	5th year

The amortization of issuance costs and discount is calculated on the straight-line method. Thus, unamortized original issuance costs and unamortized original discount are as follows:

Unamortized original issuance costs	$225,000
Unamortized original discount	$750,000

Information on New Debt:

Principal	$15,000,000
Term	20 years
Rate of interest	6% annually
Issuance costs	$ 2,323,129
Issue price	100
U.S. Treasury Obligations	6% annually

Computations of Funds Required

Old Debt	Present Values	Earnings on New Debt Proceeds	Total Future Cash Requirements
Principal	$ 7,472,582	$2,527,418	$10,000,000
Call premium	149,452	50,548	200,000
Interest	5,054,837	1,709,675	6,754,512
Proceeds required	$12,676,871	$4,287,641	$16,964,512

Gain or Loss on Advance Refunding

Amount of New Debt		$15,000,000
Less: issuance costs		2,323,129
Proceeds from new debt		$12,676,871
Carrying Amount of Old Debt:		
Principal	$10,000,000	
Unamortized issuance costs	225,000	
Unamortized discount	750,000	9,025,000
Loss on Advance Refunding		$ 3,651,871

PREFERABLE ACCOUNTING PRINCIPLES

REAL ESTATE INDUSTRY

PROFIT RECOGNITION ON REAL ESTATE TRANSACTIONS

Overview

The preferable accounting principles relating to the timing of profit recognition on real estate sales appear in the industry accounting guide entitled "Accounting for Profit Recognition on Sales of Real Estate", (hereinafter referred to as Profit Recognition Guide). This Profit Recognition Guide covers the recognition of profit on all real estate transactions except those of retail land sales. "Accounting for Retail Land Sales", is another industry accounting guide which is covered elsewhere in this publication.

The Profit Recognition Guide also applies to the sale of options involving real estate and the sale of corporate stock where the economic substance of the transaction is actually a sale of real estate (Statement of Position 75-6).

The "matching" concept requires that revenue and related costs be "matched" in determining net income for a specific period. If revenue is deferred to a future period, the associated costs of that revenue must also be deferred. Frequently, it is necessary to estimate revenue and/or costs in order to achieve a proper "matching". The result of using the matching concept in determining income or loss is called the earning process. When the earning process is complete and an exchange has taken place, only then is the realization of revenue recognized. The realization principle requires that revenue be earned before it is recorded.

GAAP require that the realization of revenue be recognized in the accounting period in which the earning process is substantially completed and an exchange has taken place (APB Statement 4). In addition, revenue is usually recognized at the amount established by the parties to the exchange except for transactions in which collection of the receivable is not reasonably assured (APB Statement 4). In the event that collection of the receivable is not reasonably assured, the installment method or cost recovery method may be used (APB-10). Alternatively, collections may be properly recorded as deposits in the event that considerable uncertainty exists as to their eventual collectibility.

More often than not, in a real estate sale, a significant portion of the sales price is represented by a long-term receivable which is not backed by the full faith and credit of the buyer. Usually, the seller can only recover the property, in the event of default by the buyer. Another unusual facet of real estate sales is the possible continuing involvement in the property by the seller. For instance, the seller may be legally bound to make certain improvements to the property or to adjacent property.

> **OBSERVATION:** *In order to assure the collection of the long-term receivable which is usually part of a real estate transaction, the Profit Recognition Guide requires minimum down payments for all real estate sales before a seller may recognize a profit. The Profit Recognition Guide emphasizes the timing of the recognition of profits but does not cover other aspects of real estate accounting.*

The preferable accounting principles in the Profit Recognition Guide are based on two main factors which usually exist in a real estate transaction:

1. The amount of the initial and continuing investment of the buyer.
2. The extent of the seller's continuing involvement with the property sold.

Buyer's Investment

The Profit Recognition Guide is quite specific in respect to the required investment in the property by the buyer. In order for a seller to recognize the full profit on a sale of real estate, (1) the buyer's initial investment must be adequate, and (2) the buyer's remaining indebtedness for the purchase price of the property, if any, must be amortized by annual level payments which include interest and principal over a specified maximum period. The specified maximum period for land is twenty (20) years, and the specified maximum for other real estate is no more than that offered for first mortgages by independent financial institutions at the time of the sale.

> **OBSERVATION:** *The required initial and continuing investment of the buyer is determined at the time of sale and*

annually thereafter. Therefore, an excess initial investment, at the time of sale, over the amount necessary, can be applied toward the annual required increase of the continuing investment of the buyer.

Buyer's initial investment   The relative size, and the composition of, the buyer's initial investment must meet specific criteria. In determining whether the buyer has made an adequate initial investment, the Profit Recognition Guide requires that the *sales value* of the property be used, instead of the stated sales price. The *sales value* is defined as the stated sales price of the property, increased or decreased for other considerations included in the sale that clearly represent additional proceeds on the sale. Additional proceeds may include but are not limited to, imputed interest and services performed without compensation. (Further discussion of "sales value" appears later).

The Profit Recognition Guide permits the use of two different methods to determine the minimum initial investment (down payment) of the buyer. The first and by far the simplest is that the minimum initial investment of the buyer be not less than twenty-five percent (25%) of the *sales value* of the property sold. The other method is that the minimum initial investment (down payment) of the buyer be the greater of:

1. the difference between the *sales value* of the property and 115% of the primary permanent commitment or loan on the property, if any, OR
2. the percentage of the *sales value* of the property as indicated on the following table:

Library of

Davidson College

	Minimum Down Payment (% of Sales Value)
Land:	
Held for commercial, industrial, or residential development to commence within two years after sale	20%[1]
Held for commercial, industrial, or residential development after two years	25%[1]
Commercial and Industrial Property:	
Office and industrial buildings, shopping centers, etc:	
Properties subject to lease on a long-term lease basis to parties having satisfactory credit rating; cash flow currently sufficient to service all indebtedness	10%
Single tenancy properties sold to a user having a satisfactory credit rating	15%
All other	20%
Other Income-Producing Properties (hotels, motels, marinas, mobile home parks, etc):	
Cash flow currently sufficient to service all indebtedness	15%
Start-up situations or current deficiencies in cash flow	25%
Multi-Family Residential Property:	
Primary residence:	
Cash flow currently sufficient to service all indebtedness	10%
Start-up situations or current deficiencies in cash flow	15%
Secondary or recreational residence:	
Cash flow currently sufficient to service all indebtedness	15%
Start-up situations or current deficiencies in cash flow	25%
Single Family Residential Property (including condominium or cooperative housing):	
Primary residence of the buyer	5%[2]
Secondary or recreational residence	10%[2]

[1]Not intended to apply to volume retail lot sales by land development companies.
[2]If collectibility of the remaining portion of the sales price cannot be supported by reliable evidence of collection experience, a higher down payment is indicated and should not be less than 60% of the difference between the sales value and the financing available from loans guaranteed by regulatory bodies, such as FHA or VA, or from independent financial institutions.

Even if the required minimum initial investment is made by the buyer, a separate assessment must be made to determine the collectibility of the receivable. In other words, there must be reasonable assurance that the receivable will be collected after the minimum initial investment is received by the seller, and if not, the sale should not be recorded. The minimum initial investment must be made by the buyer and the seller must be reasonably assured that the balance of the sales price will be collected before the real estate sale is recorded and any profits are recognized. The assessment of the receivable by the seller should include credit reports on the buyer and an evaluation of the adequacy of the cash flow from the property.

The buyer's minimum initial investment must be made at or before the time of sale in cash or cash equivalency. A buyer's note for the minimum initial investment is not acceptable unless payment of the note is unconditionally guaranteed by an irrevocable letter of credit from an established lending institution. Any funds that have been loaned or will be loaned, directly or indirectly, to the buyer by the seller must be deducted from the buyer's initial investment (down payment) to determine whether the required minimum has been met (Statement of Position 75-6). For the purposes of this provision, the seller must be exposed to a potential loss as a result of the funds loaned to the buyer (Statement of Position 75-6).

Sales value As mentioned previously, any payments by the buyer which represent additional proceeds to the seller should be included as part of the buyer's investment because additional proceeds are added to the stated sales price to determine the *sales value* of the property. The Profit Recognition Guide utilizes *sales value* and not the stated sales price. Therefore, additional proceeds enter into the determination of both the buyer's investment and the *sales value* of the property. Examples of additional proceeds are management fees, points to obtain financing, prepaid interest and principal, or payments to third parties which reduce previously existing indebtedness on the property. However, payments to third parties for improvements to the property or payments which are not verifiable cannot be considered.

The effects of an underlying land lease must also be included in computing the *sales value* of the property. If a seller sells improvements to a buyer to be built on property subject to an underlying land lease, the present value of the lease payments must be included in the *sales value* of the property. The present value of the lease payments should be computed over the actual term of the primary indebtedness of the improvements, if any, or over the usual term of primary indebtedness for the type of improvements involved. The present value of the land lease payments is tantamount to additional indebtedness on the property. If the land lease is not subordinated, the discount rate to determine the present value of the land lease payments should be comparable to interest rates on primary debt of the same nature. However, if the land lease is subordinated, a higher discount rate, comparable to secondary debt of the same nature, should be used.

XYZ, Inc. agrees to build improvements for ABC Company for a total price of $1,750,000. The improvements are to be built on land leased by ABC from a third party. The payments on the land lease are $18,000 per year, payable monthly in advance, and the lease term is for 45 years. ABC Company will pay for the improvements as follows:

Cash down payment	$ 250,000
10% Unsecured note payable in 5 annual payments of $20,000 plus interest	100,000
Primary loan from insurance company secured by improvements to the property, payable in equal monthly payments over 28 years at 8½% interest	1,400,000
Total Stated Sales Price of Improvements	$1,750,000

The computation of the *sales value,* as required by the preferable accounting principles in the Profit Recognition Guide is as follows:

Present value of land lease payments for 28 years, payable $1,500 monthly, discounted at 8½% interest	$ 193,361
Primary loan from insurance company	1,400,000
Total equivalent primary debt	$1,593,361
Unsecured note from buyer to seller	100,000
Cash down payment	250,000
Sales Value*	$1,943,361

*The buyer's minimum initial investment in the property is based on the *sales value* of the property and not on the stated sales price.

Where a land lease is between the buyer and a third party, its effects on the sales value of the property are used only to determine the adequacy of the buyer's initial investment. However, when the seller of the improvements is also the lessor of the land lease, the computation of the profit on the sale of the improvements is also affected. Since it is impossible to separate the profits on the improvements from the profits on the underlying lease, the Profit Recognition Guide requires a special computation limiting the amount of profit that can be recognized. The amount of profit which can be recognized on the improvements is equal to the *sales value* of the property less the cost of the improvements and the cost of the land. However, the present value of the lease payments in the sales value may not exceed the actual cost of the land.

The result of the limitation on the amount of profit which can be recognized on the sale of improvements is to defer any residual profit on the land from being recognized until the land is sold, or the future rental payments are actually received.

If a land lease between a buyer and a seller of improvements on the land is for a term of less than 20 years, or does not substantially cover the economic life of the improvements being made to the property, the transaction should be accounted for as a single lease of land and improvements.

Buyer's continuing investment   In addition to an adequate initial investment, the Profit Recognition Guide also requires that the buyer maintain a continuing investment in the property by increasing his investment each year. The buyer's total indebtedness for the purchase price of the property must be reduced each year in equal amounts which will extinguish the entire indebtedness (interest and principal) over a specified maximum period. The specified maximum period for land transactions is twenty (20) years. The specified maximum period for all other real estate transactions is no more than that offered at the time of sale for first mortgages by independent financial institutions.

The buyer's commitment to pay the full amount of his indebtedness to the seller becomes doubtful if the total indebtedness is not to be paid within the specified maximum period provided for by the Profit Recognition Guide.

A buyer's payments on his indebtedness must be in cash or cash equivalency. Funds provided directly or indirectly by the seller cannot be used in determining the buyer's continuing investment in the property.

Real estate agreements involving land frequently provide for the periodic release of part of the land to the buyer. The buyer obtains the released land free of any liens. The conditions for the release usually require that sufficient funds have previously been paid by the buyer to cover the sales price of the released land and often an additional sum is required to effectuate the release. In these types of transactions involving released land, the Profit Recognition Guide's requirements for a buyer's initial and continuing investment must be determined on the basis of the *sales value* of property not released or not subject to release. In other words, for a seller to recognize profit at the time of sale, a buyer's investment must be enough to pay any amounts for the release of land and still meet the specified initial and continued investment required by the preferable accounting principles in the Profit Recognition Guide. If the buyer's initial and continuing investment is not sufficient, then each release of land should be treated as a separate sale and profit recognized at that time.

Receivables subject to subordination   If, at the time of sale, a seller's receivable is subject to future subordination, no profit should be recognized because the effect of future subordination on the collectibility of a receivable cannot be reasonably evaluated. The cost recovery method should be used to recognize profit at the time of sale if the seller's receivable is subject to future subordination.

Buyer's Investment Inadequate

When it is apparent that the buyer's initial and continuing investment fails to meet the required amounts under the circumstances, an alternative method of recognizing the revenue from the sale must be used. The alternative method selected is a matter of professional judgment and should be based on the specific circumstances involved. The three methods recommended by the Profit Recognition Guide are (1) deposit accounting, (2) cost recovery method and (3) the installment sales method.

Deposit accounting   The uncertainty about the collectibility of the sales price in a real estate transaction may be so great that the effective date of the sale should be deferred and any cash received by the seller should be accounted for as a deposit. However, cash received that is designated by contract as nonrefundable interest, may be applied as an offset to existing carrying charges on the property, such as property taxes and interest, instead of being accounted for as a deposit.

All cash received except that appropriately used as an offset to the carrying charges of the property must be reflected in the seller's balance sheet as a liability (deposit on a contract for the sale of real estate). No change is made in accounting for the property subject to the contract and, if any, its related mortgage debt. However, the seller's financial statements should disclose that these items are subject to a sales contract. Depreciation expense should continue as a period cost, in spite of the fact that the property has been legally sold (Statement of Position 78-4).

Until the required buyer's initial and continuing investment are appropriately met, the seller does not report a sale and continues to report all cash received either as a deposit or in the case of nonrefundable interest, as an offset to the carrying charges of the property involved. In the event that the buyer forfeits a nonrefundable deposit, or defaults on the contract, the seller should reduce the deposit account appropriately and include such amounts in income of the period.

The terms of a real estate transaction accounted for by the deposit method may indicate that the carrying amount of the property involved is more than the sales value in the contract and that a loss has been incurred. Since the seller is using the deposit method, no sale is recorded and thus no loss. However, the information indicates an impairment of an asset which should be appropriately recorded by the seller in the period of discovery by a charge to income and the creation of a valuation allowance account for the property involved (Statement of Position 78-4).

Cost recovery method   If a seller's receivable is subject to subordination which cannot be reasonably evaluated, or uncertainty exists as to the recovery of the seller's cost on default by the buyer, the cost recovery method should be used. Even if cost has been recovered by the seller but additional collections are highly doubtful, the cost recovery method would be appropriate. Frequently, the cost recovery method is initially used for transactions which would also qualify for the installment sales method.

> **OBSERVATION:** *The cost recovery and installment sales method both defer the recognition of profit on the sale until collections are actually received.*

Under the cost recovery method all collections are applied first to the recovery of the cost of the property and only after full cost has been received is any profit recognized. The only expenses remaining to be charged against the profit are those relating to the collection process. When the cost-recovery method is used, the total sales value is included in the income statement for the period in which the sale is made. From the total sales value in the income statement, the total cost of the sale and the deferred gross profit on the sale are deducted. On the balance sheet the deferred gross profit is reflected as a reduction of the related receivable. Until full cost is recovered, principal payments received are applied to reduce the related receivable and interest payments received are added to the deferred gross profit. At any given time, the related receivable less the deferred gross profit equals the remaining cost which must be recovered. After all cost is recovered, subsequent collections reduce the deferred gross profit and appear as a separate item of revenue on the income statement.

Installment sales method   Promulgated GAAP prohibits accounting for sales by any form of installment accounting except under exceptional circumstances where collectibility cannot be reasonably estimated or assured. The doubtfulness of collectibility can be caused by the length of an extended collection period or because no basis of estimation can be established. In such cases a company can use either the cost recovery method or the installment sales method of accounting (APB-10).

The installment sales method is frequently more appropriate for real estate transactions in which collectibility of the receivable from the buyer cannot be reasonably assured because defaults on loans secured by real estate usually result in the recovery of the property sold.

Under the installment sales method of accounting, each payment collected consists of part recovery of cost and part recovery of gross profit, in the same ratio that these two elements existed in the original sale. In a real estate transaction, the original sale is equal to the *sales value* of the property sold which has already been discussed earlier in this Chapter. Thus, under the installment sales method, profit is recognized on cash payments made by the buyer to the holder of the primary debt assumed, and cash payments to the seller. The profit recognized on the cash payments is based on the percentage of total profit to total *sales value*.

Jones Company sells real property to Smith for $2,000,000. Smith will assume an existing $1,200,000 first mortgage and pay $300,000 in cash as a down payment. The balance of $500,000 will be in the form of a 12% second mortgage to Jones Company payable in equal payments of principal and interest over a ten year period. The cost of the property to Jones is $1,200,000.

Computation of Sales Value and Gross Profit:

Cash	$ 300,000
Second mortgage	500,000
First mortgage	1,200,000
Total Sales Value (which happens to be the same as the stated sales price)	$2,000,000
Less: Cost of property sold	1,200,000
Total gross profit on sale	$ 800,000
Gross profit percentage	40.0%
Profit to be recognized on down payment (40% of $300,000)	$ 120,000

Assuming that the $300,000 down payment is insufficient to meet the requirements of full profit recognition on the sale (accrual basis of accounting) Jones would recognize $120,000 gross profit at the time of sale. Assume that several months later Smith makes a cash payment of $100,000 on the first mortgage and $50,000 on the second mortgage. The amount of gross profit which Jones would recognize on these payments would be, as follows:

Payment of first mortgage	$100,000
Payment of second mortgage	50,000
Total cash payments	$150,000
Gross profit realized (40% of $150,000)	$ 60,000

The point is that even though Jones does not receive any cash on the payment of the first mortgage by Smith, gross profit is still realized because the gross profit percentage was based on the total *sales value* which included the first mortgage liability.

When the installment sales method is used, the total sales value is included in the income statement for the period in which the sale is made. From the total sales value in the income statement, the total cost of the sale and the deferred gross profit are deducted. On the balance sheet the deferred gross profit on the sale is deducted from the related receivable. As cash payments are received, the portion allocated to realized gross profit is presented as a separate item of revenue on the income statement and deferred gross profit is reduced by the same amount. At any given time, the related receivable less the deferred gross profit, represents the remaining cost of the property sold. Since realized gross profit is recognized as a portion of each cash collection, a percentage relationship will always exist between the long-term receivable and its related deferred gross profit. This percentage relationship will be the same as the gross profit ratio on the initial sales value.

Change to full accrual method   After the cost recovery or installment sales method is adopted for a real estate transaction, a periodic evaluation should be made of the collectibility of the receivable. When it becomes apparent that the seller's receivable is reasonably assured of being collected, a change to the full accrual accounting method should be made by the seller. The change is not a change in an accounting principle (Statement of Position 78-4). When the change to the full accrual accounting method is made, any remaining deferred gross profit is recognized in full in the period in which the change is made. If the change creates a material effect on the seller's financial statements, full disclosure of the effects and the reason for the change should be appropriately made in the financial statements or footnotes thereto (Statement of Position 78-4).

Seller's Continued Involvement

Real estate transactions must be carefully analyzed to determine their economic substance. Frequently, the economic substance of a real estate sale is no more than a management fee arrangement or an indication that the risks and benefits of ownership have not really been transferred in the agreement. Therefore, accounting for a real estate transaction can become quite complicated because of the many types of continuing relations that can exist between a buyer and a seller. The substance of the real estate transaction should dictate the accounting method which should be used.

As a general rule, before a profit may be recognized, a sale must occur, collectibility of the receivable must be reasonably assured, and the seller must perform all of the acts required by the contract to earn the revenue. Profit may also be recognized, at the time of the sale, on contracts which provide for the continued involvement of the seller, if the maximum potential loss of the seller is expressly limited and defined by the terms of the contract. In this event, the total profit on the sale, less the maximum potential loss which could occur because of the seller's involvement, is recognized at the time of the sale.

The two most important factors in evaluating the economic substance of a real estate sale are (1) the transfer of the usual risks and rewards of ownership in the property, and (2) the full performance by the seller of all acts required by the contract to earn the revenue. Generally, both of these factors must be accomplished before full profit may be recognized on the sale of real estate. The more common types of real estate transactions and how they should be accounted for, are discussed in the following paragraphs.

Real estate syndications   A seller forms a limited partnership to buy and hold property. The seller sells property to the limited partnership and also becomes the general partner. In this situation, the continued involvement of the seller includes:

1. As general partner the responsibility of operating the property and making distributions to the limited partners.
2. May be required to fund cash flow deficiencies of the limited partnership.
3. May be required to guarantee a return of all or part of the limited partners' investment.
4. May be required to guarantee a certain return on investment to the limited partners.

Frequently, the seller will hold a receivable from the limited partnership as a result of the purchase of the property. In this event, the collection of the receivable will depend on the successful operation of the limited partnership by the general partner who is also the seller and holder of the receivable.

Permanent financing   If the seller is responsible by contract to obtain suitable financing for the buyer, no sale or profit can be recognized until the terms of the contract are fulfilled by the seller and suitable financing is arranged.

Participation in profits   If a seller is permitted to participate in future profits from the property he sold without any risk of loss, profit may be recognized at the time of sale.

Services without compensation   As part of the contract for the sale of real estate, the seller may be required to perform services related to the property sold, without compensation or at a reduced rate. In determining profit to be recognized at the time of sale, a value should be placed on such services at the prevailing rates and deducted from the sales price of the property sold. The value of the compensation should then be recognized over the period in which the services are to be performed by the seller.

Profit-sharing, financing and leasing arrangements   In legal form a real estate transaction may be a sale, but in substance the contract may be a profit-sharing, financing or leasing arrangement. If in substance the transaction is a profit-sharing, financing or leasing arrangement, no sale or profit is recognized. If a real estate contract contains any of the following provisions it should be accounted for as a profit-sharing, financing, or leasing arrangement:

1. The return of the buyer's investment in the property is guaranteed by the seller.
2. The buyer can compel the seller to repurchase the property.
3. An option or obligation exists for the seller to repurchase the property.

Development and construction   A real estate transaction may require the seller to further develop, in the future, the property sold or adjacent property. These type of transactions may be accounted for by the percentage of completion method used in long-term construction contracts, if no significant uncertainties exist and costs and profits can be reasonably estimated from the previous experience of the seller. However, if uncertainties do exist or costs and profit cannot be reasonably estimated, the completed contract method should be used. Profit can be recognized at the time of sale for any work performed and finished by the seller prior to the date of sale. In other words, the total profit may be allocated to work performed prior to the sale and to future construction and development work. The allocation of the total profit is based on the estimated costs for each activity using a uniform rate of profit for all activities.

If a buyer has the right to defer until completion payments due for developmental and construction work, or if the buyer is financially unable to pay these amounts as they come due, the continued involvement of the seller may be presumed and no profit should be recognized until completion.

Initiating and supporting operations As part of a real estate transaction, the seller may be required to initiate or support the operations of the property for a stated amount of time, or until a certain level of operations has been achieved. In other words, the seller may agree to operate the property for a certain period, or until a certain level of rental income has been reached.

Even if there is no agreement, the Profit Recognition Guide presumes that a seller has an obligation to initiate and support operations of the property he has sold in any of the following circumstances:

1. An interest in property is sold by the seller to a limited partnership in which he is a general partner.
2. An equity interest in the property sold is retained by the seller.
3. A management contract between the buyer and seller which provides for compensation that is significantly higher or lower than comparable prevailing rates, and which cannot be terminated by either the buyer or the seller.
4. The collection of the receivable from the sale held by the seller is dependent on the operations of the property and represents a significant portion of the sales price. A significant receivable is defined as one in excess of 15% of the maximum primary financing that could have been obtained from an established lending institution.

In real estate transactions which require the seller to initiate and support operations, appropriate deferral of profits should be made for the risks and potential additional costs which may be incurred. However, in transactions in which the seller is directly or indirectly a general partner in a limited partnership which the seller sold property to, or if the seller holds a significant receivable in property which he has sold, it is doubtful whether the economic substance

of the transaction can be considered a sale. These types of transactions should appropriately be accounted for as profit-sharing,
financing, or leasing arrangements.

COSTS TO SELL AND RENT REAL ESTATE PROJECTS

Overview

Statement of Position 78-3 (SOP 78-3) contains the preferable accounting principles which should be used in accounting for costs to sell and rent, and initial rental operations of real estate projects. The initial rental operations period of a rental project is sometimes referred to as the "rent-up" period.

Whether a real estate project is being held for sale or held for rental is a decision that management must make. Since this decision affects the accounting for the real estate project, evidence contrary to management's representation should be seriously considered by the independent auditor. If management decides that a portion of the real estate project will be held for rental and a portion held for sale, then each portion should be accounted for as a separate project.

Statement of Position 78-3 does not change the preferable accounting principles for retail land sales companies, and does not apply to the following:

1. Initial direct costs of leases (FASB-17).
2. Commercial activities such as manufacturing, merchandising or service orientated activities.
3. Rental periods of less than one month in duration.

For the purposes of SOP 78-3, costs to sell real estate projects excludes the costs of amenities (tennis courts, golf courses, marinas, etc.).

The preferable accounting principles in SOP 78-3 are primarily based on the expense recognition principles advocated by APB Statement 4. The three basic expense recognition principles used in GAAP are:

1. associating cause and effect (synonymous with the "matching concept")
2. systematic and rational allocation
3. immediate recognition

When a cost is related to specific revenue, an association of cause-and-effect relationship is established. An example of this method of expense recognition is sales commissions, which are directly related to the revenue generated by the sale.

If an asset provides benefits for more than one period, its cost should be allocated in a systematic and rational manner. This method is used in the absence of a direct basis for associating cause and effect. An example of this method of expense recognition is the depreciation of fixed assets.

There are three bases for recognizing an expense immediately in the current period:

1. The cost incurred provides no future benefits.
2. Costs recorded as assets in prior periods no longer provide any future benefits.
3. Allocating the cost to future periods or directly associating it to revenue serves no useful purpose.

An example of an expense recognized in the current period is the expense of unsuccessful research and development.

Costs to Sell Real Estate Projects

Costs incurred to sell real estate should be accounted for as either (1) project costs, (2) prepaid expenses, or as (3) period costs. The preferable accounting principles in SOP 78-3 for these costs are generally based on the three basic expense recognition principles previously discussed.

Project costs are capitalized as part of the construction costs of the real estate project provided that both of the following conditions are met:

1. They are incurred for tangible assets which are used as marketing aids during the marketing period of the real estate project, or for services performed in obtaining regulatory approval for real estate sales in the project.
2. The costs incurred are reasonably expected to be recovered from sales.

Costs to sell real estate projects, less recoverable amounts from incidental operations or salvage values, include legal fees for prospectuses, sales offices, and model units, with or without furnishings.

Prepaid expenses which are sometimes called deferred charges, are capitalized and amortized over the period that is expected to benefit from the expenditure. However, if the prepaid item can be identified with certain future revenue, it should be amortized to the periods in which the future revenue is earned. Costs incurred as prepaid expenses to sell real estate projects must meet the following conditions:

1. do not qualify as project costs
2. are incurred for goods or services that will be used in future periods

Advances on commissions, future advertising costs, and unused sales brochures are examples of costs to sell real estate projects which qualify as prepaid expenses.

Period costs are charged to expense in the period incurred because they do not meet the criteria for projects costs or prepaid expenses. Costs to sell real estate projects which do not benefit future periods should be expensed in the period incurred, as period costs. Grand opening expenses, sales salaries, sales overhead and used advertising costs are examples of period costs.

Costs to Rent Real Estate Projects

Costs to rent real estate projects under operating leases are either chargeable to future periods or chargeable to the current period.

Chargeable to future periods if the costs can be identified with specific revenue, such costs should be amortized to the periods in which the specific revenue is earned. If the costs incurred are for goods not used or services not received, such costs should be charged to the future periods in which the goods are used or services are received.

If deferred rental costs can be associated with the revenue from a specific operating lease, such costs should be amortized over the lease term. On the other hand, if deferred rental costs cannot be identified or associated with the revenue from a specific operating lease, such costs should be amortized to the periods benefited.

Chargeable to the current period if the costs to rent real estate projects under operating leases do not qualify as chargeable to future periods. Thus, if costs do not meet the criteria for deferral treatment, they should be accounted for as period costs and expensed as incurred.

Initial rental operations commence at the time major construction activity is substantially completed and the real estate project is capable of producing rental revenue. A real estate rental project is considered substantially completed and available for occupancy when both of the following conditions are met:

1. Major construction activity has been completed as originally intended except for routine maintenance and clean-up.
2. Units have been offered for rental, or are presently being offered for rental.

Some portions of a real estate rental project may still require major construction for completion and other portions of the same project may be substantially completed and available for occupancy. In this event, each portion should be accounted for as a separate project.

Suspension of major construction activity may occur because of a decline in rental demand. In this event, the carrying costs of the real estate rental project may be permanently impaired and a provision for losses may be required. Impairment of the carrying cost of the real estate project may occur from insufficient rental demand even if construction is not suspended.

Once a real estate rental project is substantially completed and available for occupancy, depreciation on the entire project should be appropriately recorded.

INVESTMENTS IN REAL ESTATE VENTURES

Overview

The thrust of Statement of Position 78-9 is to extend the provisions of APB-18 (Equity Method) to unincorporated real estate ventures. Thus, if an investor includes an investment in a real estate venture in its financial statements prepared in conformity with GAAP, the real estate venture should generally be accounted for in accordance with APB-18. Regulated investment companies and other enterprises that must account for their investments at quoted market value or fair value are not required to comply with SOP 78-9.

SOP 78-9 also requires that a sale of an investment in a real estate venture meet all of the provisions set forth in the industry accounting guide entitled "Accounting for Profit Recognition on Sales of Real Estate." Thus, the sale of corporate stock in a real estate venture is in substance a sale of an interest in the underlying real property and the sale must be evaluated in this perspective.

When two or more entities own real estate together, the ownership may take several different types of legal form. SOP 78-9 cites the most common forms of ownership and their definitions, as follows:

Corporate joint venture A corporation owned and operated by a group of joint venturers for the purpose of sharing risk and rewards in a business project.

General partnership An association of two or more individuals or entities in which each partner has unlimited liability.

Limited partnership An association of two or more individuals or entities in which at lease one partner (general partner) has unlimited liability, and one partner (limited partner) has limited liability. Any remaining partners may be either general or limited.

Undivided interest Property is owned jointly by two or more owners and title is held individually to the extent of each owner's interest in the property.

Corporate joint venture, general partnership, limited partnership and undivided interest are collectively referred to in SOP 78-9 as either real estate venture or venture.

Equity Method

In order to better understand the preferable accounting principles set forth in SOP 78-9 a review of the equity method is essential.

The promulgated GAAP (APB-18) requires that the equity method be used for domestic and foreign unconsolidated subsidiaries and noncontrolled investments in voting common stock. The equity method is used in those situations where the investor can exercise significant influence over the financial and operating policies of the investee. Significant influence over the investee is presumed to occur when the investment is 20% or more of the investee (APB-18). Under the equity method, dividends are credited to the investment account and are not considered income, and after all the necessary eliminating entries are made, the investor periodically records its share of the investee's net income as a debit to the investment account and a credit to income from the investment.

An investor's share of earnings or losses from its investment is usually shown as a single amount (called a one-line consolidation) in the income statement, after the following adjustments:

1. Intercompany profits and losses are eliminated, unless realized, in the same manner as if the investee were consolidated.
2. Any difference between the underlying equity in net assets of the investee and the cost of the investment should be accounted for on a consolidated basis. Therefore, goodwill should be amortized over a period of 40 years or less.
3. The investment should be shown in the investor's balance sheet as a single amount and earnings or losses should be shown as a single amount (one-line consolidation) in the income statement, *except for the investor's share of (a) extraordinary items and (b) prior-period adjustments, which should be shown in the income statement separately.*
4. Capital transactions of the investee that affect the investor's

share of stockholders' equity should be accounted for on a consolidated basis.

5. Gain or loss is recognized when an investor sells the common stock investment, *equal to the difference between the selling price and the carrying amount of the investment at the time of sale.*

6. If the investee's financial reports are not timely enough for an investor to apply the equity method, the investor should use the most recent available financial statement, and the lag in time created should be consistent from period to period.

7. Other than temporary declines, a decrease in an investment should be recognized in the books of the investor.

8. Losses on an investment decrease the basis of the investment, which may not be reduced below zero, at which point the use of the equity method should be discontinued, unless the investor has guaranteed obligations of the investee or is committed to provide financial support. The investor should resume the equity method when the investee subsequently reports net income and the net income exceeds the investor's share of any net losses not recognized during the period of discontinuance.

9. Dividends for cumulative preferred stock of the investee must be deducted first before the investor's share of earnings or losses is computed, whether the dividend was declared or not.

10. An investor who acquires more than 20% ownership in an investee after having had less than 20% *must retroactively adjust its accounts to the equity method on the basis of a step-by-step acquisition of a subsidiary.* In this event, at the date of each step in the acquisition, the carrying value of the investment must be compared with the underlying net assets of the investee to determine whether goodwill (positive or negative) is involved.

11. If an investment in voting stock falls below the 20% level, the presumption is that the investor has lost the ability to exercise significant influence and control, in which case the equity method should be discontinued. The carrying amount at the date of discontinuance becomes the cost of the investment. Subsequent dividends are accounted for by the cost method from the date the equity method was discontinued.

12. An investor's share of earnings or losses from an investment accounted for by the equity method is based on the oustanding shares of the investee without regard to common stock equivalents (APB-15).

13. The equity method should not be used for investments of a

temporary nature, for foreign investments subject to controls and restrictions, and for those investments that are dissimilar and for which separate, supplemental information would be more meaningful.

The cost method is generally used when ownership is less than 20%. The original investment under the cost method is recorded at cost, and income is recognized from dividends received out of accumulated earnings earned after the date of acquisition.

Dividends received out of accumulated earnings prior to the date of acquisition are recorded as a return on investment and reduce the cost of the investment.

Certain factors, such as continuing operating losses, may indicate that a substantial decline in the value of the investment has occurred. If such a decline is not temporary, it should be recognized in the accounts.

Real Estate Ventures

The promulgated GAAP on the equity method of accounting (APB-18) applies only to investments held in the form of common stock. APB-18 does not cover investments in unincorporated businesses such as general partnerships, limited partnerships and investments held as undivided interests. In November 1971, an AICPA staff interpretation of APB-18 concluded that many aspects of the equity method were, in fact, quite appropriate in accounting for investments in certain unincorporated entities.

The preferable accounting principles expressed in SOP 78-9 confirm that unincorporated investments in noncontrolled real estate ventures should, as a general rule, be accounted for and reported under the equity method. The exposure to joint and several liability and the special income tax considerations of nonincorporated joint ventures are the principal differences cited by SOP 78-9 between corporate joint ventures and nonincorporated joint ventures. Some of the special problems which may arise in applying the equity method to nonincorporated real estate ventures which are not controlled are covered by SOP 78-9 and are discussed below.

Many unincorporated joint ventures are not taxable entities for income tax purposes and the tax liability is usually passed on to the individual partners or investors. In this event, the timing difference, if any, is the difference between income or loss recorded by a partner or investor using the equity method and the partner's or investor's share of distributable taxable income or loss reported by the unincorporated joint venture.

As mentioned previously, the equity method is used in those situations where the partner or investor can exercise significant influence over the operating and financial policies of the unincorporated investee, which is presumed to occur when the investment is 20% or more of the investee. However, in those situations where an investor, directly or indirectly, controls (usually 50% or more) an investee, a parent-subsidiary relationship exists and consolidated financial statements are usually required instead of the equity method. On the other hand, a limited partner's interest may be so insignificant that little, if any, influence can be exerted over the operating and financial policies of the limited partnership. When this, or a similar situation exists, it may be appropriate for the limited partner or investor to account for its investment by the cost method.

A general partner of a limited partnership should not use the equity method to account for its investment, if the limited partnership agreement provides for control of the partnership by the general partners. On the other hand, a limited partner may be in control, if it holds over 50% interest in the limited partnership.

The equity method should be used in accounting for undivided interests in real estate ventures provided that some level of joint control exists between the owners. Some level of joint control is usually present in most real estate ventures owned by undivided interests. Joint control exists where the approval of two or more owners is required to finance, develop, operate or sell the real property. An undivided interest in the assets, liabilities, revenue and expenses of a real estate venture may be present if joint control does not exist and each undivided interest is liable only for indebtedness it incurs, is entitled to only to its pro-rata share of income and is liable only for its pro-rata share of expenses.

Accounting for losses   Losses in excess of amounts invested, including loans and advances, should be recorded by partners or investors in real estate ventures in which they are jointly and severally liable. Such excess losses should be reported as a liability on the balance sheet of the partner or investor.

Sometimes a partner or investor is unable to bear its share of losses in a real estate venture and the other partners or investors may become liable. Accounting for this type of loss by a partner or investor is governed by the promulgated GAAP on contingencies (FASB-5). Therefore, if it is probable that a partner or investor in a real estate venture will have to bear a proportionate share of another partner or investor's losses, the loss should be recorded. However, the partner or investor who is unable to bear the loss, should still continue to record the losses on its books until the liability for payment has been terminated by agreement or operation of law.

Purchased goodwill The excess of cost of a real estate investment over the fair value of the underlying net assets (tangible and intangible) should be recorded as goodwill. Purchased goodwill should be amortized by systematic charges to income over the period to be benefited but not to exceed 40 years (APB-17).

Capital transactions with a real estate venture The amount of cash contributed by a partner or investor for the formation of a real estate venture should be recorded as an investment provided that all partners or investors contribute cash. A partner or investor who contributes real estate as a capital investment in a real estate venture should record as its investment the carrying cost of the real estate contributed. No profit should be recognized on a transaction that is, in economic substance, a capital contribution to a real estate venture.

Under all circumstances, a partner or investor who sells real estate to a real estate venture must comply with all of the applicable provisions of the industry accounting guide entitled "Accounting for Profit Recognition on Sales of Real Estate."

In the event a partner or investor contributes real estate to a real estate venture as a capital contribution and simultaneously receives a sum of cash from the venture which does not have to be reinvested back into the venture, the transaction is in substance an exchange to the extent of the amount of cash received. Thus, a partner or investor should recognize a profit on the amount of cash received.

The carrying amount of real estate contributed as capital by a partner or investor may exceed the proportionate amount of interest received in the venture compared to cash contributions by other partners or investors. In this event, the partner or investor contributing the real estate should recognize a loss on the transaction to the extent that a cash contribution for the same interest in the venture exceeds the carrying amount of the real estate.

Services or intangibles contributed to a real estate venture by a partner or investor should be accounted for in the same manner as that of a wholly-owned investment.

Interest income on partners' or investors' loans and advances to a real estate venture should be deferred if one of the following conditions exists:

1. The collectibility of the principal amount of the loans and advances or any remaining interest payments is in doubt.
2. The other partners or investors in the real estate venture are not reasonably expected to bear their share of present or future losses.

If both of the above conditions do not exist and the partner or investor has recorded its proportionate share of income or loss from the venture (equity method) which included interest expense on loans and advances, then the entire amount of interest income accrued on loans and advances to a real estate venture should be recorded as earned.

If none of the above conditions exist, a portion of the interest income on loans and advances should be deferred. The percentage of interest income which must be deferred is equal to the partner's or investor's percentage interest in the real estate venture.

If a real estate venture capitalizes costs of services performed by a partner or investor, the partner or investor may recognize profit on the services performed, but only to the extent of outside interests in the real estate venture and if:

1. the form and substance of the transaction are basically the same,
2. no significant uncertainties exist pertaining to completion of performance by the partner or investor, and to the total costs involved, and other partners or investors are reasonably expected to be able to share their portion of any present or future losses.

Similarly, if a partner or investor capitalizes costs of services performed by the real estate venture, the partner's or investor's share of the venture's profit on the services performed should be recorded as a reduction of the capitalized costs.

If a real estate venture sells real estate to a partner or investor, the partner's or investor's share of the venture's profit on the sale should be recorded as a reduction of the cost of the real estate purchased and not recognized as profit.

REAL ESTATE INVESTMENT TRUSTS

Overview

The preferable accounting principles for real estate investment trusts (REIT) appear in SOP 75-2 and 78-2, both entitled "Accounting Practices of Real Estate Investment Trusts".

In 1960, the Internal Revenue Code created the REIT, to eliminate double taxation of most of the taxable income of a special class of real estate ventures. Thus, the emergence of REITs is a direct result of federal tax laws.

A REIT is an unincorporated trust of at least 100 beneficiaries that hold transferable shares. In order to eliminate the double taxation on income distributed to its beneficiaries, an REIT must comply with special rules in regard to its organization, the type of income it receives, the type of assets it holds, and must distribute at least 90% of its taxable income, as defined by the IRC, to its beneficiaries.

The majority of REITs are publicly owned and invest in equity interests in real estate and real estate mortgage loans. Because of the requirement of at least 100 beneficiaries and transferable shares, most REITs are large in size and it is difficult for small real estate syndicates to become REITs.

In recent years, many REITs have experienced losses from defaulted loans. In addition, most REIT loans are not being paid on a current basis and more defaults appear to be eminent. SOP 75-2 and SOP 78-2, cover some of the accounting problems presently being encountered by REITs in connection with defaulted loans.

Preferable Accounting Principles

The preferable accounting principles in SOP 75-2 and SOP 78-2 cover the following specific items:

1. Losses on loans
2. Assets affected by troubled debt restructuring

3. Discontinuance of interest revenue recognition
4. Commitment fees
5. Operating support of the REIT by the advisor.

Each of the above topics is covered and the applicable preferable accounting principles is discussed in detail.

Losses on loans Each individual loan and its underlying real property must be separately evaluated in determining the amount which should be provided for the allowance for losses. This evaluation method should be used for both real estate held as an investment and foreclosed properties held for resale.

When the individual valuation method is used in determining the allowance for losses, the actual final loss on a particular individual property may not be the same as the estimated loss. However, the purpose of the individual evaluation method is to provide a total allowance for losses which is adequate when compared to the financial statements taken as a whole.

In evaluating the estimated amount which may be recovered on an individual loan through the disposal of its underlying real property, the estimated net realizable value must be compared to the net carrying amount of the related loan. The net carrying amount should include all recorded accrued interest and exclude any prior allowance for losses. The estimated net realizable value is equal to the estimated selling price of the underlying real property, less (1) estimated costs to improve or complete the property, (2) estimated costs of disposal, and (3) estimated costs to hold the property to the estimated time of sale. The estimated costs to improve or complete should include all costs to put the property in the condition which is assumed for the purposes of estimating the selling price. The estimated costs to hold the property to the estimated time of sale, should include, property taxes, interest expense, professional fees, and other necessary cash expenditures.

If liquidity difficulties exist, an REIT may not possess the financial resources to hold properties which have been foreclosed. In this event, the estimated selling price should be determined on the basis of the immediate liquidation of the property. However, if foreclosed property is to be held as a long-term investment, its basis is the net realizable value at the date of the foreclosure.

In computing the estimated net realizable value, the estimated period to the time of sale, should be based on the allowance of a reasonable time to attract a purchaser in the open market. Interest costs during this holding period should be based on the following guidelines which appear in SOP 75-2:

1. Interest rates should be based on the cost of all capital (debt and equity) employed by the REIT.
2. Interest rates for debt should usually be the same rate used for balance sheet purposes in recording accrued interest.
3. Full disclosure should be made by footnote of the effective interest rate used in determining estimated interest costs during the holding period.

Increases and decreases to the allowance for losses account, as determined by the individual evaluation method, should be charged or credited to current operations.

The following financial statement presentation of loans, foreclosed properties held for resale, and the related allowance for losses, is recommended by SOP 75-2:

Loans, earning	$ XX,XXX
Loans, nonearning	XXX
Foreclosed properties held for resale	X,XXX
	$XXX,XXX
Less: allowance for losses	X,XXX
Total	$XXX,XXX

SOP 75-2 contains the following conditions that establish a presumption that the recognition of interest revenue should be discontinued:

1. Principal and/or interest payments are past due.
2. The borrower has defaulted under the terms of the loan agreement.
3. The initiation of foreclosure proceedings are reasonably expected or have already been started.
4. The borrower's credit is in reasonable doubt.
5. The economic viability of the real estate project is in reasonable doubt.
6. The loan has been renegotiated.

If any of the above conditions exist, it should be presumed that further recognition of interest revenue should be discontinued. However, if other facts clearly override the presumption, the recognition of interest revenue should not be discontinued.

Commitment fees All commitment fees of a REIT should be deferred and amortized over the combined commitment period and loan period. During the commitment period amortization should be recorded by the straight-line method, and the interest method should be used for amortizing the remaining deferred commitment fees over the loan period. Obviously, income is recognized on all commitment fees if the loan is not made and the commitment period expires.

> *OBSERVATION:* *The preferable accounting principles for commitment fees accrued or received by a REIT differ from the preferable accounting principles for commitment fees accrued or received by a savings and loan association and by mortgage bankers.*
>
> *At the time a commitment actually becomes the obligation of a mortgage banker or a savings and loan association, an amount equal to the direct underwriting costs is immediately recognized in income. This appears to be quite appropriate because direct underwriting costs of making a loan are immediately expensed when incurred. SOP 76-2 advocates that a mortgage banker estimate direct underwriting costs for each loan as an amount that does not exceed the current allowable VA or FHA rates for origination fees. The industry audit and accounting guide on savings and loan associations states that an amount equal to the underwriting costs should be recognized from the commitment fee and the balance deferred.*
>
> *In addition, the SOP on REITs fails to bring to the reader's attention, the necessity of evaluating the collectibility of commitment fees which have not been collected in cash. Collectibility of commitment fees must be reasonably assured before they can be recognized as income. (Note: see chapters on Savings and Loan Associations and Mortgage Banking Industry, for a more complete discussion on commitment fees).*

Operating support of the REIT by the advisor A REIT should account for the operating support from its advisor, as follows (SOP 75-2):

1. Assets or liabilities which are transferred between the REIT and its advisor should be accounted for at current market value at the date of such transfers.
2. Operating support from the advisor should be accounted for as income or as a reduction of the advisor's fees.
3. Full disclosure should be made by the REIT of all transactions with its advisor including, (1) the relationship between the parties, and (2) the nature and amount of each transaction.

Assets affected by troubled debt restructurings FASB-15 requires that properties acquired by an REIT in a "troubled debt restructuring" must be recorded and accounted for at their fair value on the date of the restructuring. However, in subsequent periods, the allowance for losses should be determined by the individual evaluation method described earlier in this chapter.

In the event it is likely that an REIT will enter into a "troubled debt restructuring" with a debtor or creditor, the allowance for losses account should be determined under the provisions of FASB-15. Thus, in the case of a debtor, the difference between the net carrying amount of a loan and the fair value of the underlying related property is the amount which should be provided for the allowance for losses. However, in subsequent periods, the allowance for losses should be adjusted using the same method, but under no circumstances should the loan less its allowance for losses, exceed the estimated net realizable value of its underlying real property.

In a "troubled debt restructuring" with a creditor, gain, if any, on the reduction of the related payable may be included in determining the overall net loss on the identified property which is transferred to the creditor. However, under no circumstances should the identified property less the allowance for losses exceed its estimated net realizable value.

Full disclosure of "troubled debt restructurings" should be made in the financial statements of a REIT, in accordance with the provisions of FASB-15.

Discontinuance of interest revenue recognition If it is reasonable that interest revenue will not be received by a REIT, the recognition of interest revenue should be discontinued.

Some REIT advisors provide operating support by purchasing loans from the REIT at prices in excess of market, by reducing advisory fees, by forgiving of indebtedness, by making outright cash payments to the REIT, and by employing other various schemes to ensure that the REIT appears to be performing well. GAAP require that the substance of each transaction be recorded and thus, the necessity of the above rules in accounting for transactions between an REIT and its advisors.

RETAIL LAND SALES

Overview

The preferable accounting principles relating to retail land sales appear in the industry accounting guide entitled, "Accounting for Retail Land Sales", (hereinafter referred to as Retail Land Sales Guide). The Retail Land Sales Guide covers only retail land sales sold on a volume basis and does not cover wholesale or bulk sales of land. The preferable accounting principles in the Retail Land Sales Guide are very similar to those in the industry accounting guide entitled "Accounting for Profit Recognition on Sales of Real Estate," which covers the profit recognition on all real estate sales except retail land sales.

The matching concept requires that revenue and related costs be "matched" in determining net income for a specific period. If revenue is deferred to a future period, the associated costs of that revenue must also be deferred. Frequently, it is necessary to estimate revenue and/or costs in order to achieve a proper "matching". The result of using the matching concept in determining income or loss is called the earning process. When the earning process is complete and an exchange has taken place, only then is the realization of revenue recognized. The realization principle requires that revenue be earned before it is recorded.

GAAP require that the realization of revenue be recognized in the accounting period in which the earning process is substantially completed and an exchange has taken place (APB Statement 4). In addition, revenue is usually recognized at the amount established by the parties to the exchange except for transactions in which collection of the receivable is not reasonably assured (APB Statement 4). In the event that collection of the receivable is not reasonably assured, the installment method or cost recovery method may be used (APB-10). Alternatively, collections may be properly recorded as deposits in the event that considerable uncertainty exists as to their eventual collectibility.

The development of a large tract of land usually over several years is typical of a company in the retail land sales industry. Master plans are drawn for the improvement of the property which may include amenities, and all necessary regulatory approvals are obtained. Large advertising campaigns are held at an early stage which frequently result in substantial sales prior to significant development of the property. In most retail land sales, a substantial portion of the sales price is financed by the seller in the form of a long-term receivable secured by the property. Interest and principal are paid by the buyer over an extended number of years. In the event of default, the buyer usually loses his entire equity and the property reverts back to the seller. Frequently, the retail land sales contract, or existing state law, provide for a period in which the purchaser may receive a refund of all or part of any payments made. In addition, the seller usually cannot obtain a deficiency judgment against the buyer because of operation of the law. Finally, many project-wide improvements and amenities are deferred until the later stages of development when the seller may be faced with financial difficulties.

Specifically excluded from the provisions of the Retail Land Sales Guide are retail land sales which occur under the following conditions:

1. The land sold can immediately be used for construction purposes and all roads, water, sewers, and other amenities are completed and in place.
2. The seller receives at least 10% cash down payment and a first mortgage note on the property with interest at the appropriate market rate which can be legally enforced against the general credit of the buyer. The buyer receives a deed to the property at the time of sale, and the seller makes credit checks of buyers a regular business practice.
3. Local banks would lend money on the property at similar rates because of the low ratio of loan to value of the property. Also, evidence exists that the purchaser's notes are marketable to banks without substantial discounts and without recourse.

Before a retail land sale can be excluded from complying with the provisions of the Retail Land Sales Guide, all of the above conditions must exist.

Because of the small down payments, frequent cancellations and refunds, and the possibility that the retail land sales company may not be financially able to complete the project, certain specific conditions must be met before a sale can be recognized. The Retail

Land Sales Guide requires that the following conditions be met before a retail land sale may be recorded as a sale:

1. The down payment and all other subsequent payments have been made by the buyer, through and including any period of cancellation and the period for refund has expired.
2. The buyer has paid a total of 10% or more, in principal or interest, of the contract sales price.
3. The current and prospective financial capabilities of the retail land sales company (the seller) must reflect with reasonable assurance that the company is capable of completing all of its obligations under the contract.

Prior to meeting all three of the above conditions, all payments (principal and interest) received by the seller on retail land sales must be recorded as deposits. When all three conditions are met, the sale is recorded using the normal accrual accounting method or the installment sales method, according to the collectibility of the sales price. The accounting method which is selected to record the sale should be based on each company's own collection experience with each individual project. The Retail Land Sales Guide expressly prohibits the use of industry experience as a basis for determining the appropriate accounting method.

Deposit accounting method   If a retail land sale does not meet the three conditions necessary for it to be recorded as a sale, the deposit accounting method must be used. Under the deposit accounting method, the effective date of the sale is deferred and all funds received, including principal and interest are recorded as deposits on retail land sales. Any interest received which is recorded as a deposit, is credited to interest income under either the accrual or installment methods, after all three conditions have been met and the sale is ultimately recorded.

> *OBSERVATION: The Retail Land Sales Guide is silent on cash received that is designated by contract as nonrefundable interest. Statement of Position 78-4 (Application of the Deposit, Installment, and Cost Recovery Methods in Accounting for Sales of Real Estate) specifically applies to the industry accounting guide entitled "Accounting for Profit Recognition on Sales of Real Estate", and apparently does not apply to the*

> *Retail Land Sales Guide. However, SOP 78-4 states that non-refundable interest received by the seller does not have to be recorded as a deposit but can be applied as an offset to existing carrying charges on the property, such as taxes and interest. The approach appears reasonable and should probably apply to nonrefundable interest received by a seller of retail land.*

All cash received which is recorded as deposits must be reflected on the seller's balance sheet as a liability. All direct selling costs, including sales commissions, which are allocable to the retail land sales recorded as deposits, should be deferred until the sale is recorded. If the eventual sale is recorded on the accrual basis, the allocable direct selling costs at the time of recording should be charged to expense of the period. On the other hand, if the eventual sale is recorded on the installment sales basis, the allocable direct selling costs at the time of recording are deferred (see below-Installment Sales Method).

On cancellation of a retail land sale being accounted for as a deposit, the deferred selling costs are charged to expense and the deposit, less any refund, is credited to income.

> **OBSERVATION:** *The Retail Land Sales Guide is also silent about a retail land sale accounted for by the deposit method which indicates by the terms of its contract that the carrying amount of the property involved is more than the contract selling price and that a loss has been incurred. Obviously, since the deposit method of accounting is being used, no sale is recorded and thus no loss. However, SOP 78-4 which apparently does not apply to retail land sales, requires that the impairment of the asset be recognized by the seller in the period of discovery by a charge to income and the creation of a valuation allowance account for the property involved. Perhaps the applicability of SOP 78-4 should be changed to include retail land sales.*

Under the deposit accounting method no change is made to the assets on the seller's books and any depreciation expense should continue as a period cost.

Accrual accounting If a retail land sale meets the required three conditions to be recorded as a sale instead of a deposit, then certain additional conditions must be met before the sale may be recorded by the normal accrual accounting method. The additional conditions for a retail land sale to qualify for accrual accounting are, as follows:

1. At the end of the normal payment period the purchased property will clearly be useful for residential or recreational purposes. In other words, the land must be usable for the purposes represented by the seller and all improvements and amenities necessary for the purposes intended will have been made. In addition, no legal restrictions may exist which prevent the property from being used as intended.
2. Expenditure of funds have actually been made and progress on improvements have progressed beyond the preliminary stage. In addition, enough tangible evidence should exist to indicate that the project will be completed according to plans. Substantial completion of access roads and amenities is evidence of such progress.
3. The seller's receivable for the property sold is not subject to subordination of new loans. However, subordination is allowed for construction of a residence providing the project's collection experience for such subordinated receivables is approximately the same as that for those receivables which are not subordinated.
4. Collection experience for the project indicates that 90% of the receivables in force for six months after the sale is recorded will be collected in full. A down payment of 25% or more is an acceptable substitute for this collection experience test.

Unless all four of the above conditions are met for the *entire* project, the installment sales method must be used to record all sales. If the installment sales method is used initially, a change to the accrual method should be made subsequently when the above four conditions are met for the entire project. When this occurs the change should be accounted for prospectively as a change in an accounting estimate in accordance with APB-20. Effects of the change should appropriately be disclosed in the financial statements or footnotes thereto in accordance with APB-20.

Before discussing the actual procedures that must be used to record retail land sales under the accrual method of accounting, certain special factors must be given considerations.

Allowance for contract cancellations   A certain amount of contract receivables will either be cancelled or never paid. The preferable accounting principle in the Retail Land Sales Guide require that an allowance for contract cancellations be established based on regular payments which are unpaid for the following delinquency periods:

Percent of Contract Price Paid	Delinquency Period
Less than 25%	90 days
25% but less than 50%	120 days
50% and over	150 days

For the purposes of determining the adequacy of the allowance for contract cancellations, all receivables which do not conform to the criteria in the above table shall be considered uncollectible. The allowance for contract cancellations should be periodically reviewed to determine its adequacy.

If a buyer is willing to assume personal liability for his debt and apparently has the means and ability to complete all payments, the delinquency periods in the above table may be extended.

Discount on receivables   There is a general presumption that the interest stated on the face of a note, resulting from a business transaction entered into at arm's length, is fair and adequate. However, if no interest is stated or if the stated interest appears unreasonable, the substance of the transaction must be recorded (APB-21).

In retail land sales the stated interest on the long-term note receivable is usually more or less than the prevailing interest rate. The preferable accounting principles in the Retail Land Sales Guide require that the interest rate for discounting retail land sales receivables should not be less than the minimum annual rate charged by local commercial banks and established retail organizations for purchases of consumer personal property on the installment basis. Thus, if the stated interest rate on a retail land sale receivable is 10% and the rate charged locally for installment purchases of consumer personal property is 18%, the 18% rate must be used in determining the present value of the retail land sale for recording purposes.

The discount on the long-term retail land sale receivable, if any, should be amortized to income over the life of the contract. The interest method should be used in which a constant rate of interest is applied each period to the beginning balance of the related receivable.

Deferred revenue The Retail Land Sales Guide requires that the amount of revenue (discounted contract price) that is recognized under the accrual method be based on the stage of completion of the total required performance of the seller. Thus, if the seller's performance is substantially complete at the date the sale is recorded, the total revenue on the sale should be recognized. More frequently than not, performance of the seller is not complete and revenues are recognized based on the amount of cost of sales incurred to the total amount of cost of sales to be incurred. Therefore, revenue (discounted contract price) related to cost of sales not yet incurred at the time of sale must be deferred. Revenue recognized subsequently as performance is completed must be disclosed separately in the income statement from revenue recognized at the time the sale was recorded.

Because the marketing effort is generally the dominant factor in retail land sales, selling costs directly associated with the project are included in determining the amount of revenue to recognize. Although these selling costs are normally charged to expense, for the purposes of revenue recognition they are included in the computation of cost of sales incurred to total cost of sales to be incurred. In other words, they are included in determining the fraction used to compute revenue earned and revenue deferred, in spite of the fact that selling costs are not usually part of the cost of sales. The inclusion of these direct selling costs in the fraction will increase the amount of revenue recognized in the year of sale.

Prior to recording a sale on the accrual basis, some interest and other project costs may have been charged to expense and thus not included in cost of sales. In this event, these costs should also be included in the fraction used to determine the amount of revenue to recognize, and the amount of revenue which should be deferred. The inclusion of these costs in the fraction will also have the effect of increasing the amount of revenue recognized in the year of sale.

The actual procedures that must be used to record retail land sales under the accrual method of accounting are, as follows:

1. The total contract price, before any deductions, is recorded as a gross sale. The total contract price includes the total amount of principal and interest which is expected to be received on the sale.
2. The following items are recorded as deductions from the gross sale to arrive at net sales for the period:
   a. down payment
   b. allowance for contract cancellations
   c. discount on receivables

      d.   deferred portion of gross sale (to be matched with future work or performance of the seller)

3. Cost of sales should be computed on net sales for the period.
4. A sale which is made and cancelled in the same reporting period should be included in and also deducted from gross sales or appropriately disclosed in some other manner.
5. The unamortized valuation discount (discount on receivables) and the allowance for contract cancellations are shown on the balance sheet as deductions from the related receivables.
6. Deferred revenue, less any related costs, are shown on the balance sheet as a liability. Deferred revenue should be recognized in future periods as the work is performed by the seller.

Installment sales method   Promulgated GAAP prohibits accounting for sales by any form of installment accounting except under exceptional circumstances where collectibility cannot be reasonably estimated or assured. The doubtfulness of collectibility can be caused by the length of an extended collection period or because no basis of estimation can be established. In such cases a company can use either the cost recovery method or the installment sales method of accounting (APB-10). However, the Retail Land Sales Guide specifically states that the installment sales method shall be used if the sale does not qualify for normal accrual basis accounting. Thus, apparently, the cost recovery method may not be used for retail land sales, but is permitted, when appropriate, for all other types of real estate sales (see Profit Recognition on Real Estate Sales).

The actual procedures that should be used to record retail land sales under the installment sales method of accounting are, as follows:

1. The total contract price, before any deductions, is recorded as revenue in the income statement of the year the sale is recorded. The total contract price includes the total amount of principal and interest which is expected to be received on the sale.
2. Cost of sales and selling, general and administrative expenses are charged to the income statement of the year the sale is recorded. Cost of sales should include an appropriate provision for the completion of improvements and/or required performance of the seller. However, direct selling cost associated with the project are deferred in accordance with item 3.

3. The difference between revenue (total contract price) and cost of sales is the gross profit. The gross profit on installment sales, less the direct selling costs closely associated with the project, is deferred and subsequently recognized as principal payments are received. Interest payments at the stated contract rate are recorded as interest income when received. Thus, principal payments result in the recovery of cost of sales, certain deferred selling costs, and the recognition of income, while interest payments at the stated rate are recognized as interest income.

Excess selling expenses associated with the project and general and administrative expenses are treated as expenses of the period in which they are incurred. Excess selling expenses are those which result from decreases in sales volume, or from unproductive sales programs. Selling costs attributable to cancelled or delinquent contracts should not be deferred under any circumstances.

4. Unrealized gross profit should be deducted from installment contracts receivable on the balance sheet of the seller.

5. In the event that the installment and accrual methods are both being used, disclosure should be made on the income statement of the amount of sales applicable to the installment method and on the balance sheet, the total amount of installment contracts receivable should be disclosed.

6. The cancellation of an installment sales contract may precipitate one or more of the following book entries:
   a. removing the unpaid installment receivable
   b. restoring the recoverable costs of the land repossessed
   c. reduction of the liability for future improvements on the repossessed land
   d. reduction of the applicable unrealized gross profit
   e. reduction of the deferred selling costs

Retail land sales may initially be accounted for by the installment method and subsequently qualify for accrual basis accounting. When this occurs, a change must be made to the accrual basis. The change is not a change in accounting principle (Statement of Position 78-4). However, should the change create a material effect on the seller's financial statements, full disclosure of the effects and the reason for the change should be appropriately made in the financial statements or footnotes thereto (Statement of Position 78-4). The computations for the change should be made as of the beginning of the quarter in which the change is made.

Determination of Future Performance Costs

Future performance costs should be based on engineering studies and include a provision for unforeseeable costs. Unrecoverable costs of offsite improvements, amenities and facilities, should be included in cost estimates and the present value of sales of facilities should be included as recoverable costs. In addition, an inflation factor should be included in the determination of all costs.

All estimates of costs to complete improvements and other future performance costs should be reviewed at least annually. Adjustments for estimated costs should not be charged or credited to income unless the total adjusted costs exceed the related deferred income. If this occurs, the total loss is charged to income of the period in which the adjustment is required.

Capitalized Costs

Only direct costs which are required to bring the unimproved land into saleable condition are capitalized. Interest, real estate taxes, and other direct costs incurred to create the inventory of retail land sites are properly included as capitalized costs. However, capitalized interest costs are limited to those resulting from loans for which the land or construction in progress is pledged as collateral, or where the proceeds of a loan are used to improve or acquire unimproved land. All other interest, nondeferrable selling expenses, and general and administrative expenses are recorded as expenses of the period in which they are incurred. Under no circumstances, should capitalized costs exceed their net realizable value.

The cost of sales of land sites should be charged with any unrecoverable costs of developing related amenities. Amenities which are specifically developed as marketing aids, less their future sales or salvage value, should be depreciated over their estimated useful lives, or the expected selling period of the project, whichever is shorter.

Allocation of capitalized costs   The object of allocating capitalized costs of retail land projects is to appropriately match costs with related revenues. Although any reasonable method, consistently applied may be used, the Retail Land Sales Guide cites allocation based on relative sales values as the preferable method. In applying the relative sales value approach, the most valuable land sites in the project which are likely to sell first, would receive a higher allocation of the capitalized costs. The relative sales value method of allocating capitalized costs is less likely to result in deferring probable losses. Regardless of what method is used to allocate the capitalized costs, those capitalized costs which are deferred should not exceed their net realizable value.

Financial Statement Disclosure

Retail land sales companies, diversified entities with significant retail land sales operations, and investors who derive a significant portion of their income from investments involved in retail land sales, must comply with specific financial statement disclosure.

The financial statements of a retail land sales company typically reflects, (1) long-term receivables, (2) deferred revenue, and (3) deferral on income recognition. Because of these factors, a statement of changes in financial position, based on working capital, may be misleading. Therefore, the preferable accounting principles in the Retail Land Sales Guide considers a statement of changes in financial position which reflects "sources and uses of cash", more meaningful and thus, preferable. The statement of changes in financial position based on "sources and uses of cash" should be provided for all periods presented whenever earnings information is reported.

If a statement of changes in financial position is presented on a working capital basis, then only long-term receivables maturing within one year, and expenditures expected to be expended within one year for improvements and accrued commissions, should be included in working capital.

The preferable accounting principles in the Retail Land Sales Guide require the following specific disclosures in the financial statements or footnotes thereto:

Recognition of income   The method of recognizing income on each separate project should be clearly disclosed. Retail land sales, bulk lot sales, sales of amenities, and other major categories of land sales and their related cost of sales, should be separately disclosed.

Long-term receivables   The following disclosures pertaining to the long-term receivables should be made:

1. The initial valuation of the receivable and the discount rate used, if any.
2. The maturities of the gross long-term receivables for each of the five years following the date of the financial statements.
3. Method and policy used for recording retail land sales and cancelations.
4. The amount of delinquent accounts and the method used to determine delinquency.
5. The weighted average and range of stated interest rates on the long-term receivables.
6. Amount of contracts not yet recorded as sales and the amount of related receipts.

Inventories of land and improvements   The capitalization policy for amenities and carrying charges, and a description of the method used to allocate capitalized costs to sales.

Estimated liability for improvements   The following disclosures pertaining to the estimated liability for improvements should be made:

1. Estimated total cost and anticipated expenditures for each of the five years following the date of the financial statements, to improve major areas of the project from which sales are being made.
2. If any, the amount of paid-up contracts with delayed conveyance, and the amount of improvements behind construction schedule.
3. The amount of deferred profit to be matched with improvement costs (accrual basis method).
4. The method for which estimates of liability for improvements is made.

Long-term debt maturities   For each of the five years following the date of the financial statements, the maturities of long-term debt and the weighted average and range of interest rates of the long-term debt, should be disclosed.

If a debt or other liability can be satisfied solely by the surrender of property which secures the debt or other liability, without exposure to a deficiency judgment, such debt or other liability should be fully disclosed. Netting or offsetting the debt or other liability against the related asset is not acceptable.

PREFERABLE ACCOUNTING PRINCIPLES

LENDING AND OTHER FINANCIAL INSTITUTIONS

COMMERCIAL BANKING INDUSTRY

Overview

There are basically two kinds of commercial banks, those chartered by the federal government which are called "national banks", and those chartered by individual states, which are called "state banks". National banks are regulated by the federal government and are supervised by the Office of the Comptroller of the Currency. State banks are regulated by the state in which they operate and are usually supervised by a state banking department.

The Federal Deposit Insurance Corporation (FDIC) insures deposits of all of its members, up to $100,000 per depositor. All national banks are members, of the FDIC and probably 98% of all state banks are also members.

National banks are required to be members of the Federal Reserve System. State banks must meet the capital requirements of national banks and maintain specified reserve deposits, in order to be a member of the Federal Reserve System. If a state bank elects to become a member of the Federal Reserve System, it must also become a member of the FDIC. However, the reverse is not true.

Federal bank regulations generally require that commercial banks present their financial statements on the accrual basis of accounting, with the exception of revenues from the trust department which may be reported on a cash basis, if the effect is not significant on the overall fairness of the presentation.

Banks are examined by one or more different agencies according to whether they are national or state chartered, and whether they are members of the Federal Reserve System and the FDIC. Examinations are usually conducted on a surprise basis to determine (1) the bank's solvency, (2) the competence of the bank's management, and (3) the bank's compliance with banking laws and regulations. National banks are examined by the Comptroller of the Currency. State banks that are members of the Federal Reserve System are usually examined jointly by the state banking department and the Federal Reserve Bank. State banks that are only members of the FDIC are usually jointly examined by the state banking department and the FDIC. Thus, because of the fiduciary capacity in which they serve the public, all banks are subject to stringent banking laws and recurring examinations.

Most national and state banks are periodically required to file Directors' Examinations with the appropriate regulatory agency. One of the main reasons why banks obtain long-form audit reports from their independent auditors is that a great majority of the information required on a Directors' Examination appears in a long-form audit report.

Commercial banks perform many different types of services for their customers. Besides its commercial banking department a typical bank would probably have (1) an installment loan department, (2) an international department, (3) a consumer loan department, and (4) a trust department.

Preferable Accounting Principles

The preferable accounting principles for commercial banks appear in the industry audit guide and its supplement entitled "Audits of Banks", (hereinafter referred to as the Bank Guide).

The generally accepted accounting principles (GAAP) that have been promulgated for most other enterprises are also used for reporting on commercial banks. However, the Bank Guide contains a discussion of the specialized accounting principles and practices that are applicable to commercial banks.

Financial statements   The Bank Guide states that a financial report for a commercial bank that is reported in accordance with GAAP should contain (1) a balance sheet, which is frequently referred to as a statement of financial condition, (2) a statement of income, (3) a statement of changes in capital funds, and (4) all the necessary footnotes required by GAAP.

> *OBSERVATION:*   *The Bank Guide makes no reference to a statement of changes in financial condition, which is now a mandatory basic financial statement according to existing GAAP (APB-19).*

The Bank Guide states a preference for unclassified balance sheets for commercial banks. Thus, assets and liabilities do not have to be segregated between current and noncurrent for reporting purposes. In addition, the statement of income should clearly reflect the net income for the reporting period.

Valuation of investments   Investment securities should be reported at cost or at amortized cost if a premium or discount is involved. Premiums and discounts on investment securities should be initially capitalized and subsequently amortized to income. The amortization period usually starts at the date of purchase and ends at the maturity date of the security.

Investment securities should be classified in the statement of condition as (1) U. S. Government Obligations, (2) Obligations of State and Political Subdivisions, and (3) Other Investment Securities. However, if a bank is a dealer in securities, another classification should be used for trading inventory, such as Trading Account Securities.

An obligation to cover a short position in a security held as an investment should be reported as a liability, at current market value, at the date of the statement of condition. The commitment on the short position, if any, should be disclosed by a footnote to the financial statements. Short positions should not be netted against long positions for reporting purposes.

If necessary for a fair presentation, market values of investment securities should be disclosed in the financial statements or footnotes thereto. In addition, a general security reserve should be created, if necessary, by an appropriation of undivided profits. No losses should be charged against a general security reserve which should be added back to the undivided profits when no longer needed. The Bank Guide requires that the initial adoption of the amortization of discounts, if material, should be accounted for as a prior period adjustment in accordance with APB-9.

> **OBSERVATION:**   *Prior period adjustments have been narrowly defined by FASB-16, as either (1) a correction of an error in a prior period statement, or (2) an adjustment for the realization of the tax benefits of the preacquisition operating loss carryforward of purchased subsidiaries. The section of APB-9, referred to by the Bank Guide has been superceded.*

Securities gains and losses   Securities gains and losses should be recognized in accordance with existing GAAP. However, the Bank Guide states that securities gains and losses may be recognized by either the completed-transaction method, or the deferral-and amortization method. The completed-transaction method recognizes the gains and losses at the time of their realization (immediate recognition). The deferral-and-amortization method defers the gain or loss and amortizes the gain or loss over the period from the date of sale to the maturity date of the security sold. Federal bank regulations require the use of the completed-transaction method and do not allow the use of the deferral-and-amortization method.

Commercial banks that are dealers in securities, should report securities gains and losses in their trading income accounts.

Loans made on a discount basis   The unearned discount on loans made on a discount basis should be deducted from its related loan account for reporting purposes. Unearned discounts should not be reported on the statement of condition as a liability.

Loan losses   The method used to determine the provision for loan losses should provide for a systematic charge to income on a consistent basis. The journal entry to record the charge is a debit to "loan loss provision", and a credit to "reserve for loan losses".

Federal bank regulations provide that any loan loss in excess of the amount charged to operating expense ("loan loss provision"), must be charged to undivided profits. The journal entry is a debit to "undivided profits", and a credit to "reserve for loan losses".

Federal bank regulations further provide that the "reserve for loan losses" appear as a credit on the statement of condition, below total liabilities and above the equity section. Thus, undivided profits may appear in the "reserve for loan losses" account. The Bank Guide states that this presentation is acceptable under GAAP, if the affects are not material.

> **OBSERVATION:**   *Most commercial banks use the Treasury tax formula for determining the provision for loan losses. This method is used to compute the amount of loan losses that are deductible for federal income tax purposes.*

Property and equipment   Bank premises and equipment should be capitalized at acquisition cost and depreciated over the estimated useful life of the asset. Federal bank regulations require the same treatment of a bank's property and equipment.

Arbitrary write-downs, or write-offs of property and equipment are unacceptable for the purpose of GAAP.

Reserves   General contingency reserves should be created by an appropriation of undivided profits. The journal entry is a debit to undivided profits and a credit to the newly created reserve. No costs or losses should be charged to the reserve, and no part of the reserve should be transferred to income, or in any way used to effect the determination of net income for any period.

General contingency reserves should be restored to undivided profits when any part or all of the reserve is no longer considered necessary. General contingency reserves should preferably be classified in the statement of condition as part of the equity section.

Equity The equity section of a statement of condition for a commercial bank that is a corporate entity should normally include (1) capital stock, (2) capital surplus, and (3) undivided profits. However, capital notes, that are discussed later, are sometimes included in the equity section of the statement of condition for a commercial bank.

The initial capital stock of most banks is usually sold at a premium, which establishes a capital surplus account. In the banking industry, capital stock and capital surplus are considered to be part of the permanent capitalization of a commercial bank. However, compliance with banking regulations usually requires that a bank transfer part of its capital surplus to undivided profits, especially during the early days of the bank's existence. This is done to prevent a deficit in undivided profits during the early stages of the bank's existence. The practice of transferring amounts between capital surplus and undivided profits is not usually considered acceptable under GAAP. However, the Bank Guide suggests that the amount transferred from capital surplus to undivided profits be clearly disclosed and the financial statement presentation should indicate the proper amounts which should be in each account in accordance with GAAP. In addition, the Bank Guide recommends that the proper amount of capital surplus be restored as quickly as possible.

Under GAAP, a stock dividend is recorded by transferring from undivided profits to capital stock and capital surplus, the fair value of the stock dividend on the date of declaration. It has been a custom in the banking industry to capitalize only the par value of a stock dividend and not the fair value. The Bank Guide reasons that the present method used by banks to record a stock dividend is acceptable because of the peculiarities of a bank's capital accounts and the fact that an AICPA study on stockholders' equity is presently in progress.

> *OBSERVATION:*   *The present method used in the banking industry to record a stock dividend is unquestionably a departure from existing GAAP. The Bank Guide's justification for allowing this method has little, if any, foundation in accounting literature.*

Capital notes that are sometimes convertible into common stock, are issued for 20 to 30 years, and are subordinated to claims of depositors, have been issued by some large commercial banks. The capital notes are usually issued to mature in installments. In short, capital notes are, in fact, debt securities, and do not become equity unless converted.

The problem is that most banks with capital notes outstanding include the notes in the equity section of the statement of condition, in spite of the fact that these capital notes actually represent debt. Any interest paid on the notes is properly charged to operations. In addition, most bank regulations prescribe this same treatment for capital notes.

The Bank Guide describes the above treatment of capital notes as appropriate for banks and agrees with the fact that capital notes are debt securities. When capital notes are included in the equity section the Bank Guide suggests that there be a separate subsection for stockholders' equity with a total for stockholders' equity clearly shown.

> *OBSERVATION:*   *The propriety of including debt securities in the equity section of a financial statement is almost nonexistent. The argument that these capital notes are subordinated and have more of the characteristics of equity capital than of debt, is, at best, weak. Long-term subordinated debt securities are a common method of raising funds in many industries. The proper accounting for these types of debt securities is well established in GAAP.*

Consolidated financial statements   Many banks own the land and building in which they operate, but ownership may exist in the form of common stock of a subsidiary. Other types of activities that may be operated by a subsidiary include data processing and a mortgage department.

Federal bank regulations require the consolidation of all bank subsidiaries, whether or not they are majority-owned or significant. Thus, a bank must report all of its subsidiaries' activities in consolidated financial statements.

Deferred income taxes   Deferred income taxes must be provided for, when appropriate, in the financial statements of commercial banks. Deferred income taxes are a direct result of timing differences. Timing differences are merely transactions that do not appear in the financial accounting income (books) and taxable income (tax return) in the same reporting period. Thus, a difference is created between financial accounting income and taxable income, and deferred income taxes are necessary under GAAP (APB-11).

Operating revenue   Tax-exempt interest income should not be converted to a fully taxable equivalent basis for financial statement reporting purposes. In other words, tax-exempt interest should be reported in the amount actually earned and not be reported on a taxable basis. However, tax-exempt interest actually earned should be presented separately from other interest income earned.

Net occupancy expense   All items of income and expense that are applicable to the operation of the bank premises which are owned by the bank, should be reported in the financial statements as "net occupancy expense". However, if rental income from tenants is material in amount it should be parenthetically disclosed in the income statement.

If a bank does not own its premises but leases the property under a lease agreement which transfers substantially all of the benefits and risks of ownership to the bank, the leased property should be capitalized in accordance with existing GAAP (FASB-13).

Trust department activities   Trust department revenue should preferably be presented on the accrual basis as required by GAAP. However, the Bank Guide states that the cash basis is acceptable for reporting trust department revenues, if the fairness of the presentation of financial position and results of operation are not significantly affected.

As mentioned previously, federal bank regulations require the use of the accrual basis except for trust department revenue which may be reported on a cash basis if the effect on the overall fairness of the presentation of financial statements is not significant.

Restrictions on dividends   Bank regulations that restrict the amount of dividends that can be paid by a bank should be fully disclosed by a footnote to the financial statements.

Comprehensive Illustration

The following is a comprehensive illustration of the preferable accounting principles contained in this chapter.

COMMERCIAL BANK COMPANY
STATEMENT OF CONDITION
As of December 31, 1980 and 1979

	1980	1979
ASSETS		
Cash and due from banks	$ 0,000,000	$ 0,000,000
Investment securities (note 1)		
U.S. Treasury Securities	0,000,000	0,000,000
Securities of other U.S. Government agencies and corporations	0,000,000	0,000,000
Obligations of States and political subdivisions	0,000,000	0,000,000
Other securities	00,000	00,000
Loans	00,000,000	00,000,000
Bank premises and equipment—at cost (less accumulated depreciation) (note 2)	000,000	000,000
Customers' acceptance liability	000,000	00,000
Accrued interest receivable and other assets	000,000	000,000
	$00,000,000	$00,000,000
LIABILITIES		
Deposits		
Demand	$00,000,000	$00,000,000
Savings	00,000,000	0,000,000
Other time	00,000,000	0,000,000
	00,000,000	00,000,000
Mortgage indebtedness (note 3)	00,000	00,000
Acceptances outstanding	000,000	00,000
Other liabilities	000,000	000,000
	00,000,000	00,000,000
Reserve for loan losses (note 4)	000,000	000,000
Capital accounts (note 5)		
Common stock—authorized, 000,000 shares of $0 par value; issued and outstanding, 00,000 shares in 1980 and 00,000 shares in 1979	000,000	000,000
Surplus	000,000	000,000
Undivided profits	000,000	000,000
Total capital accounts	0,000,000	0,000,000
	$00,000,000	$00,000,000

See Accompanying Notes to Financial Statements

COMMERCIAL BANK COMPANY
STATEMENT OF EARNINGS
Years ended December 31, 1980 and 1979

	1980	1979
Operating income		
Interest and fees on loans	$0,000,000	$0,000,000
Income on federal funds sold	000,000	00,000
Interest and dividends on investments		
U.S. Treasury Securities	000,000	00,000
Securities of other U.S. Government		
agencies and corporations	000,000	000,000
Obligations of States and political		
subdivisions	000,000	000,000
Other securities	0,000	0,000
Service charges on deposit accounts	00,000	000,000
Other service charges, collection and ex-		
change charges, commissions and fees	000,000	00,000
Other operating income	00,000	00,000
Total operating income	0,000,000	0,000,000
Operating expenses		
Salaries	000,000	000,000
Pension and other employee benefits		
(note 6)	00,000	00,000
Interest on deposits	000,000	000,000
Expense of federal funds purchased	0,000	0,000
Occupancy expense of bank premises	000,000	00,000
Furniture and equipment, depreciation,		
rental costs, servicing, etc.	00,000	00,000
Provision for loan losses (note 4)	00,000	00,000
Other	000,000	000,000
Total operating expenses	0,000,000	0,000,000
Earnings before income taxes and		
securities gains	000,000	000,000
Income taxes	00,000	00,000
Earnings before securities gains	000,000	000,000
Securities gains less related income tax effect		
of $0,000 in 1980 and $00,000 in 1979	0,000	00,000
Net earnings	$ 000,000	$ 000,000
Earnings per common share (note 8)		
Earnings before securities gains	$0.00	$0.00
Securities gains	.00	.00
Net earnings	$0.00	$0.00

See Accompanying Notes to Financial Statements

COMMERCIAL BANK COMPANY
STATEMENT OF CHANGES IN CAPITAL ACCOUNTS
Years ended December 31, 1980 and 1979

1979	Common stock	Surplus	Undivided profits
Balance January 1, 1979	$000,000	$000,000	$000,000
Net earnings for the year			000,000
Issuance of 0,000 shares of common stock for 00% stock dividend	00,000		(00,000)
Issuance of 0,000 shares of common stock for 0% stock dividend	00,000		(00,000)
Cash dividends declared ($.00 per share)			(00,000)
Transferred to reserve for loan losses less tax effect of $00,000 (note 4)			(00,000)
Other changes			(0,000)
Balance December 31, 1979	000,000	000,000	000,000
1980			
Net earnings for the year			000,000
Issuance of 0,000 shares of common stock for 0% stock dividend (note 5)	00,000		(00,000)
Proceeds from sale of 00,000 shares of common stock (note 5)	00,000	000,000	
Transferred to reserve for loan losses less tax effect of $0,000 (note 4)			(0,000)
Transfer of amount originally allocated to undivided profits at Bank's inception (note 5)		000,000	(000,000)
Other changes			(000)
Balance December 31, 1980	$000,000	$000,000	$000,000

See Accompanying Notes to Financial Statements

COMMERCIAL BANK COMPANY
STATEMENT OF CHANGES IN FINANCIAL POSITION
Years ended December 31, 1980 and 1979

	1980		1979	
Source of funds				
From operations				
Net earnings		$ 000,000		$ 000,000
Depreciation and amortization (note 2)		00,000		00,000
Increase (decrease) in reserve for loan losses (note 4)		0,000		(0,000)
		000,000		000,000
Provision for loan losses charged to undivided profits net of tax effect (note 4)		(00,000)		(00,000)
Increase in deposits				
Demand	$0,000,000		$0,000,000	
Savings	0,000,000		0,000,000	
Other time	0,000,000	00,000,000	0,000,000	0,000,000
Acceptances outstanding		000,000		0,000
Other changes		000,000		00,000
Proceeds from sale of common stock (note 5)		000,000		—
		$00,000,000		$0,000,000
Application of funds				
Net additions to bank premises and equipment		$ 000,000		$ 00,000
Increase (decrease) in loans		0,000,00u		(000,000)
Increase in securities				
Taxable	$0,000,000		$0,000,000	
Non-taxable	0,000,000	0,000,000	0,000,000	0,000,000
Increase in cash and due from banks		0,000,000		0,000,000
Cash dividends		—		00,000
Other changes		000,000		000,000
		$00,000,000		$0,000,000

NOTES TO FINANCIAL STATEMENTS

Note 1—Investment Securities

Investment securities are stated at cost less amortization of premiums. The carrying value of securities pledged to secure public funds and for other purposes as required by law amounted to $0,000,000 at December 31, 1980 and $0,000,000 at December 31, 1979.

Note 2—Bank Premises and Equipment

Bank premises and equipment are stated at cost less accumulated depreciation and amortization of $00,000 at December 31, 1980 and $00,000 at December 31, 1979. Depreciation and amortization are provided for in amounts sufficient to relate the cost of depreciable assets to operations over their estimated service lives, principally on a straight-line basis.

Note 3—Mortgage Indebtedness

The 0% first mortgage note is collateralized by a portion of the Bank's real estate that composes the bank site. The note is payable $000 monthly and is due in 1984.

Note 4—Reserve for Loan Losses

Transactions in the reserve account were as follows:

	1980	1979
Balance at beginning of year	$000,000	$000,000
Provision charged to operating expenses	00,000	00,000
Transferred from undivided profits	00,000	00,000
	000,000	000,000
Less loans charged off, net of recoveries of $0,000 and $0,000	00,000	000,000
Balance at end of year	$000,000	$000,000

The loan-loss provision charged to operating expenses is based on the Bank's past loan-loss experience and such other factors which, in management's judgment, deserve current recognition in estimating possible loan losses and also meets the minimum provision required under the formula computed on the basis of net charge-offs to total loans over the past five years as prescribed by the Comptroller of the Currency. The amount transferred from undivided profits represents an additional provision allowed for tax and other purposes and is not in anticipation of any unusual losses.

Note 5—Capital Account Transactions

A 0% stock dividend was paid to stockholders of record January 31, 1980, with the aggregate par value of the stock issued being transferred from undivided profits to common stock. In 1980, 00,000 shares of common stock were offered to stockholders under a preemptive rights provision. The excess of the amount received over the par value of the stock was credited to surplus.

During the current year, the stockholders approved an employee stock option plan under which a total of 0,000 shares of common stock was made available for granting through February 17, 1991. During 1980, options for 0,000 shares were issued. The option price of $00 per share was based on the stock offering mentioned above.

At the Bank's inception, $000,000 of the original capitalization was allocated to undivided profits, a generally accepted practice in the banking industry for the early years of a bank's operations. In 1971, this amount was transferred to surplus in accordance with the regulations of the Comptroller of the Currency.

A 00% stock dividend was declared to stockholders of record December 31, 1980, to be issued on January 15, 1981.

The Bank intends to offer to stockholders of record March 31, 1981, 00,00 shares of common stock, subject to the approval by the Comptroller of the Currency. Each stockholder would be entitled to approximately one additional share of stock for each four shares owned.

Note 6—Retirement Plan

The Bank has a non-contributory retirement plan which covers full-time employees who have completed one year of service and who have attained the age of twenty-one but have not attained their sixtieth birthday. Total pension cost approximated $00,000 and $00,000 for 1980 and 1979 respectively. There is no unfunded liability for past service costs.

Note 7—Commitments

The Bank leases a substantial portion of the land that composes the Bank site. Expiration of the leases range from 2001 through 2070 and provide aggregate annual rentals of approximately $00,000. The Bank intends to build additional facilities on land covered by a lease expiring in 2001. Construction is expected to commence in 1981, at an estimated cost of $000,000.

Note 8—Earnings per Common Share

Earnings per common share has been computed based on the weighted average of shares outstanding, after giving retroactive effect to stock dividends issued.

SAVINGS AND LOAN ASSOCIATIONS

Overview

The preferable accounting principles for savings and loan associations appear in the audit and accounting guide entitled "Savings and Loan Associations" (hereinafter referred to as the S&L Guide).

Generally accepted accounting principles (GAAP) and practices that have been promulgated for commercial enterprises are also used in reporting on savings and loan associations. The S&L Guide discusses the application of existing GAAP to savings and loan associations.

Most savings and loan associations are mutual companies which are owned by the depositors and borrowers of the association. In the minority, are capital stock associations, which issue and sell capital stock to investors. The capital stock which is usually considered permanent equity is called "guaranty stock", "guarantee stock", or "permanent reserve shares."

A savings and loan association is chartered either by the Federal Home Loan Bank Board (FHLBB), or by a state. Those chartered by the FHLBB are federal associations and are subject to the rules and regulations of the FHLBB, the Federal Savings and Loan Insurance Corporation (FSLIC), and the Federal Home Loan Bank (FHLB). Savings and loan associations chartered by a state are subject to the rules and regulations of the state in which they operate and the Federal Home Loan Bank. State-chartered associations are also subject to the rules and regulations of the FSLIC if they are insured by the FSLIC. Federal associations are required to insure savings accounts with the FSLIC, while state-chartered associations are not usually required to insure their savings accounts with the FSLIC, but can if they desire.

In states which allow capital stock associations, regulations have been promulgated by the FHLBB that permit federally insured mutual associations to convert to capital stock associations.

The capital stock of a capital stock association may be owned, in whole or in part, by a corporation which is not a savings and loan association. These corporations are called "holding companies" and they exist only in those states which permit capital stock associations. Holding companies of capital stock associations are subject to the same rules and regulations of regular savings and loan associations. All acquisitions of capital stock associations by holding companies are subject to the approval of many different regulatory agencies.

The Office of Examinations and Supervision (OES) of the FHLBB is charged with the responsibility of performing examinations of all federal and state-chartered associations whose accounts are insured by the FSLIC. State-chartered institutions which are not insured by the FSLIC are examined periodically by the states in which they operate. Thus, as a general rule, all savings and loan associations whether insured or not, undergo some sort of periodic examination.

Generally, both federal and state regulations require that savings and loan associations prepare their financial statements on the accrual basis.

Preferable Accounting Principles

Generally accepted accounting principles and practices which have been promulgated for commercial enterprises are also used in reporting on savings and loan associations. The S&L Guide contains the specialized application of GAAP to savings and loan associations.

Investments in securities   The types of investment securities that savings and loan associations can acquire and hold are restricted by state and federal regulations. As a general rule, savings and loan associations must invest most of their available funds in U.S. Government Debt Securities. However, some states do permit savings and loan associations to invest in equity securities. Debt securities are not covered by FASB-12 (Accounting for Certain Marketable Securities).

The preferable accounting principles in the S&L Guide require that investments in securities be recorded at cost and presented in the financial statements at amortized cost (net carrying value). Discounts and premiums should be amortized against investment income, using the "interest method". Market values of investments in securities not covered by FASB-12 should be disclosed parenthetically in the financial statements. Permanent declines in market value below amortized cost should be recognized as a loss to income in the period in which the permanent decline is discovered. The intent and ability of the savings and loan association to hold an investment security to its maturity should be included as a factor in determining whether a permanent decline in market value has occurred.

Short-term loans are frequently made to other members of the Federal Reserve System which are called "federal funds". The duration of these loans is usually for one or two days. Separate disclosure of "federal fund" loans should be made in the financial statements if they are material.

Savings and loan associations may enter into agreements called "repos", or "reverse repos". A "repo" transaction occurs when a savings and loan association invests funds on a short-term basis at a stated rate of interest. To secure the loan, the borrower "sells" the savings and loan association certain specified securities and agrees, at the same time, to repurchase the exact same securities at the exact same price at which they were sold. The savings and loan association must sell the securities back to the borrower and thus the securities actually represent collateral. The amount of securities involved almost always exceeds the amount of funds involved to provide the lender with a cushion. The interest rate on a "repo" is negotiated and any interest or dividends received on the securities involved belong to the borrower. Only in the event of a default by the borrower can the savings and loan association (lender) exercise ownership rights in the securities involved. In addition, the securities involved remain under the control of the borrower. "Repo" transactions can be made for one day or several months and actually represent a loan transaction, at a specified rate of interest, which is secured by collateral in excess of the loan amount.

A "reverse repo" is exactly the opposite of a "repo". A savings and loan association will borrow a sum of money at a stated rate of interest and concurrently sell to the lender under an agreement of repurchase, certain specified securities owned by the savings and loan association.

In a "repo", or "reverse repo", the borrower is always the party who sells the securities under an agreement to repurchase the same securities. In substance a "repo", or "reverse repo", represents a loan transaction because the securities involved are only sold in legal form but never actually change hands unless a default occurs. Thus, these transactions should be accounted for in substance, not in legal form. The borrower records the transaction as a liability and the lender records the transaction as a loan receivable. No entry is made on either the borrower's or lender's books for the securities involved and, in fact, the securities never change hands. However, to comply with regulations the borrower does record a "memo entry" that the securities involved have been sold.

Material amounts of "repos", or "reverse repos" should be separately disclosed in the financial statements or footnotes thereto.

Savings and loan associations may invest in bonds which are backed by mortgages. This type of investment security represents packages of real estate loans which are easily brought or sold on existing markets.

The Federal National Mortgage Association (FNMA) issues these types of bonds which are authorized by the Government National Mortgage Association (GNMA). FNMA issues these bonds in fixed principal amounts at a stated rate of interest, for a specified term. These bonds are properly classified as investment securities.

The Chicago Board of Trade operates the GNMA futures market where savings and loan associations may hedge their actual positions by buying or selling future contracts. However, regulations do not allow federal savings and loan associations to speculate in the futures market.

Gain or loss on hedge transactions in GNMA futures should be deferred and amortized over the estimated life of the related loan or group of loans.

Loans Mortgage loans secured by real estate, represent the major business activity of savings and loan associations. All associations are restricted by regulations on the amount and the type of mortgage loan they can make. An important restriction is the loan-to-value restriction, which may be based on the geographic lending area and the specific type of loan. Generally, the loan-to-value restriction limits the amount of mortgage loan which can be made to a certain percentage of the market value of the real property securing the loan.

A "straight construction loan" is one which is made only for the period of construction, and is due to be repaid, in full, at the end of the construction period. The other major type of construction loan is one which is made for the period of construction and then converted by the terms of the loan, into a permanent mortgage loan. Frequently, the savings and loan association holds the construction funds and only makes disbursements on presentation of proof that certain specified work has been satisfactorily completed and a "waiver of lien" has been obtained from the subcontractor or supplier. The "waiver of lien" is a legal document which provides the savings and loan association with protection that the subcontractor or supplier will not file a lien on the property for the completed work or services.

> *OBSERVATION: The S&L Guide is silent on how mortgage loan receivables secured by real estate should be valued for reporting purposes by savings and loan associations.*
>
> *Since mortgage loan receivables held by a mortgage banker for long-term investment purposes, or held for sale in the ordinary course of business, are exactly the same as those held by savings and loan associations, it is logical to assume that the preferable accounting principles be the same.*
>
> *The preferable accounting principles for mortgage loan receivables held by mortgage bankers can be found in the chapter on the Mortgage Banking Industry.*

Savings and loan associations make loans which are secured by a savings account. The savings account is held as collateral by the association to secure the loan. If the loan is not paid when due, the savings and loan association may use the funds in the collateral savings account to pay off the loan.

Other types of loans which a savings and loan association may be permitted to make are (1) land development loans, (2) property improvement loans, (3) educational loans, (4) consumer loans, and (5) loans on mobile homes.

Mortgage servicing fees Most all types of loans must be serviced. The process of collecting, sending notices, maintaining mortgage records, and other related chores are referred to as "servicing". An owner of a loan, or portfolio of loans may perform the "servicing function" itself, or may engage someone else to perform such services (see chapter on the Mortgage Banking Industry). An entity which performs the "service function" for mortgage loans, usually charges a fee based on a percentage of the unpaid principal balance of the loan. Servicing revenue may be quite substantial.

As a general rule, most savings and loan associations "service" their own outstanding loans and may also service loans for others.

A problem may arise when a savings and loan association sells a loan or portfolio of loans and agrees to continue servicing the loans at a fee which is significantly different from prevailing servicing rates.

Ordinarily, when a loan or portfolio of loans is sold and the buyer assumes the servicing function, no problem arises. Gain or loss on the sale of loans is the difference between the sales price and the net carrying amount of the loans. However, when loans are sold and the seller continues the servicing function for the buyer, a problem arises if the servicing fee charged is significantly different from that of the prevailing servicing rates. In this event, gain on the sale must be decreased to provide a normal profit on future servicing income based on estimated prevailing rates. For example, if the estimated prevailing fee for servicing revenue is 1% of the unpaid principal balance of the loans and the estimated future costs for servicing are .4%, the normal profit on the future servicing revenue would be estimated to be .6%. If the agreement for the sale of the loans included a total servicing fee of .5% of the unpaid principal balances, normal estimated profit on servicing revenue would be reduced to .1%. Therefore, the future servicing revenue must be increased by the difference between the normal estimated profit of .6% and the estimated profit of .1%, for a total of the .5%. The adjustment is made in the amount of the present value of the difference. Thus, if one million dollars in loans were involved in the sale, the adjustment would be the present value of .5% of one million dollars. The journal entry to record the adjustment is a debit to the gain on the sale of loans and a credit to deferred servicing revenue. The deferred servicing revenue is amortized to income over the life of the related loans, so that each future period will theoretically receive a normal profit on the servicing revenue. In the case of a loss on the sale of loans, the loss would be increased by the amount of the present value of the adjustment necessary to increase future servicing revenue to yield a normal profit.

It is very important to note that the adjustment to future servicing revenue profits is only made when the impact on operating results is significant (SOP 74-12).

The preferable accounting principles for excessive or deficient servicing fees is covered by SOP 74-12 (Accounting Practices in the Mortgage Banking Industry).

Premium or discount on sales of loans A savings and loan association may sell an entire portfolio of loans or a participation in a portfolio of loans, or a single loan. According to the S&L Guide, when a participation is sold and the buyer agrees to pay the face amount of the loans but also agrees to pay a rate of interest which is more or less than the average rate of interest stated on the loans (after taking into consideration servicing fees, if any), the transaction should be accounted for in accordance with APB-21 (Interest on Receivables and Payables). Thus, a premium or discount will result on the transaction.

> *OBSERVATION: Apparently, the industry audit and accounting guide entitled "Savings and Loan Associations" is incorrect because APB-21 expressly excludes from its provisions any transaction arising in the ordinary course of business of any lending institution.*

Pass-through certificates Savings and loan associations pool certain qualifying VA and FHA mortgage loans and issue pass-through certificates which represent participation in the pool. The pass-through certificates are issued at a stated rate of interest on the unpaid principal and are usually guaranteed by GNMA. The pooled mortgage loans must be of equal interest rates and all have the same approximate maturity date. Similar pass-through certificates are issued by the Federal Home Loan Mortgage Corporation.

Pass through certificates are repaid in fixed amounts of principal and interest over the life of the certificate. Repayment on principal and interest is usually made monthly and the issuing association keeps records of the individual certificate holders. In addition, if loans are paid off before maturity, the issuing association will usually make a pro-rata distribution of principal.

Although pass-through certificates are similar to investment securities, they more closely resemble a participating interest in real estate loans. Thus, investments in pass-through certificates by savings and loan associations should be accounted for as participation interests in real estate and not as investment securities.

For tax purposes, pass-through certificates have been ruled, by the Internal Revenue Service, to meet the qualifications of (1) "loans secured by an interest in real property", and (2) as "qualifying real property loans".

If a savings and loan association has issued mortgage backed securities and the amount is material, disclosure of the amount, type, interest rate, and all other pertinent facts should be made in the financial statements or footnotes thereto.

Loans in process This account is used usually by savings and loan associations to record the disbursements of mortgage loans. The gross amount of each mortgage loan and all disbursement to the mortgagor are recorded in this account. Any undisbursed portions of any mortgage loan will appear in the "loans in process" account. Undisbursed balances of mortgage loans are deducted from the related loans for financial statement purposes. Treatment of the "loans in process" account for regulatory purposes sometimes conflicts with GAAP.

Loan commitments   If loan commitments are material in relationship to total assets, they should be disclosed in the financial statements. While loan commitments are not recorded in the books of accounts, a file of outstanding loan commitments is usually maintained by each savings and loan association. Income from loan commitments is discussed later in this chapter.

Troubled debt restructuring   All savings and loan associations must comply with the provisions of FASB-15 (Accounting by Debtors and Creditors for Troubled Debt Restructuring).

   Real estate that is acquired or reacquired by a savings and loan association which is not covered by FASB-15, should be carried at the lower of cost or estimated net realizable value. All direct holding costs are properly capitalized, but the total carrying amount must not exceed the estimated net realizable value.

Gains and losses on real estate sales   GAAP should be followed in reporting gains and losses on sales of real estate by savings and loan associations. The S&L Guide mentions the following pronouncements which may be applicable to real estate sales by savings and loan associations:

1. APB-21 (Interest on Receivables and Payables)
2. Industry Accounting Guide entitled "Accounting for Profit Recognition on Sales of Real Estate"
3. Industry Accounting Guide entitled "Accounting for Retail Land Sales"
4. SOP 75-6 (Questions Concerning Profit Recognition on Sales of Real Estate)
5. SOP 78-2 (Accounting Practices of Real Estate Investment Trusts)

   The S&L Guide does not mention the following pronouncements which are certainly as applicable to real estate sales as the above pronouncements:

1. SOP 75-2 (Accounting Practices of Real Estate Investments Trusts)
2. SOP 78-3 (Accounting for Costs to Sell and Rent, and Initial Rental Operations of, Real Estate Projects)
3. SOP 78-4 (Application of the Deposit, Installment, and Cost Recovery Methods in Accounting for Sales of Real Estate)

> *OBSERVATION:* *All of the above pronouncements may be found elsewhere in this publication except APB-21 (Interest on Receivables and Payables). As mentioned previously, APB-21 specifically excludes lending institutions from its provisions. Thus, the S&L Guide is apparently incorrect in stating that savings and loan associations must comply with the provisions of APB-21. If the FASB agrees with the application of APB-21 to savings and loan associations as stated in the S&L Guide, then it should either amend or interpret APB-21.*

Investments in real estate ventures   The S&L Guide states that savings and loan associations should comply with SOP 78-9 (Accounting for Investments in Real Estate Ventures).

> *OBSERVATION:* *SOP 78-9 may be found elsewhere in this publication. Briefly, SOP 78-9 deals with the Equity Method and its application to unincorporated entities.*

Savings accounts   The main resources of a savings and loan association are derived from savings accounts. Many different types of savings accounts exists, including passbook accounts, money-market certificates, vacation club accounts, Christmas Club accounts, and other special purpose savings accounts. Federal regulations on the rate of interest which may be paid on savings accounts are contained in regulation "Q".

The total amount of savings accounts should be broken down by interest rates and disclosed in the notes to the financial statements.

Escrow accounts   In addition to the regular periodic payments of interest and principal, a borrower may be required by the terms of the mortgage loan, to also make periodic payments for taxes and insurance on the mortgaged property. These payments are held by the savings and loan association in an escrow account from which the actual payments for insurance and taxes are made as they become due.

Escrow accounts should be reported as a liability on the statement of financial condition (balance sheet), or disclosed in a note to the financial statements.

Deferred income taxes   A savings and loan association may qualify for special tax consideration which appears in subchapter H of the Internal Revenue Code. The two most important benefits of subchapter H are (1) a special method of computing the allowance for bad debts, and (2) foreclosure on real estate properties is not a taxable event.

To qualify for the special method of computing bad debts, the loans of a savings and loan association must meet the Internal Revenue Code's definition of "qualifying real property loans". In general, the special method allows the deduction for bad debt to be a percentage of taxable income, subject to certain limitations. The allowance for bad debts computed under the special method differs significantly with the same allowance determined in accordance with GAAP.

The special treatment of foreclosures on real estate properties is allowed by the Internal Revenue Code if the loans qualify as "loans secured by an interest in real property". If the loans do meet the required definition, no gain or loss is recognized for tax purposes in the event of a foreclosure. For tax purposes, the foreclosed property has the same character as the loan it secured. In other words, foreclosure is not a taxable event and the tax basis of the foreclosed property is the same as that of its related foreclosed loan (substituted basis). In addition, for tax purposes any provision for losses for either the loan or the foreclosed property, and any gain or loss on the eventual disposition of the foreclosed property are not included in taxable income, but are charged or credited to the allowance for bad debt.

Because of the special tax treatment for the allowance for bad debt and gain or loss on foreclosed mortgages, a difference will exist between taxable income (per tax return) and pre-taxed financial accounting income (GAAP).

Bad debt allowances of savings and loan associations that create a difference between taxable income and pretax financial accounting income are usually considered permanent differences, because the company controls the events that create the tax consequence. However, if circumstances dictate that income taxes will be paid because of a reduction in the bad debt allowance, a tax expense should be accrued on such reductions in the period they occur. In effect, these reductions do create a timing difference when they occur and should not be accounted for as an extraordinary item.

Disclosure of bad debt allowances should be made in the financial statements or in footnotes, as follows:

1. the purpose of the allowance account and the rules and regulations pertaining thereto
2. the fact that income taxes may become payable, if the allowance account is used for other purposes
3. the total amount of the allowance account for which income taxes have not been accrued

These disclosure requirements also apply to the parent company of the savings and loan association.

Debentures and subordinated debt   Savings and loan associations are permitted by federal regulations to issue subordinated debt securities for a term of up to seven years. This type of debt is sometimes reflected as part of "equity" for regulatory purposes. However, for purposes of GAAP these debt securities must be appropriately classified as a liability.

Capital stock   As mentioned previously, most savings and loan associations are not stock companies. However, capital stock is accounted for as provided for under existing GAAP.

Mutual savings and loan associations have no capital stock and are owned by their depositors and borrowers. The equity section in the statement of financial condition for a mutual association does not reflect any capital stock. Usually, the only account that appears in the equity section of a mutual association is retained earnings, and any additions or deductions from retained earnings.

Retained earnings   In the statement of financial condition (balance sheet) of a savings and loan association, retained earnings should be shown as a single amount. Material restrictions on retained earnings (and there usually are) should be disclosed in the financial statements. It may be desirable to disclose regulatory restrictions on retained earnings separately from other restrictions.

If retained earnings are substantially restricted, a notation should be placed next to the retained earnings account in the statement of financial condition to that effect.

Disclosure should be made in a note to the financial statements describing the amount and type of statutory and supervisory reserves which have been treated as an appropriation of retained earnings.

Revenues   The largest portion of the revenues of a savings and loan association is derived from interest income. The interest income is earned on the many types of loans that an association will have outstanding.

Loan commitment fees   Loan commitment fees probably represent the second largest source of revenue, after interest income. Most loan commitment fees are nonrefundable and represent a charge which the savings and loan associations makes for entering into a binding agreement to furnish a loan. Underwriting costs are those which the savings and loan association incurs in processing loans. Direct underwriting costs include, direct loan personnel salaries, appraisals, site inspection, loan processing costs, and other direct related costs. Loan commitment fees may also include a charge for earmarking the funds for the prospective borrower, sometimes at a specific interest rate.

A loan commitment is usually a written representation from the savings and loan association, to lend funds for a specific purpose, and term. A "floating rate commitment" is one in which the interest rate to be charged on the loan is determined by the prevailing rate at the time the loan is drawn upon. A "fixed rate commitment" is one in which the interest rate is specified in the commitment.

The recognition of revenue from loan commitment fees varies with the type and substance of the commitment. Obviously, income is recognized on all commitment fees if the loan is not made and the commitment period expires. In this event, the association has no obligation to perform and the loan commitment fee is earned.

At the time a commitment actually becomes an obligation of the savings and loan association, an amount of the commitment fee equal to the direct underwriting costs should be recognized as income. Any amount of a commitment fee which is compensation for earmarking the necessary funds for the loan, should be deferred and amortized, by the straight-line method, over the term of the commitment. Any amount of a commitment fee which is charged for possible changes in interest rates should be deferred until the loan is actually drawn. At the time the loan is drawn, the interest rate in the commitment is compared to the market rate and if it is the same, or less, the amount should be recognized as income at that time. However, if the market rate of interest is higher than that specified in the loan commitment, the amount of fee should be deferred and amortized at a constant rate (interest method) over the life of the loan.

When a commitment fee exceeds the direct underwriting costs and such excess can only be attributed to an adjustment of the yield on the loan, the excess should be deferred and amortized over both the commitment term and loan period. During the commitment term the amortization should be on a straight-line basis and during the loan period the amortization should be at a constant rate (interest method).

Unamortized loan commitment fees on completed loans should be deducted from their related loan receivable in the statement of financial condition.

When a savings and loan association originates an in-house loan it usually receives an "origination fee", which is generally equal to the direct underwriting costs to make the loan. Origination fees are accounted for in a similar manner as loan commitment fees. Thus, if the origination fee is equal to the direct underwriting costs it is recognized as income at the time the loan is closed. (For a discussion on how origination and loan commitment fees are accounted for by mortgage bankers, see chapter on the Mortgage Banking Industry).

Expenses   Interest paid on savings accounts is usually the largest expense that is incurred by a savings and loan association. Existing GAAP should be followed in accounting for interest expense.

Business combinations   Existing GAAP, including APB-16 (Business Combinations), and FASB Interpretation-9 (Applying APB-16 and 17, When a Savings and Loan Association or a Similar Institution is Acquired in a Business Combination Accounted for by the Purchase Method), should be followed in accounting for business combinations of savings and loan associations.

When a savings and loan association is acquired in a business combination accounted for by the purchase method, the assets and liabilities acquired are recorded at their fair values on the date of acquisition. This is called the "separate valuation method", as opposed to the "net spread method", which values the purchase as a whole, based on the spread between interest rates received on the mortgage portfolio and interest rates paid on savings accounts. The net spread method is unacceptable for GAAP purposes.

Any portion of the purchase price that cannot be assigned to specifically identifiable tangible and intangible assets acquired by a savings and loan association, less liabilities assumed, shall be recorded as goodwill. Goodwill must be amortized by the straight-line method (APB-17) unless both the following conditions are met:

1. Part or all of the recorded goodwill includes one or more of the following factors which could not be separately determined:
    a. capacity of existing savings accounts and loan accounts to generate future income and/or additional business or new business
    b. nature of territory served
2. The anticipated benefits to be received from the factors in 1 above are expected to decline over their estimated lives.

Only in those cases where both of the above conditions are met can accelerated methods be used to amortize the purchased goodwill (FASB Interpretation-9).

Comprehensive Illustration

The following is a comprehensive illustration of the preferable accounting principles contained in this chapter.

SAVINGS AND LOAN ASSOCIATION
STATEMENT OF CONDITION
As of December 31, 1980 and 1979

	1980	1979
ASSETS		
Cash	$ 00,000,000	$ 00,000,000
United States government and other securities, at amortized cost, partially pledged (market: 1980, $00,000,000; 1979, $00,000,000) (notes 7 and 8)	00,000,000	00,000,000
Loans receivable (notes 2 and 4)	0,000,000,000	0,000,000,000
Interest receivable, less allowance for delinquent interest: 1980, $000,000; 1979, $000,000	00,000,000	00,000,000
Real estate owned (notes 3 and 4)	0,000,000	0,000,000
Premises and equipment (note 6)	00,000,000	00,000,000
Investment in Federal Home Loan Bank stock and Secondary Insurance Reserve, at cost (note 8)	00,000,000	00,000,000
Accounts receivable and other assets	0,000,000	0,000,000
Excess of cost over value assigned to net assets of associations acquired, less amortization	0,000,000	0,000,000
	$0,000,000,000	$0,000,000,000
LIABILITIES AND STOCKHOLDERS' EQUITY		
Savings accounts (note 7)	$0,000,000,000	$0,000,000,000
Advances from Federal Home Loan Bank (note 8)	000,000,000	000,000,000
Commercial paper (note 8)	000,000,000	0,000,000,000
Other borrowings (note 8)	00,000,000	00,000,000
Taxes on income (deferred: 1980, $00,000,000; 1979, $00,000,000) (note 9)	00,000,000	00,000,000
Other liabilities and accrued expenses	00,000,000	00,000,000
Unearned income	00,000,000	0,000,000
	0,000,000,000	0,000,000,000
Stockholders' equity (see separate statement)	00,000,000	00,000,000
Contingencies and commitments (notes 9 and 12)		
	$0,000,000,000	$0,000,000,000

SAVINGS AND LOAN ASSOCIATION
STATEMENT OF OPERATIONS
Years Ended December 31, 1980 and 1979

	1980	1979
INCOME:		
Interest on loans	$000,000,000	$000,000,000
Loan origination fees	00,000,000	0,000,000
Other fees	0,000,000	0,000,000
Income on investments	00,000,000	0,000,000
Real estate operations, net (note 3)	(00,000)	(00,000)
Other income (note 5)	0,000,000	000,000
	000,000,000	000,000,000
EXPENSES:		
Administrative and general:		
Salaries and related personnel costs	00,000,000	00,000,000
Equipment and office occupancy expense (note 6)	0,000,000	0,000,000
Advertising	0,000,000	0,000,000
Other expenses	0,000,000	0,000,000
	00,000,000	00,000,000
Interest on savings accounts	000,000,000	00,000,000
Interest on borrowings	00,000,000	00,000,000
Provision for losses (note 4)	000,000	000,000
	000,000,000	000,000,000
Income before taxes on income	00,000,000	00,000,000
Taxes on income (note 9)	0,000,000	00,000,000
Net income	$ 00,000,000	$ 00,000,000
Net income per common share (note 11)	$0.00	$0.00

See Accompanying Notes to Financial Statements

SAVINGS AND LOAN ASSOCIATION
STATEMENT OF STOCKHOLDERS' EQUITY
Years Ended December 31, 1980 and 1979

	Common Stock (Note 11) $0 Par Value Per Share Authorized 00,000,000 Shares		Paid-in Capital	Retained Earnings—Substantially Restricted (Note 10)	Common Stock in Treasury		Total Stockholders' Equity
	Shares Issued	Par			Shares	Cost	
Balance at December 31, 1978	0,000,000	$0,000,000	0,000,000	00,000,000	(000,000)	($0,000,000)	00,000,000
Treasury stock sold at market to Employee Stock Ownership Plan	—	—	00,000	—	00,000	00,000	000,000
Treasury stock issued upon exercise of stock options	—	—	00,000	—	00,000	00,000	000,000
Cash dividends paid $.00 per share	—	—	—	(0,000,000)	—	—	(0,000,000)
Adjustment to investment in subsidiary	—	—	—	(0,000)	—	—	(0,000)
Net income for the year ended December 31, 1979	—	—	—	00,000,000	—	—	00,000,000
Balance at December 31, 1979	0,000,000	0,000,000	0,000,000	00,000,000	(000,000)	(0,000,000)	00,000,000
Treasury stock sold at market to Employee Stock Ownership Plan	—	—	000,000	—	00,000	00,000	000,000
Treasury stock issued upon exercise of stock options	—	—	00,000	—	00,000	—	000,000
Cash dividends paid, $.00 per share	—	—	—	(0,000,000)	—	—	(0,000,000)
Adjustment to investment in subsidiary	—	—	—	(0,000)	—	—	(0,000)
Net income for the year ended December 31, 1980	—	—	—	00,000,000	—	—	00,000,000
Balance at December 31, 1980	0,000,000	$0,000,000	0,000,000	00,000,000	(000,000)	($0,000,000)	00,000,000

See Accompanying Notes to Financial Statements

SAVINGS AND LOAN ASSOCIATION
STATEMENT OF CHANGES IN FINANCIAL POSITION
Years Ended December 31, 1980 and 1979

	1980	1979
Funds provided by:		
Operations:		
Net income	$ 00,000,000	$ 00,000,000
Charges (credits) to income not requiring funds:		
Deferred income taxes (note 9)	0,000,000	0,000,000
Depreciation and amortization (note 6)	0,000,000	0,000,000
Net increase in deferred fee income	0,000,000	0,000,000
Provision for losses, net (note 4)	(0,000,000)	000,000
Reversal of unused portion of liability established in 1976 (note 5)	(0,000,000)	—
Funds provided by operations	00,000,000	00,000,000
Loan principal repayments:		
Monthly amortization	00,000,000	00,000,000
Cash payoffs	000,000,000	00,000,000
Sale of loans	000,000,000	000,000,000
Increase in savings accounts:		
Net deposits	000,000,000	000,000,000
Interest credited to savings accounts	00,000,000	00,000,000
Real estate loans foreclosed	000,000	0,000,000
Sales of real estate owned	00,000,000	0,000,000
Increase in borrowings	000,000,000	00,000,000
Net decrease in cash and investment securities	00,000,000	—
	$000,000,000	$000,000,000
Funds used for:		
Loan originations	$000,000,000	$000,000,000
Purchases of loans	00,000,000	00,000,000
Loans refinanced	(00,000,000)	(00,000,000)
Increase in undisbursed loan funds	(0,000,000)	(00,000,000)
Loan disbursements	000,000,000	000,000,000
Net increase in cash and investment securities	—	00,000,000
Purchase of GNMA loan certificates	00,000,000	—
Additions to real estate owned	0,000,000	0,000,000
Increase in Federal Home Loan Bank stock	00,000,000	0,000,000
Dividends paid	0,000,000	0,000,000
	$000,000,000	$000,000,000

NOTES TO FINANCIAL STATEMENTS

Note 1—Summary of Significant Accounting Policies

The accounting and reporting policies of Savings and Loan Association (Company) and its subsidiary, Save-Much Savings and Loan Association (Saver) conform to generally accepted accounting principles and to general practice within the savings and loan industry and are as follows:

Consolidation   The Consolidated Financial Statements include those of the Company and its subsidiary Saver. All material intercompany accounts and transactions have been eliminated in consolidation.

Deferred Fee Income   Loan origination fees in excess of 0% of the loan plus $000 for construction loans and 0% of the loan plus $000 for other loans are deferred and amortized to income by the straight-line method over 10 years or until the loan is paid off or sold.

Commitment Fees   Non-refundable fees received for commitments to make loans are deferred, except for the portion representing underwriting costs, and recognized as income as follows:

1. Commitments to make loans at the market rate of interest: The fee is amortized by the straight-line method over the term of the commitment.

2. Commitments to make loans up to a maximum or at a fixed interest rate: The fee is amortized to income during the commitment period by the straight-line method using a life of the combined commitment period and estimated loan life. When loans are funded at a below market interest rate, the balance of the fee is amortized over the life of the loan as a yield adjustment. When loans are funded at a market interest rate, or the commitment expires unused, the remaining balance of the fee is recognized at that time.

Provision For Losses   Provisions for losses are established by a charge to earnings when a liability can be reasonably estimated or, in the case of loans and property owned, when Saver's investment in such assets is greater than their estimated realizable value. When it is anticipated that real estate will be held for an extended period of time, holding costs, including a discount factor to give effect to the cost of money, are considered in providing valuation allowances. Additionally, an overall provision for possible losses on loans has been provided based on the loss experience of prior periods and current economic trends.

Loan Sales   Additional funds are obtained by selling loans and participating interests therein. Any gains or losses on these sales are recognized at the time of sale. Saver generally continues to service the loans sold, paying the buyer an agreed yield which is normally less than the interest rate paid by the borrowers, the difference being retained by Saver as a service fee. These service fees are included in Interest on Loans in the Consolidated Statements of Operation.

Investment Securities   These securities partially fulfill certain regulatory liquidity requirements and are carried at amortized cost, as it is generally management's intention to hold them to maturity thereby recovering their carrying value.

Premises and Equipment   Depreciation and amortization of premises and equipment are computed on the straight-line basis over the estimated useful lives as follows:

Buildings	20 to 50 years
Leaseholds	Term of the lease
Furniture and equipment	3 to 50 years

Maintenance and repairs are charged to expense and improvements are capitalized. The cost and accumulated depreciation relating to property and equipment retired or otherwise disposed of are eliminated from the accounts and any resultant gains and losses are credited or charged to earnings.

Federal Home Loan Bank System   As a member of the Federal Home Loan Bank System, Saver is required to invest an amount equal to the larger of 1% of its outstanding residential loans or 1/20 (1/12 prior to December, 1979) of its outstanding advances in capital stock of the Federal Home Loan Bank.

Eligible savings accounts of Saver are insured up to $00,000 ($000,000 per public agency) by the Federal Savings and Loan Insurance Corporation (FSLIC). In addition to the annual premium for this insurance, the FSLIC has required deposits to be made to a secondary insurance reserve under the control of FSLIC. This reserve is being refunded over a ten year period, starting in 1975, by cash payments and by credits against a portion of the annual insurance premium.

Dividends received by Saver on its FHLB capital stock and interest earned on its secondary reserve are included in Income on Investments in the Consolidated Statements of Operations.

The Excess of Cost over Value Assigned to Net Assets of Associations Acquired This deferred charge attributable to associations acquired in 1971 and prior is being amortized by charges to income, using the straight-line method, over periods of 20 to 40 years from the date of acquisition.

Taxes on Income Deferred income taxes have been provided on earnings reported for financial statement purposes but which are deferred for tax purposes. The Company takes the investment tax credit, which is not material, into income as a reduction in income taxes in the year after it is used as a tax credit.

Note 2—Loans Receivable

Loans receivable at December 31 are summarized as follows:

	1980	1979
Real estate loans secured by first deeds of trust:		
Residential–Single family	$0,000,000,000	0,000,000,000
Residential–Two to four units	000,000,000	000,000,000
Residential–Over four units	000,000,000	000,000,000
Commercial	000,000,000	000,000,000
Land	0,000,000	0,000,000
	0,000,000,000	0,000,000,000
Property improvement and other loans	00,000,000	00,000,000
Loans on savings accounts	00,000,000	00,000,000
	0,000,000,000	0,000,000,000
Less:		
Allowance for losses (note 4)	0,000,000	0,000,000
Undisbursed portion of loans in process	00,000,000	00,000,000
Unamortized loan fees	0,000,000	0,000,000
	$0,000,000,000	0,000,000,000

At December 31, 1980 real estate loans with outstanding principal balances of $00,000,000 (1979—$0,000,000) were in a non-interest bearing status because they were three or more months past due or in the process of foreclosure.

Certain loans secured by first deeds of trust are pledged as collateral for borrowings as set forth in Note 8.

At December 31, 1980 Saver was servicing $000,000,000 of loans and participating interests in loans owned by others (1979—$000,000,000).

Note 3—Real Estate Owned

Real estate owned consisted of the following at December 31:

	1980	1979
Acquired in settlement of loans, at cost	$ 0,000,000	0,000,000
Acquired for investment, at cost	0,000,000	0,000,000
	0,000,000	00,000,000
Less allowance for loss (note 4)	0,000,000	0,000,000
	$ 0,000,000	0,000,000

Net gain or loss from real estate operations is summarized as follows:

	Year Ended December 31	
	1980	1979
Foreclosed real estate:		
Net gain on sales	$000,000	00,000
Cost of funds and holding expense charged to allowance for loss	00,000	00,000
Expenses, net of rental income	(000,000)	(000,000)
	0,000	(000,000)
Properties held for investment:		
Net gain (loss) on sales	(000,000)	00,000
Cost of funds and holding expense charged to allowance for loss	00,000	00,000
Expenses, net of rental income	(00,000)	(00,000)
	(00,000)	00,000
Net loss	$(00,000)	(00,000)

Note 4—Allowances for Losses

The following is a summary of charges and credits to the allowances for losses on loans, real estate owned and other:

	Loans	Real Estate Owned	Other
Balance at December 31, 1978	$0,000,000	0,000,000	000,000
Additions charged to income	000,000	—	000,000
Reductions at sale credited to real estate operations	—	(00,000)	—
Transfers at foreclosure	(000,000)	000,000	—
Holding and selling expenses and cost of funds charged against the allowance	(00,000)	(00,000)	—
Settlement of proposed legal action	—	—	(00,000)
Balance at December 31, 1979	0,000,000	0,000,000	000,000
Additions charged to income	00,000	—	000,000
Reductions at sale credited to real estate operations	—	(000,000)	—
Holding and selling expenses and cost of funds charged against the allowance	—	(00,000)	—
Settlement of litigation	—	—	(00,000)
Unused allowances credited to real estate operations and other income, respectively	(000,000)	(000,000)	(000,000)
Allowance offset against amount receivable	—	—	(000,000)
Balance at December 31,1980	$0,000,000	0,000,000	000,000

The "other" allowance for loss is for certificates of deposit in a closed bank, in an amount equal to such certificates, and for estimated liabilities in connection with lending and other operating procedures. These items are included in the captions 'Accounts Receivable and Other Assets' and 'Other Liabilities and Accrued Expenses' in the accompanying Statements of Condition.

Note 5—Liabilities Assumed

In 1976, Saver received proceeds upon the liquidation of certain savings and loan associations and assumed certain liabilities from these associations. Provision was made for these liabilities assumed and income in the amount of $0,000,000 was recognized.

In 1980, the unused portion of this provision in the amount of $0,000,000 was recognized as income and is included in Other Income in the Consolidated Statement of Operations.

Note 6—Premises and Equipment

Premises and equipment consisted of the following at December 31:

	1980	1979
Land	$ 0,000,000	0,000,000
Buildings and leasehold improvements	00,000,000	00,000,000
Furniture, fixtures and equipment	00,000,000	0,000,000
Total cost	00,000,000	00,000,000
Less accumulated depreciation and amortization	0,000,000	0,000,000
	$00,000,000	00,000,000

The following expenses relating to premises and equipment have been charged to the Consolidated Statements of Operations:

	Year Ended December 31	
	1980	1979
Maintenance and repairs	$0,000,000	0,000,000
Depreciation and amortization of premises and equipment	0,000,000	0,000,000
Rents—Branch locations and office equipment	0,000,000	0,000,000
Other	000,000	000,000
	$0,000,000	0,000,000

Note 7—Savings Accounts

Savings accounts as of December 31, are summarized as follows:

	1980		1979	
	Amount	Percent	Amount	Percent
Certificate accounts:				
Average rate	00.00%		0.00%	
Maturity:				
Current year	$ 000,000,000	00.0%	$ 000,000,000	00.0%
1 to 2 years	000,000,000	0.0	00,000,000	0.0
2 to 3 years	000,000,000	0.0	000,000,000	0.0
3 to 4 years	00,000,000	0.0	000,000,000	0.0
4 to 5 years	00,000,000	0.0	00,000,000	0.0
Over 5 years	00,000,000	0.0	00,000,000	0.0
	0,000,000,000	00.0	000,000,000	00.0

Passbook accounts 0.0% (1979–0.00%)	000,000,000	00.0	000,000,000	00.0
Bonus accounts 0.0% and 0.00%	00,000,000	0.0	00,000,000	0.0
Total savings	$0,000,000,000	000.0%	$0,000,000,000	000.0%
Out of state savings accounts	$ 00,000,000		00,000,000	
Percent to total savings	0.0%		0.0%	

The average interest rate on savings based on stated interest rates, was 0.00% at December 31, 1980 (1979–0.00%). The weighted average interest rate, based on actual interest expense and the average monthly balance, was 0.00% for 1980 and 0.00% for 1979.

Investment securities with an approximate market value of $0,000,000 (1979–$0,000,000) and real estate loans with outstanding principal balances of approximately $000,000,000 (1979–$000,000,000) were pledged as security for certain state and local government agency deposits at December 31, 1980.

Note 8—Borrowings

Borrowings at December 31 are summarized as follows:

	1980	1979
Advances from Federal Home Loan Bank:		
Fixed rate	$000,000,000	000,000,000
Variable rate, 00% at December 31, 1980	000,000,000	—
	000,000,000	000,000,000
Interest range on fixed rate advances	0.0-0.00%	0.0-00.0%
Average interest rate, all advances	00.0%	0.00%
Commercial paper, net of unamortized discount: 1980, $0,000,000; 1979, $00,000	000,000,000	0,000,000
Average interest rate	00.0%	00.00%
Other Borrowings:		
Reverse repurchase agreements	00,000,000	0,000,000
Notes payable to banks:		
Secured	—	00,000,000
Unsecured	—	00,000,000
	00,000,000	00,000,000
Average interest rate	00.00%	00.00%
Total borrowings	$000,000,000	000,000,000

Highest month end balance	000,000,000	000,000,000
Average monthly borrowings, based on month end balances	000,000,000	000,000,000
Weighted average interest rate, based on the above balances and actual interest expense	00.00%	0.00%
Maturing in years ending December 31:		
1979	—	000,000,000
1980	000,000,000	00,000,000
1981	00,000,000	00,000,000
1982	00,000,000	0,000,000
1983	00,000,000	0,000,000
1984	0,000,000	0,000,000
	$000,000,000	000,000,000

Advances from the Federal Home Loan Bank are secured by the stock of the Federal Home Loan Bank and by pledges of certain real estate loans of Saver with outstanding principal balances of approximately $000,000,000 at December 31, 1980.

The reverse repurchase agreements at December 31, 1980 are secured by GNMA loan certificates totaling $00,000,000 (1979–by pledged securities with an approximate market value of $0,000,000).

The notes payable to banks at December 31, 1979 were secured by pledges of certain real estate loans of Saver and by 000,000 shares of the guarantee capital stock of Saver owned by the Company.

Note 9—Taxes on Income

The charge for taxes on income in the Consolidated Statements of Operations is comprised of the following items:

	Federal	*State*	*Total*
Year Ended December 31, 1980:			
Current tax expense	$0,000,000	000,000	0,000,000
Deferred tax expense	0,000,000	0,000,000	0,000,000
	$0,000,000	0,000,000	0,000,000
Year ended December 31, 1979:			
Current tax expense	$0,000,000	0,000,000	0,000,000
Deferred tax expense	0,000,000	000,000	0,000,000
	$0,000,000	0,000,000	00,000,000

Deferred tax expense results from timing differences in the recognition of income and expenses for tax and financial statement purposes. The sources of these differences and their tax effects are as follows:

	Year Ended December 31	
	1980	1979
Loan fee income deferred for tax purposes	$0,000,000	0,000,000
Increase in commitment fee income deferred on the books	(0,000,000)	(000,000)
Income and expense recognized on the accrual basis for financial statements but on the cash basis for tax returns	0,000,000	0,000,000
Effect of allowable federal bad debt deduction, net of preference tax	(0,000,000)	(000,000)
Miscellaneous	(000,000)	(0,000,000)
	$0,000,000	0,000,000

Combined federal and state income tax expense was less than that calculated by applying the statutory federal rate of 00% (1979–00%) to income before taxes on income. A reconciliation of the difference, expressed in percentages is as follows:

	Percent of Pre-tax Income	
	1980	1979
Statutory tax rate (federal)	00.0%	00.0%
State franchise tax, net of federal income tax benefit	0.0	0.0
Federal bad debt deduction based on a percentage of income, net of applicable preference tax	(00.0)	(00.0)
Miscellaneous	(0.0)	—
Effective tax rate	00.0%	00.0%

During 1979 and 1980 Saver qualified for a special bad debt deduction under the Internal Revenue Code related to additions to tax bad debt reserves established for the purpose of absorbing losses. The allowable deduction was 00% in 1979 and is 00% for 1980 and subsequent years. Generally, the amount of this deduction in excess of the normal federal income tax liability is subject to the 00% minimum tax on tax preference items. See also Notes 10 and 12.

The Internal Revenue Service has completed audits of the Company's consolidated income tax returns for the years 1974 through 1979 and has proposed certain adjustments related principally to timing differences in reporting of income for tax and financial statement purposes. The adjustments to the 1976-1979 returns, which are not material, have been agreed to by the Company. The proposed adjustments to the 1975 return are being disputed by the Company and while the ultimate outcome is presently undeterminable, management believes that final assessments, if any, will not materially affect the Company's consolidated financial statements.

Note 10—Restricted Retained Earnings

Retained earnings at December 31, 1980 include $00,000,000 (1979–$00,000,000), which has been allocated by Saver on an accrual basis to bad debt reserves for federal income tax purposes and for which no provision for income taxes has been made. If, in future periods, this amount is used for any purpose other than absorbing losses from bad debts, Saver will be liable for federal income tax at the then current corporate tax rate. The Company does not anticipate using this amount in a manner which will create federal income tax liability.

In connection with the insurance of accounts, Saver is required to maintain a federal insurance reserve which may be used only to absorb possible losses. Saver is also subject to the reserve requirements of the State. These requirements have been met. The regulatory reserves are not related to amounts of losses actually anticipated and therefore the appropriations to these reserves have not been charged against earnings.

The above allocations and requirements limit the amount of retained earnings available for distribution to stockholders as cash dividends as follows:

| | December 31, | |
	1980	1979
Retained earnings restricted by statutory reserve requirements	$00,000,000	00,000,000
Additional retained earnings subject to federal income tax	0,000,000	00,000,000
	00,000,000	00,000,000
Retained earnings not subject to federal income tax	00,000,000	00,000,000
Total retained earnings	$00,000,000	00,000,000

Note 11—Common Stock

Earnings per common share have been computed on the basis of the average number of shares of common stock and common stock equivalents outstanding during the year (1980–0,000,000 and 1979–0,000,000).

The Company has adopted a qualified and a non-qualified stock option plan, each plan covering 000,000 shares of the Company's common stock. The options under both plans expire five years from the date of grant and are exercisable 00% per annum on an accumulative basis during the five year option period. Additionally, under the non-qualified plan, the Company may provide that the options be exercisable in full throughout the option period. Option prices under the plans must be fixed by the Company at the date of grant and, under the qualified plan, must be at least equal to the market value of the stock on the date of grant.

The option prices and fair market values at the grant dates of options outstanding under the plans at December 31, 1980 are:

Grant Date	Number of Shares	Option Price		Fair Market Value at Grant Date	
		Per Share	Aggre-gate	Per Share	Aggre-gate
Qualified plan:	None				
Non-qualified plan: Exercisable in full throughout the option period:					
August 26, 1977	00,000	0.000	00,000	0.00	00,000
June 23, 1978	00,000	0.000	000,000	0.000	000,000
December 20, 1978	0,000	0.000	00,000	0.000	00,000

The following is a summary of options which became exercisable in 1979 and 1980:

	Number of Shares	Option Price		Fair Market Value at Date Exercisable	
		Per Share	Aggre-gate	Per Share	Aggre-gate
				0.00-	
1979: Qualified plan	0,000	$0.00	00,000	0.00	00,000
Non-qualified plan	0,000	0.00	00,000	0.00	00,000
1980: Non-qualified plan	0,000	0.00	00,000	0.000	00,000

Options exercised in 1979 and 1980 were:

	Number of Shares	Option Price		Fair Market Value at Date Exercised	
		Per Share	Aggre-gate	Per Share	Aggre-gate
				0.00-	
1979: Qualified plan	0,000	$0.00	00,000	0.00	00,000
Non-qualified plan	00,000	0.00	000,000	0.00- 00.00	000,000
1980: Non-qualified plan	00,000	. 0.00	000,000	0.00- 00.00	000,000

Unoptioned shares available for granting options under the plans at December 31 were as follows:

	1980	1979
Qualified plan	000,000	000,000
Non-qualified plan	00,000	00,000

Note 12—Contingencies and Commitments

Saver had outstanding commitments to make loans amounting to $000,000,000 at December 31, 1980 and $000,000,000 at December 31, 1979.

Saver is committed to various operating leases for premises and equipment aggregating $00,000,000 with approximate minimum payments as follows:

1981	$0,000,000	1986-1989	$0,000,000
1982	0,000,000	1990-1994	0,000,000
1983	000,000	1995-1999	0,000,000
1984	000,000	After 1999	000,000
1985	000,000		

The Company and Saver are defendants in certain legal proceedings and Saver is one of the numerous savings and loan association defendants in a class action suit challenging the imposition of late charges.

In the opinion of the management of the Company and Saver, the outcome of litigation will not have a material adverse effect on the financial position of the Company or Saver.

Note 13—Employee Stock Ownership Plan

The Company has an employee stock ownership plan (the Plan) which all employees of the Company and its subsidiary are eligible to join after completing a full year of service, subject to working a minimum number of hours. All contributions to the Plan are to be made by the Company and allocated to each employee covered by the Plan in the ratio their salary bears to the total salaries of all covered employees. The employees right to receive benefits under the Plan vest at 00% per annum after three years of service. In 1980, the Company sold at market 00,000 (1979–00,000) shares of its common stock held in treasury to the Plan. The Board of Directors of the Company has authorized a $000,000 contribution to the Plan for 1980.

Note 14—Quarterly Summary of Operations (Unaudited)

Quarterly operating results for the two years ended December 31, 1980 are summarized as follows:

	Income	Expense	Net Income Amount	Net Income Per Share
1980:				
First Quarter	$ 00,000	00,000	0,000	.00
Second Quarter	00,000	00,000	0,000	.00
Third Quarter	00,000	00,000	0,000	.00
Fourth Quarter	00,000	00,000	0,000	.00
Total	$000,000	000,000	00,000	0.00
1979:				
First Quarter	00,000	00,000	0,000	.00
Second Quarter	00,000	00,000	0,000	.00
Third Quarter	00,000	00,000	0,000	.00
Fourth Quarter	00,000	00,000	0,000	.00
Total	$000,000	000,000	00,000	0.00

(000's omitted except per share data)

Net income for the fourth quarter of 1980 includes a reduction of approximately $000,000, or $.00 per share, in taxes on income accrued in 1979 and the first three quarters of 1980 upon the determination in December, 1980 by the State Franchise Tax Board of the 1979 State franchise tax rate for financial institutions.

Note 15—Analysis of the Effect of Inflation on Selected Financial Data (Unaudited)

All segments of the American economy have been, and continue to be, impacted by the effects of inflation. In recent years, many attempts have been made to measure the effect of inflation on business enterprises, but none of the methods proposed have received general support.

In September, 1979, the Financial Accounting Standards Board issued FASB Statement No. 33, Financial Reporting and Changing Prices. This Statement requires that large business enterprises start reporting the effect of inflation on accounting data and prescribes the measurement methods and reporting formats.

The accompanying schedule shows a five-year comparison of selected financial data on a historical cost basis and as adjusted for changing prices, or inflation. Historical cost, as required by generally accepted accounting principles, is the basis of measurement used in preparing all other financial statements and related data in this Annual Report: This traditional accounting measurement does not take into account any changes over time in the relative purchasing power of money. The historical cost data has been converted to average 1980 dollars by applying factors obtained from the Consumer Price Index for All Urban Consumers (CPI) issued by the

U.S. Department of Labor. These adjusted numbers are generally referred to as constant dollars. Supporters of this method consider that a comparison between historical cost and constant dollar amounts show the effect of inflation on a business enterprise. However, there are differences of opinion as to the value of this comparison and as to whether the CPI is the appropriate index for measuring inflation.

Monetary assets and liabilities are those, such as loans and savings deposits, which will be converted into a fixed number of dollars regardless of inflation. Non-monetary assets and liabilities, such as premises and equipment, are those the monetary value of which fluctuates depending on the influence of a number of factors including inflation and supply and demand. The loss from effect of inflation on net monetary assets reflected in the accompanying schedule is based on the theoretical concept that all monetary assets decrease in value at the rate of the CPI and all liabilities are reduced at the rate of the CPI. Since a financial institution's monetary assets exceed monetary liabilities, when the CPI is increasing financial institutions will generally show a loss due to inflation.

In contrast to an industrial company, substantially all the assets and liabilities of a financial institution are monetary in nature. Consequently, a financial institution's performance may be significantly influenced by changes in interest rates. Interest rates do not necessarily move in the same direction or at the same rate as the CPI.

Comparisons of the constant dollar data included in the attached schedule are most meaningful in terms of trends and relationships between the periods. Comparisons of constant dollar to historical cost amounts should be made with caution as the constant dollar amounts can vary significantly, depending on the choice of base period.

FIVE-YEAR COMPARISON OF SELECTED FINANCIAL DATA AS ORIGINALLY REPORTED AND AS ADJUSTED FOR THE EFFECTS OF CHANGING PRICES (UNAUDITED)
(Dollars in millions, except per share amounts)

	1980	1979	1978	1977	1976
Average consumer price index (1967 = 100)	000.0	000.0	000.0	000.0	000.0
Percentage increase in average CPI	00.0 %	0.0 %	0.0 %	0.0 %	0.0 %
Gross revenues—					
as reported	$000.0	000.0	000.0	00.0	00.0
as adjusted	000.0	000.0	000.0	000.0	00.0
Interest expense—					
as reported	000.0	000.0	00.0	00.0	00.0
as adjusted	000.0	000.0	00.0	00.0	00.0
Net income—					
as reported	00.0	00.0	00.0	0.0	0.0
as adjusted	00.0	00.0	00.0	0.0	0.0
Stockholders' equity—					
as reported	00.0	00.0	00.0	00.0	00.0
as adjusted	00.0	00.0	00.0	00.0	00.0
Loss from effect of inflation on net monetary assets (stockholders' equity)	00.0	0.0	0.0	0.0	0.0
Earnings per share—					
as reported	0.00	0.00	0.00	0.00	.00
as adjusted	0.00	0.00	0.00	0.00	0.00
Cash dividends per share—					
as reported	.00	.00	.00	.00	—
as adjusted	.00	.00	.00	.00	—
Market price per share—					
as reported	0.00	0.00	0.00	0.00	0.00
as adjusted	0.00	0.00	0.00	0.00	0.00

Note: The adjusted amounts are based on a historical cost/constant dollar method of accounting. Net nonmonetary assets are not material so all assets and liabilities have been treated as monetary for the purposes of these computations. Current cost data have not been included because current cost amounts do not differ materially from historical cost/constant dollar amounts.

FINANCE COMPANIES

Overview

The preferable accounting principles for finance companies appear in the industry audit guide entitled "Audits of Finance Companies", (hereinafter referred to as the Finance Guide).

Generally accepted accounting principles (GAAP) and practices which are used for commercial enterprises are also used in reporting on finance companies. The Finance Guide sets forth the application of existing GAAP to finance companies.

Generally, finance companies compete on a limited basis with commercial banks, credit unions, savings and loan associations, and large retail enterprises which operate their own captive finance company affiliate. A finance company may specialize in one or two particular types of loans or may make many different types of loans. The three major categories of finance companies are (1) sales finance companies, (2) consumer loan companies, and (3) commercial finance companies.

Sales finance companies This type of finance company finances retail sales of consumer goods, such as automobiles, television sets, mobile homes, major appliances, and household goods. A sales finance company may be captive or independent. A captive sales finance company is usually one which is owned by a major retail enterprise and all of its financing business is generated by the major retail enterprise. Thus, the finance company has a "captive" market in which to obtain its business. Most major retailers of consumer goods have captive finance companies.

An independent sales finance company is one which does not have a captive market and must generate its business from many different sources. Usually, an independent finance company makes continuing arrangements with many small and medium size retailers in an area, and occasionally a consumer will finance a purchase directly with the finance company.

The majority of a sales finance company's business comes from the purchase of retail contracts. The retailer sells the consumer goods on an installment basis and the purchaser signs a contract or notes which specifies the rate of interest, the amount of each payment, and the number of payments. The contract also sets forth all of the terms and conditions of the sale and usually provides for repossession of the consumer goods on default of the contract by the purchaser. These conditional sales contracts are usually referred to as "three party paper", because the retailer (dealer), the purchaser (borrower), and the finance company are all involved.

After the sale is made and the conditional sales contract is executed by the purchaser, the retailer sells the contract, with or without recourse, to the sales finance company. More frequently than not the retailer will sell the conditional sales contract to the sales finance company at an interest yield which is less than that stated in the contract. Thus, the retailer usually makes a profit on the sale of the contract. This profit is usually held by the finance company in a "dealer's reserve account", and disbursed to the dealer in accordance with the terms of the recourse or nonrecourse agreement.

In some agreements between the finance company and the dealer, the finance company has the responsibility to check the purchaser's credit and decide whether the risk is acceptable.

It is not unusual for captive sales finance companies to also furnish wholesale financing (floor-plan loans) to their affiliates, when necessary. Thus, a large automobile manufacturer would likely have a captive finance company which would furnish floor-plan loans to dealers to help finance automobiles in stock and also purchase the dealer's conditional sales contracts.

Wholesale financing loans (floor-plan loans) are usually collateralized by specific items of inventory held by the dealer. When the specific item of inventory is sold by the dealer, the wholesale loan must usually be repaid. Thus, the collateral is an important factor in wholesale financing.

Consumer loan companies   This type of finance company usually makes cash loans to consumers for personal needs. Consumer loan companies are still referred to as "small loan companies".

Cash loans to consumers by consumer loan companies may be collateralized, but frequently are not. Regulatory statutes exist in all states governing consumer loan companies. The amount of loan, interest rates, and repayment terms are all usually regulated. However, the regulations vary from state to state.

When cash loans are not collateralized, the borrower's creditworthiness becomes the primary consideration for granting the loan.

Commercial finance companies   This type of finance company makes various different types of loans to business entities. The more important types of business loans are usually collateralized by inventory, accounts receivable, or plant and equipment.

Some businesses which are short of working capital will factor their accounts receivables. Factoring is a process by which a company can convert its receivables into cash by assigning them to a factor either with or without recourse. "With recourse" means that the assignee can return the receivable to the company and get back the funds paid if the receivable turns out to be uncollectible. "Without recourse" means that the assignee assumes the risk of any losses on collections. Under factoring arrangements, the customer may or may not be notified.

Regulation of finance companies   Every state has its own regulations for finance companies. These regulations are not uniform and in one state the maximum annual interest rate on a consumer loan may be 36%, and in another state the maximum may only be 15%. There is also a great deal of disparity between states on the maximum amount of a loan and the maximum repayment period.

Federal regulation of finance companies is uniformly applied in every state. The most significant federal regulation for finance companies is the Federal Reserve Regulation "Z" which is usually called the "Truth in Lending Act". This Act requires the full disclosure of the finance charge and the annual percentage rate of interest by all companies covered by the law. Thus, the borrowing consumer can more easily compare the different credit terms available.

PREFERABLE ACCOUNTING PRINCIPLES

Finance Receivables

Finance receivables from direct cash loans may be the result of interest bearing loans, or loans made on a discount basis. In an interest bearing loan the face amount of the note does not include any interest. However, in a loan made on a discount basis, the face amount of the note does include the interest.

Receivables from direct cash loans are initially recorded at the face amount of the note. In the case of an interest bearing loan the amount of cash disbursed by the finance company is equal to the face amount of the note and the journal entry to record the loan is:

Finance receivable	$X,XXX	
Cash		$X,XXX

In the case of a loan made on a discount basis, the amount of cash disbursed by the finance company is not the same as the face amount of the note and the difference is credited to deferred finance income, as follows:

Finance receivable	$X,XXX	
Cash		$X,XXX
Deferred finance income		XX

As mentioned previously, conditional sales contracts are purchased by a finance company from the retailer (dealer) at a discount. Thus, the gross balance of the contract is more than the amount of cash disbursed by the finance company. Since these types of contracts are initially recorded by a finance company at their gross balances, the difference between the gross balances and the purchase prices is deferred finance income.

Commercial loans are usually collateralized and are initially recorded by a finance company at the amount of cash advanced on the loan.

Obviously, finance receivables represent a major asset of finance companies and the aging of such receivables is extremely important. The two most common methods used to age receivables are (1) contractual due dates and (2) recency of payment.

Contractual Due Dates

In this method, receivables are aged in accordance with the contractual due dates in the contract. This is the method that most accountants are familar with. The aging of conditional sales contracts is usually based on the contractual due dates because the value of the collateral is considered important. The older the collateral gets, such as an automobile, the more its value declines.

Recency of Payments

The recency of payments method of aging receivables is based upon how recent the last payment was received. If a borrower made a payment within the last thirty days, his recency of payment would be thirty days, even if several payments were missed prior to the last payment.

In direct cash loans the ability of the borrower to make payments is paramount because these type of loans are seldom collateralized. Thus, the age of the loan is not as important as the recency of the borrower's last payment.

Finance Income

As discussed previously, deferred finance income is recorded at the inception of a discount basis loan because of the difference between the gross receivable and the actual cash disbursed. Deferred finance income is not recorded at the inception of an interest bearing loan because the receivable and the cash disbursed are the same.

Finance income on interest bearing loans should be recognized in current operations when collected. An accrual for uncollected finance income may also be appropriate at a balance sheet date. In addition, the methods described below for recognizing finance income on discount basis loans may also be used on interest bearing loans.

The combination method of recognizing the deferred finance income on discount basis loans is considered preferable. However, the effective yield method without transfer and the pro-rata method with transfer, are also acceptable in recognizing deferred finance income on discount basis loans. In order to understand how to apply these three methods, a discussion of the various costs involved in acquiring and maintaining a loan is necessary.

Acquisition Costs

Certain types of direct and indirect costs exist in the initial acquisition of a loan. These costs should include an allowance for loan losses based on a percentage of the face amount of a loan. A calculation is made of the total acquisition costs per loan, based on prior experience and all known existing factors.

Servicing and Operating Costs

Certain types of direct and indirect costs exist in the servicing of a loan during the term of the loan. These costs include collection expenses and operating costs incurred in servicing a loan. A calculation is made, of the total servicing, collecting, and operating costs, on a per loan basis. These type of costs can be reasonably estimated from budget data and prior experience.

Cost of Borrowed Funds

Certain costs are incurred in obtaining borrowed funds that are directly related to the unpaid balances of loans outstanding. A reasonable estimate must be made on a per loan basis, of the cost of borrowed funds directly related to outstanding unpaid loans.

Profit Before Taxes

To determine the total estimated costs of a single loan, the total costs per loan are added together. Thus, on a per loan basis, the (1) acquisition costs, (2) servicing and operating costs, and (3) costs of borrowed funds, are all added together. If we then subtract these total estimated costs for a single loan from the deferred finance income on that single loan, the estimated profit before taxes on the particular loan is calculated.

With an understanding of the above costs which are incurred in the finance industry, we can now proceed with a discussion of the three acceptable methods of recognizing deferred finance income.

Combination Method

Of the three methods of recognizing deferred finance income, the combination method is preferred. The combination method more closely matches revenue with related costs.

In the combination method the total deferred finance income at the inception of the loan is split-up and recorded in three separate deferred accounts, as follows:

1. acquisition costs
2. servicing, collecting and operating costs
3. cost of borrowed funds and profit before taxes

The cost of borrowed funds and profit before taxes does not actually have to be computed on a per loan basis because it is the remainder of the deferred finance income on a loan after deducting the acquisition costs per loan and the servicing, collecting and operating costs per loan.

In the combination method the deferred finance income at the inception of a loan is eliminated and in its place are three separate deferred accounts.

The three separate deferred accounts are subsequently accounted for, as follows:

Acquisition costs   Acquisition costs per loan are credited to current operations in the month in which the loan is initially recorded. The assumption is that actual acquisition costs per loan will be charged to current operations in the month in which the loan is initially recorded.

Servicing, collecting, and operating costs   Servicing, collecting, and operating costs per loan are credited to subsequent operations on a pro-rata basis or on a straight-line basis. The amortization credit may be made on the accrual basis (standard rate per month), or on the collection basis (per payment received).

Cost of borrowed funds and profit before taxes   Cost of borrowed funds and profit before taxes is credited to subsequent operations by the effective yield method. The amortization (credit) may be made on the accrual basis (declining amount per month), or on the collection basis (per payment received). (Note: The effective yield method is described below).

If the estimated costs per loan excluding profit before taxes, exceed the total deferred finance income on a loan, a loss on the loan is indicated. In this event, the loss on the loan is recognized in the month the loan is initially recorded.

Allocation of the three categories of costs used in the combination method may be applied (1) on a per loan basis, or (2) in aggregates based on weighted average terms of loans by major types of loan receivables.

Effective Yield Method Without Transfer

At the inception of a loan the deferred finance income is recorded. In subsequent months the deferred finance income is credited to operations in declining amounts, either on the accrual basis (balance of the term of the loan), or on the collection basis (balance of the loan outstanding). The sum-of-digits method is usually used in calculating the amounts under both the accrual basis and the collection basis.

In the effective yield method the amount of the loan outstanding is used to determine the amount of deferred finance income which should be recognized.

Without transfer, merely means that deferred finance income is not broken down into (1) acquisition costs, (2), servicing, collecting and operating costs, and (3) cost of borrowed funds and profit before taxes. Under the effective yield method without transfer, the entire deferred finance income is credited to subsequent operations. Thus, acquisition costs are not matched with a credit from deferred finance income in the inception month of the loan, and costs incurred equally over the life of the loan are also not matched.

The effective yield method should not be used for loan maturities of over seven years, because sum-of-digit calculations over long periods tend to produce significantly different amounts than those obtained by more precise mathematical methods.

Pro-Rata Method with Transfer

At the inception of the loan the portion of the deferred finance income attributable to acquisition costs is transferred to current operations. The balance remaining in deferred finance income is then credited to subsequent operations in relation to the amount of collections received. Thus, the deferred income is credited to subsequent operations in an increasing amount which is exactly opposite to the effective yield method without transfer.

Indirect acquisition costs should be excluded in determining the amount of transfer from deferred finance income at the inception of the loan. The reason for this is that indirect acquisition costs are not easily isolated and estimates may not be realistic.

Under any method, if a loss on a loan is evident at the inception of the loan, the loss should be recognized immediately in current operations. A finance company should make periodic evaluations of its loan portfolios. In the event, that a reduction of a loan portfolio is necessary, a provision for losses should be provided.

Allowance for Losses

In the finance industry losses may arise from either expected sources and from unexpected sources. Losses which are usually experienced on loans should be determined by the category of loan based on known factors and prior experience. Changes in business conditions and other unexpected conditions may result in adjustments to original anticipated allowances.

It is important to segregate loan receivables by the type of loan in order to properly evaluate the adequacy of the allowance for losses account. As a general rule, prior loss experience on loans and general economic conditions are the two most influential factors in evaluating the allowance for losses.

The preferable method of accounting for losses on loans written off is the net basis and financial statements should be prepared to reflect the net basis.

On the balance sheet the allowance for losses should be deducted from its related loans receivable. The income statement (statement of earnings) should reflect the provision for losses as a separate item of expense.

Repossessions

According to the terms of their agreement, either the finance company or the dealer may be responsible for repossessing the collateralized property, when necessary. If the agreement calls for full recourse, the dealer must pay the finance company any unpaid balance after applying any proceeds from the sale of the repossessed property, if any. On the other hand, no recourse requires that the finance company absorb any loss incurred.

Repossession expenses should be charged to the debtor's loan account, and insurance cancellation proceeds, unearned finance income, and proceeds if any, from the disposition of repossessed property should be credited to the debtor's account.

Repossessed property should be carried at the lower of cost or estimated net realizable value and, if material, should be separately disclosed in the financial statements.

Acquisitions and Bulk Loan Purchases

Existing GAAP (APB-16) should be applied in the acquisition of a subsidiary or the bulk purchase of loan receivables. Intangible assets arising from a business combination should be accounted for in accordance with APB-17 (Intangible Assets).

Branch Office Start-Up Costs

Start-up costs of new loan offices or branch offices may be deferred on a limited basis. Deferred start-up costs should be limited to costs incurred up to the end of the month before the office is opened. All deferred start-up costs should be amortized to operations over a very short period.

Dealer's Reserves

An agreement between a finance company and a dealer may provide for additional income for the dealer. The income may be computed on the basis of a percentage of the total loans purchased by the finance company, or may be a stated flat fee per loan for each contract. The agreement will most likely provide for the finance company to accumulate this additional income in a dealer reserve account. The finance company usually has the right to charge losses back to the dealer's reserve account. When a dealer's reserve exceeds a specified amount, the finance company usually sends the dealer a check for the excess.

In rare cases, the agreement between the finance company and the dealer calls for immediate payment of the dealer's portion of the finance charges. In this event, the amount to be paid to the dealer should not be credited to the dealer's reserve account.

Unless, a debit balance in a dealer's reserve account is reasonably assured of being collected, it should be charged against the allowance for losses account.

For financial statement purposes, dealer's reserves may be combined into one account and shown as a liability.

Insurance Commissions

Many finance companies require that all borrowers purchase insurance to cover certain risks involved in their loans. Also, many borrowers desire to have certain risks covered which are inherent in some loans. Life insurance coverage on the borrower's life can provide for full payment of any remaining unpaid balance at the time of death, and health insurance provides for loan payments to be automatically made during a borrower's period of disability or illness. In addition, property used as collateral for a loan should be insured against fire and casualty. Many finance companies have affiliated insurance companies which provide all or part of the necessary insurance.

The commissions received by a finance company from insurance companies should be deferred and amortized to income over the term of the insurance coverage. The amortization method should be consistent with methods used for premium recognition for insurance companies.

Financial Statements

The Finance Guide includes a discussion of the financial statement presentation of certain items which may be significant, as follows:

Consolidation   Insurance subsidiaries of finance companies should be consolidated.

Classification of balance sheet A nonclassified balance sheet is required of all finance companies, except those whose receivables are all contractually due within one year.

Subordinated long-term debt It is unacceptable to use the terminology "subordinated long-term debt and stockholders' equity". It is obvious that stockholders' equity does not include subordinated long-term debt and such a presentation is unacceptable because it is misleading.

Changes in financial position Since a finance company does not have a classified balance sheet, the statement of changes in financial position cannot be presented on a working capital basis. Thus, the statement of changes in financial position of a finance company will not reflect any increase or decrease in working capital, but should reflect any increases or decreases in cash. However, the Finance Guide recommends that in all other respects the sources and uses of funds of finance companies fully comply with existing GAAP (APB-19) on the statement of changes in financial position. Thus, all financing and investing activities should be included on a gross basis in the statement.

Finance receivables The composition of the total finance receivables should be disclosed in the financial statements along with the maximum terms and maturities of all loans. If the majority of direct cash loans are not expected to be paid in accordance with the contractual maturities, disclosure should be made of that fact. Also, cash collection experience of all significant loan classifications should be disclosed in a footnote to the financial statements.

Interest rates on receivables The Finance Guide recommends that interest rates on loan receivables should not be disclosed.

Line of credit and compensating balances The Finance Guide recommends that disclosure of lines of credit and compensating balances be limited to balances and credit lines supported by written valid agreements. Also, restrictions and conditions imposed on the use of compensating balances and credit lines may be disclosed, if significant.

Commercial loans receivable   Commercial loans receivable should be reported on the balance sheet at the unpaid balance of the cash advanced on the loan. Accounts receivables held as collateral by a finance company to secure a commercial loan should not be shown on the balance sheet of the finance company, under any circumstances.

In addition, disproportionate credit risks assumed by a finance company in a participation loan agreement should be fully disclosed in the financial statements.

Revenue   The disclosure, in the financial statements, of the sources of revenue of a finance company is required by the Finance Guide. In particular, gross revenue derived from finance loan receivables should be disclosed.

Loss experience and insurance losses   The loss experience on loans of a finance company is an extremely important barometer of the company's ability to collect outstanding loans. Thus, the loss experience should not be distorted by including other losses in computing the loss expense.

The Finance Guide states that it has been common practice in the past for finance companies to include insurance losses with losses on loans in a caption entitled "Insurance losses and loss expenses". Thus, it is important that the loss expense be reported separately in the statement of earnings of a finance company, and insurance losses should also be separately reported.

> *OBSERVATION:*   *The illustrative statement of consolidated earnings and retained earnings on page 82 of the Finance Guide is apparently incorrect because the presentation shows loss expense and insurance losses combined on one line entitled "insurance losses and loss expense". This is apparently in violation of the Finance Guide's requirement that the loss experience of a finance company be shown separately from insurance losses in the statement of earnings.*

Comprehensive Illustration

The following is a comprehensive illustration of the preferable accounting principles contained in this chapter.

FINANCE COMPANY
·BALANCE SHEET
As of December 31, 1980 and 1979

	in millions	
	1980	*1979*
ASSETS		
Cash (Note 2)	$ 00.0	$ 00.0
Finance Receivables (Note 3)	0,000.0	0,000.0
Less: Unearned Finance Charges	(000.0)	(000.0)
Principal of Finance Receivables	0,000.0	0,000.0
Less: Reserve for Credit Losses	(000.0)	(000.0)
Insurance Policy and Claim Reserves Applicable to Finance Receivables	(000.0)	(000.0)
Net Finance Receivables	0,000.0	0,000.0
Net Receivables Acquired from XYZ	000.0	—
Acquired Assets to be Divested	000.0	—
Investments—Securities (Note 4)	000.0	000.0
Equity in Net Assets of Non-Consolidated Subsidiaries	00.0	00.0
Property and Equipment	00.0	00.0
Other Assets (Note 5)	000.0	000.0
Total	$0,000.0	$0,000.0
LIABILITIES AND SHAREHOLDERS' EQUITY		
Short-Term Debt (Note 6)	$ 000.0	000.0
Deposits Payable	00.0	00.0
Accounts Payable and Accrued Liabilities (Note 7)	000.0	000.0
Insurance Policy and Claim Reserves (applicable to risks other than finance receivables)	000.0	000.0
Long-Term Debt	0,000.0	0,000.0
Total Liabilities	0,000.0	0,000.0
Redeemable Preferred Stock	000.0	—
Other Preferred Stock (Note 10)	000.0	000.0
Common Stock (00.0 shares authorized, 00.0 and 00.0 shares issued and outstanding) (Note 10)	00.0	00.0
Capital Surplus	00.0	00.0
Net Unrealized Loss on Equity Securities (Note 4)	(00.0)	(0.0)
Retained Earnings (Note 8)	000.0	000.0
Total	$0,000.0	$0,000.0

FINANCE COMPANY
STATEMENT OF RETAINED EARNINGS
Years Ended December 31, 1980 and 1979

	(in millions)	
	1980	*1979*
Balance, Beginning of Period	$000.0	$000.0
Net Income	000.0	00.0
Total	000.0	000.0
Dividends on Capital Stock		
Preferred	00.0	0.0
Common	00.0	00.0
Total Dividends	00.0	00.0
Balance, End of Period	$000.0	$000.0

See Accompanying Notes to Financial Statements.

FINANCE COMPANY
STATEMENT OF CHANGES IN FINANCIAL POSITION
Years Ended December 31, 1980 and 1979

	(in millions)	
	1980	1979
Source of Funds		
Operations		
Net Income	$ 000.0	$ 00.0
Non-cash charges (credits) to income		
Provision for credit losses (before offsetting recoveries)	000.0	00.0
Increase (decrease) in unpaid expenses	00.0	00.0
Increase (decrease) in insurance reserves	00.0	00.0
Depreciation, amortization, and other	00.0	0.0
Unrealized foreign exchange loss (gain)	(0.0)	0.0
Deferred income taxes	0.0	0.0
Undistributed net loss (income) of non-consolidated subsidiaries	(00.0)	(0.0)
Funds provided by operations	000.0	000.0
Collections of principal of finance receivables	0,000.0	0,000.0
Increase (decrease) in short-term debt	000.0	000.0
Increase (decrease) in accounts payable	00.0	00.0
Redeemable preferred stock issued	000.0	—
Long-term debt issued	0,000.0	000.0
Other	(000.0)	(00.0)
	$0,000.0	$0,000.0
Application of Funds		
New Funds lent to customers	0,000.0	$0,000.0
Principal of finance receivables purchased	000.0	00.0
Increase (decrease) in investments— securities (at carrying amount)	000.0	000.0
Long-term debt paid	000.0	00.0
Capital acquisitions	000.0	—
Dividends on capital stock	00.0	00.0
	$0,000.0	$0,000.0

FINANCE COMPANY
STATEMENT OF INCOME
Years Ended December 31, 1980 and 1979

	(in millions)	
	1980	*1979*
Revenue	$000.0	$000.0
Expenses		
Interest (Notes 1, 15 and 16)	000.0	000.0
Less Interest Income from		
Non-Consolidated Subsidiaries	(0.0)	(0.0)
Interest (net)	000.0	000.0
Salaries and Employee Benefits	000.0	000.0
Provision for Credit Losses		
(after offsetting recoveries)	000.0	00.0
Insurance Benefits Provided	000.0	00.0
Other	000.0	000.0
Total	000.0	000.0
Operating Income	000.0	000.0
Foreign Exchange Gain (Loss)		
(Notes 1 and 9)	.0	(0.0)
Income Before Income Taxes	000.0	000.0
Provision For Income Taxes (Note 12)	00.0	00.0
Net Income	$000.0	$ 00.0

Earnings Per Common Share

(Note 14)		
Earnings Available for		
Common Stock	$ 00.0	$ 00.0
Average Outstanding Shares	00.0	00.0
Net Income	$ 0.00	$ 0.00
Dividends Per Common Share	$ 0.00	$ 0.00

See Accompanying Notes to Financial Statements.

NOTES TO FINANCIAL STATEMENTS

Note 1—Significant Accounting Principles and Practices

Basis of Consolidation The consolidated financial statements include, after inter-company eliminations, the accounts of all significant subsidiaries. Certain prior year amounts have been reclassified to conform to 1979 presentation.

Finance Operations The financial statements, except for consumer finance revenue, are prepared on the accrual basis.

Unearned finance charges generally are taken into income as earned and collected under the Rule of 78ths method. Income from interest-bearing direct cash loans is taken into income as collected.

Receivables considered uncollectible or to require disproportionate collection costs are charged monthly to the Reserve for Credit Losses, but collection efforts generally are continued.

Valuation of Investments—Securities Debt securities are carried at amortized cost. Equity securities (substantially all marketable) generally are carried at market value. The carrying amount of marketable equity securities is adjusted from cost to market value through a valuation allowance, the change in which is not reflected in Net Income but directly in Shareholders' Equity. (See Note 4.)

Translation of Foreign Currencies Assets, including immaterial amounts of property and equipment and related accumulated depreciation, and liabilities in foreign currencies are translated to U.S. dollar equivalents at the market rates at each Balance Sheet date. Translation of foreign operating results is at the average market rates for each period covered by the Statement of Income. The net gain or loss is credited or charged to income.

Interest Expense, after Income Taxes, Related to Investment in Subsidiaries Interest expense related to investment in subsidiaries which are not a part of the company is removed from interest expense of the company and is shown, net of taxes, as a separate item. Similarly, interest expense related to the investment in the Insurance Group has been removed from interest expense of the Consumer Finance Group, but remains in expense (see Note 15).

The aggregate expense reflects the cost of funds used to acquire various subsidiaries as well as interest on funds borrowed by the parent company to pay dividends applicable to those subsidiaries to the extent that the subsidiaries have not paid dividends at the same payout ratio as the parent company.

Amortization of Excess Cost of Net Assets Acquired   Excess Cost for acquisitions before November 1, 1970 is not being amortized. For significant acquisitions subsequent to that date, Excess Cost is being amortized over 40 years.

Note 2—Cash

Cash at December 31 consists of the following:

	(in millions)	
	1980	1979
On Hand and Unrestricted Deposits	$00.0	$ 0.0
Compensating Balances	00.0	00.0
Total Cash	$00.0	$00.0

Compensating balance requirements in 1980 and 1979 generally have been the greater of 00% of the bank line of credit or 00% of actual borrowings. Effective December 31, 1980 such requirements generally are 0% compensating balances on one-half the bank line of credit with a 0% per annum fee on the remainder.

Note 3—Finance Receivables and Receivables Purchased From XYZ

The amount of and maximum term in months (from origination) of Finance Receivables at December 31 are as follows:

	Amount (in millions)		Maximum Term (months)	
	1980	1979	1980	1979
Direct Cash Loans:				
Dollar-cost	$0,000	$0,000	000	000
Interest-bearing	0,000	000	000	000
All Loans	0,000	0,000		
Sales Finance Contracts	000	000	00	00
Bank Credit Card Receivables	00	00	00	00
Lease Receivables	000	00	000	00
Total Finance Receivables	$0,000	$0,000		

Scheduled contractual payments of Finance Receivables, excluding bank credit card receivables, to be received after December 31, 1980 are as follows:

	1981	1982	1983	1984	beyond
Direct Cash Loans:					
Dollar-cost	00%	00%	00%	0%	0%
Interest-bearing	00	00	00	00	00
All loans	00	00	00	0	0
Sales Finance Contracts	00	00	0	0	0
Lease Receivables	00	00	00	00	00
Total	00	00	00	0	0

The above tabulation of scheduled contractual payments is not a forecast of collections. Collections of principal of Finance Receivables amounted to $0,000.0 million for 1980 and $0,000.0 million for 1979.

The percentage of monthly cash principal collections to average monthly balances was 4.37% for 1980 and 4.43% for 1979.

The Company purchases receivables from XYZ with recourse. The reserve for credit losses applicable to these receivables is maintained by XYZ. The accounts had a weighted average remaining maturity of 10 months at December 31, 1980.

Note 4—Investments—Securities

These are held principally by the Insurance Group as long-term investments. Equity securities had a cost of $00.0 million at December 31, 1980 and $00.0 million at December 31, 1979.

Investments—Securities at December 31 consist of the following.

	(in millions)			
	1980		1979	
	Carrying Amount	Market Value	Carrying Amount	Market Value
Debt Securities:				
Certificates of Deposit	$ 00.0	$ 00.0	$ 00.0	$ 00.0
Commercial Paper	00.0	00.0	00.0	00.0
U.S. Government Obligations	00.0	00.0	0.0	0.0
Foreign Government and Agency Obligations	00.0	00.0	00.0	00.0

Municipal Bonds	000.0	000.0	000.0	000.0
Convertible Bonds	00.0	00.0	00.0	00.0
Non-Convertible Bonds	000.0	000.0	00.0	00.0
Other	00.0	00.0	0.0	0.0
	000.0	000.0	000.0	000.0

Equity Securities:

Preferred Stocks	00.0	00.0	00.0	00.0
Convertible Preferred Stocks	0.0	0.0	.0	.0
Common Stocks	00.0	00.0	00.0	00.0
	00.0	00.0	00.0	00.0
Total Investments— Securities	$000.0	$000.0	$000.0	$000.0

Net Unrealized Loss on Equity Securities at December 31 is as follows:

in millions

	1980	1979
Unrealized Losses	$00.0	$0.0
Less Unrealized Gains	(.0)	(.0)
Net Unrealized Loss	$00.0	$0.0

Realized gains and losses, determined on the specific cost identification basis, are not material.

Note 5—Other Assets

At December 31 these consist of the following:

	in millions	
	1980	1979
Accrued Interest on Investments	$ 00.0	$ 00.0
Deferred Income Tax Benefits	00.0	0.0
Excess Cost of Net Assets Acquired	000.0	00.0
Insurance Premiums Receivable	00.0	00.0
Unamortized Insurance Policy Acquisition Costs	00.0	00.0
Unamortized Long-Term Debt Expense	00.0	00.0
Other	00.0	00.0
Total Other Assets	$000.0	$000.0

The remaining Excess Cost of Net Assets Acquired being amortized at December 31, 1980 and 1979 is $000.0 million and $00.0 million.

Note 6—Short-Term Debt

At December 31 such debt consists of the following:

	in millions	
	1980	*1979*
Banks:		
Line of Credit Loans	$000.0	$000.0
Demand Master Note	00.0	0.0
	000.0	000.0
Commercial Paper	000.0	000.0
	000.0	000.0
Total Short-Term Notes	000.0	000.0
Employee Thrift Accounts	00.0	00.0
Total Short-Term Debt	$000.0	$000.0

The average interest rates on Short-Term Notes outstanding December 31, without giving effect to compensating balances at banks, and maturities were as follows:

	1980	*1979*
Average Interest Rates:		
Banks:		
U.S. dollars	00.00%	00.00%
Foreign currencies	00.00	0.00
Overall	00.00	00.00
Demand Master Note	00.00	00.00
Commercial Paper:		
U.S. dollars	00.00	00.00
Foreign currencies	00.00	00.00
Overall	00.00	00.00
Maturities (in days):		
Banks	0-000	0-000
Commercial Paper	00-000	00-000

At December 31 bank lines of credit are as follows:

	in millions	
	1980	*1979*
Loans	$ 000.0	$000.0
Unused Portion	000.0	000.0
Total Bank Lines	$0,000.0	$000.0

Note 7—Accounts Payable and Accrued Liabilities

At December 31 these consist of the following:

	in millions	
	1980	*1979*
Accrued Interest	$ 00.0	$ 00.0
Dealer Reserves	00.0	00.0
Income Taxes Payable	00.0	0.0
Insurance Premiums Payable	00.0	00.0
Other	00.0	00.0
Total Accounts Payable and Accrued Liabilities	$000.0	$000.0

Note 8—Debt Restrictions on Use of Surplus

Certain of the indentures and agreements relating to the Company's long-term debt contain covenants restricting payment of dividends (other than stock dividends) and the purchase and retirement of the Company's capital stock. At December 31, 1980 and 1979 the amounts of all unrestricted surplus (Capital Surplus and Retained Earnings), under the most restrictive of these covenants, are approximately $000 million and $000 million.

Note 9—Foreign Operations

Significant data at December 31 regarding amounts denominated in foreign currencies and foreign operations for the years then ended, after translation to U.S. dollar equivalents, are:

	in millions	
	1980	*1979*
Assets	$000.0	$000.0
Liabilities	000.0	000.0
Net Assets	$ 00.0	$ 00.0
Income before Foreign Exchange Gain (Loss):		
Before Income Taxes	$00.0	$00.0
After Income Taxes	$00.0	$00.0

Note 10—Capital Stock

At December 31 the number of shares of capital stock is as follows:

Issued and Outstanding	*1980*	*1979*
Preferred—no par value (issuable in series). Authorized, 000,000: 0.00% Series Redeemable Preferred	000,000	None
0% Cumulative Preferred— $00 par value. Authorized, 000,000	000,000(a	000,000(a
$0.00 Dividend Cumulative Convertible Preferred— no par value—$00 stated value (each share convertible into 0.0 shares of Common; maximum liquidation value, $00.0 million and $00.0 million). Authorized, 0,000,000	000,000	000,000
$0.00 Dividend Cumulative Preferred—$000 par value. Authorized, 000,000	000,000	000,000
$0.00 Dividend Cumulative Preferred—no par value— $000 stated value. Authorized, 0,000,000	000,000	000,000
Common—$0 par value. Authorized, 00,000,000	00,000,000(b	00,000,000(b
After deducting treasury shares:		
a)	000,000	000,000
b)	0,000,000	0,000,000

Of the authorized shares shown above as of December 31, 1980, a total of 000,000 shares of Common is issuable upon conversion of $0.00 Preferred.

Note 11—Employee Retirement Plans

Substantially all employees of the Company and consolidated subsidiaries are covered by one or more of several retirement plans. The plans are fully funded, except for immaterial amounts of unfunded past service costs resulting from the merger of the retirement plan of a subsidiary with the Company's retirement plan. The assets of the retirement plan of the subsidiary exceed vested benefits. Total expense for the plans was $0.0 million for 1980 and $0.0 million for 1979.

Note 12—Taxes on Income

The Company files a consolidated U.S. federal income tax return with all eligible subsidiaries, including the eligible merchandising subsidiaries. The Provision for Income Taxes is comprised of:

	1980	1979
United States:		
Current	$00.0	$00.0
Deferred	(0.0)	0.0
Investment Tax Credit Deferred	00.0	—
Total U.S.	00.0	00.0
Foreign:		
Current	0.0	0.0
Deferred		(0.0)
Total Foreign	0.0	0.0
Total U.S. and Foreign	00.0	00.0
State and Local	0.0	0.0
Total	$00.0	$00.0

Deferred taxes result from timing differences in the recognition of income and expense for tax and financial statement purposes and relate to:

	(in millions)	
	1980	1979
Differences between cash and accrual basis	$ 0.0	$(0.0)
Insurance Benefits Provided	.0	(.0)
Insurance Policy Acquisition Costs	0.0	0.0
Reserve for Credit Losses	(0.0)	—
Unrealized Foreign Exchange Gain (Loss)	(0.0)	0.0
Other	(.0)	(.0)
Total	$(0.0)	$0.0

A reconciliation between the expected and the effective U.S. and foreign tax rates on Income before Income Taxes follows:

	1980	*1979*
Expected Tax Rate	00.0%	00.0%
Increases (Decreases) in Tax Rate		
Resulting from:		
Income of insurance subsidi-		
aries taxed at lower effective rates	(0.0)	(0.0)
State and local income taxes	(0.0)	(0.0)
Unrealized and untaxed foreign		
exchange gains and losses	(.0)	0.0
Application of foreign tax credits	—	(0.0)
Investment tax credit	(.0)	(.0)
Other	(.0)	0.0
Effective Tax Rate	00.0%	00.0%

U.S. income taxes generally have not been provided on retained earnings of foreign subsidiaries, as such retained earnings are expected to be permanently invested in foreign countries.

Note 13—Leases

There are 0,000 real estate leases which generally have an original term of five years with renewal option for a like term. Data processing equipment lease terms range from one to seven years and generally are renewable. The minimum rental commitments under non-cancelable leases at December 31, 1980 are as follows:

	(in millions)
1981	$00.0
1982	00.0
1983	0.0
1984	0.0
1985 thru 1989	0.0
Thereafter	.0
Total	$00.0

Note 14—Earnings Per Common Share

Earnings per Common Share is computed on the basis of average shares outstanding and their equivalents after deducting dividend requirements on Preferred Stocks. None of the Preferred Stocks are common stock equivalents.

Note 15—Interest Expense, after Income Taxes, Related to Investment in Subsidiaries

The effect of the treatment for interest expense as set out in Note 1 for the years ended December 31 is summarized as follows:

	(in millions)	
	1980	1979
Net Income:		
Consumer Finance Group	$ 00.0	$ 00.0
Insurance Group	00.0	00.0
Interest Expense, after Income Taxes, Related to Investment in Insurance Group	(0.0)	(0.0)
Income	00.0	000.0
Interest Expense, after Income Taxes, Related to Investment in Non-Consolidated Subsidiaries	(00.0)	(00.0)
Total	$000.0	$ 00.0

Note 16—-Capitalization of Interest Cost

Financial Accounting Standards Board Statement No. 34 requires interest to be capitalized on assets being constructed for an enterprise's own use, effective January 1, 1980. In 1980 the Company began construction of office buildings, expected to be ready for occupancy in 1982, and has elected to begin capitalization of interest in 1980, as permitted. During 1980 the total amount of interest cost incurred was $000.0 million, of which $.0 million has been capitalized.

MORTGAGE BANKING INDUSTRY

Overview

The preferable accounting principles for the mortgage banking industry appear in Statement of Position 74-12 entitled "Accounting Practices in the Mortgage Banking Industry", and in Statement of Position 76-2 entitled "Accounting for Origination Costs and Loan Commitment Fees in the Mortgage Banking Industry".

The primary business activity of a mortgage banker is to bring together investors and those who seek long-term financing. Most mortgage bankers deal in both residential loans and commercial loans. The second largest business activity of mortgage bankers is the servicing of loans. Servicing includes the collection of payments, sending notices, maintaining records, and other related chores. Servicing revenue is generally based upon a percentage of the unpaid principal balance of the loan.

Some mortgage bankers have ancillary operations such as property management, selling insurance, and real estate development activities.

Generally, a mortgage banker receives a commitment from a long-term investor for a block of mortgage loans secured by real estate. The commitment contains the total amount of loans to be acquired, the maximum amount of each individual loan, the minimum interest yield, and other related information. In addition, the commitment will also usually state whether the loans will be subsequently serviced by the mortgage banker or by some other party. Of course, whenever possible a mortgage banker would prefer to service the mortgages which he originates. The largest single group which services mortgage loans, both residential and commercial, in the United States is probably mortgage bankers.

Many mortgage bankers acquire mortgage loans on speculation with the intent of packaging a portfolio of loans and selling them to a long-term investor while retaining the servicing function for themselves. Occasionally a mortgage banker will retain some mortgage loans on a long-term basis. Thus, a mortgage banker may acquire mortgage loans for (1) long-term investors under a commitment, (2) speculation with the intent of selling in the near future, and (3) a long-term mortgage portfolio. Most mortgage loans are classified as either, (1) residential or (2) commercial.

Some mortgage loans are acquired by the mortgage banker directly from the ultimate borrower. However, the more frequent sources of mortgage loans that mortgage bankers originate are from real estate developers, realtors, and other related entities.

A mortgage loan can be guaranteed by a federal agency such as FHA or VA, or can be a "conventional" loan which is not guaranteed. Due to their low interest rates some federally guaranteed mortgages sell at a discount. SOP 74-12 states that the preferable method of accounting for any discounts as income is to defer them until the mortgage loan has been sold and transferred to the permanent investor.

The permanent investors that a mortgage banker is apt to sell mortgage loans to include insurance companies, pension funds, individual investors, and savings and loan associations. In addition, a mortgage banker may package a portfolio of mortgage loans and sell them to the Federal Home Loan Mortgage Corporation or to the Federal National Mortgage Association (FNMA).

A mortgage banker must process the loans that he originates which can take up to a period of six months. The processing is necessary whether the loans were obtained under a firm commitment for a permanent investor or not. Any risks, such as changes in interest rates which are not specifically covered by a firm commitment must be borne by the mortgage banker during the processing period. In addition, the mortgage banker must service the loans during this period.

Frequently, a mortgage banker will obtain a "warehouse loan" on the amount of loans in process, to ease the financial strain of carrying large amounts of mortgage loans. The loans are pledged as collateral to a bank for this short-term financing.

Because of the length of the processing period, mortgage loans receivables usually constitute the largest asset on the financial statements of a mortgage banker

Preferable Accounting Principles

One of the more difficult problems in accounting for the mortgage loan receivables of mortgage bankers is their valuation for reporting purposes. According to SOP 74-12 the valuation of these mortgage loan receivables depends upon whether they are held for sale or for long-term investment. However, it should be noted that SOP

74-12 states that almost all mortgage loans of a mortgage banker are held for sale in the ordinary course of business. Valuation of mortgage loan receivables for reporting purposes should be determined as at the balance sheet date.

Held for long-term investment purposes   Mortgage loans held by a mortgage banker for long-term investment should be reported at cost for financial statement purposes (GAAP). However, the intent of the mortgage banker must be to hold the mortgage loans for long-term investment, and the following conditions should exist at the time the investment decision is made, to verify the mortgage banker's intent:

1. The accounting records and financial reports of the mortgage banker must reflect these mortgage loans separately as long-term investments.
2. Documentary evidence should exist, such as a corporate resolution that these mortgage loans will be held for an extended period of time, or to maturity.
3. In classified balance sheets of the enterprise, if any, the mortgage loans will be reflected as noncurrent assets.
4. Evidence of financial strength of the mortgage banker should exist to substantiate that the mortgage loans can be held for an extended period, or until maturity.

In other words, SOP 74-12 makes it perfectly clear that almost all mortgage loans held by mortgage bankers are usually held for sale. However, if a mortgage loan passes the test for classification as a long-term investment it should be reported at cost.

When a mortgage loan receivable held for sale is reclassified as a long-term investment, the transfer must be made at the lower of cost or market on the date of transfer. In the event of a permanent impairment in the value of a mortgage loan classified as a long-term investment, its carrying value should be further reduced. Any difference between the carrying value of a mortgage loan held as a long-term investment and its par value should be amortized to income over the estimated life of the loan.

Held for sale   All mortgage loans receivable held for sale should be valued at the lower of cost or market as defined in accordance with the type of mortgage loan. Separate computations should be made for residential and commercial mortgage loans and the lower of cost or market can be determined on the total of all mortgage loans in a particular category, or on an individual mortgage loan basis for a particular category

Loans Covered by Commitments

Market value for loans covered by commitments should be the prices specified in the commitment. This is because the mortgage banker is, at least, guaranteed those prices agreed on in the commitment. Thus, lower of cost or market for loans covered by commitments is the lower of cost or the specified price in the commitment.

Mortgage loans which do not meet the required specifications in the commitment must be considered as loans not covered by commitment.

Loans not Covered by Commitments

Market value for loans not covered by commitments is the actual market value of the loans as determined by reference to the normal market in which the mortgage banker operates.

Quotation supplied by GNMA or the FNMA Free Market System, or other public markets should be used when appropriate. If no established market quotations are available, then market prices should be determined by the enterprise's normal market outlets.

GNMA Mortgage Backed Securities not Covered by Commitments

GNMA Mortgage Backed Securities may be held by a mortgage banker for the purpose of trading on the open market. The current market value of the underlying mortgage loans which are pledged by the mortgage banker as collateral for the GNMA securities is usually the same as the current market value of the securities themselves. In other words, the actual market value of the mortgage loans held in trust as collateral for the GNMA securities, should certainly be approximately the same value at which the GNMA securities are being traded. Thus, the GNMA securities are traded on the open market but the underlying collateralized mortgage loans are not traded.

Market value, for GNMA Mortgage Backed Securities, for the purposes of lower of cost or market, depends upon whether the trust agreement which covers the mortgage banker's underlying mortgage loans, can be terminated on short notice and the mortgage loans sold on the open market. In this event, market value for the GNMA securities is either the current market value of the GNMA securities or the current market value of the underlying mortgage loans. The choice of which current market to use should be preferably based on whether the mortgage banker intends to terminate the trust or not. If the mortgage banker does not intend to terminate the trust, market value for the purposes of lower of cost or market, should be the current market value of the GNMA securities. If the mortgage banker intends to terminate the trust, market value for the purposes of lower of cost or market, should be the current market value of the underlying mortgage loans.

If the trust cannot be terminated on short notice by the mortgage banker, then market value of the GNMA securities for the purposes of lower of cost or market, should be based on the published GNMA securities yield.

Block purchases of mortgage loans   Block purchases of mortgage loans have been made by mortgage bankers from GNMA or other investors. Certain costs incurred in block purchases of mortgage loans, which can be associated with future servicing income may be capitalized and amortized over the estimated average term of the mortgage loans. When these costs are appropriately capitalized they should be added to the valuation of the loans after cost, or the lower of cost or market is determined. However, if the cost have been inappropriately capitalized they must be included as part of cost, or the lower of cost or market, of the mortgage loans.

Market value recovery   Recoveries in market values in subsequent periods should be recorded but total market value may not exceed total cost. Frequently, a mortgage banker will value mortgage loans at the lower of cost or market and market is lower. However, in a subsequent period market value recovers. In this event, the mortgage banker records the recovery of market value, but only to the extent that market value does not exceed cost. The journal entry to record the recovery of market value is a debit to mortgage loans receivable and a credit to an income account.

Short-term interest expense   Historically, short-term interest rates have always been less than long-term interest rates. Thus, when a mortgage banker paid interest on short-term warehouse loans the interest received on the pledged mortgage loans receivable always exceeded the amount paid to carry them on a short-term basis. The difference between the short-term and long-term interest rates creates a "positive spread" for the mortgage banker. However, in recent years the trend in interest rates has reversed and now short-term rates exceed long-term rates. The result is a "negative spread" in interest rates for the mortgage banker.

The cost of warehousing mortgage loans by a mortgage banker is primarily a financing activity. Thus, "negative spreads" in interest rates should be charged, as incurred, to current operations.

Mortgage servicing fees   As mentioned previously, all types of mortgage loans must be serviced. The process of collecting, sending notices, maintaining mortgage records, and other related chores are referred to as "servicing". An owner of a loan, or portfolio of loans may perform the "servicing function" itself, or may engage someone else to perform such services. An entity which performs the servicing for mortgage loans usually charges a fee based on a percentage of the unpaid principal balance of the loans. Servicing revenue can be quite substantial.

As a general rule, most mortgage bankers service their own outstanding loans and may also service a large number of mortgage loans for others.

A problem may arise when a mortgage banker sells a loan or a portfolio of loans and agrees to continue servicing the loans at a fee which is significantly different from prevailing servicing rates.

Ordinarily, when a loan or portfolio of loans is sold and the buyer assumes the servicing function, no problem arises. Gain or loss on the sale of loans is the difference between the sales price and the net carrying amount of the loans. However, when loans are sold and the seller continues the servicing function for the buyer, a problem arises if the servicing fee charged is significantly different from that of the prevailing servicing rates. In this event, gain on the sale must be decreased to provide a normal profit on future servicing income based on estimated prevailing rates. For example, if the estimated prevailing fee for servicing revenue is 1% of the unpaid principal balance of the loans and the estimated future costs for servicing are .4%, the normal profit on the future servicing revenue would be estimated to be .6%. If the agreement for the sale of the loans included a total servicing fee of .5% of the unpaid principal balances, normal estimated profit on servicing revenue would be reduced to .1%. Therefore, the future servicing revenue must be increased by the difference between the normal estimated profit of .6% and the estimated profit of .1%, for a total of .5%. The adjustment is made in the amount of the present value of the difference. Thus, if one million dollars in loans were involved in the sale, the adjustment would be equal to the present value of .5% of one million dollars. The journal entry to record the adjustment is a debit to the gain on the sale of loans and a credit to deferred servicing revenue. The deferred servicing revenue is amortized to income over the life of the related loans, so that each future period will theoretically receive a normal profit on the servicing revenue. In the case of a loss on the sale of loans, the loss would be increased by the amount of the present value of the adjustment necessary to increase future servicing revenue to yield a normal profit.

It is very important to note that the adjustment to future servicing revenue profits is only made when the impact on operating results is significant (SOP 74-12).

Transactions with affiliates   Special treatment is afforded sales of mortgage loans by mortgage bankers to affiliated companies.

A mortgage banker should record the sale of mortgage loans to an affiliated company at the lower of cost or market at the measurement date. The lower of cost or market shall be determined at the measurement date in accordance with the provisions of SOP 74-12. The loss, if any, is charged to income in the period of transfer and should not be eliminated in consolidation. No gain and no additional loss may be recognized by the mortgage banker on the sale of the mortgage loans to an affiliated company.

The measurement date is the first date that management decides that the sale shall take place. The measurement date must be supported by formal approval of the sale by the purchasing affiliate and the issuance of a binding commitment. The binding commitment must be approved and accepted by the selling mortgage banker.

A mortgage banker may act in the capacity of an agent for an affiliated company. In the capacity of an agent the mortgage banker will originate certain specified types of loans for the affiliated company. Under these circumstances the mortgage banker may charge an origination fee for services rendered in acquiring the loans. However, all risks of ownership must be assumed by the affiliated company in order to constitute an agency relationship. The affiliated company should record the loans acquired at the mortgage banker's acquisition cost.

Agreements, or arrangements which do not bind the affiliated company to purchase the loans originated by the affiliated mortgage banker, such as "right of first refusal" contracts, do not establish an agency relationship.

SOP 74-12 states that, in the sale of mortgages from an affiliated mortgage banker to another affiliated company, there is a presumption that the purchasing affiliate is acquiring the mortgage loans for long-term investment purposes. Thus, if a repurchase, or similar agreement exists between the affiliated mortgage banker and the affiliated purchaser, the presumption that the mortgage loans are being acquired for long-term investment purposes cannot be supported. In this event, the transaction between the two affiliates may have to be accounted for as an intercompany loan, collateralized by the mortgage loans.

Balance sheet presentation   Inasmuch as normal working capital ratios mean little, if anything, when applied to the mortgage banking industry, many argue that classified balance sheets are not necessary. For the purposes of GAAP, SOP 74-12 allows the use of either classified or unclassified balance sheets when reporting on entities in the mortgage banking industry.

Whether a classified or unclassified balance sheet is used for reporting purposes by a mortgage banker, mortgages held for sale, and mortgages held for long-term investment must be separately disclosed.

Origination Costs for Mortgage Loans (SOP 76-2)

As mentioned previously, revenue from servicing mortgage loans is one of the main sources of income for a mortgage banker. In an effort to increase revenue from servicing loans, a mortgage banker will sometimes incur more origination costs than origination income. Another method of increasing servicing revenue is to purchase the existing rights from another company to service specific mortgage loans. In this event, part of the purchase price may be appropriately allocated to the right to receive future servicing income.

Still another method in which a mortgage banker can increase servicing revenue is by purchasing blocks of mortgage loans from federal agencies, such as FNMA and GNMA.

Origination costs for obtaining mortgage loans usually consist of direct personnel costs and other direct costs such as appraisals and site inspection fees. However, many mortgage bankers include general and administrative expenses and costs of short-term financing (warehousing mortgage loans in process) in the category of origination costs.

Identifying origination costs to specific loans is almost impossible, and the cost to do so is usually prohibitive.

For the purposes of GAAP, SOP 74-12 requires that all costs incurred in originating in-house mortgage loans, of a mortgage banker, must be charged to current operations. Origination costs should include general and administrative expenses and short-term financing costs which are incurred during the origination of in-house mortgage loans. The deferral of any origination costs for in-house mortgage loans is not acceptable under GAAP (SOP 74-12).

Bulk purchases or sales Mortgage bankers sometimes acquire blocks of mortgages in bulk purchases from GNMA, FNMA and other governmental agencies. Part of the bulk purchase price may be attributable to the right to receive future servicing income. In this event, the amount directly attributable to the right to receive future servicing income, may be deferred. However, the amount deferred may not be more than the difference between the market value of the mortgage loans at the date of purchase and the total purchase price paid for the loans. Market value must be determined in accordance with the provisions of SOP 74-12. In addition, the following conditions must be met:

1. Prior to the date of the bulk purchase, the mortgage banker had obtained commitments from investors to purchase the mortgage loans acquired in the bulk purchase, or obtains such a commitment no later than 30 days after the date of the bulk purchase. The commitments must provide for the mortgage

banker to continue servicing the mortgage loans.

2. If the sales price to the permanent investors exceeds the market value of the mortgage loans at the date of the bulk purchase, the difference must be used to reduce the amount deferred for the right to receive future servicing income.

3. The total amount deferred for any reason may not exceed the present value of future net servicing income from the mortgage loans purchased in bulk. Future net servicing income is the difference between estimated future servicing revenue and estimated future servicing costs.

4. Amortization of any amount deferred must be made in proportion to the estimated net servicing income expected to be earned from the bulk purchase of mortgage loans.

Issuance costs for GNMA securities   Costs of up to one month's interest that is incurred in connection with the issuance of GNMA Mortgage Backed Securities may be deferred.

Amortization of any amount deferred must be in proportion to the estimated net servicing income expected to be earned from the related underlying mortgage loans.

The total amount deferred for issuance costs, or any other reason, may not exceed the present value of the future net servicing income from the underlying mortgage loans. Future net servicing income is the difference between estimated future servicing revenue and estimated future servicing costs.

> **OBSERVATION:**   *A mortgage banker may use either the concurrent method (15 days), or the internal reserve method (45 days), to pay the holder of GNMA Mortgage Backed Securities. Under the internal reserve method, a cost equivalent to one month's interest is incurred on the issuance of the securities. Under the concurrent dates method, no additional interest cost is incurred. The additional one month's interest incurred may be deferred and amortized in proportion to the estimated future net servicing income on the related underlying mortgage loans.*

Rights to servicing mortgage loans   In a business combination, part of the purchase price may be properly allocable to the rights to receive future servicing revenue. However, under no circumstances may the amount allocated to such rights exceed the present value of the estimated future net servicing income. The future net servicing income is the difference between the estimated future servicing revenue and the estimated future servicing costs.

The amortization of the rights to receive future servicing revenue should be made in proportion to the estimated future net servicing income.

Other intangible assets acquired by a mortgage banker in a business combination should be accounted for under existing promulgated GAAP (APB-16 and 17). However, SOP 76-2 implies that amounts capitalized for the "future relationship of the new investor" with the mortgage banker, are practically impossible to determine, even if the new investor agrees to purchase future mortgage loans and to give the mortgage banker the related servicing revenue. Thus, amounts allocated to the value of a future relationship with a new investor should usually not be capitalized by the mortgage banker.

Origination, placement and commitment fees   These type of fees represent a primary source of revenue to the mortgage banker. In addition, a mortgage banker may pay a fee to a permanent investor for a commitment for the permanent investor to purchase certain specified mortgage loans from the mortgage banker during a specific term.

An origination fee is charged a prospective borrower, which represents reimbursement to the mortgage banker for the underwriting costs incurred in processing a loan. Underwriting costs include direct loan personnel salaries, appraisals, site inspection, loan processing costs, and other direct related costs. Since direct underwriting costs are charged to expense as incurred, origination fees should be included in income as they are collected. However, origination fees in excess of reimbursement of direct underwriting costs should be accounted for as commitment fees and recognized as income only on completion of the sale of the mortgage loan to a permanent investor.

The cost of isolating direct underwriting costs to a specific loan, as discussed previously, is very difficult. Thus, SOP 76-2 advocates that a mortgage banker estimate direct underwriting costs for each origination fee as an amount that does not exceed the current allowable VA or FHA rates for origination fees. However, origination fees in excess of the current allowable VA or FHA rate should be accounted for as commitment fees and recognized in income on completion of the sale of the mortgage loans to a permanent investor.

A placement fee is earned by a mortgage banker when he acts as a middleman (agent) by bringing together an investor and a borrower. The placement fee is recognized as earned when the mortgage banker has performed substantially all of the obligations required of him under the terms of the placement agreement.

All fees received by mortgage bankers for services rendered, such as site inspection or appraisals, should be recognized as revenue in the period in which the services are rendered.

A loan commitment is usually a written representation from the mortgage banker to a borrower, to lend funds for a specific purpose and term. A commitment term may be for as little as one week or possibly as much as one year or longer. A "floating rate commitment" is one in which the interest rate to be charged on the loan is determined by the prevailing rate of interest at the time the loan is drawn upon. A "fixed rate commitment" is one in which the interest rate is specified in the commitment.

The recognition of revenue from loan commitment fees varies with the type and substance of the commitment. Obviously, income is recognized on all commitments if the loan is not made and the term of the commitment expires. In this event, the mortgage banker has no obligation to perform and the loan commitment fee is earned.

All commitment fees received or paid by a mortgage banker for the purpose of funding a residential or commercial loan should be deferred and recognized as revenue on completion of the sale of the mortgage loans to a permanent investòr. In the case of commitment fees received or paid for blocks of mortgage loans, the mortgage banker should recognize as revenue only that portion of the fee attributable to those individual mortgage loans which have been completed.

Standby and gap loan commitment fees involve a commitment term and a standby gap loan period. In addition, land acquisition, development and construction loan fees also involve a combined commitment and loan period. These types of fees should be deferred and amortized to income over the combined commitment and loan period. During the commitment period amortization should be made by the straight-line method and during the loan period, the interest method should be used. On the sale of these types of loans to a permanent investor, any remaining unamortized commitment or loan fee is recognized in the period of completion of the sale to the permanent investor.

Under any circumstances, if an origination, placement, or commitment fee has not been collected in cash, an evaluation of the collectibility of the fee must be made. Collectibility of these fees must be reasonably assured before they can be recognized as income.

> *OBSERVATION:* *Savings and loan associations and mortgage bankers provide similar services to prospective borrowers in certain mortgage lending activities. Thus, the preferable accounting principles for mortgage loans, origination fees, placement fees and loan commitment fees are comparable.*
>
> *The preferable accounting principles for savings and loan associations appear in the audit and accounting guide entitled "Savings and Loan Associations". The preferable accounting principles for mortgage bankers appear in SOP 74-12 (Accounting Practices in the Mortgage Banking Industry) and SOP 76-2 (Accounting for Origination Costs and Loan and Commitment Fees in the Mortgage Banking Industry). (Note: The preferable accounting principles for these two industries may be found in this publication in the Chapters on the "Mortgage Banking Industry", and "Savings and Loan Associations").*

Comprehensive Illustration

The following is a comprehensive illustration of the preferable accounting principles contained in this chapter.

MORTGAGE BANKING COMPANY
STATEMENT OF FINANCIAL POSITION
As of June 30, 1980 and 1979

	(in thousands)	
	1980	*1979*
ASSETS		
Current Assets		
Cash and short-term investments—Note 1	$ 00,000	$ 00,000
Receivables:		
Commissions and premiums, less allowance for doubtful accounts (1980—$000; 1979—$000)	00,000	0,000
Sundry notes and accounts	0,000	0,000
Prepaid expenses	0,000	0,000
Total Current Assets	00,000	00,000
Real Estate Loans and Property—Note 2		
Construction loans	0,000	00,000
Federally insured and conventional real estate loans	00,000	00,000
Residential property equity loans	0,000	0,000
Residential property acquired for sale	0,000	000
Property held for development and/or sale	0,000	000
Less allowance for potential losses	(000)	(000)
	00,000	00,000
Other Assets		
Commissions and fees receivable, due after one year	0,000	0,000
Deposits, employee advances and sundry	0,000	0,000
Deferred income taxes—Note 6	0,000	0,000
Goodwill	00,000	0,000
Investment in affiliated company	0,000	
	00,000	00,000
Property and Equipment—Note 4		
Land	0,000	0,000
Buildings and improvements	00,000	00,000
Furniture and equipment	00,000	00,000
	00,000	00,000
Less allowances for depreciation and amortization	00,000	00,000
	00,000	00,000
	$000,000	$000,000

LIABILITIES AND STOCKHOLDER'S EQUITY

Current Liabilities		
Accounts payable and accrued expenses	$ 00,000	$ 0,000
Commissions payable	0,000	0,000
Salaries, payroll taxes and amounts withheld		
from employees	0,000	0,000
Dividends payable	000	000
Income taxes	000	0,000
Portion of long-term debt due within one year	0,000	0,000
Total Current Liabilities	00,000	00,000
Real Estate Loans Payable—Note 2		
Secured by:		
Construction loans	0,000	00,000
Federally insured and conventional real		
estate loans	00,000	00,000
Residential property equity loans	0,000	0,000
Residential property acquired for resale	000	00
Property held for development and/or sale	000	
	00,000	00,000
Long-Term Debt—less portion due within one		
year—Note 4	00,000	00,000
Other Liabilities		
Deferred compensation—Note 10	00,000	00,000
Commissions payable, due after one year	000	000
Deferred income	000	00
	00,000	00,000
Stockholders' Equity—Note 5		
Common Stock, no par value, authorized		
00,000,000 shares—stated value	000	000
Additional paid-in capital	0,000	0,000
Retained earnings	00,000	00,000
	00,000	00,000
Commitments and Contingent		
Liabilities—Notes 7, 8, 9, and 10		
	$000,000	$000,000

See Accompanying Notes to Financial Statements

MORTGAGE BANKING COMPANY
STATEMENT OF STOCKHOLDERS' EQUITY
Years Ended June 30, 1980, and 1979

(in thousands)

| | Common Stock | | Additional Paid in Capital | Retained Earnings |
	Shares	*Amount*		
Balance at July 1, 1978	0,000,000	$000	$0,000	$00,000
Exercise of stock options	00,000	00	000	
Cash dividends declared ($.00 per share)				(0,000)
Repurchased and retired Common Stock	(00,000)			(000)
Net income for year				0,000
Other			00	0
Balance at June 30, 1979	0,000,000	000	0,000	00,000
Exercise of stock options and related transactions	00,000	00	000	
Cash dividends declared ($.00 per share)				(0,000)
Investment in affiliated company	00,000	00	0,000	
Net income for year				00,000
Other				(0)
Balance at June 30, 1980	0,000,000	$000	$0,000	$00,000

See Accompanying Notes to Financial Statements

MORTGAGE BANKING COMPANY
STATEMENT OF CHANGES
IN FINANCIAL POSITION
Years Ended June 30, 1980 and 1979

	(in thousands)	
	1980	1979
Source of Funds:		
From operations:		
Net income	$00,000	$ 0,000
Add (deduct) items not affecting funds:		
Depreciation and amortization	0,000	0,000
Deferred compensation	0,000	0,000
Deferred income taxes	(0,000)	(0,000)
Funds Provided from Operations	00,000	00,000
Proceeds from sale of property and equipment	0,000	000
Proceeds from issuance of long-term debt	0,000	0,000
Increase (decrease) in:		
Accounts payable and accrued expenses	0,000	0,000
Commissions payable	000	000
Salaries, payroll taxes and amounts withheld		
from employees	0,000	0,000
Dividends payable	000	000
Income taxes payable	(0,000)	000
Portion of long-term debt due within one year	000	0,000
	00,000	00,000
Use of Funds:		
Acquisition of property and equipment	00,000	0,000
Cash dividends declared on Common Stock	0,000	0,000
Reduction of long-term debt	0,000	0,000
Companies purchased, less net current assets		
acquired (1980—$000, 1979—$000):		
Property and equipment	000	000
Goodwill	0,000	0,000
Other assets and liabilities—net	00	000
Investment in affiliated company	0,000	
Increase in receivables	0,000	000
Increase in prepaid expenses	000	000
Other, net	(0,000)	0,000
	00,000	00,000
Increase in cash and short-term investments	0,000	0,000
Cash and short-term investments, beginning of		
year	00,000	00,000
Cash and Short-Term Investments, End		
of Year	$00,000	$00,000

MORTGAGE BANKING COMPANY
STATEMENT OF INCOME
Years Ended June 30, 1980 and 1979

	(in thousands)	
	1980	1979
Revenues:		
Real estate brokerage commissions on sales and leases	$000,000	$000,000
Mortgage loan fees	0,000	0,000
Property management fees	0,000	0,000
Development services fees	000	000
Asset management fees	000	0,000
Escrow fees	0,000	0,000
Title insurance fees	000	
Appraisal and consultation fees	0,000	0,000
Insurance commissions	0,000	0,000
Real estate sales	00	0,000
Other commissions, interest and sundry	00,000	0,000
	000,000	000,000
Commissions, fees and other costs	000,000	00,000
Total Revenues	000,000	000,000
Operating expenses:		
General and administrative expenses	000,000	00,000
Interest	0,000	0,000
	000,000	00,000
Income before Income Taxes	00,000	00,000
Income taxes—Note 6	00,000	0,000
Net Income	$ 00,000	$ 0,000
Net income per average share of Common Stock outstanding (giving effect to shares issuable on the exercise of stock options)	$0.00	$0.00

See Accompanying Notes to Financial Statements

NOTES TO FINANCIAL STATEMENTS

Note 1—Summary of Significant Accounting Policies

Industry Information   The Company is an integrated real estate-related service organization engaged in brokerage, mortgage loan, property management and associated activities.

Principles of Consolidation   The consolidated financial statements include the accounts of the Company and its subsidiaries. All significant intercompany transactions and balances have been eliminated in consolidation.

Investment in Affiliated Company   Investment in affiliated company is reported on the equity method.

Income Recognition   Real estate sales commissions are credited to income upon close of escrow or upon transfer of title. Other commissions and fees are credited to income at the time the related services have been performed by the Company unless significant future contingencies exist.

Expenses   Sales commissions are recorded concurrently with the income transactions to which they relate. Drawings by sales personnel are charged to expense as paid. New office start-up costs are expensed as incurred.

Property and Depreciation   Property is stated at historical cost. Depreciation is calculated principally on the straight-line method; estimated useful lives range primarily from 6 to 45 years for buildings and improvements and 3 to 10 years for furniture and equipment. Leasehold improvements are amortized over the shorter of the life of the lease, excluding options to renew, or the estimated useful life.

Maintenance and repairs are charged against operations as incurred. Renewals and betterments are capitalized.

The cost of assets sold or otherwise disposed of and related accumulated depreciation are removed from the accounts at the time of disposal and the resultant gain or loss is transferred to operations.

Investment Tax Credits   The investment tax credits are recognized on the flow-through method as a reduction of the provision for federal income taxes.

Short-Term Investments   Short-term investments consist primarily of certificates of deposit, treasury bills and commercial paper which are carried at cost (approximate market). At June 30, 1980 and 1979, certificates of deposit were $00,000,000 and $0,000,000 respectively. Other short-term investments were $00,000,000 and $0,000,000 respectively.

Goodwill   Goodwill represents the excess of cost over net assets acquired and is being amortized over a 00-year period.

Note 2—Real Estate Loans, Commitments and Property

The Company held governmental insured and guaranteed loan commitments covering the federally insured real estate loans of $00,000,000 and $00,000,000 at June 30, 1980 and 1979, respectively. In fiscal 1980, the Company initiated a conventional residential real estate loan program with private commitments covering most of these loans. At June 30, 1980 and 1979, conventional residential real estate loans outstanding were $0,000,000 and $000,000, respectively.

Construction loans, federally insured real estate loans and conventional real estate loans are collateralized by first deeds of trust on the related properties. Residential property equity loans are collateralized primarily by second deeds of trust on the related properties.

In connection with its residential real estate marketing program, the Company acquires residential property for resale, assuming all underlying debt. These properties are generally resold within six months of acquisition and gains or losses are included in sundry revenues.

The average interest rate on real estate loans payable was 00.0% and 0.0% at June 30, 1980 and 1979, respectively. The following information relates to such debt for the years ended June 30:

	(Dollars in thousands)	
	1980	1979
Maximum amount outstanding at any month-end	$00,000	$00,000
Average amount outstanding (total of daily outstanding principal balances divided by 365)	$00,000	$00,000
Weighted average interest rate (actual interest expense on debt divided by average debt outstanding)	0.0%	0.0%

Note 3—Business Acquisitions

During fiscal 1979 and 1980 the Company acquired companies primarily engaged in residential real estate brokerage activities. The acquisitions were accounted for by the purchase method and, accordingly, operating results from the dates of acquisition have been included in the accompanying financial statements.

The following table summarizes on a pro forma basis the combined results of operations of the Company and its subsidiaries, as though the above acquisitions had been made at July 1, 1978.

| | *(In thousands, except per share data)* | |
	1980	*1979*
Revenue	$000,000	$000,000
Net income	$ 00,000	$ 0,000
Net income per share	$0.00	$0.00

Note 4—Long-Term Debt

Long-term debt consists of the following:

| | *(In thousands)* | |
	1980	*1979*
Trust deed notes payable, interest rates from 00% to 00%, due in varying installments to 2004, secured by real property having a carrying value of $00,000,000	$ 0,000	$ 0,000
Unsecured notes payable, interest rates from 0% to 00%, due in varying installments to 1988	00,000	0,000
Other	000	000
	00,000	00,000
Less portion due within one year	0,000	0,000
	$00,000	$00,000

Aggregate amounts of long-term debt maturing in the succeeding four years are as follows: $0,000,000 in 1981, $0,000,000 in 1982, $0,000,000 in 1983, and $0,000,000 in 1984.

Interest on long-term debt amounted to $0,000,000 for 1980 and $0,000,000 for 1979.

The Company had unused lines of credit amounting to $00,000,000 and $00,000,000 at June 30, 1980 and 1979, respectively. In connection with the line of credit agreements with certain banks, the Company has agreed to maintain unrestricted average compensating balances, based upon bank ledger balances adjusted for uncollected funds at various rates. Based upon outstanding borrowings and the total lines of credit at June 30, 1980 and 1979, the Company should have maintained average compensating balances of approximately $00,000,000 and $0,000,000, respectively (including $00,000,000 and $0,000,000, respectively, relating to its unused lines of credit). Under the credit agreements, the compensating balance requirements may be met, and are substantially met, by escrow, agency and fiduciary funds (see Note 8).

Note 5—Capital Stock and Stock-Related Plans

In April 1980, the Board of Directors authorized an amendment to the Articles of Incorporation increasing the number of authorized shares, no par value, from 0,000,000 to 00,000,000 and authorized a 2-for-1 split in the Common Stock, each effective May 18, 1980. Proportional adjustments to the terms of various stock-related employee benefit and incentive plans were also authorized. All references herein to outstanding stock, to per-share information or such stock-related plans have been restated retroactively where applicable to present all such information on a consistent basis.

The amended 1968 and 1976 Stock Option Plans provide for the granting to key employees of options covering shares of the Company's unissued Common Stock at prices not less than the fair market value of the stock on the date of grant. The options are not exercisable until one year after date of grant and become exercisable thereafter as determined by the Compensation Committee over a period generally not to exceed five years from date of grant. All of the options granted after February 28, 1976 are, and all of the options to be granted in the future must be, nonqualified options under present income tax laws.

As permitted by the amended Plans, stock appreciation rights (SARS) have been made available solely to officers and employee-directors of the Company, who are subject to certain limitations on disposition of option stock under federal securities laws. These rights permit the optionee to surrender exercisable options in exchange for cash and/or stock equal in value to the difference between the option price and the market value of shares covered by surrendered options. At June 30, 1980 such rights were outstanding with respect to exercisable installments covering 00,000 shares at exercise prices ranging from $0.000 to $00.00, for which the potential obligation of $000,000 is classified as a current liability.

Note 6—Income Taxes

The provision for income taxes consists of the following:

	(In thousands) 1980	1979
Currently payable:		
Federal	$00,000	$00,000
State	0,000	0,000
Deferred	(0,000)	(0,000)
	$00,000	$ 0,000

The deferred amounts included in the provision above consist primarily of deferred compensation not deducted for tax purposes.

The reasons for the difference between income tax expense and the amount computed by applying the statutory federal income tax rate to income before income taxes are as follows:

	(In thousands)			
	1980		1979	
Computed "expected" federal tax expense	$00,000	00.0%	$0,000	00.0%
Increase (reduction) in taxes resulting from:				
State income tax, net of federal income tax benefit	000	0.0	000	0.0
Investment tax credit	(000)	(0.0)	(000)	(0.0)
Other	(00)	(0.0)	0	—
	$00,000	00.0%	$0,000	00.0%

Note 7—Litigation

The Company and/or its subsidiaries are defendants or codefendants under certain lawsuits. Based upon the opinions of counsel, the Company believes that any liability which may result from disposition of these lawsuits will not have a material effect on the financial statements.

Note 8—Escrow, Agency, and Fiduciary Loans

The financial statements do not include the assets and liabilities of escrow, agency, and fiduciary funds which amounted to $00,000,000 and $00,000,000 at June 30, 1980 and 1979, respectively.

Note 9—Leases

Total rental expense under various operating leases amounted to $0,000,000 in 1980 and $0,000,000 in 1979.

Future minimum rental commitments as of June 30, 1980, for all non-cancellable operating leases are $0,000,000 in 1981, $0,000,000 in 1982, $0,000,000 in 1983, $0,000,000 in 1984 and $00,000,000 after July 1, 1984.

The leases for premises may generally be renewed for five year periods. The Company has no significant capital leases.

Note 10—Profit Sharing, Deferred Compensation, Bonus and Similar Plans

The Company has two profit sharing retirement plans to which it contributes annually a percentage, as determined by the Board of Directors, of operating income. Substantially all employees are eligible to participate.

The Company has entered into incentive compensation agreements with certain key executives of recently acquired companies. Aggregate incentive compensation in each case is related to the amount by which operating profits of the acquired company during the three years following acquisition exceed a specified cumulative amount. Such incentive compensation is generally payable not more than four years following the specified three-year period.

The Company's Performance Share Incentive Plan and related obligations are described in Note 5.

The Company awards annual cash bonuses to key salaried employees based on corporate earnings and individual performance. Such employees are also offered the opportunity, by appropriate advance election, to defer receipt of a limited portion of any such annual bonus, to be paid in installments after termination of employment. Amounts so deferred are credited (subject to vesting provisions) with certain increments in value measured principally by dividends declared and by increases in market price of the Company's stock. A similar plan is offered to sales personnel achieving prescribed levels of commission earnings.

The aggregate amounts charged to expense for the plans and agreements described above were $00,000,000 in 1980 and $0,000,000 in 1979.

The liability for deferred compensation at June 30 consists of the following:

	(In thousands)	
	1980	1979
Incentive compensation	$ 0,000	$ 0,000
Performance shares	0,000	000
Bonuses	0,000	0,000
Sales commissions	0,000	0,000
	$00,000	$00,000

INVESTMENT COMPANIES

Overview

The preferable accounting principles for investment companies appear in the industry audit guide entitled "Audits of Investment Companies" (hereinafter referred to as Investment Companies Guide), and the following Statements of Position (SOP):

SOP 74-11, Financial Accounting and Reporting by Face-Amount Certificate Companies

SOP 77-1, Financial Accounting and Reporting by Investment Companies

SOP 79-1, Accounting for Municipal Bond Funds

Although the accounting principles and practices set forth in the Investment Companies Guide are generally applicable to all investment companies, the Investment Companies Guide is primarily directed to mutual funds and closed-end investment companies registered with the Securities and Exchange Commission (SEC) in accordance with the Investment Company Act of 1940.

Accounting changes   The Investment Companies Guide requires that adjustments resulting from compliance with its provisions be reported as prior period adjustments as required by paragraph 18 of APB-9.

> *OBSERVATION: A change in, or a new, promulgated GAAP, or the issuance of an industry audit guide by the AICPA constitutes sufficient support for a change in an accounting principle (FASB Interpretation-20). However, the correction of an error in previously issued financial statements is not an accounting change (APB-20).*
>
> *Corrections of errors in previously issued financial statements may be made as a prior period adjustment (FASB-16). However, a change in an accounting principle is usually ac-*

counted for by reflecting the "cumulative effects" of the change in the income statement of the year the change is made. Thus, it is doubtful whether adjustments resulting from compliance with the Investment Companies Guide can appropriately be made as prior period adjustments.

Background

Investment companies generally raise funds by selling their capital stock to the investing public. Most investment companies have predetermined investment objectives, such as income, growth, or a combination of both. An income fund attempts to maximize periodic income and usually invests in high yield securities. A growth fund attempts to maximize periodic growth and usually invests in securities that have high potential for capital appreciation. A fund which attempts to maximize both income and growth, is called a "balanced fund". An investment company can be described as a vehicle for smaller investors to pool their funds which are then invested by a team of professional investment advisors.

As mentioned previously, the Investment Companies Guide was written primarily for mutual funds and closed-end investment companies. Mutual fund is the common everyday name used for an open-end investment comany defined in the Investment Company Act of 1940. Generally, there is no trading market for shares of a mutual fund or open-end investment company, because the company itself will redeem its own shares at any time, at current net asset value. In addition, a mutual fund or open-end company will offer its capital shares to the public on a continuous basis even though not required to do so. The offering price is the current net asset value, sometimes increased by a sales commission. A fund which sells its capital shares at current net asset value, is called a "no-load fund", and if a sales commission is added on, the fund is called "loaded". Generally, capital shares of all funds are redeemed at current net asset value, but occasionally some funds will charge a premium for redemption.

A "closed-end" management investment company's capital shares are traded on an open market and prices are determined by demand and supply (as opposed to an "open-end" company whose shares are not traded on an open market). However, the current net asset value of the capital shares of a "closed-end" company are reported in financial publications and certainly affect the market price of the shares. A "closed-end" fund may offer its capital shares on a continuous basis, but usually limits such sales to the reinvestment of capital gains distributions. As a general rule, a "closed-end" fund does not redeem its capital shares because of the established open market on which its shares are traded.

Small business investment companies (SBIC) and venture capital investment companies are usually "closed-end" and their investment objectives are usually capital growth. A venture capital investment company invests its resources in young companies developing new patents, processes, or products. It is not unusual for a venture capital company to supply managerial and technical advice. An SBIC may be a finance company or a venture capital investment company. In addition, an SBIC may be licensed by the Small Business Administration (SBA) and be registered under the Investment Company Act of 1940.

An investment company, created by a trust indenture, is called a "unit investment trust". Securities in a "unit investment trust" are redeemable and represent an individual interest in a unit of specified securities. A "contractual plan" or "top trust" is a unit investment trust in which all of the assets are securities issued by a management investment company. These unit investment trusts differ from those whose assets consist of a number of portfolio securities. A sponsor corporation forms a "contractual plan" for the purposes of selling shares in a particular mutual fund. In addition to the sponsor, a "contractual plan" usually has a custodian and, of course, investors. The investors agree to make single or periodic payments over a specified period. The custodian receives the investors' payments and also acts as custodian of the assets in the trust. Thus, "contractual plans" are a method for investors to accumulate shares of a particular mutual fund under a periodic or single payment plan, and also a method for a sponsor to sell shares of a particular mutual fund.

Portfolio management, recordkeeping and custodianship, and selling and administration, are the major functions which must be provided for an investment company. These functions are usually performed by outsiders and not the investment company itself. A manager is retained by the investment company who provides research, investment advice, and certain administrative services. The manager's fee is usually based on a percentage of the average net assets of the investment company. Sometimes the manager's fee is based on the company's performance compared to the average performance of the stock market or some other financial indicator. The Investment Company Act of 1940 requires that investment advisory service contracts be approved in a certain manner by "disinterested" directors of the company and the stockholders of the company.

A distributor is retained by the investment company to sell, either as agent or principal, the capital shares of the fund. Sales are made at current net asset value plus a sales commission unless the fund is a "no-load" fund. Sales commissions are regulated by the National Association of Securities Dealers (NASD). The Investment Advisor Act of 1940 also requires that a distributor's contract be approved in a specific manner.

A custodian is retained by an investment company to take custody of all cash and securities. The custodian's responsibilities are the receipt, delivery, and safekeeping of all cash and securities owned by the investment company. The custodian is more frequently than not, a bank or other type of financial institution.

Capital shares of an investment company must be issued, transferred, redeemed and accounted for, and these duties are usually handled by a transfer agent under agreement with the investment company.

Besides the securities acts of 1933 and 1934, and the various "blue sky" laws enacted by all the states, investment companies whose shares are publicly traded, may be subject to the following statutory law:

Investment Company Act of 1940 contains the rules and regulations for the fiduciary and other responsibilities of investment companies.

Investment Advisory Act of 1940 regulates the conduct, contracts, and compensation of those who render investment advice.

Small Business Investment Act of 1958 provides for government funds to be loaned by the Small Business Administration to SBIC (small business investment company) which are licensed under the Investment Company Act of 1940.

Financial statements of regulated investment companies must be submitted to stockholders and the SEC twice a year, and annual financial statements must be audited. The financial statements must contain a (1) balance sheet, (2) schedule of investments, (3) statement of income and expenses, and (4) a statement of surplus. In lieu of a balance sheet and statement of surplus, most investment companies include a "statement of assets, liabilities and net assets" and a "statement of changes in net assets".

Rules and regulations are prescribed in the various statutory laws for accounting records and financial reports which regulated investment companies must keep and submit to the authorities.

Preferable Accounting Principles

The largest group of assets which appears on an investment company's statement of assets and liabilities is the portfolio investment in securities. As a result of its large investments in securities, an investment company will also have income from dividends, interest, and gains or losses (realized and unrealized) from the sale or exchange of investments.

An investment company may be limited by its charter or other legal document as to the amount and types of securities in which it can invest. It may be prohibited from owning real estate or similar types of investments and on the other hand, may be required to invest in certain industries.

The trade date for a security transaction is the date on which the securities are sold or purchased. The settlement date is the date on which a security is to be delivered and paid for. The settlement date is used by securities brokers and dealers to record a transaction. However, it is established industry practice for investment companies to use the trade date for the purchase or sale of any securities. As a result of this practice, receivables from brokers for securities sold but not yet delivered may appear on the statement of assets and liabilities of an investment company. The reverse is also true, and payables to brokers for securities purchased but not yet received may also appear on the statement of assets and liabilities. Outside of the regular investing channels, investment companies record transactions on the date an enforceable right exists to demand the securities, or to collect the proceeds of a sale.

Valuation of securities Investment securities portfolios should be reported at "value". "Value" is defined as (1) the quoted market price for securities that have readily available market quotations, and (2) in respect to other securities and assets, fair value as determined by the board of directors of the investment company. This definition of value is spelled out in the Investment Company Act of 1940. In addition, the aggregate cost of the securities portfolio should be disclosed parenthetically on the statement of assets and liabilities, as follows:

Investment in securities at value
(Identified cost $23,456,778) $27,465,432

The portfolio of investments in securities should reflect the individual investments by either industry groups or some other meaningful arrangement. The total portfolio of investments in securities should be shown at value with cost shown parenthetically.

It is customary for investment companies to list their investments in securities as the first item on the statement of assets and liabilities because of its importance.

For financial accounting purposes, the cost of investment securities of investment companies is specific identification on a FIFO, LIFO, or average cost method. However, the method used must be consistently applied from year to year.

> **OBSERVATION:** *The valuation method for portfolios of investment securities described in the Investment Companies Guide generally agrees with FASB-12 (Marketable Securities) as it applies to specialized industry practices.*

Realized and unrealized gain or loss on security transactions Realized gains or losses are grouped together and unrealized gains or losses are grouped together and the total net realized and unrealized gain or loss is presented in the statement of operations (statement of income and expense). The presentation follows the determination of net investment income, as follows:

Net investment income		$1,234,567
Realized and Unrealized Gain		
or (Loss) on Investments:		
Realized Gain or (Loss):		
Proceeds from sales	$12,000,000	
Cost of securities sold	10,000,000	
	$ 2,000,000	
Provision for taxes	200,000	
Net realized gain		$1,800,000
Unrealized Gain or (Loss):		
Beginning of period	$ 6,000,000	
End of period	5,000,000	
(Decrease) in unrealized		
appreciation		(1,000,000)
Net realized and		
unrealized gain or		
(loss) on investments		$ 800,000

Dividend income   Cash dividends are recorded as income as of the ex-dividend date. The ex-dividend date is used because the quoted market price of a security usually decreases on the ex-dividend date to reflect the amount of dividend. The purchaser of securities on an ex-dividend date does not receive the dividend.

Since an investment company's equity interest in a particular security is not changed by a stock split or stock dividend in the particular security, no income is recorded. Dividends received in property are usually recorded at fair value of the property received.

Interest income   Interest income is accrued on a daily basis. Amortization of bond discount or premium has no effect on the net asset value of an investment company because investments are reported at market value.

Net asset value   The Investment Company Act of 1940 requires that all open-end investment companies determine their net asset values on a daily basis. The purpose of determining the net asset value is for redemptions and sales. Some closed-end investment companies, although not required, also compute their net asset values on a daily, or less frequent basis. Since the investment portfolio in securities is the largest portion of an investment company's assets, recordkeeping is done on a daily basis.

Equalization theory   The application of this theory protects the rights of the continuing shareholder in the undistributed income of an investment company. Since sales and redemptions are made on a daily basis the amount of undistributed net investment income must be computed on a daily basis. Thus, the net asset value of each share repurchased or sold will consist of the following items, on any given day:

1. par value of the stock
2. paid in capital, if any
3. other surplus, if any
4. undistributed net investment income

Under the equalization theory each share of capital stock retains the same amount of undistributed net investment income it has earned or acquired. A simple illustration will demonstrate, in detail, how the equalization theory works.

On a given day, an investment company had 100,000 shares of capital stock outstanding (500,000 authorized), and the following net worth:

Capital stock, par value	$1,000,000
Paid-in capital, excess over par	500,000
Unrealized appreciation of investments	500,000
Undistributed net investment income	100,000
Net asset value ($21.00 per share)	$2,100,000

Assuming that the investment company sold 1,000 shares on this day at $21.00 per share, the journal entry using an equalization account, would be:

Cash	$21,000	
Capital stock		$10,000
Paid-in capital		10,000
Equalization account		1,000

Now, lets assume that the investment company also repurchased 2,000 shares on the same day, the journal entry would be:

Capital stock	$20,000	
Paid-in capital	20,000	
Equalization account	2,000	
Cash		$42,000

Discussion

The original information reflects $100,000 of undistributed net investment income and 100,000 shares of capital stock outstanding before the two transactions. This indicates that each share of capital stock was entitled to $1.00 of undistributed net investment income before the two transactions occurred. If an equalization account was not used in the first transaction the $1,000 would have been credited to paid-in capital. Thus, there would still be $100,000 in undistributed net investment income to divide between 101,000 shares of capital stock (100,000 original shares plus 1,000 sold). The result would be that the undistributed net investment income per share would be reduced from $1.00 per share to $0.99 per share. However, by using an equalization account in the first transaction $1,000 is credited to this account and the dilution of the continuing shareholders in the undistributed net investment income is completely avoided.

Taxes The Internal Revenue Code (subchapter M) provides for special tax treatment for investment companies registered under the Investment Company Act of 1940. If an investment company qualifies as a "regulated" investment company, its investment income and capital gains are taxable only to the shareholders. In other words, the investment company acts as a "conduit", pays no federal income taxes on investment income and capital gains, and the investment income is taxed only once. The qualifications, in brief, for this favorable tax treatment of investment companies, is as follows:

1. The investment company must be a domestic corporation registered during the entire year under the Investment Company Act of 1940.

2. The investment company must make a valid election by computing taxable income as a regulated investment company. Such an election is irrevocable.
3. 90% or more of the investment company's gross income must be from dividends, interest, and gains from the sale or exchange of securities (losses are not considered for this 90% test).
4. Less than 30% of the investment company's gross income must be from gains on the sale or exchange of securities held for less than three months (losses are not considered for this 30% test.)
5. 90% or more of the investment company's income (as defined by the IRC) for the taxable year must be paid out to its shareholders.

In addition to the above requirements, certain diversification of assets must be maintained at the close of each quarter of the taxable year.

Equity method of accounting   APB-18 (Equity Method of Accounting for Investments in Common Stocks) specifically excludes from its coverage any investment company registered under the Investment Company Act of 1940, or those who would otherwise qualify as investment companies.

Face-amount certificate companies   SOP 74-11 amends the Investment Companies Guide by excluding face-amount certificate companies from its classification of investment companies in spite of the fact that these companies may be subject to the Investment Company Act of 1940. Therefore, face-amount certificate companies should not be classified as investment companies for the purposes of applying the Investment Companies Guide.

The most important reason given for this change is that there are only four or five such companies in existence and they do not sell their shares to the public.

Money-market funds   SOP 77-1 defines a money-market fund as an open-end investment company which is subject to the provisions of the Investment Companies Guide. A modification of the format for the statement of changes in net assets is recommended, as well as changes in (1) supplementary information and (2) reporting gains and losses on short term investments.

Other changes in SOP 77-1 A brief description of other changes recommended by SOP 77-1 are:

Put and Call Options recommends how puts and calls should be accounted for by investment companies subject to the Investment Companies Guide.

Development Stage Companies investment companies in the development stage should comply with FASB-7 (Accounting and Reporting for Development Stage Enterprises).

Amortization of Deferred Costs deferred costs of investment companies are subject to the same accounting principles as those used by conventional enterprises, in amortizing deferred costs.

Municipal bond funds Municipal bond funds are now subject to the provisions of the Investment Companies Guide (SOP 79-1). Investment companies that invest primarily in tax-exempt municipal bonds are called municipal bond funds. As a result of the Revenue Act of 1978, most municipal bond funds can qualify as "regulated investment companies". Thus, investment income and capital gains can be passed on to shareholders who pay federal income taxes instead of the investment company.

The two major types of municipal bonds are (1) general obligation and (2) revenue. General obligation bonds are backed by the full faith and credit of the governmental unit issuing the bonds. Revenue bonds are payable from a specific source of revenue and are not general obligations of the governmental unit. As a general rule, interest on municipal bonds is tax-exempt.

SOP 79-1 requires that municipal bonds be valued, for accounting purposes, at value. This is the same method recommended by the Investment Companies Guide. Value is defined as (1) with respect to securities for which market quotations are readily available, the quoted market value, and (2) with respect to other securities and assets, fair value as determined in good faith by the board of directors.

> **OBSERVATION:** *Although SOP 79-1 describes several ways in which market value can be determined for municipal bonds, no change is made in the underlying definition. Some of the ways that SOP 79-1 recommends for determining market value are (briefly):*
>
> 1. *obtain bid and asked prices*
> 2. *retain a bond dealer (at a fee)*
> 3. *daily bond quotations*

SOP 79-1 recommends that municipal bonds be grouped together by states or specific municipalities, whichever is more meaningful, for financial statement presentations.

Comprehensive Illustration

The following is a comprehensive illustration of the preferable accounting principles contained in this chapter.

OPEN ENDED TRUST COMPANY
STATEMENTS OF ASSETS AND LIABILITIES
As of December 31, 1980

Assets:

Investments, at value (Note 1) (average cost, $000,000,000)		$0,000,000,000
Cash		000,000
Receivable for investments sold		0,000,000
Receivable for shares sold		000,000
Dividends and interest receivable		0,000,000
Prepaid expenses		00,000
Total assets		$0,000,000,000

Liabilities:

Capital gain distribution ($0.000 a share) on shares requesting payment in cash, payable January 2, 1980	$0,000,000	
Payable for shares reacquired	0,000,000	
Accrued expenses	000,000	
Total liabilities		00,000,000

Net Assets for 000,000,000 shares of beneficial interest outstanding (including 0,000,000 shares to be issued on January 2, 1980 in payment of capital gain distribution)	$0,000,000,000
Net Asset Value Per Share	$0.00

See Accompanying Notes to Financial Statements

OPEN ENDED TRUST COMPANY
STATEMENT OF OPERATIONS
Year Ended December 31, 1980

Investment Income:

Income:

Dividends		$00,000,000
Interest		0,000,000
Total income		$00,000,000

Expenses:

Investment advisory fee (Note 2)	$0,000,000	
Compensation of Trustees not affiliated with the investment adviser	00,000	
Transfer and dividend disbursing agent fees	000,000	
Custodian fee	000,000	
Printing and postage	000,000	
Legal and auditing services	00,000	
Miscellaneous	000,000	
Total expenses		0,000,000
Net investment income		$00,000,000

Realized and Unrealized Gain (Loss) on Investments:

Realized gain from investment transactions (average cost basis):

Proceeds from sales (Note 3)	$000,000,000	
Cost of investments sold	000,000,000	
Net realized gain		$00,000,000

Unrealized appreciation of investments:

Beginning of year	$000,000,000	
End of year	000,000,000	
Increase in unrealized appreciation		00,000,000
Net realized and unrealized gain (loss) on investments		$00,000,000

See Accompanying Notes to Financial Statements

OPEN ENDED TRUST COMPANY
STATEMENT OF CHANGES IN NET ASSETS
Years ended December 31, 1980 and 1979

	1980	1979
From Investment Activities:		
Income:		
Net investment income	$ 00,000,000	$ 00,000,000
Deduct: Undistributed net investment income included in price of shares reacquired and sold (Note 1)	00,000,000	00,000,000
Total	$ 00,000,000	$ 00,000,000
Deduct: Dividends to shareholders	00,000,000	00,000,000
Increase in undistributed net investment income	$ 000,000	$ 000,000
Principal:		
Net realized gain on investment transactions	$ 00,000,000	$ 00,000,000
Deduct: Distributions to shareholders	00,000,000	00,000,000
Total	$ (000,000)	$ (0,000,000)
Increase (decrease) in unrealized appreciation of investments	$ 00,000,000	$ (000,000,000)
Increase (decrease) in net assets from investment activities	$ 00,000,000	$ (000,000,000)
From Trust Share (Principal) Transactions (Note 4) (Exclusive of amounts allocated to net investment income):		
Cost of shares reacquired	$ (000,000,000)	$ (000,000,000)
Net proceeds from sale of shares	00,000,000	00,000,000
Net asset value of shares issued or issuable to shareholders in payment of distributions from net realized gain on investment transactions	00,000,000	00,000,000

Decrease in net assets from Trust share transactions	$ (000,000,000)	$ (00,000,000)
Net decrease in net assets	$ (00,000,000)	$ (000,000,000)

Net Assets:

At beginning of year	0,000,000,000	0,000,000,000
At end of year (including un-distributed net investment in-come of $0,000,000 and $0,000,000, respectively)	$0,000,000,000	$0,000,000,000

Supplementary Information
(For a Share Outstanding Throughout Each Year)

Year Ended December 31,

	1980	1979	1978	1977	1976
Investment income	$ 0.000	$ 0.000	$ 0.000	$ 0.000	$ 0.000
Expenses	0.000	0.000	0.000	0.000	0.000
Net investment income	$ 0.000	$ 0.000	$ 0.000	$ 0.000	$ 0.000
Dividends from net invest-ment income	(0.000)	(0.000)	(0.000)	(0.000)	(0.000)
Net realized and unrealized gain (loss) on invest-ments	0.000	(0.000)	0.000	0.000	(0.000)
Distributions from net real-ized gain on investment transactions	(0.000)	(0.000)	(0.000)	(0.000)	—
Net increase (decrease) in net asset value	$ 0.000	$(0.000)	$ 0.000	$ 0.000	$(0.000)
Net asset value:					
Beginning of year	0.000	00.000	0.000	0.000	00.000
End of year	$ 0.000	$ 0.000	$00.000	$ 0.000	$ 0.000
Ratio of expenses to average net assets	0.00%	0.00%	0.00%	0.00%	0.00%
Ratio of net investment in-come to average net as-sets	0.00%	0.00%	0.00%	0.00%	0.00%
Portfolio turnover	00%	00%	00%	00%	0%
Number of shares outstand-ing at end of year (000 omitted)	000,000	000,000	000,000	000,000	000,000

See Accompanying Notes to Financial Statements

NOTES TO FINANCIAL STATEMENTS

Note 1—Significant Accounting Policies

The Trust is registered under the Investment Company Act of 1940, as amended, as a diversified, open-end, management investment company. The following is a summary of significant accounting policies consistently followed by the Trust in the preparation of its financial statements.

Investment Security Valuations   Securities listed on securities exchanges are valued at closing sale prices. Unlisted securities or listed securities for which closing sale prices are not available are valued at closing bid prices. However, listed debt securities may be valued on the basis of over-the-counter prices without regard to exchange prices when over-the-counter prices are believed more accurately to reflect the value of such securities. Short-term obligations are valued at amortized cost, which approximates value. Securities, if any, for which there are no such quotations or valuations are valued at fair value as determined in good faith by or at the direction of the Trustees.

Federal Income Taxes   The Trust complies with the provisions of the Internal Revenue Code available to investment companies and distributes to shareholders each year all of its taxable income, including any net realized gain on investments. Accordingly, no provision for Federal income tax is provided.

Equalization   The Trust follows the accounting practice known as equalization by which a portion of the proceeds from sales and costs of reacquisitions of Trust shares equivalent, on a per-share basis, to the amount of undistributed net investment income on the date of the transaction is credited or charged to undistributed net investment income. As a result, undistributed net investment income per share is unaffected by sales or reacquisitions of Trust shares.

Other   Investment transactions are accounted for on the date the investments are purchased or sold. Dividend income, distributions to shareholders, and shares issuable to shareholders electing to receive capital gain distributions in shares are recorded on the ex-dividend date.

Note 2—Investment Advisory Fee and Other Transactions with Affiliates

The investment advisory fee paid to Open Ended Financial Services Company is based upon a percentage of the average daily net assets plus a percentage of the gross income. The annual rates are reduced as average daily net assets and gross income exceed certain levels. For the year ended December 31, 1980, the effective annual rate, based on average daily net assets, was 0.000% and, based on gross income, was 0.000%. The fee, as compensation for overall investment advisory and administrative services, and general office facilities, amounted to $0,000,000. The Trust pays no compensation directly to its Trustees who are affiliated with the Investment Adviser or to its officers, all of whom receive remuneration for their services to the Trust from the Investment Adviser. Open Ended Financial Services Company, as principal underwriter, also received $000,000 as its portion of the sales charge on sales of shares of the Trust. Certain of the Trustees and officers of the Trust are partners of Open Ended Financial Services Company.

Note 3—Purchases and Sales of Investments

Purchases and sales of investments, other than short-term obligations, aggregated $000,000,000 and $000,000,000, respectively.

Note 4—Shares of Beneficial Interest

At December 31, 1980, there were authorized 000,000,000 shares of beneficial interest, having a par value of $0.00 each. Capital paid in aggregated $000,000,000, after deducting the excess of distributions over accumulated net realized gain on investments, computed on the basis of average cost. Transactions in shares were as follows:

| | Year Ended December 31 | |
	1980	1979
Shares reacquired	(00,000,000)	(00,000,000)
Shares sold	0,000,000	0,000,000
Shares issued or issuable to shareholders in payment of distributions from net realized gain on investment transactions	0,000,000	0,000,000
Net decrease	(00,000,000)	(0,000,000)

PREFERABLE ACCOUNTING PRINCIPLES

INSURANCE INDUSTRY

PROPERTY AND LIABILITY INSURANCE COMPANIES

Overview

The preferable accounting principles and practices for property and liability insurance companies appear in the following publications:

SOP (Note-1), Revision of Form of Auditor's Report

SOP 78-6, Accounting for Property and Liability Insurance Companies

Industry Audit Guide, Audits of Fire and Casualty Insurance Companies (hereinafter referred to as the Casualty Insurance Guide).

Note-1 This Statement of Position was never given a number and its date of issuance was July 1974.

SOP 78-6 specifically excludes title insurance companies from its provisions. However, the Casualty Insurance Guide is silent on its coverage of title insurance companies. For the purposes of this publication, it is presumed that title insurance companies are excluded from SOP 78-6 and the Casualty Insurance Guide. In addition, SOP 78-6 recommends that the term property and liability insurance companies be used instead of fire and casualty insurance companies.

The Casualty Insurance Guide does not prescribe the method that should be used for accounting changes which result from its implementation. Thus, it is presumed that all accounting changes that result from the implementation of the Casualty Insurance Guide should be accounted for in accordance with existing GAAP (APB-20, Accounting Changes).

> **OBSERVATION:** *Most industry audit guides and statements of position do prescribe the treatment of accounting changes that result from implementing their provisions.*

SOP 78-6 substantially amends the Casualty Insurance Guide and requires that the implementation of its provisions be accounted for as a prior period adjustment and financial statements presented for prior periods must be restated.

> **OBSERVATION:** *A change in, or a new promulgated GAAP, or the issuance of an industry audit guide by the AICPA, constitutes sufficient support for a change in an accounting principle (FASB Interpretation-20). However, the correction of an error in previously issued financial statements is not an accounting change (APB-20).*
>
> *Prior period adjustments have been narrowly defined by FASB-16, as either (1) a correction of an error in a prior-period statement, or (2) an adjustment for the realization of the tax benefits of the preacquisition operating-loss carryforward of purchased subsidiaries.*
>
> *Thus, it is doubtful whether adjustments resulting from compliance with SOP 78-6 can, under existing promulgated GAAP, be made as prior-period adjustments.*

As will be discussed later, the insurance industry is highly regulated. Thus, accounting principles and practices prescribed by insurance regulatory agencies may differ significantly from GAAP. As a rule, insurance companies must prepare one set of financial statements using regulatory accounting principles and practices, and one set of financial statements utilizing GAAP.

Property and liability companies are very similar to life insurance companies. The big difference is that property and liability insurance companies cover risks incurred on property or liability and life insurance companies cover risks involving the death or disability of the insured. Both types of insurance companies collect premiums and usually pay commissions to agents or sales personnel. In addition, both types of insurance companies have underwriting departments and utilize other insurance companies to spread excess or specialized risks (reinsurance).

Background

A property and liability insurance company may be organized as (1) a stock company, (2) a mutual company, or (3) a reciprocal or inter-insurance exchange.

A stock property and liability insurance company is owned by its stockholders, and is organized as a corporation. Because of the corporate form, stockholders' liability is usually limited to the amount of their investment in capital stock.

In a mutual property and liability insurance company the current policyholders are the owners at any given time and they share in the earnings and have the right to vote for the members of the board of directors. Upon liquidation of a mutual company, the current policyholders receive any remaining assets after payment of all liabilities. Most mutual companies issue nonassessable insurance policies that limit the liability of the policyholders in the event of bankruptcy, or lack of capital.

A reciprocal insurance exchange is comprised of subscribers who sign subscribers agreements. The subscribers' agreements provide, among other things, for an attorney-in-fact who has the power to underwrite insurance for the subscribers. However, each subscriber's liability is several and not joint. Thus, the liability of each subscriber is limited by the amount stated in the subscriber's agreement. Subscribers may be individuals, corporations, trusts, or partnerships. Compensation is paid to the attorney-in-fact based either on a percentage of premium income, or some other appropriate method.

A property and liability insurance company may underwrite one line of insurance business, or may be licensed to sell multiple lines of insurance. The lines of property and liability insurance are usually grouped as (1) fire and similar perils, (2) general liability, (3) marine perils, (4) automobile liability and property damage, (5) homeowners' insurance, (6) accident and health, (7) workman's compensation, (8) fidelity, (9) theft, (10) glass, (11) surety, (12) boiler and equipment, and other miscellaneous commercial insurance.

From an economic standpoint insurance is a method which is used to spread a specific risk among policyholders. The insurance company assumes the specific risk and charges a premium based on past loss experiences for the specific risk. The premiums collected by the insurance company are used to pay current losses and operational costs, and the balance is invested. Thus, the two main sources of income for a property and liability insurance company are (1) premiums, and (2) investment income.

An owner of an insurance contract must have an insurable interest in the subject matter of the policy in order for the contract to be valid. An insurable interest in life insurance need only exist at the time the policy is issued, while an insurable interest in property insurance must exist at the time of the loss.

An insurable interest is a test of financial relationship. A wife may insure the life of her husband, an employer the life of an employee, a creditor the life of his debtor, and a partner the life of his copartners. In life insurance the insurable interest must exist only at the time the policy is issued and if subsequently the relationship is broken (divorce of a marriage, dissolution of a partnership) the owner may still collect the benefits of the insurance contract.

A landlord may insure his property and a homeowner his or her home. However, in property insurance the insurable interest must exist at the time a loss is incurred. If a landlord sells his or her property, they have no further insurable interest and are not entitled to collect for any losses on the property sold.

The departmental functions of a typical property and liability insurance company would usually consist of (1) an agency department, (2) an underwriting department, (3) a policy service department, and (4) an investment department.

The agency department is responsible for the marketing functions of the insurance company. Supervision and training of sales personnel, sales promotion, and other selling activities are handled by the agency department.

The underwriting department is responsible for evaluating the risks which are undertaken by the insurance company, and also controls the issuance of all policies. Premium rates are determined by past loss experiences for specific types of risks. In addition, the underwriting department determines all reinsurance arrangements.

The policy service department is responsible for the bookkeeping activities, such as premium notices and collection, changes in address, beneficiary and similar changes, and the payment of loss claims.

The insurance company's investments are managed by the investment department.

Usually, insurance companies keep their general ledgers on a cash basis, because this is exactly how they do business. Another reason why the cash basis is used is that some reports required by regulatory agencies must be prepared on a cash basis, particularly details of income and expense. Assets that have been recorded on the books of an insurance company are called "ledger assets". Assets that are not recorded on the books are called "nonledger assets". Nonledger assets arise from the adjusting journal entries which are necessary to convert the cash basis trial balance to the accrual basis. Liabilities are referred to in the same manner, so that those that are recorded on the books, are called "ledger liabilities" and those not recorded on the books, are called "nonledger liabilities".

Because insurance companies use the cash basis, very few liabilities are recorded and consequently most liabilities are "nonledger". However, most assets arise from cash transactions and thus an insurance company will have few "nonledger assets".

When adjusting journal entries are made for workpapers, to convert the cash basis trial balance to the accrual basis, they are not posted to the books. Therefore, the books of insurance companies are always on the cash basis. This procedure makes it necessary for the insurance company to keep certain other records, such as a "claims register", so that information is available to adjust easily to the accrual basis. The claims register keeps track of claims pending, paid, negotiated, and rejected, while the cash basis trial balance will only reflect the claims actually paid. The claims register is used to prepare some of the necessary adjusting journal entries for conversion to the accrual basis.

All insurance companies theoretically have a maximum financial capacity or limit as to the amount of insurance it should underwrite. In addition, many insurance companies set their own limit on the amount of risk they are willing to undertake and thus, the amount of insurance they will underwrite. However, even if an insurance company has reached its theoretical financial capacity or self-imposed limit, the company can still write additional business and utilize reinsurance to keep within its established limits. Reinsurance is where one insurance company (the ceding company) transfers one or more of its policies to another insurance company (the reinsurer). The reinsurer charges the ceding company a premium for the amount of risk it has assumed and agrees to pay its share of any losses. In practice, some insurance companies have entered into agreements with other insurance companies for automatic reinsurance. Automatic reinsurance means that a specific portion, or percentage of the total business written by the ceding company is automatically reinsured by one or more other insurance companies. On the other hand, "facultative reinsurance" is where the ceding company submits each individual risk or portion of risk to the reinsurer who then has the choice of accepting or rejecting each individual risk.

Another form of reinsurance occurs when one insurance company sells all or part of its insurance in force to another insurance company. However, this form of reinsurance almost always includes the transfer of policy service responsibilities to the assuming company. Thus, the assuming company takes over the actual bookkeeping responsibilities, such as premium notices and collections. Frequently, a sale of insurance policies in force will require the approval of local regulatory agencies.

Every state has statutory laws governing the insurance industry. The insurance department of each state is charged with the responsibility of making sure that insurance companies remain solvent and deal fairly with policyholders. In addition, most states require some sort of periodic uniform financial report from insurance companies. Insurance companies are also restricted as to the types of investments that they can make.

The National Association of Insurance Commissioners (NAIC) is an organization comprised of the insurance commissioners from each state. The NAIC meets semi-annually and makes recommendations for new rules and procedures which are almost always adopted by all of the states. The NAIC is very concerned with financial reporting and auditing of insurance companies. The results have been the establishment of uniform annual reports and the development of an examiners manual which is written in the form of an audit program for insurance companies.

Property and liability insurance companies obtain their business through (1) direct writing, (2) brokers, (3) local and regional agents, and (4) general agents. In obtaining its· business through direct writing, an insurance company usually has salaried or commission sales personnel who do not have the power to bind the company on any insurance risks. The sales personnel who work directly for the company must submit all policies sold to a branch or home office for approval. Insurance brokers are usually independent agents who represent many insurance companies. Brokers can submit policies which they have sold to any insurance company they wish and the insurance company may accept or reject the broker's business as they see fit. Local and regional agents usually report to a branch or home office and are appointed on a nonexclusive territory basis. They are generally paid a commission based on a percentage of the premiums they produce. General agents are also compensated on a percentage of the premiums that they produce. However, the percentage is almost always higher for a general agent than for any other type of insurance solicitor. General agents usually sign contracts with the insurance company, and agree to maintain a sales force and promote the insurance company's business. In addition, a general agent agrees to pay its own expenses and often agrees to obtain subagents. In exchange, the insurance company usually grants an exclusive territory to the general agent.

Many property and liability insurance companies handle their own policy claims through salaried employees. These employees often investigate a claim and propose a settlement with the claimant. However, in most cases, settlements must be approved by the home office.

Another method used by insurance companies to investigate, adjust, and settle policy claims is through an adjustment bureau. Adjustment bureaus consist of several insurance companies who are all members of the adjustment bureau. The expenses of a bureau are paid by the members, usually based on the number of claims handled, or the dollar value of the claims. Final approval of all settlements made by an adjustment bureau is usually exercised by the insurance company. Members are not obligated to use the bureau.

Independent insurance adjustors, who work on a fee basis, are another alternative which an insurance company may use to investigate, adjust, and settle policy claims.

Preferable Accounting Principles

Most of the accounting and statistical data used by a property and liability insurance company appears in the "daily reports". A "daily report" is a copy of a section of the insurance policy that was sold, and it contains practically all of the accounting and statistical data necessary to record the transaction. Copies of the "daily reports" are distributed to several departments at the home office of the insurance company. The underwriting department receives a copy of the "daily report" from which the correct premium for the policy is computed.

Recognition of premium revenues The preferable accounting principles (SOP 78-6) require that premium revenue be recognized in proportion to the insurance company's performance under the contract. The insurance company's performance under the contract is the coverage of the risks that are insured. Thus, in those insurance policies in which coverage is provided evenly over the term of insurance, the premiums should be recognized evenly over the term of the insurance. However, if the period of coverage (risk) is different from the term of the insurance contract, then the premium should be recognized over the period of coverage. In other words, the premium income must be "matched" to the period of risk (coverage) during which the insurance company is exposed to potential loss. In the event the amount of insurance declines over the term of the insurance, the premium should be recognized in proportion to the amount of insurance over the term of the insurance.

> **OBSERVATION:** *The method of recognizing premium income in accordance with the preferable accounting principles is a classic example of the use of the "matching concept".*

In some types of insurance, such as workman's compensation, the final premium is not determined until after the term of the insurance contract because the premium is based on the total amount of compensation paid to employees. The insurance company receives a premium deposit at the inception of the policy and after the term of the insurance, a premium adjustment is made. In this event, an estimate of the final premium adjustment is necessary in order to recognize the total premium revenue over the term of insurance coverage.

Over the term of an insurance policy, the premiums are expected to pay for losses, if any, operational expenses, and still provide the insurance company with a profit. The amount of losses that a single insurance policy may incur is based on the law of averages. In other words, the possible loss that a single policy may incur is based on the loss experience of many policies. As long as an insurance policy is outstanding, there may be a claim for a loss. Thus, the unearned portion of a premium, at any time, should be sufficient to pay losses, operational expenses and a margin for profit. Statutory laws, in most states, provide that insurance companies must maintain reserves for possible losses equal to the unearned premiums of all insurance policies outstanding. The most common method used to determine unearned premiums is the "monthly pro rata fractional basis". This method assumes that the same dollar amount of insurance business is written each day of every month. Thus, the mean of all insurance business written in any month is the middle of the month. One year is divided into 24 periods, and a fraction is assigned to each month, as follows: January 1/24, February 3/24, March 5/24, April 7/24, May 9/24, June 11/24, and so forth. The appropriate fraction is then applied to the total original premium to determine the amount of earned and unearned premium.

Most state statutes require that insurance companies maintain their records in a manner in which a determination can be made annually on December 31, of the (1) premiums in force on direct insurance business and any reinsurance business, and the (2) premiums in force on insurance business that has been ceded on a reinsurance basis to other insurance companies.

Deferred acquisition costs Since the "matching concept" is applied to the recognition of premium revenue, it is only logical that the same principle be used in accounting for the costs incurred in obtaining the premium revenue. Thus, the preferable accounting principles provide that variable costs that are directly or indirectly related to the production of new or renewal premium revenue, should be deferred and amortized as a charge against income as the related premium revenue is earned. Costs that are directly related to the production of insurance business include all direct costs and indirect costs, such as underwriting and policy issuance expenses. Collection expenses, professional fees, depreciation, and general administrative expenses are not directly related to, nor vary directly with, the production of new or renewal insurance business and should be expensed as incurred.

Deferred acquisition costs should be amortized as a charge to income in the same manner as the related premium revenue is earned. The method of amortization should be consistently applied from year to year.

Premium deficiencies Premium revenue is supposed to be sufficient to pay losses, operational expenses, and provide a margin for profit. At any given time, unamortized unearned premiums should also be sufficient to pay losses, operational expenses, including deferred acquisition costs, and provide a margin for profit. Whenever premium revenue, or unearned premium revenue is not sufficient to pay losses and operational expenses, including unamortized deferred acquisition costs, a loss results which is referred to as a premium deficiency.

The preferable accounting principles (SOP 78-6) recommends that premium deficiencies be determined by reasonable groupings of business that is consistent with a company's manner of acquiring, servicing, and measuring profitability for its insurance business. In addition, SOP 78-6 requires that:

a. A provision for anticipated premium deficiencies should be provided when unearned premiums are insufficient to cover all related costs and expenses. Related costs and expenses should include, expected losses and loss adjustment expenses, expected policyholder dividends, unamortized deferred acquisition costs, and any anticipated expenses that are expected to be incurred subsequent to the inception date of the policy. If a cost, subsequent to the inception date of the policy, is direct or can be attributed to maintaining the policy in force, it should be included in the determination of the premium deficiency.

b. Although the issue has not been settled, anticipated investment income may be included in the determination of a premium deficiency but disclosure should be made, along with its effects on the financial statements, in the note on accounting policies.

c. Premium deficiencies should be recognized in the financial statements. Recognition should be made by reducing unamortized deferred acquisition costs by a charge to income in the amount necessary. If the unamortized deferred acquisition costs are smaller than the amount of premium deficiency, all of the unamortized deferred acquisition costs should be charged to income and an additional separate liability for the balance of the premium deficiency should be created by a charge to income.

Unpaid losses   Provision must be made in the financial statements for reported losses in the process of settlement, and unreported losses incurred but not reported. The provision for reported losses in the process of settlement may be made by estimating each reported loss on an individual basis. However, because of their large number, smaller losses may be estimated by an average dollar loss per case. Thus, the provision for smaller losses is frequently made by multiplying the number of smaller cases by the estimated average loss per case.

Unreported losses incurred but not reported are more difficult to determine and are usually estimated on a formula basis. Formulas are usually determined on the basis of statistics on actual loss experience for prior years which is then adjusted for current trends and other factors. This is usually accomplished by specific types of insurance policies for a selected period and then relating the loss experience to the premiums in force for the specific type of insurance policies. Formulas are only used for normal losses which are expected to reoccur. Large losses resulting from catastrophies are not included in the statistics used in determining formulas but are estimated separately, usually on the basis of judgment. Thus, a formula will usually consist of the loss experience determined for a prior period adjusted for current trends and also a factor for large catastrophic losses.

Statutory Formula Reserves are required by most states for bodily injury liability and workmen's compensation insurance. In addition, several states require minimum reserves for unreported losses incurred on surety and fidelity insurance policies.

The preferable accounting principles (SOP 78-6) require that provisions be made in the financial statements for reported losses in the process of settlement and unreported losses incurred but not reported. The provision for unpaid losses may include the effects of inflation and other economic factors and be based on the best estimate of the cost of settlement, arrived at by using past loss experience adjusted for current trends. The cost of settlement may be reduced by any estimated salvage and/or subrogation expected to be recovered from the case. Amounts of salvage and/or subrogation should be deducted from the liability for unpaid losses in the balance sheet and the amount deducted should be disclosed in a footnote to the financial statements.

No conclusion was reached by SOP 78-6 as to whether estimated unpaid losses should be presented in the balance sheet at their present values. However, if a company elects to present estimated unpaid losses at their present value on its balance sheet, it should be disclosed, along with its effects on the financial statements, in the note on accounting policies.

Loss adjustment expense   The provision for reported losses in the process of settlement and the provision for unreported losses incurred but not reported, involve the estimation of the amount of loss. The loss adjustment expense provides for the future costs involved in settling the reported and unreported losses. Loss adjustment expense may be classified as allocated or unallocated. Allocated loss adjustment expenses are those that can be directly identified to a specific loss. Unallocated loss adjustment expenses are those that cannot be identified to a specific loss and include indirect salaries, stationery, postage, rent, travel, and other similar expenses.

The provision for loss adjustment expense is generally determined by a formula based on expenses incurred in the settlement of losses in prior periods. In other words, the formula is based on past experience which may be adjusted for new and current trends.

The preferable accounting principles (SOP 78-6) require that a provision for loss adjustment expense be provided for all reported losses in the process of settlement and all unreported losses incurred but not reported.

Reinsurance   When one insurance company reinsures part or all of an outstanding policy with one or more other insurance companies it is called reinsurance. If a loss is incurred on a policy that has been reinsured, the reinsurers will have to pay their portion of the settlement. Thus, amounts recoverable from reinsurers should be included in the determination of (1) the provision for losses in the process of settlement, (2) the provision for unreported losses incurred but not reported, and (3) the provision for loss adjustment expense.

The preferable accounting principles (SOP 78-6) require that amounts recoverable from reinsurers be accounted for, as follows:

a. Amounts recoverable for losses and loss adjustment expense that have already been paid should be accounted for as a receivable (asset) from the reinsurers.
b. Amounts recoverable for losses and loss adjustment expense that have not been paid should be deducted from the liability for unpaid losses and loss adjustment expense, and the amount of the deduction should be disclosed in a footnote to the financial statements.
c. Collectible premiums that have been ceded to a reinsurer are not considered receivables and they should be netted against their related unearned premiums.
d. It is preferable that receivables and payables to the same reinsurer be offset against each other.
e. Premiums ceded to a reinsurer should be deducted from the related earned premiums in the income statement.
f. Recovery of losses from reinsurers should be deducted from the related incurred losses in the income statement.

In addition, an insurance company should disclose in its financial statements all of the pertinent facts concerning its reinsurance activities. This should include, (1) the amount of reinsurance premiums which have been ceded or assumed that are included in earned premiums for the period, (2) reinsurance premiums paid on catastrophe-type contracts that have been deducted from the related earned premiums for the period, and (3) reinsurance recoveries on catastrophe-type contracts that have been deducted from the related losses incurred for the period.

Policyholder dividends   Policyholder dividends must be accrued and reported in the financial statements. If the amount is not known, the use of reasonable estimates is required by the preferable accounting principles (SOP 78-6).

> **OBSERVATION:** *SOP 78-6 makes a direct reference to the necessity of accruing policyholder dividends. However, the accrual basis of accounting is required under GAAP.*

Contingent commissions   Insurance companies usually agree to pay additional commissions to their brokers and agents if the business they generate results in a favorable loss experience. Therefore, these additional commissions are contingent on whether or not a favorable loss experience occurs.

The preferable accounting principles (SOP 78-6) require that contingent commissions (receivable or payable) be appropriately accrued and appear in the income. statement of the periods in which the related profits are recognized.

Valuations of investments   The valuations of investments of property and liability insurance companies are almost identical with those of life insurance companies, as follows:

Bonds
If the insurance company has the ability and intent to keep bonds to maturity, the bonds should be carried at amortized cost, providing that there has been no permanent decline in the market value of the bonds below amortized cost. Bonds held for speculation should be carried at market value and unrealized gains or losses should be recognized.

Common and Nonredeemable Preferred Stock
Common and nonredeemable preferred stock should be carried at market value. If the insurance company has the ability and intent to keep redeemable preferred stock until redemption, the preferred stock should be carried at amortized cost, providing that there has been no permanent decline in the market value of the preferred stock below amortized cost.

Mortgages
Mortgages should be carried at the balance of the unpaid principal. Mortgages purchased at a discount or premium should be carried at amortized cost.

Real Estate Investments

Real estate investments should be carried at depreciated cost. Amortization, depreciation and other related costs or credits should be included in the determination of investment income.

Real estate should be classified in accordance with its predominant use either as property used in business or as an investment. Real estate operating expenses, including depreciation, should be classified consistent with the related asset as either investment expense or operating expense. Real estate that is used in business by the insurance company should not be accounted for as investment income with a corresponding charge to operations for rental expense. In other words, an insurance company cannot include rental income in its financial statements for property it uses in the regular course of business.

Real estate is always classified as an investment for regulatory accounting purposes, regardless of its use. Rental expense is charged to operations and rental income is included in investment income for real estate used by the insurance company in its own business.

Realized gains and losses All realized gains and losses on all assets held for investment should appear, net of related taxes, in the income statement below operating income. Realized gains and losses applicable to property used in business should be included as part of operating income.

Unrealized investment gains and losses should not be included in the determination of net income, but are recognized, net of related taxes, as an addition to, or reduction of, stockholders' equity.

Permanent declines in security investments, below cost or amortized cost, should be recognized as realized losses. These security investments should be written down to their net realizable values, which subsequently becomes their new cost basis.

Valuation accounts should not be used for bonds, common stocks, or preferred stocks, which are publicly traded.

Nonadmitted assets Certain assets are not permitted to be shown on the balance sheet of an insurance company under regulatory accounting practices. Nonadmitted assets are charged to surplus and thus eliminated from the regulatory balance sheet. The following is a list of the more common types of nonadmitted assets:

1. furniture and equipment
2. automobiles
3. prepaid and deferred expenses
4. goodwill and other intangible assets
5. unauthorized investments
6. investments in excess of authorized amounts
7. receivables from agents (debit balances)
8. receivables from employees and officers
9. accrued income on investments in default
10. receivables from unauthorized reinsurers

Some states allow furniture and equipment as admitted assets up to certain amounts based on a percent of total assets. In most states, as a general rule, only the undepreciated balance of furniture and equipment are treated as "nonadmitted assets". Thus, insurance companies that charged depreciation expense to operations are allowed to do so as only the undepreciated balances are considered nonadmitted assets.

Nonadmitted assets must be restored in presenting financial statements in conformity with GAAP. This is accomplished by debiting the various assets and crediting retained earnings (surplus). However, care must be exercised in determining the collectibility of receivables which are restored.

Stockholders' equity It may be necessary to reclassify an insurance company's equity accounts for the purposes of financial statements presented in conformity with GAAP. As mentioned above, nonadmitted assets must be restored by a credit to retained earnings. If an insurance company has increased its statutory reserves by a direct charge to surplus, the transaction will have to be redone to be in conformity with GAAP.

STOCK LIFE INSURANCE COMPANIES

Overview

The preferable accounting principles and practices for stock life insurance companies appear in the following publications:

SOP (Note-1) Confirmation of Insurance Policies in Force
SOP 79-3 Accounting for Investments of Stock Life Insurance Companies
Industry Audit Guide, Audits of Stock Life Insurance Companies (hereinafter referred to as the Stock Life Guide)
Note-1, This Statement of Position was never given a number and its date of issue was August 4, 1978.

The Stock Life Guide covers stock life insurance companies only and does not apply to mutual life insurance companies.

The Stock Life Guide requires that accounting changes resulting from its implementation should be reported as prior period adjustments as stated in paragraph 18 of APB-9.

> *OBSERVATION: A change in, or a new promulgated GAAP, or the issuance of an industry audit guide by the AICPA, constitutes sufficient support for a change in an accounting principle (FASB Interpretation -20). However, the correction of an error in previously issued financial statements is not an accounting change (APB-20).*
>
> *Corrections of errors in previously issued financial statements may be made as a prior period adjustment (FASB-16). However, a change in an accounting principle is usually accounted for by reflecting the "cumulative effect" of the change in the income statement of the year the change is made. Thus, it is doubtful whether adjustments resulting from compliance with the Stock Life Guide can appropriately be made as prior period adjustments.*

It must be clearly understood that accounting practices prescribed by insurance regulatory agencies may differ significantly from GAAP. Thus, insurance companies must usually prepare one set of financial statements using regulatory accounting principles, and one set of financial statements utilizing generally accepted accounting principles (GAAP).

Background

The proceeds of a life insurance policy usually provide some degree of financial security to one or more beneficiaries named in the policy. Upon death of the insured, the insurance company pays the face amount of the policy, less any outstanding indebtedness, to the beneficiary. However, the proceeds of the insurance policy are not always paid in a lump-sum at the time of death of the insured. Many different elections are available as to how the proceeds will be paid. For example, an election can be made for the insurance company to pay certain periodic amounts to the beneficiary, or to pay the proceeds when the beneficiary reaches a specified age. In this event, the proceeds held by the insurance company will usually earn interest. Almost any type of arrangement can be made with a life insurance company for the payment of a policy's proceeds.

An owner of an insurance contract must have an insurable interest in the subject matter of the policy in order for the contract to be valid. An insurable interest in life insurance need only exist at the time the policy is issued, while an insurable interest in casualty insurance must exist at the time of the loss.

An insurable interest is a test of financial relationship. A wife may insure the life of her husband, an employer the life of an employee, a creditor the life of his debtor, and a partner the life of his copartners. In life insurance the insurable interest must exist only at the time the policy is issued and if subsequently the relationship is broken (divorce of a marriage, dissolution of a partnership) the owner may still collect the benefits of the insurance contract.

A landlord may insure his property and a homeowner his home. However, in casualty insurance the insurable interest must exist at the time a loss is incurred. If a landlord sells his property, he has no further insurable interest and is not entitled to collect for any losses on the property sold.

From an economic standpoint insurance is a method which is

used to spread a specific risk among many individuals. The insurance company assumes the specific risk, such as death, and charges a premium based on actuarial calculations. In the case of death, mortality tables have been established which take into consideration the frequency of deaths among individuals in various age groups. The premiums collected by the insurance company are used to pay current benefits and costs and the balance is invested to yield investment income. Theoretically, if an individual dies in the year that the mortality tables predict, the accumulated net premiums collected by the insurance company, plus the investment earned on the accumulated premiums, should be sufficient to pay the face amount of the policy and still leave a profit. These accumulated premiums and investment income are reflected on the balance sheet of an insurance company as "policy reserves".

An annuity insurance policy is one that the insured does not have to die to collect. It is more like a fixed compulsory saving plan. The insured pays premiums for a stated period, after which, the insurance company makes fixed payments to the insured either for a specified time, or for the balance of the insured's life.

Accident and health insurance policies are issued on an individual or group basis. In these types of policies the insurance company pays for hospital and medical care, and sometimes for the loss of income during periods that the insured is incapacitated.

The important thing to remember is that revenues of an insurance company are usually derived from premiums and investment income.

The two most common types of insurance companies are (1) stock companies, and (2) mutual companies. Stock companies are formed to earn profit for its shareholders. A stock life insurance company may issue participating and nonparticipating insurance policies. Participating policyholders share in the earnings created by their policies. These earnings, if any, are returned to the participating policyholders in the form of dividends. Nonparticipating policyholders do not share in any earnings of the company.

As a general rule, mutual insurance companies issue only participating policies. Thus, all of the policyholders share in the earnings and all have the right to vote for the members of the board of directors.

The departmental functions of a typical life insurance company would consist of (1) an agency department, (2) an underwriting department, (3) a policy service department, (4) an actuarial department, and (5) an investment department.

The agency department is responsible for the marketing functions of the insurance company. Supervision and training of sales personnel, sales promotion, and other selling activities are handled by the agency department.

The underwriting department is responsible for evaluating the risks which are undertaken by the insurance company, and also controls the issuance of all policies.

Premium rates are determined by the actuarial department as well as calculation of the dividends on participating policies. Long-range planning and the calculation of the adequacy of policy reserves are also the responsibility of the actuarial department.

The policy service department is responsible for the bookkeeping activities, such as premium notices and collection; changes in address, beneficiary and similar changes; and the payment of claims or benefits.

The insurance company's investments are managed by the investment department.

Usually, insurance companies keep their general ledger on a cash basis, because this is exactly how they do business, on a cash basis. Another reason why the cash basis is used is that some reports prepared for regulatory agencies require detail of income and expense items on a cash basis. Assets that have been recorded on the books of a life insurance company are called "ledger assets". Assets that are not recorded on the books are called "nonledger assets". Nonledger assets arise from the adjusting journal entries which are necessary to convert the cash basis trial balance to the accrual basis. Liabilities are referred to in the same manner, so that those that are recorded on the books are called "ledger liabilities", and those not recorded on the books, are called "nonledger liabilities".

Because insurance companies use the cash basis, very few liabilities are recorded and consequently most liabilities are "nonledger". However, most assets arise from cash transactions and thus an insurance company will have few "nonledger assets".

When adjusting journal entries are made for workpapers, to convert the cash trial balance to the accrual basis, they are not posted to the books. Therefore, the books of insurance companies are always on the cash basis. This procedure makes it necessary for the insurance company to keep certain other records, such as a "claims register", so that information is available to adjust easily to the accrual basis. The claims register keeps track of claims pending, paid, negotiated, and rejected, while the cash trial balance will only reflect the claims actually paid. The claims register is used to prepare the necessary adjusting journal entries for conversion to the accrual basis.

Another large liability which does not appear on the cash trial balance is the policy reserve account. The policy reserve account and reserves for other contract liabilities are maintained in a separate subsidiary ledger.

All insurance companies theoretically have a maximum financial capacity as to the amount of insurance it should underwrite. In addition, many insurance companies set their own limit on the amount of risk they are willing to undertake and thus, the amount of insurance they will underwrite. However, even if an insurance company has reached its theoretical financial capacity or self-imposed limits, the company can still write additional business and utilize reinsurance to keep within its established limits. Reinsurance is where one insurance company (the ceding company) transfers one or more of its policies to another insurance company (the reinsurer). The reinsurer charges the ceding company a premium for the amount of risk it has assumed, and agrees to pay its share of any losses. In practice, some insurance companies have entered into agreements with other insurance companies for automatic reinsurance. Automatic reinsurance means that a specific portion, or percentage of the total business written by the ceding company is automatically reinsured by one or more other insurance companies. On the other hand, "facultative reinsurance" is where the ceding company submits each individual risk or portion of risk to the reinsurer who then has the choice of accepting or rejecting each individual risk.

Another form of reinsurance occurs when one insurance company sells all or part of its insurance in force to another insurance company. However, this form of reinsurance almost always includes the transfer of policy service responsibilities to the assuming company. Thus, the assuming company takes over the actual book-keeping responsibilities, such as premium notices and collections; address and beneficiary changes; and the payment of benefits. Frequently, a sale of insurance policies in force will require the approval of local regulatory agencies.

Every state has statutory laws governing the insurance industry. The insurance department of each state is charged with the responsibility of making sure that insurance companies remain solvent and deal fairly with policyholders. In addition, most states require some sort of periodic uniform financial report from insurance companies. Insurance companies are also restricted as to the types of investments that they can make.

The National Association of Insurance Commissioners (NAIC) is an organization comprised of the insurance commissioners from each state. The NAIC meets semi-annually and makes recommendations for new rules and procedures which are almost always adopted by all of the states. The NAIC is very concerned with financial reporting and auditing of insurance companies. The results have been the establishment of uniform annual reports and the development of an examiners manual which is written in the form of an audit program for insurance companies.

Generally, life insurance companies are exempt from registration under the Securities Exchange Act of 1934. However, many insurance companies have established "holding companies" which are not considered life insurance companies and thus must be registered under the 1934 Act. In addition, some insurance companies have registered their shares under the 1934 Act so that the shares can be listed and traded on a national stock exchange. Public offerings of life insurance companies' stock must be registered under the Securities Act of 1933.

If an insurance company has registered under either of the securities acts, it must comply with annual and periodic reporting requirements and proxy solicitation rules.

The Life Insurance Business

An insurance company receives its revenues from premiums and investment income. Premium income may be derived directly from the owner of the policy or from reinsurance agreements with other insurance companies. Investment income is regulated by insurance statutes which set forth the types of investments that may be made.

Life insurance companies generally sell (1) life insurance, (2) annuity contracts, and (3) accident and health contracts. There are many different types of life insurance coverage, the more common are discussed below.

Whole-life policies benefits are paid only upon death of the insured. Benefits are usually equal to the face amount of the policy, less loans or indebtedness owed to the insurance company. Whole-life policies usually accumulate a cash surrender value which increases as each year passes. The owner of the policy can usually borrow from the insurance company or a bank using the cash surrender value as collateral.

Premiums for whole-life insurance are generally level, that is, they are the same amount each year. They are payable annually but more frequent payments can be made by payment of a small service fee. A whole-life policy can be paid in one lump-sum payment at the beginning of the policy term, but this is an exception, as most policies are paid either quarterly, semi-annually, or annually. A "straight-life" policy (also called "ordinary life") requires that premiums be paid during the entire life of the insured. A limited-payment policy requires that premiums be paid over a specified period which is usually ten, twenty, or thirty years. As a result, the premiums on a limited-payment policy are always higher than those of a straight-life policy, but the total cost of the policy is usually less.

Term insurance policies   are issued for a specific period and death benefits are paid only if the insured dies during the specified period. Benefits are usually equal to the face amount of the policy. Term insurance policies generally do not accumulate any cash surrender value, and thus, no loans can be made against them.

Term insurance policies are written for short periods, usually one to five-years. However, in most cases the policyholder is granted the right to renew a term insurance policy up to a maximum age (60 or 65) without having to submit additional evidence of insurability. The term policy may also grant the right to the policyholder to convert the term insurance to whole-life or some other type of coverage.

Premiums for term insurance policies usually increase with the age of the insured. Payment must be made annually, but may be made at interim periods during the year for an additional service charge.

Since term insurance does not usually accumulate any cash value, the premiums constitute payment for insurance protection only. Thus, most people feel that term insurance is best in those cases where protection is sought.

Besides individual term policies, an insurance company may issue group term life insurance policies. A group term policy insures a specific group of individuals under a single master contract, usually for one-year. Premiums are calculated on the basis of the ages of the individuals in the group.

Endowment insurance policies   are issued for a specific time, called the endowment period, and have a maturity date on which the insured receives the face amount of the policy, less any indebtedness owed to the insurance company. However, if the insured dies during the endowment period the insurance company pays the face amount, less any indebtedness, to the beneficiary of the policy. Thus, the insured has insurance protection during the endowment period and, if living at the maturity date, receives the face amount of the policy, less any indebtedness due to the insurance company. Endowment policies accumulate a cash value which increase with time. The cash value may be used as collateral for a loan.

Premiums for endowment policies can be on a single lump-sum payment or on a limited-payment basis, but are generally payable over the endowment period specified in the policy.

Basic insurance policies can be expanded by the use of riders which are attached to and made part of, the insurance contract. A nonforfeiture rider can be attached to a policy which provides that in the event the policyholder fails to make a premium payment, the insurance company may use the cash value of the policy to make the premium payment. Another type of nonforfeiture rider provides for the entire policy to be converted to a term insurance policy in the event that a premium payment is not made on time. Thus, the policyholder is given extended protection instead of having the insurance protection lapse.

Still another type of common rider provides for the waiver of all premiums during periods of disability that the insured might experience. An accidental death benefit rider (double indemnity) provides that the insurance company will pay twice the face amount of the policy, if the insured dies by accidental means.

Obviously, each rider has its price which increases the overall premium on the insurance policy.

In an annuity contract, the insurance company guarantees to pay the annuitant for as long as he lives, a periodic sum of money. The annuity can begin immediately or at some specified future date. Annuity contracts can be issued on an individual or group basis and group annuities are often utilized to fulfill a company's pension plan obligations. Premiums for annuities are based on the amount of the periodic payment, the date the payments begin, and the age of the annuitant.

Straight-life annuity   the annuitant receives guaranteed periodic payments as long as he or she lives. No further payments are made by the insurance company after the date of death of the annuitant.

Life annuity—period certain exactly the same as a straight-life annuity except that the insurance company agrees to make the guaranteed payments for a specified time. Thus, if the annuitant dies before the end of the specified time, the annuitant's beneficiary continues to receive the guaranteed payments until the specified time comes to an end.

Joint and survivorship annuity involves two or more annuitants and provides for guaranteed periodic payments to any surviving annuitant.

Variable annuity the periodic annuity payment varies in accordance with investment experience. Investments for variable annuities are kept in a separate fund and the amount of the periodic annuity is based on the performance of the investments. Variable annuities may or may not include a minimum death benefit during the accumulation period.

There are many types of accident and health insurance policies available today. However, most of the coverage is provided by group contracts. The more common types provide for reimbursement of medical expenses and for loss of income during periods of partial or total disability. Medical coverage is frequently broken down into hospital expenses and reimbursement for doctor bills. Health insurance policies almost always contain a "deductible clause", which requires that the insured pay a stipulated amount of losses before the coverage is effective.

Preferable Accounting Principles

There are significant differences in accounting principles and practices used in reporting to insurance regulatory agencies and generally accepted accounting principles. The following are some of the more important exceptions to GAAP which are used in regulatory accounting practices:

1. Increasing the "policy reserves" account by a direct debit to unassigned surplus (retained earnings) instead of a charge to income.
2. Charging unassigned surplus with prior service costs of pension plans instead of a charge to income.

3. Netting liabilities against related assets.
4. Debiting unassigned surplus for only the par value of certain stock dividends.

Premiums are calculated by actuaries to provide policy benefits, selling and other expenses, and a profit for the insurance company. The information used by the actuaries to calculate the premium on an insurance policy are called "actuarial assumptions". For example, the mortality tables contain expected life spans for both men and women, and the actuary must use an expected rate of return for invested funds.

Generally, an insurance company must compute a gross premium and a net premium for each policy issued. The gross premium is the amount charged to the policyholder, and the net premium is used in the determination of the statutory reserve liability. The difference between the gross and net premium does not necessarily represent an amount for expenses and profit, and although misleading the difference is called "loading".

Recognition of premium revenues The preferable accounting principles require that premium revenue be recognized over the life of the insurance contract in proportion to performance under the contract. In certain types of insurance contracts the life of the contract is the same as the premium-paying period.

Recognition of Costs

An insurance company pools the risks of many individuals and businesses. Thus, the undertaking of risks is the primary business of an insurance company. However, the real risk that an insurance company takes is that actual experience will be worse than the actuarial assumptions used in calculating the premium. When this occurs, the insurance company loses money. Thus, it is important that insurance companies be reasonably conservative in their basic assumptions which should include a provision for the "risk of adverse deviation."

The normal costs of an insurance company include the payment of policy benefits and the expenses of doing business. These costs must be matched to their related premium revenue.

Acquisition expenses Acquisition expenses consist of all costs incurred to acquire new business. The two broad categories of acquisition expenses are those related to the (1) actual sale of insurance, and (2) processing of insurance business.

Acquisition expenses which are related to, and vary with, the production of new business should be deferred and amortized, as a charge to income, in proportion to the recognition of the related premium revenue. The method of amortization for acquisition expenses must be in proportion to the premium revenue recognized. All other acquisition expenses should be recognized in the period incurred.

Under regulatory accounting practices, all acquisition expenses are charged against income in the period incurred.

Actual acquisition expenses should be compared to those used in the actuarial assumptions and when possible the actual acquisition expenses should be used in the actuarial assumptions instead of estimates. When estimates are used to determine the amount of acquisition expenses which should be deferred, it is necessary to adjust such estimates to actual amounts if the differences are significant.

As mentioned previously, regulatory accounting practices require that all acquisition expenses be charged to income when incurred. Thus, a significant difference between regulatory accounting practices and GAAP is the deferral and amortization of acquisition expenses. This difference is reflected in stockholders' equity and net income determined under regulatory accounting practices and stockholders' equity and net income determined under GAAP.

Unamortized acquisition expenses should be disclosed in a separate presentation on the balance sheet and should be classified as a deferred charge.

Other expenses Other expenses of insurance companies are treated in accordance with existing GAAP. Thus, if an expenditure benefits future periods, it may be deferred and charged to the periods benefited. However, all other expenses, such as policy maintenance and general overhead, which are not directly related to the production of new business, should be charged to operations in the period incurred.

Loss recognition As mentioned previously, the actuarial assumptions for each policy or group of policies must include a provision for the payment of benefits. These provisions are reflected in the balance sheet as liabilities, and are called "policy reserve accounts". The "Reserve for Life Policies and Contracts" should contain an estimated amount which is adequate to provide future guaranteed benefits as they become payable. In life insurance contracts, the two most important factors that affect the policy reserves are the mortality rate and assumptions as to future interest rates.

At any given time, the policy reserve reflects the present value of future guaranteed benefits, less the present value of future net premiums. In addition, the policy reserve should be sufficient to cover any unamortized acquisition expenses.

As long as the original actuarial assumptions are met compared to actual experience no adjustment to the policy reserve is necessary. However, when actual experience is significantly different than the assumptions an adjustment is required. The adjustment is computed by using the actual experience information, as follows:

Computation of Gross Premium Reserve
December 31, 1979

Present value of future benefits and related expenses	$40,000
Less: present value of future gross premiums	36,000
Gross premium reserve	$ 4,000
Actual reserve on valuation date	3,500
Addition to reserve before acquisition expenses	$ 500
Add: unamortized acquisition costs	900
Reserve deficiency	$ 1,400

The reserve deficiency must be recognized as a loss against current operations and the policy reserve account increased by the amount of the reserve deficiency. The revised assumptions should then be used to determine any future reserve additions.

The gross premium reserve computation should be periodically compared to the actual reserve balance, and any reserve deficiency should be charged to period income.

Investments in subsidiaries   Investments in subsidiaries should be accounted for as a purchase or pooling of interests in accordance with existing GAAP (APB-16). Unconsolidated subsidiaries should be accounted for by the equity method (APB-18) where appropriate. In a purchase transaction, any cost in excess of acquired assets should be accounted for as goodwill under the provisions of APB-17 (Accounting for Intangible Assets).

Under regulatory accounting practices, life insurance companies can not consolidate subsidiaries. Subsidiaries must be carried at the values prescribed in the NAIC manual published by the subcommittee on valuations of securities.

Deferred income taxes   The Life Insurance Company Act of 1959 covers the taxation of life insurance companies for federal tax purposes. For the purposes of GAAP, life insurance companies must comply with existing promulgated pronouncements, and thus, must determine deferred income taxes when appropriate.

Other Important Matters

SOP 79-3 (Accounting for Investments of Stock Life Insurance Companies) replaces the section in the Stock Life Guide entitled "Valuation of Investments and Recognition of Related Realized and Unrealized Gains or Losses". SOP 79-3 provides that insurance companies should value investments, as follows:

Bonds   If the insurance company has the ability and intent to keep bonds to maturity, the bonds should be carried at amortized cost, providing that there has been no permanent decline in the market value of the bonds below amortized cost. Bonds held for speculation should be carried at market value and unrealized gains or losses should be recognized.

Common and nonredeemable preferred stock   should be carried at market value. If the insurance company has the ability and intent to keep redeemable preferred stock until redemption, the preferred stock should be carried at amortized cost, providing that there has been no permanent decline in the market value of the preferred stock below amortized cost.

Mortgages should be carried at the balance of the unpaid principal. Mortgages purchased at a discount or premium should be carried at amortized cost.

Real estate investments should be carried at depreciated cost. Amortization, depreciation and other related costs or credits should be included in the determination of investment income.

Real estate should be classified in accordance with its predominant use as either property used in business or as an investment (SOP 79-3). Real estate operating expenses, including depreciation, should be classified consistent with the related asset as either investment expenses or operating expenses. Real estate that is used in business by the insurance company should not be accounted for as investment income with a corresponding charge to operations for rental expense. In other words, an insurance company cannot include rental income in its financial statements for property it uses in the regular course of business.

Real estate is always classified as an investment, for regulatory accounting purposes, regardless of its use. Rental expense is charged to operations and rental income is included in investment income for real estate used by the insurance company in its own business.

Realized gains and losses all realized gains and losses on all assets held for investment should appear, net of related taxes, in the income statement below operating income. Realized gains and losses applicable to property used in business should be included as part of operating income.

Unrealized investment gains and losses should not be included in the determination of net income, but are recognized, net of related taxes, as an addition or reduction of stockholders' equity.

Permanent declines in security investments, below cost or amortized cost, should be recognized as realized losses. These security investments should be written down to their net realizable values, which subsequently becomes their new cost basis.

Valuation accounts should not be used for bonds, common stocks, or preferred stocks, which are publicly-traded.

Commitment fees   Commitment fees for mortgage loans which exceed those fees that are currently being charged in the industry, should be accounted for as a reduction of the effective rate of the permanent financing. Normal commitment fees, less direct costs and related expenses should be recognized as income over the commitment period. Unamortized commitment fees should be included in income in the period in which the company's obligation no longer exists.

Mandatory securities valuation reserve   A Mandatory Securities Valuation Reserve (MSVR) is required to be established in most states in accordance with a NAIC formula. Unassigned surplus is debited and a reserve account is credited. This procedure is unacceptable under GAAP.

Under GAAP the MSVR represents an appropriation of retained earnings (surplus) which should be included in the equity section of the balance sheet.

Nonadmitted assets   Certain assets are not permitted to be shown on the balance sheet of an insurance company under regulatory accounting practices. Nonadmitted assets are charged to surplus and thus eliminated from the regulatory balance sheet. The following is a list of the more common "nonadmitted assets":

1. furniture and equipment
2. automobiles
3. prepaid and deferred expenses
4. goodwill and other intangible assets
5. unauthorized investments
6. investments in excess of authorized amounts
7. receivables from agents (debit balances)
8. receivables from employees and officers
9. accrued income on investments in default
10. receivables from unauthorized reinsurers

Some states allow furniture and equipment as admitted assets up to certain amounts based on a percent of total assets. In most states, as a general rule, only the undepreciated balance of furniture and equipment is treated as "nonadmitted assets". Thus, insurance companies that charge depreciation expense to operations are allowed to do so as only the undepreciated balances are considered "nonadmitted assets".

Nonadmitted assets must be restored in presenting financial statements in conformity with GAAP. This is accomplished by debiting the various assets and crediting retained earnings (surplus). However, care must be exercised in determining the collectibility of receivables which are restored.

Stockholder's equity   It may be necessary to reclassify an insurance company's equity accounts for the purposes of financial statements presented in conformity with GAAP. As mentioned previously, nonadmitted assets must be restored by a credit to retained earnings. If an insurance company has increased its policy reserves by a direct charge to surplus, the transaction will have to be redone to be in conformity with GAAP. Care must also be exercised in segregating appropriated surplus from unassigned surplus for financial statement purposes.

Disclosure   Besides the disclosure of the principal accounting policies and practices of stock life insurance companies, the following additional disclosures should be considered:

1. Method of recognizing premium revenue and related expenses.
2. The nature of, method of amortizing, and the amount of amortization of deferred acquisition costs.
3. The methods employed to compute policy reserves and a description of the assumption used.
4. Method of accounting for dividends to policyholders and the amount of participating business in force.
5. Treatment of mandatory securities valuation reserve and nonadmitted assets.
6. The amount of stockholders' equity which is restricted by statutory requirements.
7. The amount of current and deferred income taxes.
8. Amounts and expiration dates of unused operating loss carryforwards.
9. The amount of retained earnings in excess of statutory requirements upon which no income tax provision has been made.
10. Reinsurance transactions of significant nature and their affects on the financial statements.

Accounting Changes

SOP 79–3 states that its conclusions should be applied retroactively and financial statements presented for prior years should be restated.

> *OBSERVATION: SOP 79-3 apparently conflicts with existing GAAP (APB-20, Accounting Changes). As a general rule, a change in an accounting principle or practice is accounted for by including the "cumulative effect" of the change in net income of the period of change (APB-20). The "cumulative effect" is shown in the income statement, net of related taxes, between extraordinary items and net income. The effect of the change in accounting principle or practice for the current period is not included in the "cumulative effect", but the net income for the current period is reported on the basis that includes the newly adopted accounting principle or practice (APB-20).*
>
> *The issuance of an industry audit guide or statement of position by the AICPA constitutes sufficient support for a change in accounting principle or practice and how to report such changes (FASB Interpretation-20).*

Comprehensive Illustration

The following is a comprehensive illustration of the preferable accounting principles contained in this chapter.

STOCK LIFE INSURANCE COMPANY
BALANCE SHEET
As of December 31, 1980 and 1979

ASSETS	1980	1979
Cash	$ 0,000,000	$ 0,000,000
Investments:		
Bonds, at amortized cost (approximate market, $000,000,000 in 1980 and $000,000,000 in 1979)	000,000,000	000,000,000
Preferred stocks (note 1)	00,000,000	00,000,000
Common stocks, at market (cost $00,000,000 in 1980 and $00,000,000 in 1979)	00,000,000	00,000,000
Mortgage loans on real estate (net of allowance for uncollectible loans of $000,000 in 1980 and $000,000 in 1979)	00,000,000	00,000,000
Real estate (including home office), at cost, partially pledged (net of accumulated depreciation of $0,000,000 in 1980 and $00,000,000 in 1979) (note 5)	00,000,000	00,000,000
Policy loans, secured by cash values	00,000,000	00,000,000
Premium notes, substantially secured (notes 7 and 8)	0,000,000	00,000,000
Other invested assets (net of accumulated depletion of $0,000,000 in 1980 and $0,000,000 in 1979)	000,000	000,000
Total investments	000,000,000	000,000,000
Accrued investment income	00,000,000	00,000,000
Receivables (net of allowance for uncollectible accounts of $0,000,000 in 1980 and $0,000,000 in 1979) (note 8)	0,000,000	0,000,000
Furniture and equipment (net of accumulated depreciation of $0,000,000 in 1980 and $0,000,000 in 1979	0,000,000	0,000,000
Unamortized policy acquisition costs	000,000,000	000,000,000
Premium notes sold to bank (note 7)	00,000,000	00,000,000
	$000,000,000	$000,000,000

LIABILITIES AND STOCKHOLDERS' EQUITY

	1980	*1979*
Future policy benefit reserves (note 3)	$000,000,000	$000,000,000
Policy and contract claims	0,000,000	0,000,000
Policyholders' funds	00,000,000	00,000,000
Mortgage notes payable (note 5)	0,000,000	0,000,000
Premium note commissions in escrow (note 7)	0,000,000	0,000,000
Other liabilities	0,000,000	0,000,000
Deferred Federal income taxes (note 4)	00,000,000	00,000,000
Premium notes sold to bank (note 7)	00,000,000	00,000,000
Total liabilities	000,000,000	000,000,000
Stockholders' equity (notes 1, 2 and 9): Capital stock of $0 par value Authorized 0,000,000 shares; issued and outstanding 0,000,000 shares	0,000,000	0,000,000
Net unrealized loss on investment in stocks	(0,000,000)	(000,000)
Retained earnings	000,000,000	000,000,000
Total stockholders' equity	000,000,000	000,000,000
	$000,000,000	$000,000,000

See Accompanying Notes to Financial Statements

STOCK LIFE INSURANCE COMPANY
STATEMENT OF STOCKHOLDERS' EQUITY
Years Ended December 31, 1980 and 1979

	1980	1979
Capital Stock	$ 0,000,000	$ 0,000,000
Net unrealized loss on investment in stocks (note 1):		
Beginning of year	(000,000)	000,000
Net unrealized investment loss during the year (net of deferred Federal income tax benefit of $000,000 in 1979)	(0,000,000)	(000,000)
End of year	(0,000,000)	(000,000)
Retained earnings:		
Beginning of year	000,000,000	000,000,000
Net earnings	00,000,000	00,000,000
Cash dividends to stockholders ($0.00 per share in 1980 and $0.00 per share in 1979)	(0,000,000)	(0,000,000)
End of year	000,000,000	000,000,000
Total stockholders' equity	$000,000,000	$000,000,000

See Accompanying Notes to Financial Statements.

STOCK LIFE INSURANCE COMPANY
STATEMENT OF EARNINGS
Years ended December 31, 1980 and 1979

	1980	1979
Income:		
Premiums and other considerations	$ 00,000,000	$ 00,000,000
Investment income:		
Interest on bonds	00,000,000	00,000,000
Dividends on preferred stocks	0,000,000	000,000
Dividends on common stocks	0,000,000	0,000,000
Interest on mortgage loans	0,000,000	0,000,000
Real estate income (net)	0,000,000	0,000,000
Interest on policy loans	0,000,000	0,000,000
Interest on premium notes (net)	000,000	0,000,000
Net investment income	00,000,000	00,000,000
Other income	000,000	000,000
Total income	000,000,000	000,000,000
Policyholder benefits and expenses:		
Death and disability benefits	0,000,000	0,000,000
Policyholders' dividends and coupons	0,000,000	0,000,000
Increase in future policy benefit reserves	00,000,000	00,000,000
Cost of operations:		
Commissions	00,000,000	00,000,000
General insurance expense and taxes	00,000,000	00,000,000
Increase in unamortized policy acquisition costs	(0,000,000)	(0,000,000)
Total policyholder benefits and expenses	00,000,000	00,000,000
Earnings from operations before Federal income taxes	00,000,000	00,000,000
Federal income taxes (note 4):		
Current	0,000,000	0,000,000
Deferred	0,000,000	0,000,000
	0,000,000	0,000,000
Earnings from operations	00,000,000	00,000,000
Realized investment gains and losses (note 1)	00,000	00,000
Net earnings	$ 00,000,000	$ 00,000,000
Per share of capital stock:		
Earnings from operations	$ 0.00	$ 0.00
Net earnings	$ 0.00	$ 0.00

STOCK LIFE INSURANCE COMPANY
STATEMENT OF CHANGES IN FINANCIAL POSITION
Years Ended December 31, 1980 and 1979

	1980	*1979*
Funds provided:		
From operations:		
Net earnings	$ 00,000,000	$ 00,000,000
Charges (credits) to earnings not affecting funds:		
Depreciation and depletion	0,000,000	0,000,000
Amortization of policy acquisition costs	00,000,000	00,000,000
Decrease in premium notes	0,000,000	0,000,000
Increase in accrued investment income	(0,000,000)	(0,000,000)
Decrease (increase) in receivables	000,000	(000,000)
Increase in future policy benefit reserves	00,000,000	00,000,000
Increase in policyholders' funds	0,000,000	0,000,000
Deferred Federal income taxes	0,000,000	0,000,000
Decrease in premium note commissions in escrow and other liabilities	(0,000,000)	(00,000)
Other (net)	(000,000)	000,000
Funds provided from operations	00,000,000	00,000,000
(Increase) decrease in cash	(0,000,000)	000,000
From investments sold or matured:		
Bonds	000,000,000	000,000,000
Preferred stocks	0,000,000	0,000,000
Common stocks	0,000,000	0,000,000
Mortgage loans on real estate	0,000,000	0,000,000
Real estate	00,000,000	0,000,000
Other invested assets	0,000	0,000
	000,000,000	000,000,000
Premium notes sold to bank	0,000,000	0,000,000
	$000,000,000	$000,000,000

Funds used:		
Increase in policy loans	$ 0,000,000	$ 0,000,000
Cost of investments purchased:		
Bonds	000,000,000	000,000,000
Preferred stocks	0,000,000	00,000,000
Common stocks	0,000,000	0,000,000
Mortgage loans on real estate	00,000,000	0,000,000
Real estate	0,000,000	000,000
Other invested assets	000,000	
	000,000,000	000,000,000
Policy acquisition costs (including commissions of $00,000,000 in 1980 and $00,000,000 in 1979)	00,000,000	00,000,000
Retirements of mortgage notes payable	000,000	0,000,000
Premium notes repurchased from bank	0,000,000	0,000,000
Dividends to stockholders	0,000,000	0,000,000
Other (net)	00,000	000,000
	$000,000,000	$000,000,000

See Accompanying Notes to Financial Statements

NOTES TO FINANCIAL STATEMENTS

Note 1—Summary of significant accounting policies

The accompanying financial statements have been prepared on the basis of generally accepted accounting principles (GAAP) in accordance with the American Institute of Certified Public Accountants' Audit Guide for Stock Life Insurance Companies. The significant GAAP accounting principles and practices are as follows:

Recognition of premium revenues, benefits and expenses   Premium revenue is reported as earned when collected by cash or premium note and benefits and expenses are associated with premium revenue so as to result in recognition of profits over the life of contracts. This association is accomplished by means of the provision for future policy benefit reserves and the amortization of policy acquisition costs.

Unamortized policy acquisition costs   The costs of acquiring new business, principally commissions, production bonuses, and certain expenses of the policy issuance and underwriting departments have been deferred. These deferred acquisition costs are being amortized over the premium paying period of the related policies (not to exceed twenty-five years from policy issue date) using the same interest assumptions as were used for computing future policy benefit reserves.

Future policy benefit reserves   Future policy benefit reserves have been computed by a net level premium method based upon estimated future investment yield, mortality and withdrawals. For the composition of future policy benefit reserves and the more significant assumptions pertinent thereto, see note 3.

Participating policies   Participating business approximates 0 percent of the Company's ordinary life insurance in force. The amount of dividends to be paid is determined annually by the Board of Directors. The policy benefit reserves include a provision for such dividends based upon dividend scales contemplated at the time the policies were issued.

Depreciation   Investment real estate is being depreciated principally on a straight-line basis over lives ranging from twenty to forty years. Depreciation is provided on a straight-line basis for furniture and equipment over lives ranging from three to ten years.

Federal income taxes   Deferred Federal income taxes have been provided for timing differences between the reporting of earnings for financial statement and tax purposes. Such timing differences are principally related to the deduction of policy acquisition costs and the provisions for future policy benefit reserves (see note 4).

Investments   Bonds are carried at amortized cost.
Preferred stocks: sinking fund issues at cost, non-sinking fund issues at market.
Common stocks are carried at market value.
At December 31, 1980 and 1979, gross unrealized gains (losses) were as follows:

	1980	1979
Gains	$ 000,000	$ 0,000,000
Losses	(0,000,000)	(0,000,000)
Net unrealized losses	$ (0,000,000)	$ (000,000)

Net realized investment gains (losses) included in the determination of net earnings for 1980 and 1979 were as follows:

	1980	1979
Bonds	$ (0,000,000)	$ (000,000)
Preferred stocks	(00,000)	00,000
Common stocks	000,000	(0,000)
Mortgage loans	(000,000)	—
Real estate	0,000,000	000,000
	00,000	00,000
Related Federal income taxes	—	(0,000)
Net realized gains	$ 00,000	$ 00,000

See Accompanying Notes to Financial Statements

Note 2—Reconciliation of net earnings and stockholders' equity

A reconciliation of net earnings and stockholders' equity of the Company, as reported to state and regulatory authorities, to that included in the accompanying financial statements is as follows:

	Net earnings year ended December 31,		Stockholders' equity December 31,	
	1980	*1979*	*1980*	*1979*
As reported for statutory purposes	$00,000,000	00,000,000	00,000,000	00,000,000
Adjustments:				
Future policy benefit reserves and deferred premiums	0,000,000	0,000,000	(0,000,000)	(0,000,000)
Unamortized policy acquisition costs	0,000,000	0,000,000	000,000,000	000,000,000
Participating policy-holders' interests	00,000	00,000	0,000,000	0,000,000
Non-admitted assets	---	---	0,000,000	0,000,000
Mandatory securities valuation reserve	---	---	0,000,000	0,000,000
Federal income taxes	(0,000,000)	(0,000,000)	(00,000,000)	(00,000,000)
Other	000,000	(00,000)	(000,000)	000,000
As reported herein	$00,000,000	00,000,000	000,000,000	000,000,000

The excess of retained earnings over statutory unassigned surplus (amounting to $00,000,000 at December 31, 1980 and $00,000,000 at December 31, 1979) is not available for the payment of dividends to stockholders.

Note 3—Future policy benefit reserves

The composition of future policy benefit reserves at December 31, 1980 and 1979 and the more significant assumptions pertinent thereto are as follows:

	December 31, 1980		December 31, 1979		Years of issue	Interest rate	Mortality table	Withdrawal assumption
	Insurance in force (thousands omitted)	Benefit reserve	Insurance in force (thousands omitted)	Benefit reserve				
Individual life	$0,000,000	00,000,000	0,000,000	0,000,000	0000-00	0-0.0%	0000-00 basic	Company's experience
Individual life	0,000,000	000,000,000	0,000,000	000,000,000	0000-00	0.0-0%	0000-00 basic	Company's experience
Individual life	000,000	00,000,000	000,000	00,000,000	0000-00	0.0%	0000-00 basic	Company's experience
Individual life	00,000	00,000,000	00,000	00,000,000	0000-00	0-0%	0000-00 basic	Linton BA
Individual life	0,000	0,000,000	0,000	0,000,000	0000-00	0.0-0.0%	American men	Linton BA
Group life	00,000	00,000	000,000	000,000	Various	0%	0000 CSO	
Subtotal for life policies	0,000,000	000,000,000	0,000,000	000,000,000				
Annuities	—	00,000,000	—	00,000,000	Various	0%	Standard Annuitant	
Supplementary contracts with life contingencies	—	000,000	—	000,000	Various	0%	Standard Annuitant	
Accidental death benefits	—	0,000,000	—	0,000,000	Various	0%	0000 ADB	
Disability benefits	—	0,000,000	—	0,000,000	Various	0%	0000 Disability Study	
Supplementary contracts without life contingencies	—	0,000,000	—	0,000,000	Various	0%		
Gross benefit reserve and in force	0,000,000	000,000,000	0,000,000	000,000,000				
Less reinsurance ceded	000,000	000,000	000,000	000,000				
Net benefit reserve and in force	$0,000,000	000,000,000	0,000,000	00,000,000				

Note 4—Federal income taxes

Pursuant to the Life Insurance Company Income Tax Act of 1959, life insurance companies are taxed on the lesser of taxable investment income or gain from operations plus one-half of any excess of gain from operations over taxable investment income. One-half of the excess (if any) of the gain from operations over taxable investment income, an amount which is not currently subject to taxation, plus special deductions allowed in computing the gain from operations, is placed in a special memorandum tax account known as the "policyholders' surplus account." The accumulated amount of income subject to current taxation, less the tax thereon, is placed in another special memorandum tax account designated the "shareholders' surplus account." These accounts are purely tax memoranda accounts and appear only on the returns. They are not related in any way to unassigned surplus as that term is used in insurance accounting. As of December 31, 1980, the "policyholders' surplus account" balance was approximately $0,000,000. This balance, as well as any future accumulations in the account, would become subject to Federal income tax at then prevailing rates only when distributions are considered to be paid out of the "policyholders' surplus account," or when the balance of the "policyholders' surplus account" exceeds prescribed limitations. However, the Company does not anticipate any transactions that would cause any part of this amount to become taxable.

Deferred Federal income taxes result from timing differences in the recognition of certain expenses for financial statement and tax purposes. The sources of these differences and the approximate tax effect of each are as follows:

	1980	1979
Adjustments to statutory financial statements for policy acquisition costs and future policy benefit reserves	$ 0,000,000	$ 0,000,000
Effect of special life insurance company tax deductions	(0,000,000)	(0,000,000)
Differences in computing tax and statutory future policy benefit reserves	0,000,000	0,000,000
Other	(000,000)	00,000
	$ 0,000,000	$ 0,000,000

A reconciliation of Federal income tax expense computed by applying the United States Federal income tax rate of 00.0% to earnings from operations before Federal income taxes in the statements of earnings follows:

	1980		1979	
	Amount	Percent of pretax income	Amount	Percent of pretax income
Computed normal tax expense	$00,000,000	00.0%	00,000,000	00.0%
Decreases:				
Special life insurance company tax deductions	(0,000,000)	(00.0)	(0,000,000)	(00.0)
Dividends received deduction	(000,000)	(0.0)	(000,000)	(0.0)
Other	(000,000)	(.0)	(00,000)	(.0)
	$ 0,000,000	00.0%	0,000,000	00.0%

Note 5—Mortgage notes payable

Mortgage notes at interest rates of 0% to 0% ($0,000,000 and $0,000,000 secured by home office building and $000,000 and $000,000 secured by investment real estate in 1980 and 1979 respectively) are due in monthly installments to 1999. Principal payments due in one year are $000,000 at December 31, 1980 and $0,000,000 at December 31, 1979.

Note 6—Employee benefit plans

The Company has various pension and profit-sharing retirement plans which cover substantially all employees. Total contributions for 1980 and 1979 were $000,000 and $000,000 respectively. The Company's policy is to fund current service costs as accrued. Prior service costs are completely funded.

Note 7—Premium notes

The Company's marketing policies provide that certain first year premiums may be financed with the Company. In addition, the Company finances second and third-year premiums under certain marketing plans. At December 31, 1980 and 1979, approximately 00% of the premium notes are for other than first year premiums.

The Company has sold certain of its premium notes to a bank (the

Company and the bank have certain common Directors) with recourse in the event of default by the notemaker. The historical policy of the Company has been to repurchase all notes from the bank between the second and third years following original issuance, when statutory policy reserves have accrued in amounts equal to the principal of the notes; but no obligation exists to make such repurchases. At December 31, 1980 premium notes at the bank mature principally in 1982 and 1983. The Company pays interest monthly at the prime lending rate as quoted on a daily basis applied to the outstanding balance of premium notes. All rights to accrued interest on the premium notes are retained by the Company and all premium notes are serviced by the Company. Although these premium notes are owned by the bank, these transactions are treated as if they are loans from the bank for purposes of reporting in accordance with generally accepted accounting principles.

Note 8—Receivables

Amounts included in receivables are principally amounts due from agents and premium notes associated with lapsed policies which have been guaranteed by agents.

Note 9—Stock option plan

In 1975, the shareholders approved a stock option plan for key executives of the Company. Options to purchase an aggregate of 0,000 shares at $00.00 per share and 0,000 shares at $00.00 per share (market value on the dates of grant) have been issued. A total of 000,000 shares of authorized but unissued shares have been reserved for the plan.

Note 10—Statutory financial information

Following is condensed financial information as reported to insurance regulatory authorities.

STATUTORY STATEMENTS OF FINANCIAL CONDITION
Years ended December 31, 1980 and 1979

	1980	1979
Admitted Assets		
Cash	$ 0,000,000	$ 0,000,000
Investments	000,000,000	000,000,000
Accrued investment income	0,000,000	0,000,000
Home office building and equipment	00,000,000	00,000,000
Deferred and uncollected premiums (net)	00,000,000	00,000,000
	000,000,000	000,000,000
Liabilities and Stockholders' Equity		
Policy benefit reserves	000,000,000	000,000,000
Policy and contract claims	0,000,000	0,000,000
Policyholders' funds	0,000,000	0,000,000
Other liabilities	00,000,000	00,000,000
Mandatory securities valuation reserve	0,000,000	0,000,000
Total liabilities	000,000,000	000,000,000
Capital stock	0,000,000	0,000,000
Unassigned surplus	00,000,000	00,000,000
	$000,000,000	$000,000,000

STATUTORY STATEMENTS OF INCOME
Years ended December 31, 1980 and 1979

	1980	1979
Income:		
Premiums and other considerations	$ 00,000,000	$ 00,000,000
Net investment income	00,000,000	00,000,000
Other income	000,000	000,000
	000,000,000	000,000,000
Policyholder benefits and expenses:		
Death, disability and other policyholder benefits	00,000,000	00,000,000
Increase in policy benefit reserves	00,000,000	00,000,000
Cost of operations	00,000,000	00,000,000
	000,000,000	000,000,000

Policyholders' dividends	000,000	000,000
Income before Federal income taxes	00,000,000	00,000,000
Provision for Federal income taxes	0,000,000	0,000,000
Net income	$ 00,000,000	00,000,000

STATUTORY STATEMENTS OF STOCKHOLDER'S EQUITY
Years ended December 31, 1980 and 1979

	1980	1979
Capital stock	$ 0,000,000	$ 0,000,000
Unassigned surplus:		
Balance, beginning of year	00,000,000	00,000,000
Add (deduct):		
Net income	00,000,000	00,000,000
Realized investment gains (net)	000,000	00,000
Unrealized investment losses (net)	(0,000,000)	(0,000,000)
Cash dividends ($0.00 per share in 1980 and $0.00 per share in 1979)	(0,000,000)	(0,000,000)
Change in mandatory securities valuation reserve	000,000	000,000
Change in nonadmitted assets	0,000,000	0,000,000
Other	(0,000,000)	(0,000,000)
Balance, end of year	00,000,000	00,000,000
Statutory stockholders' equity	$00,000,000	$00,000,000

TITLE INSURANCE COMPANIES

Overview

The preferable accounting principles for title insurance companies appear in Statement of Position 80-1 (SOP 80-1). The section on "title plant" which appears in SOP 80-1 is applicable to any entity that utilizes a "title plant" in its regular business operations.

Title insurance companies are regulated in the same manner as other insurance companies. Also, as with other insurance companies, regulatory accounting practices for title insurance companies may differ significantly from GAAP. SOP 80-1 contains a discussion of these differences and the recommendations which should be used in reporting on title insurance companies.

The main business activity of a title insurance company is to issue title insurance policies. Title insurance provides protection against loss or damage that results from liens or defects in the ownership document to a parcel of real estate. Thus, if a buyer obtains title insurance on real estate that is being purchased and subsequently a loss is incurred because of a lien or defect in the title to the property, the title insurance company will pay any loss or damage. Generally, every mortgage lender will require a title insurance policy on the property being purchased before they will lend any funds as a mortgage.

A title insurance policy is very unique inasmuch as the premiums are usually not refundable and the term of the policy is indefinite. However, the amount of title insurance and the date of title search are stated in the policy. Thus, any loss in excess of the amount of title insurance and any loss which occurs because of a lien or defect that did not exist up to the date of the title search will not be covered by the policy.

When an application for title insurance is received by the insurance company a title search is made. A title search consists of reviewing and scrutinizing the chain of ownership of the property being insured up to the date of the title search. Some title searches may go back several hundred years. Each change of ownership is examined to make sure it was properly made and that no unpaid liens or defects exist against the title to the property. If a lien or defect is discovered, the title insurance policy is still usually issued but the discovered lien or defect is cited in the policy and not covered. In this event, the buyer may be able to cancel the purchase of the property or compel the seller to take care of the existing lien or defect. Most contracts for the sale of real property contain a provision to the effect that the property is being sold free of any liens and/or defects, and that the buyer has a specified period to determine whether any liens or defects do exist against the property being purchased.

The records that a title insurance company uses to search the chain of ownership of a parcel of real estate is called the "title plant". The "title plant" consists of the public records of a specific geographic area (town, city, county, etc.) that have been appropriately indexed and integrated so that an individual parcel of real property may be easily located. From the "title plant" the insurance company can prepare an abstract on any piece of real estate in the particular geographic area. An abstract is a short summary of the ownership history of a specific parcel of real property.

A "title plant" is usually kept up-to-date on a daily basis. A well maintained "title plant" will usually increase in value over time and seldom, if ever, decreases in value. In addition, the estimated useful life of a "title plant" is generally indefinite. These unusual characteristics make a "title plant" quite unique.

Preferable Accounting Principles

The preferable accounting principles that appear in SOP 80-1 cover the following specific topics pertaining to title insurance companies: (1) recognition of premium revenue, (2) provision for losses, (3) loss adjustment expense, (4) title plant, (5) valuation of investments, and (6) realized and unrealized gains or losses.

Recognition of premium revenue   When the title insurance company is legally or contractually entitled to the premium, revenue is recognized as earned. The effective date of the title insurance policy or the date of the binder are the likely dates that the insurance company is legally or contractually entitled to collect the premium.

> **OBSERVATION:** *The reasoning behind recognizing the entire title insurance premium on the effective date of the policy*

is because the insurance company has performed all of the acts necessary to earn the revenue. *If a subsequent loss occurs it will be because the insurance company did not find the cause of the loss at the time of the title search.*

A portion of the premium revenue is usually deferred under regulatory accounting practices.

Provision for losses A provision for estimated losses should be made at the time the premium revenue is recognized. Estimated losses should include unpaid losses which have been reported as well as unreported losses that may be incurred. Estimates should be based on all available information and include a factor for inflation, if necessary. Available information may include past experience that is adjusted for current trends and information.

The provision for losses must be periodically reviewed and adjustments should be recognized as a charge or credit to income in the period in which the adjustment is required.

In a settlement of a claim, a title insurance company may acquire the ownership to the insured real property. The acquired property should be recorded as an asset at its estimated net realizable value and the provision for losses should be reduced by the same amount. The acquired real estate should not be reported as an investment on the balance sheet but should be presented separately. Gain or loss on the disposition of acquired real estate should be reported as an increase or decrease to claims incurred.

No conclusion was reached in SOP 80-1 as to whether estimated unpaid losses should be presented in the balance sheet at their present values (discounted). However, a title insurance company that presents estimated unpaid losses at their present values on its balance sheet should disclose the fact along with the effects, if any, on the financial statements.

A provision for reported losses is usually required in regulatory accounting practices. However, a specific provision for unreported losses that have been incurred is not required by existing regulatory accounting practices.

Loss adjustment expense The estimate provision for losses does not include future costs involved in settling claims. These costs are included in the loss adjustment expense and usually consist of internal and external costs. The external costs are generally legal expenses. External costs should be estimated and accrued at the same time as the related provision for losses is recorded. Internal costs incurred in settling claims should be expensed as period costs when incurred.

Title plant   Direct costs incurred to acquire, organize or construct a title plant should be capitalized. Subsequent costs incurred to maintain the title plant should be expensed as incurred.

SOP 80-1 expressly states that capitalized costs of a title plant should not be depreciated. Thus, unless there is an impairment in the carrying value of the title plant, the undepreciated capitalized costs are reported as an asset indefinitely on the balance sheet.

Part or all of a title plant which is purchased should be recorded at acquisition cost. Costs incurred to modernize or modify a title plant should be separately deferred and not added to the carrying value of the title plant. Such deferred costs should be amortized over their estimated useful lives in a systematic manner.

The outright sale of a title plant, the sale of an undivided interest in a title plant, and a sale of a copy of a title plant, should all be presented in the income statement as a separate component of revenue, net of their related carrying amounts and costs. However, in the sale of a copy of the title plant there should be no allocation of the carrying amount of the title plant. Also, no carrying amount of the title plant should be allocated to an agreement to use the title plant.

The preferable accounting principles in SOP 80-1 clearly state that a title plant is a tangible asset that has an indeterminable life and its value does not decrease with the passage of time, unless there has been an impairment in the value of the tangible asset. In the event of an impairment in the value of the title plant, it should be written down to its net realizable value.

Valuation of investments   The valuations of investments of title insurance companies are almost identical with those of other types of insurance companies, as follows:

Bonds
If the insurance company has the ability and intent to keep bonds to maturity, the bonds should be carried at amortized costs, providing that there has been no permanent decline in the market value of the bonds below amortized cost. Bonds held for speculation should be carried at market value and unrealized gains or losses should be recognized.

Common and Nonredeemable Preferred Stock

Common and nonredeemable preferred stock should be carried at market value. If the insurance company has the ability and intent to keep redeemable preferred stock until redemption, the preferred stock should be carried at amortized cost, providing that there has been no permanent decline in the market value of the preferred stock below amortized cost.

Mortgages

Mortgages should be carried at the balance of the unpaid principal. Mortgages purchased at a discount or premium should be carried at amortized cost.

Real Estate Investments

Real estate investments should be carried at depreciated cost. Amortization, depreciation and other related costs or credits should be included in the determination of investment income.

Real estate should be classified in accordance with its predominant use as either property used in business or as an investment. Real estate operating expenses, including depreciation, should be classified consistent with the related asset as either investment expense or operating expense. Real estate that is used in business by the insurance company should not be accounted for as investment income with a corresponding charge to operations for rental expense. In other words, an insurance company cannot include rental income in its financial statements for property it uses in the regular course of business.

Real estate is always classified as an investment for regulatory accounting purposes, regardless of its use. Rental expense is charged to operations and rental income is included in investment income for real estate used by the insurance company in its own business.

Realized gains and losses All realized gains and losses on all assets held for investment purposes should appear, net of related taxes, in the income statement, below operating income. Realized gains and losses applicable to property used in business should be included as part of operating income.

Unrealized investment gains and losses should not be included in the determination of net income, but are recognized, net of related taxes, as an addition to, or reduction of, stockholders' equity.

Permanent declines in security investments, below cost or amortized cost, should be recognized as realized losses. These security investments should be written down to their net realizable values, which subsequently becomes their new cost basis.

Valuation accounts should not be used for bonds, common stocks, or preferred stocks, which are publicly traded.

Transition

SOP 80-1 is effective for fiscal years beginning after December 31, 1980. However, earlier compliance is encouraged. SOP 80-1 also requires that an accounting change resulting from the implementation of SOP 80-1 should be made retroactively by restating the financial statements of prior periods.

> **OBSERVATION:** *Under existing promulgated GAAP a change in accounting principle is usually accounted for by determining the "cumulative effect" of the change in accounting principle and including this amount, net of related taxes, in net income of the period of change under a separate caption below income from continuing operations. Thus, SOP 80-1 is recommending that existing GAAP be violated to effectuate its implementation.*

Comprehensive Illustration

The following is a comprehensive illustration of the preferable accounting principles contained in this chapter.

TITLE INSURANCE COMPANY
BALANCE SHEET
As of December 31, 1980 and 1979

	1980	1979
ASSETS		
Cash and accounts receivable:		
Cash	$ 0,000,000	$ 0,000,000
Accounts receivable for title insurance premiums, abstracts and service fees	0,000,000	0,000,000
Less allowance for cancellations	000,000	000,000
	0,000,000	000,000
Miscellaneous receivables	000,000	00,000
Total cash and accounts receivable	0,000,000	0,000,000
Investments (Note 3):		
Municipal bonds	0,000,000	0,000,000
Stocks:		
Common	0,000,000	0,000,000
Preferred	000,000	00,000
Time deposits in insured financial institutions	0,000,000	0,000,000
Mortgage loans and contracts	000,000	00,000
Other	000,000	000,000
Total investments	0,000,000	0,000,000
Other assets:		
Notes receivable, less allowance for possible losses in collection of $000,000 at both dates	000,000	000,000
Land and building, at cost less accumulated depreciation of $0,000	000,000	
Office equipment and leasehold improvements, at cost less accumulated depreciation of $000,000 and $000,000	000,000	000,000
Special deposits and misc	00,000	00,000
Total other assets	0,000,000	000,000
Title records, indexes and intangibles,	0,000,000	0,000,000
	$00,000,000	$00,000,000

LIABILITIES AND STOCK-HOLDERS' EQUITY

	1980	1979
Notes payable:		
Demand notes payable to banks	$ 000,000	
0% installment note, payable in semi-annual installments of $0,000, plus interest, through November 1, 1982	00,000	$ 00,000
Total notes payable	000,000	00,000
Other payables:		
Accounts payable and accrued expenses	000,000	000,000
Claims for losses on title insurance policies, including estimated adjustment expenses	000,000	000,000
Dividends payable	000,000	000,000
Federal taxes on income	000,000	000,000
Total other payables	0,000,000	0,000,000
Unearned title insurance premiums (Note 1)	0,000,000	0,000,000
Unrealized Appreciation of Stocks	0,000,000	0,000,000
Stockholders' equity:		
Capital stock, par value $0.00 a share:		
Authorized 0,000,000 shares		
Issued 000,000 shares	0,000,000	0,000,000
Capital surplus	000,000	000,000
Earned surplus (Note 1)	0,000,000	0,000,000
	0,000,000	0,000,000
Less treasury stock at cost, 00,000 shares	0,000,000	0,000,000
Total stockholders' equity	0,000,000	0,000,000
	$00,000,000	$00,000,000

See Accompanying Notes to Financial Statements

TITLE INSURANCE COMPANY
STATEMENT OF SOURCE AND APPLICATION OF FUNDS
Years Ended December 31, 1980 and 1979

	1980	1979
Source of funds:		
Operations:		
Net earnings	$ 000,000	$0,000,000
Unearned premiums, net	000,000	000,000
Depreciation	00,000	00,000
Gain realized on exchange of portfolio securities for treasury stock		(0,000,000)
	0,000,000	0,000,000
Increase (decrease) in notes payable	000,000	(000,000)
Increase in other payables	000,000	00,000
	0,000,000	0,000,000
Application of funds:		
Cash dividends declared	000,000	000,000
Increase (decrease) in accounts receivable	000,000	(00,000)
Additions to property, net	000,000	00,000
Increase in investments, net of unrealized appreciation	000,000	000,000
Increase in title records, indexes and intangibles	000,000	00,000
Other, net	0,000	(00,000)
	0,000,000	000,000
Increase in cash	$ 00,000	$ 000,000

See Accompanying Notes to Financial Statements

TITLE INSURANCE COMPANY
STATEMENT OF EARNINGS
Years Ended December 31, 1980 and 1979

	1980	1979
Title insurance premiums earned	$0,000,000	$0,000,000
Abstract, escrow and service fees	0,000,000	0,000,000
	0,000,000	0,000,000
Expenses and title insurance losses:		
Salaries, commissions and personnel costs	0,000,000	0,000,000
Other operating expenses	0,000,000	0,000,000
Title insurance losses and loss adjustment expenses	000,000	000,000
	0,000,000	0,000,000
Earnings from operations	0,000,000	0,000,000
Investment income, less advisory expenses	000,000	000,000
Other income	00,000	00,000
Earnings before federal taxes on income and extraordinary item	0,000,000	0,000,000
Federal taxes on income (Note 7)	000,000	000,000
Earnings before extraordinary item	000,000	0,000,000
Extraordinary item—gain realized on exchange of portfolio securities for treasury stock		0,000,000
Net earnings	$ 000,000	$0,000,000
Per share of capital stock:		
Earnings before extraordinary item	$ 0.00	$ 0.00
Extraordinary item		0.00
Net earnings	$ 0.00	$0,0000.00

See Accompanying Notes to Financial Statements

TITLE INSURANCE COMPANY
STATEMENT OF EARNED SURPLUS
Years Ended December 31, 1980 and 1979

	1980	1979
Balances at beginning of year	$0,000,000	$0,000,000
Net earnings	000,000	0,000,000
	0,000,000	0,000,000
Cash dividends declared,		
$.00 a share each year	000,000	000,000
Balances at end of year	$0,000,000	$0,000,000

See Accompanying Notes to Financial Statements

NOTES TO FINANCIAL STATEMENTS

Note 1—Consolidation and Accounting Policies

The consolidated financial statements include the accounts of the parent company and all subsidiaries except one corporation which is not significant and which the Company does not expect to retain. The investment in the unconsolidated subsidiary is carried at equity.

Pursuant to laws of the state of incorporation, 00 percent of all title insurance premiums received must be designated as unearned premiums and recognized as income ratably over a period of twenty years. This statutory method of accounting for title insurance premiums corresponds reasonably with generally accepted accounting principles requiring simultaneous recognition of revenues and applicable losses and expenses. Additional statutory loss reserves are required by the laws of certain other states with respect to policies written in such states. As these statutory loss reserves are in addition to unearned premium reserves required with respect to the same policies, they are reported as appropriations of earned surplus. The amounts of appropriated surplus at December 31, 1980 and December 31, 1979 were $000,000 and $000,000, respectively.

Note 2—Acquisition

During October, 1980, the Company acquired for cash all of the outstanding stock of Title Insurance Company of the Region. This acquisition has been treated as a purchase for accounting purposes.

Note 3—Investments

Investments are valued in accordance with valuations prescribed by the National Association of Insurance Commissioners (stocks at quoted market prices and bonds at amortized cost).

Bonds stated at $0,000,000 were on deposit with the insurance departments of various states at December 31, 1980, as provided by law for the protection of policyholders.

Note 4—Escrow Funds

Segregated cash accounts and the offsetting liabilities to escrow depositors in the same amounts ($0,000,000 at December 31, 1980 and $0,000,000 at December 31, 1979) are not included as assets or liabilities in the accompanying balance sheet as the escrow funds are not available for regular business use.

Note 5—Pension Plan for Employees

The Company's noncontributory pension plan was amended as of July 1, 1980 to provide increased pension benefits. As a result of these changes in the plan, pension costs were increased for 1980. Total pension costs charged to operations were approximately $000,000 for 1980 and $000,000 for 1979. Prior service costs and fluctuations in market value of investments are being amortized over a period of twenty years. Transitional adjustments related to the December 1, 1977 amendment to the pension plan are being amortized over a period of ten years. The Company's policy is to fund pension costs accrued. The actuarially computed value of vested benefits as of December 31, 1980 exceeded the total of the pension fund by approximately $000,000.

Note 6—Leases

The Company has leases for office space which expire on various dates, principally 1978 and 1983. Annual rentals of approximately $000,000 are payable under these leases.

Note 7—Federal Taxes on Income

The provision for taxes on income does not bear a normal relationship to earnings before taxes on income, principally because of the 85 percent dividend credit and tax-exempt interest income.

PREFERABLE ACCOUNTING PRINCIPLES

ENTERTAINMENT INDUSTRY

CABLE TELEVISION COMPANIES (CATV)

Overview

The preferable accounting principles for cable television companies appear in Statement of Position 79-2 (SOP 79-2).

The Addendum to APB-2 requires that the financial statements of a regulated business should be based on existing GAAP with appropriate recognition given to the rate-making process. Thus, existing GAAP applies to companies in regulated industries. SOP 79-2 states (¶ 47) that ". . . the addendum to APB-2 does not apply to the financial statements of cable TV companies".

> *OBSERVATION: SOP 79-2 is not clear in its reference to the addendum to APB-2 not applying to financial statements of cable TV companies. However, SOP 79-2 contains a discussion to the effect that some states have regulated cable TV companies in spite of the fact that CATV systems are not similar to public utilities.*
>
> *Perhaps, the statement in SOP 79-2 means to communicate to the reader that cable TV companies should not be recognized as a regulated industry for accounting purposes in spite of the fact that some states have adopted legislation regulating CATV systems. Thus, the entire provisions of SOP 79-2 apparently apply to all cable TV companies whether they are regulated or not.*

SOP 79-2 also requires that the implementation of its provisions be accounted for retroactively by restating financial statements of prior periods that are presented in a financial report.

> *OBSERVATION: The FASB has delegated to the AICPA the power to issue Statements of Position on how to report accounting changes (FASB Interpretation-20). However, it is doubtful whether the FASB also delegated to the AICPA the power to amend or promulgate new GAAP.*
>
> *Existing GAAP (APB-20, Accounting Changes) generally require that a change in accounting principle be accounted for*

> by adopting the change in accounting principle in the year of change and including the "cumulative effect" of the change in accounting principle for prior years, as a separate item, in the income statement of the current year. Restatement of prior years' financial statements are only permitted for such accounting changes as (1) a change from the LIFO method of inventory pricing to another method, (2) a change in accounting for long-term construction-type contracts, and (3) two other exceptions which are not encountered very often.
>
> APB-20 (Accounting Changes) does require a "pro forma" presentation of net income and EPS data which presents the (1) current year reflecting the new accounting principles, and (2) pro forma amounts for any prior years presented reflecting the effect of the new accounting principle.
>
> Thus, SOP 79-2 cannot require the restatement of financial statements to effect its implementation, unless existing GAAP is amended or new GAAP is promulgated by the FASB.

Cable TV companies are required under existing copyright laws to pay royalty fees based on a percentage of gross receipts that it receives from its subscribers.

Background

CATV systems are organized and built to provide uninterrupted program entertainment, usually not available on regular commercial television. The distribution of the television programs by a CATV system is usually made over coaxial cables or satellites to a defined area. A CATV system network may cover a small community or a major metropolitan area.

Usually, a cable TV company obtains a franchise from a local governmental authority which permits the distribution of CATV programs in a specified area. The franchise agreement usually provides for payment of fees to the granting authority and contains, among other provisions, the maximum fees that the company can charge a subscriber. In addition, franchise agreements may include many provisions pertaining to the type and quality of service that must be provided, number of TV channels, type of construction, and duration of the franchise. If all of the terms of the franchise agreement are not met, the governmental authority may retain the right to terminate the contract with the cable TV company.

The operation of a CATV system begins with the purchase of

program entertainment from a cable service company or a production company. Program entertainment is usually acquired on a long-term contract with one or more cable service companies. The transmission signals of the cable service company are picked up by the CATV system by microwave relay, antennas, or satellite, then amplified and distributed to subscribers via coaxial cables. The subscriber usually pays an initial hookup charge and thereafter, a monthly subscription fee.

The size of the franchise area and the density of the population will usually determine the construction period required to install a CATV system. However, the type of system being built may also affect the period of construction. For example, if the coaxial cables must be installed underground, rather than on utility poles, the period of construction will likely take longer. The construction period is completed when all of the equipment used to receive transmissions (head-end equipment) is installed, all main (head-end) and distribution cables are in place, and most subscriber drops (installation hardware) are installed. The CATV system is "energized" when the first transmission is made to subscribers. It is not unusual to "energize" part of a CATV system before the entire system is built because large CATV systems are generally built in sections over several years. When this occurs, a "prematurity period" is established. A "prematurity period" is the period that begins when the first subscriber's revenue is earned and ends when construction of the system is completed or when the first major stage of construction is completed. The "prematurity period" will vary in direct relationship to the size of the franchise and the density of the population.

The capital investment that is necessary, even for a small CATV system, is quite substantial. The acquisition of a franchise and the cost of the physical facilities are expensive and the operating overhead during the construction period requires a great deal of working capital. Space on utility poles or underground ducts is usually leased from utility companies.

Preferable Accounting Principles

Generally accepted accounting principles which have been promulgated for commercial companies are also used in reporting on cable TV companies. However, SOP 79-2 contains the specialized methods of applying existing GAAP to cable TV companies.

Initial recording of assets   In the construction of a cable TV company the "prematurity period" begins on the date that subscribers' revenue is earned, and ends on the date that the construction of the CATV system is completed or when the first major stage of construction is completed. However, some cable TV companies have determined that the "prematurity period" begins on the date that subscribers' revenue is earned and ends on the date that a predetermined number of subscribers is reached.

All costs of constructing the physical facilities of a CATV system should be capitalized. However, during the "prematurity period" some subscribers are receiving service while construction continues on the CATV system. Thus, during the "prematurity period" a distinction must be made between costs related to (1) the current period, (2) future periods, and (3) both current and future periods.

Costs Related to the Current Period

Selling, marketing and administrative expenses and all costs related to current subscribers should be accounted for as period costs.

Costs Related to Future Periods

During the "prematurity period" all costs of constructing the physical facilities of the CATV system should continue to be capitalized.

Costs Related to Both Current and Future Periods

Tangible and intangible costs which are incurred and capitalized or deferred during the "prematurity period" are related to both current and future periods. The cost of leases on utility poles or underground ducts, leases on satellite or microwave installations, capitalized interest costs on construction, and so forth, are costs that have to be amortized or depreciated over their estimated useful lives or the life of the franchise whichever is less. Thus, during the "prematurity period" a portion of these costs must be "matched" with current revenue from subscribers.

During the "prematurity period", SOP 79-2 recommends that depreciation and amortization charges should be allocated to both current and future periods based on a fraction. The denominator of the fraction is the total expected subscribers at the end of the "prematurity period", and the numerator of the fraction is the estimated number of subscribers at the end of each month of the "prematurity period". The amount of depreciation or amortization which results from the fraction is charged to expense and the balance is capitalized.

During the "prematurity period" depreciation on the cost of the physical facilities of the CATV system should also be allocated by the same fraction. However, instead of computing depreciation on the costs incurred to date, the total depreciable base of the physical facilities is estimated and depreciation is determined by applying the depreciation method normally used by the company. After the total depreciation expense is computed on the total estimated cost of the completed physical facilities, the fraction is applied to arrive at the amount of depreciation expense that should be charged to the current period.

After the "prematurity period" is over, depreciation and amortization should be based on the life of the franchise, unless the economic useful life is shorter. The only justification for the use of an economic useful life which is greater than the life of the franchise is the likely renewal of the franchise or that the asset has a recoverable value at the end of the life of the franchise.

Periodic review of recoverability   Capitalized assets not only benefit a future period, but their costs should be recoverable from expected future revenue. When expected future revenue is insufficient to cover expected future operating expenses, including depreciation and amortization, then further costs should not be capitalized. In this event, it may be necessary to write-down the assets involved to their recoverable amounts.

Hookup revenue   Hookup revenue should be included in current revenue but only to the extent of direct selling costs. Direct selling costs include those which are incurred in obtaining and processing new subscribers. Hookup revenue in excess of direct selling costs should be deferred and amortized to revenue over the estimated average subscription period.

If the cost of a previous customer's hookup has been amortized, a new customer hookup at the same location should be deferred. However, if the old customer's hookup costs have not been amortized, the new customer's hookup costs should be charged to expense.

Purchased franchises The acquisition of a CATV system accounted for as purchase should be recorded and reported in accordance with existing GAAP (APB-16). Goodwill arising in a purchase transaction should be accounted for under existing GAAP (APB-17).

Capitalized interest costs SOP 79-2 was released prior to the promulgation of FASB-34 (Capitalization of Interest Costs) and only requires that companies that do not capitalize interest costs prior to "energizing" their CATV system should not do so in subsequent periods.

FASB-34 allows the capitalization of certain interest costs incurred in the acquisition of assets which require longer than one year to complete for their intended use. The pertinent provisions of FASB-34, are as follows:

> Certain interest costs may be capitalized and added to the acquisition cost of assets which require longer than one year to complete for their intended use. The cost of assets to which capitalized interest may be allocated include the cost of both those assets acquired for a company's own use and those acquired for sale in the ordinary course of business. Thus, inventory items which require a long time to produce, such as aged whiskey, qualify for capitalization of interest costs. However, interest costs should not be capitalized for inventories which require more than one year to complete for their intended use, if such inventories are routinely produced in large quantities on a repetitive basis.
>
> Imputing interest costs on equity funds is specifically prohibited.
>
> The interest capitalization period commences with the first expenditure for the asset and continues through the acquisition period. Interest is not capitalized during delays or interruptions, other than brief, which occur during the acquisition or development stage of the qualifying asset. When the qualifying asset is substantially complete and ready for its intended use, the capitalization of interest ceases.
>
> The capitalized interest costs are equal to the actual interest costs incurred during the acquisition period of the qualifying asset which would not have been incurred if the asset was not acquired.

Total capitalized interest costs for any particular period may not exceed the total interest costs actually incurred during that particular period. In consolidated financial statements, this limitation on the total amount of interest costs which may be capitalized in a period, should be applied on a consolidated basis.

Capitalized interest costs for a particular period are determined by applying an interest rate to the average amount of accumulated expenditures during the period for the qualifying asset. The interest rate paid on borrowings during a particular period should be used to determine the amount of interest costs which should be capitalized for the period. Where a qualifying asset is related to a specific new borrowing, the allocated interest cost is equal to the amount of interest incurred on the new borrowing. However, if the average accumulated expenditures outstanding for the period exceed the amount of the related specific new borrowing, interest cost should be computed on the excess. The interest rate that should be used on the excess is the weighted average interest rate for other borrowings of the company.

Progress payments received from the buyer of a qualifying asset must be deducted in the computation of the average amount of accumulated expenditures during a period. Nonetheless, the determination of the average amount of accumulated expenditures for a period may be reasonably estimated.

Should existing GAAP require the recognition of a value for the qualifying asset which is less than acquisition cost, interest capitalization should not cease. However, the provision necessary to reduce the qualifying asset to the lower value should be increased.

Capitalized interest costs become an integral part of the acquisition costs of an asset and should be accounted for as such in the event of disposal of the asset.

The total amount of interest costs incurred and charged to expense during the period and, if any, the amount of interest costs which have been capitalized during the period, should be disclosed in the financial statements or footnotes thereto.

Television exhibitions   Internally produced programs by a cable TV company should be accounted for in accordance with the established preferable accounting principles (see chapter entitled "Motion Picture Films"). Externally purchased program material should be accounted for in accordance with the established preferable accounting principles (see chapter entitled Broadcasting Companies).

Financial Statements

Financial statements of cable TV companies may contain either classified or unclassified balance sheets (SOP 79-2).

A CATV system that is distinctly separate from affiliated systems should be accounted for as a separate system. Some of the facts that would distinguish a separate system are (1) geographic location, (2) separate accountability, (3) separate physical facilities, and (4) separate management and/or investment policies.

Some separate CATV systems have been referred to in the industry as "segments". SOP 79-2 refers to these separate systems as "portions", because of the use of the word "segments" in FASB-14 (Financial Reporting for Segments of a Business).

Costs that are capitalized in accordance with the preferable accounting principles (SOP 79-2) should be separately identified and classified under the caption "plant and equipment". The ending date of the "prematurity period" should be disclosed, if applicable, and the amount of costs capitalized during a reporting period which falls within the "prematurity period" should be disclosed.

Comprehensive Illustration

The following is a comprehensive illustration of the preferable accounting principles contained in this chapter.

CABLE TELEVISION COMPANY
STATEMENT OF FINANCIAL POSITION
As of May, 31, 1980 and 1979

	(In Thousands)	
	1980	*1979*
Assets		
Cash, including certificates of deposit of $0,000,000 in 1980 and $000,000 in 1979	$ 0,000	$ 0,000
Marketable securities at cost, which approximates market	0,000	—
Receivables, less allowance for doubtful receivables of $000,000 in 1980 and $000,000 in 1979	000	000
Prepaid expenses and deferred charges (Note 1)	0,000	000
Investments in and advances to affiliated companies (Notes 2 and 3)	000	0,000
Receivables from sales of assets	0,000	0,000
Investment in cable television system (Notes 1, 2, 3 and 8)		
Property, plant and equipment, at cost	00,000	00,000
Less accumulated depreciation	(00,000)	(00,000)
	00,000	00,000
Excess cost over net tangible assets of subsidiary at acquisition, net of amortization	00,000	0,000
Deferred cable television permit costs, net of amortization	000	000
Total investment in cable television system	00,000	00,000
	$00,000	$00,000
Liabilities & Stockholders' Equity		
Accounts payable	$ 0,000	$ 0,000
Subscriber prepayments and deposits	0,000	0,000
Accrued liabilities	0,000	0,000
Debt (Note 3)	00,000	00,000
Total liabilities	00,000	00,000
Deferred Federal income taxes (Note 4)	0,000	000
Commitments (Note 7)		
Common stock, $.00 par value, authorized 0,000,000 shares; issued 0,000,000 shares in 1980 and 0,000,000 shares in 1979 (Notes 3 and 5)	000	000
Additional paid-in capital	00,000	00,000
Retained earnings (deficit) (Note 3)	0,000	(0,000)
Total stockholders' investment	00,000	00,000
	$00,000	$00,000

CABLE TELEVISION COMPANY
STATEMENT OF STOCKHOLDERS' EQUITY
Years Ended May 31, 1980 and 1979

	Common Stock Issued		Stated in Thousands		Common Stock in Treasury	
	Shares	*Amount*	*Additional Paid-in Capital*	*Retained Earnings (Deficit)*	*Shares*	*Amounts*
Balances, May 31, 1978	0,000	$000	$00,000	($0,000)	—	$ —
Proceeds from stock options exercised (Note 5)	00	0	00		—	—
Purchase of stock for treasury	—	—	—	—	00	000
Issuance of stock to acquire minority interest in subsidiary	0	0	000	—	—	—
Net earnings	—	—	—	0,000	—	—
Balances, May 31, 1979	0,000	000	00,000	(0,000)	00	000
Proceeds from stock options exercised (Note 5)	00	0	000	—	—	—
Purchase of warrants	—	—	(00)	(000)	—	—
Net earnings	—	—	—	0,000	—	—
Dividends paid	—	—	—	(000)	—	—
Balances, May 31, 1980	0,000	$000	$00,000	$0,000	00	$000

See Accompanying Notes to Financial Statements

CABLE TELEVISION COMPANY
STATEMENT OF CHANGES IN FINANCIAL POSITION
Years Ended May 31, 1980 and 1979

	(Stated in Thousands)	
	1980	1979
Sources of cash and marketable securities:		
Operations:		
Net earnings	$ 0,000	$ 0,000
Items not requiring (providing) cash:		
Depreciation and amortization	0,000	0,000
Deferred Federal income taxes	000	(000
Gain from retirement of debt	—	(000)
Other	(000)	(00)
Total from operations	0,000	0,000
Change in payables, accruals and other, net	(000)	000
Debt refinancing (Note 3):		
Proceeds	00,000	—
Less repayment of existing indebtedness	(00,000)	—
Net proceeds from refinancing	0,000	—
Proceeds from borrowings	00,000	—
Collections on notes receivable from sales of assets	00	0,000
Proceeds from stock options exercised	000	00
Total sources	$00,000	$ 0,000
Uses of cash and marketable securities:		
Repayment of debt:		
Scheduled payments	$ 0,000	$ 0,000
Revolving credit loan	—	0,000
Retirement of note	—	0,000
	0,000	0,000
Purchase of:		
Property, plant and equipment	00,000	0,000
Additional interest in CATV-SUB system	0,000	—
Stock purchase warrants	000	—
Treasury stock	—	000
Payment of dividends	000	—
Additional investments in and advances to affiliated companies	—	000
Total uses	00,000	00,000
Increase (decrease) in cash and marketable securities	$ 0,000	$ (0,000)

CABLE TELEVISION COMPANY
STATEMENT OF INCOME
Years Ended May 31, 1980 and 1979

	(Stated in Thousands Except Per Share Data)	
	1980	*1979*
Revenues:		
Service	$00,000	$00,000
Other	000	000
	00,000	00,000
Operating expenses, exclusive of items shown below	00,000	0,000
General and administrative expenses	0,000	0,000
	00,000	00,000
Operating income before interest, depreciation and amortization	00,000	0,000
Other income (expense):		
Interest expense	(0,000)	(0,000)
Depreciation and amortization	(0,000)	(0,000)
Earnings before income taxes and extraordinary item	0,000	0,000
Income tax provision (Note 4):		
Current (all state)	000	00
Deferred Federal	000	000
	0,000	000
Earnings before extraordinary item	0,000	0,000
Extraordinary gain from retirement of debt (Note 3)	—	000
Net earnings	$ 0,000	$ 0,000
Earnings per common and common equivalent shares:		
Primary:		
Earnings before extraordinary item	$0.00	$0.00
Extraordinary item	—	.00
Net earnings	$0.00	$0.00
Fully-diluted:		
Earnings before extraordinary item	$0.00	$ .00
Extraordinary item	—	.00
Net earnings	$0.00	$0.00
Average number of common and common equivalent shares:		
Primary	0,000	0,000
Fully-diluted	0,000	0,000

NOTES TO FINANCIAL STATEMENTS

Note 1—Summary of Significant Accounting Policies

Principles of Consolidation The accompanying consolidated financial statements include the accounts of the Company and all of its majority-owned subsidiary companies. Investments in and results of operations of 20% to 50% owned corporations and partnerships are presented on the equity basis of accounting. All significant intercompany accounts and transactions have been eliminated.

Property, Plant and Equipment Costs of cable television systems (or segments in the case of large systems requiring extensive construction over a long period of time) include all net costs (including interest and operating losses) prior to the time the respective system or segment becomes operational, defined as when 00% of the homes passed by cable are connected or one year after the first subscriber connection is made, whichever occurs first. Initial subscriber connection costs are capitalized as part of the distribution system and disconnects and reconnects are expensed.

Depreciation is determined on a composite basis using the straight-line method over the following estimated service lives:

Buildings	20-25 years
Distribution systems and equipment	8-12½ years
Microwave equipment	12½ years
Transportation equipment	4 years
Other property, plant and equipment	10 years

Replacements, renewals and improvements are capitalized and maintenance and repairs are charged to expense as incurred. The cost and cumulated depreciation related to other than routine retirements or disposals are removed from the accounts and the resulting gain or loss is reflected in the statement of operations.

Excess Cost Over Net Tangible Assets of Subsidiaries At Acquisition This item includes all costs of purchased subsidiaries in excess of the fair values of net tangible assets acquired. Such costs related to businesses acquired prior to November 1, 1970, are not being amortized since it is anticipated such assets will be of benefit to the Company indefinitely. In accordance with Accounting Principles Board Opinion No. 17, costs related to businesses acquired after that date are being amortized over 40 years.

Deferred Permit Costs Costs incurred in obtaining cable television permits are deferred and amortized over the lives of the permits, beginning with the dates the systems become operational. If and when it becomes apparent that a permit will not be obtained, related deferred costs are charged to operations.

Deferred Charges Deferred debt expense ($000,000 at May 31, 1980) is amortized over the life of the related debt on a straight-line basis.

Deferred subscriber acquisition costs ($000,000 at May 31, 1980) represent costs incurred during the initial direct sales program in a new system and are amortized over a three-year period.

Income Taxes Provision is made for deferred Federal income taxes arising from timing differences in the determination of income reported for financial statement and tax purposes, principally depreciation, amounts capitalized as property, plant and equipment and subscriber acquisition costs.

Investment tax credits are accounted for on the "flow-through" method.

Note 2—Acquisition

Cable Television Subsidiary Company (CATV-SUB) In 1972, the Company acquired a 00% interest in certain franchise rights and agreed to construct and operate the new system. The other 00% owners included the Company's president who acquired his 00% interest in 1965, prior to his affiliation with the Company. The system was constructed in two major segments. The first segment was built from 1973 to 1975 and the final segment was substantially completed during fiscal 1980.

The Board of Directors approved the purchase of the remaining 00% of CATV-SUB in January 1980 for $0,000,000. An independent appraisal, based on projected first-year cash flow, supported the cash purchase price as representative of the fair market value of the interest acquired. The acquisition was accounted for as a purchase. Accordingly, the net tangible assets acquired were recorded at the estimated fair value of those assets and the remainder of the purchase price, $0,000,000 was recorded as "excess cost over net tangible assets of subsidiaries at acquisition". CATV-SUB's operating results have been consolidated effective January 1, 1980. Previously, the investment in CATV-SUB was recorded on the equity method. The following summary presents the consolidated results of operations of the Company on a pro forma basis, as though the acquisition had taken place at the beginning of fiscal 1979:

	Year Ended May 31,	
	1980	1979
	(In Thousands)	
Revenues	$00,000	$00,000
Earnings before extraordinary item	0,000	0,000
Net earnings	0,000	0,000
Earnings per common and common equivalent share:		
Primary	0.00	0.00
Fully diluted	0.00	0.00

Note 3—Debt

Debt consists of the following:

	May 31,	
	1980	1979
	(In Thousands)	
General Credit Indebtedness:		
Revolving Credit Agreement	$ —	$ 0,000
00% of Senior Notes due in escalating annual installments from 1983 to 1994	00,000	—
00% Senior Notes due in equal annual installments from 1981 to 1988	0,000	0,000
Other	0,000	0,000
	00,000	00,000
Limited Recourse Indebtedness, refinanced in 1980:		
1982 Series notes	—	0,000
1988 Series notes	—	0,000
Note payable to bank	—	0,000
	—	0,000
Total debt	$00,000	$00,000

Installments due on debt principal for the four years ending May 31, 1981 through 1984 respectively, are: $0,000,000, $0,000,000, $0,000,000, and $0,000,000.

The Company's revolving credit and term loan agreement provides for maximum revolving credit loans of $00,000,000 through May 30, 1981, at which time any outstanding balance may be converted into term loans.

The Company must maintain average compensating balances equal to 00% of the outstanding borrowings. A fee of prime plus 0% must be paid on any compensating balance deficiency computed on a six-month average.

In May 1980, the Company completed arrangements with two insurance companies for $00,000,000 in long-term financing, the proceeds of which were used primarily to retire existing indebtedness.

The Company's loan agreements include various covenants and restrictions, certain of which relate to the payment of dividends or other distributions to stockholders, redemptions of capital stock, advances to certain subsidiaries and others, the incurrence of additional indebtedness, mortgaging, pledging or disposition of major assets and maintenance of specified net worth and working capital ratios.

Note 4—Income Taxes

The total income tax provision applicable to earnings before income taxes and extraordinary items is reconciled with the normally expected income tax provision for the two years ended May 31, 1980, as follows:

(In Thousands)	1980	1979
Computed "normally expected" income tax provision at statutory rates	$0,000	$0,000
Increases (reductions) in taxes resulting from:		
Investment credit recognized	(0,000)	(000)
State income taxes, net of Federal income tax benefit	00	00
Other, net	(00)	00
Total income tax provision	$0,000	$ 000

As of May 31, 1980, the Company's tax returns reflect unused investment credit and loss carry-overs which, under certain conditions, may be used to reduce Federal income taxes payable in the years 1981 to 1987. The potential tax benefits of these carry-overs in future years which have not yet been recognized by the Company could be in excess of $0,000,000.

Note 5—Common Stock Options

Under the Company's qualified stock option plan, options may be granted to purchase shares of common stock at the market value on date of grant. Options become exercisable in a single installment or in such installments as determined by the committee administering the plan and expire 1981 through 1983. Data concerning qualified stock options follows:

	1980	1979
Available for grant May 31	0,000	00,000
Outstanding May 31	00,000	000,000
Exercisable May 31	0,000	00,000
Price range, per share	$0.00 to $00.00	$0.00 to $0.00
Granted during year	00,000	—
Terminated during year	0,000	00,000
Exercised during year	00,000	00,000

Under the Employees' Stock Purchase Plan of 1971, options to purchase 00,000 shares of common stock may be granted to regular employees. Exercise prices are to be 00% of the fair market value of the common stock (at date of grant or at time of exercise, whichever is less). No options have been granted under this plan.

Note 6—Retirement Plan

Substantially all employees of the Company and its subsidiaries are covered by a retirement plan adopted in 1976. Total pension expense, which was $00,000 in 1980 and $00,000 in 1979, includes current costs and amortization of prior service costs over 30 years. The Company's policy is to fund pension costs accrued. As of June 1, 1979, unfunded prior service costs were $000,000, plan assets totaled $000,000 and there were no vested benefits.

Note 7—Commitments

The Company rents office space, microwave services and other facilities under various long-term lease arrangements. A summary of noncancellable long-term lease commitments follows:

Year Ending May 31:

1981	$000,000
1982	000,000
1983	000,000
1984	000,000
1985-1989	000,000
Thereafter	000,000

Rental expense for the years ended May 31, 1980 and 1979, totaled approximately $0,000,000 and $0,000,000, respectively.

Budgeted capital expenditures for fiscal 1981 are $00,000,000.

Note 8—Property, Plant and Equipment

The cost of property, plant and equipment consists of the following:

	(In Thousands) May 31,	
	1980	1979
Land	$ 000	$ 000
Buildings	0,000	0,000
Distribution systems and equipment	00,000	00,000
Microwave equipment	000	000
Transportation equipment	0,000	0,000
Other property, plant and equipment	0,000	0,000
	$00,000	$00,000

BROADCASTING COMPANIES

Overview

A broadcasting station may be completely independent, or may be affiliated with a network. Independent broadcasters must purchase or otherwise provide for all of their programming, while a network affiliated broadcaster obtains much of its programming from its affiliated network.

Revenue of broadcasters arise from the sale of advertising time. Independent broadcasters must sell all of their advertising time while much of an affiliated broadcasters advertising time is sold by the network. When the broadcaster airs the sponsor's advertising, revenue is recognized. Network affiliated broadcasters receive revenue from their affiliated networks on a monthly basis. The revenue is based on a formula, and the networks submit weekly reports of revenue to their affiliates.

Advertising rates are usually based on the size of the estimated audience reached by the broadcaster and the quality of the station's programming. Rates vary significantly from market to market. Local and regional rates are generally less than national advertising rates. Rate cards that contain the advertising rates of a broadcaster are determined during rating periods in which the size and demographics of the broadcaster's audience is measured along with the quality of the broadcaster's programming. Rate cards are usually broken down into broadcasting time periods and are revised on a regular basis.

A broadcaster may exchange advertising time for services or products. Such barter transactions should not conflict with a broadcaster's regular advertising business.

Programming costs are usually the largest expense of television broadcasters. Independent broadcasters must obtain all of their programming, while network affiliated broadcasters obtain much of their programming from their affiliated networks. Programming costs are generally higher for independent broadcasters than they are for network affiliated broadcasters. Program material for television broadcasters is purchased under television licenses from producers or distributors. These producers and distributors generally package several films and license the broadcaster for one or more exhibitions or for a specified period, at which time, the license expires. The license agreement usually provides for installment payments over a period which is almost always less than the license period. Thus, the producer or distributor receives all of its money for the license prior to the expiration of the license.

Many television broadcasters produce some of their programming material either live or on video tape. Local news broadcasts and local interview shows are popular programs produced by television broadcasters.

Television and radio broadcasters are regulated by the Federal Communications Commission (FCC). Broadcasters are licensed for three years to use frequencies in a specific area which are assigned by the FCC. In licensing a broadcaster the FCC may consider the (1) financial position of the broadcaster, (2) advertising policies, (3) quality of the programming, and (4) contribution made to the community in which the broadcaster operates. Advertising rates are not regulated by the FCC, but guidelines have been established for advertising rates by the National Association of Broadcasters.

The major assets of a broadcaster are its FCC license and its network affiliation. Thus, network affiliated broadcasters are usually more valuable than independent broadcasters.

Preferable Accounting Principles

The preferable accounting principles for the broadcasting industry appear in SOP 75-5 (Accounting Practices in the Broadcasting Industry). The three specific areas in the broadcasting industry which SOP 75-5 covers are (1) television film license agreements, (2) barter transactions, and (3) intangible assets.

Television film license agreements   SOP 75-5 requires that broadcasters record the assets and liabilities that are involved in a television film license agreement when the following conditions are met:

1. The cost of each film is known.
2. The broadcaster has accepted the film in accordance with the conditions in the license agreement.
3. The licensor can deliver the film rights and the broadcaster can exercise the rights. Availability of the film exists when a film may be shown for the first time under a licensing agreement (SOP 79-4).

Costs of the television film license agreement should be postponed if an option or any other condition creates a doubt as to the ability or obligations of both parties to perform.

> *OBSERVATION: If a long-term liability arises from the purchase of film rights which is either noninterest bearing or an unreasonable rate of interest is stated, the provisions of APB-21 (Interest on Receivables and Payables) should be applied. Thus, the present value of the long-term liability will be recorded as an asset and the difference between the present value and the face amount of the liability will be recorded as deferred interest expense.*

Amortization of the film rights should be computed on the estimated number of times that the film will be aired by the broadcaster. An accelerated method of amortization must be used when the first broadcast of a film is more valuable than its reruns. Thus, the straight line method of amortization should only be used when each broadcast is expected to produce approximately the same amount of revenue.

Feature films should be amortized on an individual basis. However, series film and similar programs should be amortized on a series basis. Film rights purchased for unlimited broadcasts may be amortized over the term of the film rights agreement. The cost of rights to a film package should be allocated to each film right in the package based on the relative value of each film right to the broadcaster.

Unamortized film rights and film rights of unrecorded film license agreements should not exceed their net realizable values. In the event that film rights do exceed their net realizable values they should be written down to net realizable values by a charge to current income. Film rights should be reflected in the balance sheet at the lower of their amortized cost or their net realizable values.

SOP 75-5 requires that the balance sheet of a broadcaster be classified. Thus, assets and liabilities should be classified as current or noncurrent based on the normal operating cycle of the industry. SOP 75-5 specifies that one year should be used as the normal operating cycle in the broadcasting industry.

Unrecorded firm commitments for film rights should be disclosed in a footnote to the financial statements.

Barter transactions   SOP 75-5 requires that all barter transactions be recorded in accordance with existing GAAP (APB-29, Accounting for Nonmonetary Transactions). The transaction should be recorded at the time the broadcaster airs the commercial. If the services or products have not been received at the date the commercial is aired, a receivable should be recorded.

APB-29 requires that nonmonetary exchanges be accounted for at the fair value of the assets or services received or surrendered, whichever is more clearly evident. In the event that fair value is indeterminable, the only valuation available may be the recorded book value of the nonmonetary assets exchanged. When barter revenue is significant, it should be disclosed in the financial statements or footnotes thereto.

Intangible assets   SOP 75-5 requires that intangible assets in the broadcasting industry should be accounted for in accordance with existing GAAP (APB-17, Intangible Assets). Thus, intangible assets in the broadcasting industry must be amortized by the straight-line method over a period not to exceed forty years.

If a network affiliation is terminated, any unamortized network affiliation costs should be charged to expense unless a replacement agreement exists. In this event, if the fair value of the replacement agreement exceeds the unamortized network affiliation costs of the terminated agreement, no gain is recognized. However, if the fair value of the replacement agreement is less than the unamortized network affiliation costs of the terminated agreement, a loss is recognized to the extent of the difference.

A change in network affiliation is not, by itself, justification to support a change in the amortization method used by a broadcaster.

Comprehensive Illustration

The following is a comprehensive illustration of the preferable accounting principles contained in this chapter.

BROADCASTING COMPANY
BALANCE SHEET
As of December 31, 1980 and 1979

	($Thousands)	
	1980	*1979*

ASSETS

Current Assets

Cash and short-term cash investments	$ 0,000	$ 0,000
Notes and accounts receivable (Net of allowance for doubtful accounts of $000 in 1980, and $000 in 1979)	00,000	00,000
Television film exhibition rights (Note 1)	00,000	00,000
Prepaid expenses	0,000	0,000
	$ 00,000	$ 00,000

Investments and Noncurrent Receivables

Investment in ABC Corporation (Note 1)	$ —	$ 0,000
Notes, accounts, deposits and other investments	0,000	0,000
	$ 0,000	$ 0,000

Property, Plant and Equipment-At Cost

Land and land improvements	$ 0,000	$ 0,000
Buildings and improvements to buildings	00,000	00,000
Broadcast and related equipment	00,000	00,000
	$000,000	$000,000
Less allowance for depreciation and amortization	00,000	00,000
	$ 00,000	$ 00,000

Intangible Assets (Notes 1 and 2)

	$ 00,000	$ 00,000

Deferred Charges and Other Assets

Television film exhibition rights (Note 1)	$ 00,000	$ 00,000

Franchise rights, less allowance for amortization of $0,000 in 1980, and $0,000 in 1979	00,000	00,000
Other assets (Notes 1 and 5)	0,000	0,000
	$ 00,000	$ 00,000
	$000,000	$000,000

LIABILITIES AND STOCKHOLDERS' EQUITY

Current Liabilities

Notes payable (Note 3)	$ 0,000	$ 0,000
Accounts payable - trade	0,000	0,000
Film contracts payable (Notes 1 and 3)	0,000	0,000
Accrued expenses (Interest $0,000, Compensation $000 Payroll taxes and other $0,000)	00,000	00,000
Federal, state and local taxes payable (Note 6)	0,000	0,000
	$ 00,000	$ 00,000

Long-Term Liabilities

Notes payable (Note 3)	$ 00,000	$ —
Subordinated debentures payable (Note 3)	00,000	00,000
Film contracts payable (Notes 1 and 3)	00,000	00,000
Deferred income taxes (Note 6)	0,000	0,000
	$ 00,000	$ 00,000

Commitments and Contingencies (Note 4)
Stockholders' Equity (Note 5)

Common stock, par value $0.00 per share; authorized 0,000,000 shares, issued 0,000,000 outstanding 0,000,000 in 1980, and 0,000,000 in 1979	$ 0,000	$ 0,000
Paid-in capital	00,000	00,000
Retained earnings	000,000	000,000
Less cost of treasury stock, 000,000 in 1980, and 000,000 in 1979	00,000	00,000
	$000,000	$000,000
	$000,000	$000,000

See Accompanying Notes to Financial Statements

BROADCASTING COMPANY
STATEMENT OF INCOME
Years Ended December 31, 1980 and 1979

	($Thousands)	
	1980	1979
Net Revenues		
Broadcast Stations	$000,000	$ 00,000
Other Broadcast Related (Note 1)	0,000	0,000
	$000,000	$000,000
Operating Expenses		
Broadcast Stations (Note 1)	00,000	00,000
	$ 00,000	$ 00,000
Selling, Administrative and General Expenses		
Broadcast Stations	00,000	00,000
Other Broadcast Related	0,000	0,000
General Corporate Expenses	0,000	0,000
	$ 00,000	$ 00,000
Total Operating Income	$ 00,000	$ 00,000
Other Income (Expense)		
Amortization-Intangibles (Note 1)	$ (000)	$ (000)
Interest Expense	(0,000)	(0,000)
Gain on Sale of Broadcast Facility	—	0,000
Gain on Repurchase of Subordinated Debentures (Note 3)	000	000
Interest Income	000	000
Gain on Sale of Securities (Note 1)	0,000	—
Miscellaneous, Net	(000)	(000)
	$ (0,000)	$ 000
Income Before Provision For Income Taxes	$ 00,000	$ 00,000
Provision For Income Taxes (Note 6)	00,000	00,000
Net Income	$ 00,000	$ 00,000
Net Income Per Share (Note 7)		
With No Dilution	$0.00	$0.00
Fully Diluted	$0.00	$0.00

BROADCASTING COMPANY
STATEMENT OF CHANGES IN FINANCIAL POSITION
Years Ended December 31, 1980 and 1979

	($Thousands)	
	1980	*1979*
Source of Working Capital:		
Net Income	$00,000	$00,000
Charges Not Requiring Working Capital:		
Depreciation and Amortization—		
Property and Franchise Rights	00,000	0,000
Other	000	—
Deferred Income Taxes	(00)	000
Working Capital Provided from Operations	$00,000	$00,000
Issuance of Treasury Shares in Connection with:		
Restricted Stock Plan	000	—
Corporate Acquisitions	0,000	—
Disposal of Property, Plant and Equipment	000	000
Decrease in Notes, Accounts, Deposits and Other Investments	00	000
Issuance of Long-term Notes	00,000	—
Sale of ABC Corporation Securities	0,000	—
Increase (Decrease) in Film Contracts Payable	0,000	(00)
	$00,000	$00,000
Use of Working Capital:		
Additions to Property, Plant and Equipment	$00,000	$00,000
Dividends Paid	0,000	0,000
Reduction of Long-term Notes	0,000	000
Purchase of Treasury Stock	0,000	—
Purchase of Subordinated Debentures	0,000	0,000
Increase (Decrease) in Television Film Exhibition Rights	0,000	(0,000)
Acquisitions:		
Intangible Assets	00,000	—
Property and Equipment	0,000	—
Franchise Rights	0,000	—
Other Assets	000	—
Other	000	—
	$00,000	$00,000
(Decrease) Increase in Working Capital	($0,000)	$ 000

The Major Changes in Working Capital Were As Follows:

(Decrease) in Cash and Short-term Cash Investments	($0,000)	($0,000)
Increase in Receivables	0,000	0,000
(Decrease) Increase in Television Film Exhibition Rights and Film Contracts	(000)	0,000
(Increase) in Accounts Payable	(0,000)	(000)
(Decrease) Increase in Net Other Assets and Liabilities	(0,000)	000
(Increase) Decrease in Federal, State and Local Taxes	(0,000)	0,000
(Decrease) Increase in Working Capital	($0,000)	$ 000

See Accompanying Notes to Financial Statements

BROADCASTING COMPANY
STATEMENT OF STOCKHOLDERS' EQUITY
Years Ended December 31, 1980 and 1979

	Common Stock	($ Thousands) Paid In Capital	Retained Earnings	Treasury Stock
Balance December 31, 1978	$0,000	$00,000	$000,000	($00,000)
Net Income			00,000	
Dividends Paid			(0,000)	
Balance December 31, 1979	0,000	00,000	000,000	(00,000)
Net Income			00,000	
Dividends Paid			(0,000)	
Shares Issued in Connection With:				
Restricted Stock Plan (Note 5)		000		000
Corporate Acquisitions (Note 5)		0,000		0,000
Purchase of Treasury Stock (Note 5)				(0,000)
Balance December 31, 1980	$0,000	$00,000	$000,000	($00,000)

See Accompanying Notes to Financial Statements

NOTES TO FINANCIAL STATEMENTS

Note 1—Significant Accounting Policies

Principles of Consolidation   The consolidated balance sheets, from which intercompany transactions and accounts have been eliminated, include all of the Company's subsidiaries.

The consolidated statements of income include the results of the Company and all of its subsidiaries. Intercompany revenues and expenses not eliminated in the statements of income consist of Other Broadcast Related revenues earned by the Company's national sales subsidiary from Company-owned television stations in the amount of $0,000,000 in 1980 and $0,000,000 in 1979. Such revenues and expenses have not been eliminated in consolidation since the Company's operations are presented on a business segment basis.

Investment in ABC Corporation   The investment in ABC Corporation at December 31, 1979 consisted of 00,000 shares of common stock with a market value of $0,000,000. The investment was sold in 1980 resulting in a pre-tax gain of $000,000.

Intangible Assets and Franchise Rights   Intangible assets represent the excess of the cost of certain broadcast properties acquired over the amounts assigned to the net tangible assets and franchise rights at dates of acquisition. No amortization has been charged to income for intangible assets acquired prior to October 31, 1970 ($00,000,000) since, in the opinion of the Company, there has been no decrease in their value. Intangibles arising subsequent to that date and franchise rights are being amortized on a straight-line basis over forty years.

Depreciation and Amortization   For financial reporting purposes, depreciation is provided over the estimated lives of the properties, principally on the declining balance method for broadcasting facilities, studio and office buildings and improvements.

	Years
Transmitter buildings and improvements	20
Equipment	6–7
Towers	20
Furniture, fixtures and automobiles	3–10
Studio and office buildings	20–40

The cost of improvements to premises not owned but occupied under lease agreements is being amortized on the basis of the terms of the respective leases. The Company charges expenditures for maintenance and repairs against income. Expenditures for betterments and major renewals are capitalized. The carrying amounts of assets sold or retired and related allowances for depreciation and amortization are eliminated from the accounts in the year of disposal. Gains and losses resulting from such disposals are included in income.

Depreciation expense, and amortization of broadcast intangibles are as follows:

Year	Depreciation	Amortization of Broadcast Intangibles
1980	$00,000,000	$000,000
1979	0,000,000	000,000

Television Film and Syndicated Series Exhibition Rights   Television film and syndicated series exhibition rights acquired under license agreements and the related obligations incurred are recorded as assets and liabilities at the time the Company enters into the agreements. Such rights are amortized generally on a straight-line basis over the contract period or estimated number of showings, whichever results in the greater aggregate monthly amortization.

The estimated costs of film contracts to be charged to operations during the next year have been classified as a current asset.

Stock Options   Proceeds from the sale of common stock issued under stock options are credited to common stock at par value and the excess of the option price over par value is credited to paid in capital. There are no charges to income with respect to these options. In 1985, the options on all shares expire; no options were exercised in 1980 or 1979.

Investment Tax Credits   Investment tax credits are recognized as reductions of income tax expense for the period in which the expenditures for property create tax benefits.

Pension Plan   The Company maintains a non-contributory pension plan covering substantially all full-time employees who meet certain eligibility requirements. It is the policy of the Company to fund pension costs accrued. Pension expense amounted to $0,000,000 and $0,000,000 in 1980 and 1979, respectively, which includes amortization of the unfunded prior service cost over 20 years. The actuarially computed value of vested benefits for the plan exceeded the actuarial value of the assets of the plan by approximately $0,000,000 at the latest valuation date, December 31, 1979. Estimated unfunded prior service cost as of December 31, 1979 was approximately $0,000,000.

Note 2—Acquisitions

During 1980, the Company completed its acquisition of radio station WKKK-FM for approximately $0,000,000 in cash. Of the purchase price $0,000,000 has been allocated to intangible assets.

Operations of purchased companies are included from the dates of their acquisition. Consolidated operating results would not have been significantly different if the purchased companies had been included for the entire two-year period presented.

Note 3—Notes, Subordinated Debentures and Film Contracts Payable

At December 31, 1980, the Company had outstanding $0,000,000 principal amount of notes issued for the purchase of CATV systems. These notes bear interest at the rate of 0%. Principal amounts of notes, other than to banks, and film contracts maturing over the next five years are as follows:

	Notes Payable—Other	Film Contracts
	($ Thousands)	
1981	$000	$00,000
1982	000	0,000
1983	000	0,000
1984	000	0,000
1985	000	000
Thereafter	—	000

In connection with a revolving credit agreement with a group of banks, the Company has commitments to borrow up to $00,000,000 at the prime rate of a New York bank at any time prior to January 1, 1981. There were no borrowings under the agreement at December 31, 1979 and $0,000,000 in borrowings were outstanding at December 31, 1980. The agreement provides for a commitment fee of ½ of 1% per annum on the daily average unused amount. The Company has informally agreed with the lending banks to maintain cash balances in its accounts in amounts which, when viewed over a period of time, are sufficient to justify the banks' extension of credit under this revolving credit agreement. It is estimated that the average cash balances maintained on deposit with the lending banks in 1980 used for operations and to support such credit approximated $0,-000,000.

At December 31, 1980, $00,000,000 principal amount of 0% convertible subordinated debentures were outstanding. These debentures will mature on January 1, 1990, with provision for a mandatory sinking fund with annual payments of $0,000,000. The debentures are convertible, at the option of the holders, at any time before January 1, 1990, into common stock of the Company at $00.00 per share.

Note 4—Commitments

The Company and subsidiaries are committed to make payments for exhibition rights to sporting events and lease certain facilities, principally office space. Expense included in the consolidated statements of income for the years 1980 and 1979 is as follows:

| | ($ Thousands) | |
	1980	1979
Sporting event exhibition rights	$0,000	$0,000
Rental of facilities and property	0,000	0,000
	$0,000	$0,000

The following summary sets forth the annual commitments under non-cancellable contracts for exhibition rights to sporting events and operating leases for the rental of facilities and property:

| | ($ Thousands) | | |
	Exhibition Rights to Sporting Events	Rental of Facilities and Property	Total
Year ending December 31,			
1981	$0,000	$ 000	$ 0,000
1982	000	000	0,000
1983	000	000	0,000
1984	000	000	0,000
1985	000	000	0,000
Thereafter	—	0,000	0,000
Total minimum future rentals	$0,000	$0,000	$00,000

Note 5—Capital Stock

At December 31, 1980, the Company has 000,000 shares of common stock reserved for debenture conversions (000,000) and issuance under a restricted stock plan (00,000). In April, 1980, the Company adopted a restricted stock plan for officers and key employees. The aggregate number of shares which may be granted under the plan is 00,000 with a maximum of 0,000 shares granted to any one employee. The shares are issued without cash consideration when granted and are held in escrow until certain employment conditions have been satisfied. At December 31, 1980, 00,000 shares had been issued with a maximum of 00,000 additional shares to be granted over the next three years if the Company achieves certain performance levels. Shares of restricted stock issued based only upon employment conditions (00,000 shares) have been recorded at the closing price ($00.00) on the New York Stock Exchange at the date of grant by a charge to deferred compensation; for those additional shares earned based on the attainment of performance levels (0,000 shares in 1980, of which 0,000 have not been issued), compensation is measured by the closing market price ($00) at the date such performance levels are attained (December 31, 1980). The deferred compensation ($000,000) is being amortized over a three year restriction period ($000,000 amortized in 1980).

During 1980, the Company purchased 00,000 shares of common stock in the open market for general corporate purposes, at a cost of $0,000,000; and 000,000 treasury shares were issued as follows: 00,000 under the restricted stock plan and 000,000 for corporate acquisitions. Specific certificate identification is used to credit the cost of the respective treasury shares issued.

Note 6—Provision for Income Taxes

The provision for income taxes for 1980 and 1979 is composed of the following elements:

	Current	Investment Credits	Deferred	Total
		($ Thousands)		
1980:				
Federal	$00,000	($0,000)	($ 00)	$00,000
State and local	0,000	—	—	0,000
	$00,000	($0,000)	($ 00)	$00,000
1979:				
Federal	$00,000	($0,000)	$000	$00,000
State and local	0,000	—	—	0,000
	$00,000	($0,000)	$000	$00,000

Total income tax expense when related to income before taxes differs from the U.S. statutory income tax rate of 00% due to the following reasons:

	% of Pre-tax income	
	1980	1979
Computed "expected" tax expense	00%	00%
State and local income taxes, net of		
Federal income tax benefit	0	
Investment tax credits	(0)	(0)
Capital gains	(0)	(0)
Amortization of intangibles	0	0
Other, net	—	0
	00%	00%

Note 7—Net Income Per Share

In computing net income per share with no dilution, all stock options have been excluded since they are anti-dilutive or their inclusion would not have an effect on the calculation. The convertible debentures are not common stock equivalents in this calculation. The average shares outstanding in 1980 and 1979 were 0,000,000 and 0,000,000, respectively.

Fully diluted net income per share gives effect to the dilution which would result from the conversion of the Company's convertible debentures, but excludes all options since their inclusion would not have an effect on the calculation. For purposes of this computation, actual debenture interest expense and amortization of issue costs, net of tax effects, were added to income. Average shares used in this computation were 0,000,000 in 1980 and 0,000,000 in 1979.

Note 8—Quarterly Financial Information (unaudited)

Selected financial data relating to the results of operations for each quarterly period in 1980 and 1979 is as follows:

	($ Thousands, except per share data) Quarter Ending			
	March 31	June 30	September 30	December 31
1980				
Net revenues	$00,000	$00,000	$00,000	$00,000
Operating income	$ 0,000	$00,000	$ 0,000	$00,000
Net income	$ 0,000	$ 0,000	$ 0,000	$ 0,000

Net income per share:				
With no dilution	$ .00	$0.00	$ .00	$0.00
Fully diluted	$ .00	$0.00	$ .00	$0.00
1979				
Net revenues	$00,000	$00,000	$00,000	$00,000
Operating income	$ 0,000	$ 0,000	$ 0,000	$00,000
Net income	$ 0,000	$ 0,000	$ 0,000	$ 0,000
Net income per share:				
With no dilution	$ .00	$ .00	$ .00	$0.00
Fully diluted	$ .00	$ .00	$ .00	$0.00

Note 9—Replacement Cost Information (unaudited)

The Company's annual report for 1980 to the Securities and Exchange Commission on Form 10-K (a copy of which will be available upon request after March 31, 1981) will contain unaudited data regarding the estimated year-end replacement cost of broadcast facilities and equipment with related data on estimated depreciation expense based on such replacement costs.

Inflation and technological advances have resulted in higher replacement costs of these assets and, accordingly, assumed replacement of plant and equipment would require greater capital investment than the historical cost reflected in the balance sheet.

MOTION PICTURE FILMS

Overview

The industry accounting guide entitled "Accounting for Motion Picture Films" (hereinafter referred to as Motion Picture Guide), and Statement of Position (SOP) 79-4, establish the *preferable accounting principles* for motion picture companies, and enterprises that distribute such products.

The exhibition rights to a film are usually licensed by the licensor who may be the original producer of the film or a distributor of the film. The rights licensed may be for one showing of the film, or for multiple showings of the film over a specified period. Generally, only one first-run telecast of a film is licensed in a given market, at a given time.

A film starts with the acquisition of a story property (book, stage play, original screen play, etc.), goes through the various stages of producing the film, and last the film is distributed for exhibition. The production-to-distribution cycle can be as short as a few months, and sometimes exceeds three years, depending on the nature and length of the film. Films can be produced for television, or theaters, or eventually be exhibited in both medias.

Revenue Recognition

Revenue recognition for motion picture film rights is recognized in accordance with the basic realization principle embodied in GAAP. However, the Motion Picture Guide requires that certain events occur before revenue may be recognized. Revenue recognition from theatrical exhibitions is discussed separately from television exhibitions.

Theatrical exhibitions In larger markets, exhibition rights are sold on a percentage of box office receipts, sometimes with a non-refundable guarantee. In smaller markets, the film rights are usually sold on a flat-fee basis. In foreign markets, nonrefundable guarantees are generally considered outright sales because additional revenues based on percentage of box office receipts are seldom, if ever, remitted to the licensor. This is particularly true in foreign markets where the licensor has no control over distribution. Thus, nonrefundable guarantees which are essentially outright sales, should be recognized as revenue on the execution of a noncancellable agreement.

Under normal conditions, revenue should be recognized for percentage and flat-fee contracts, on the date the film is exhibited by the licensee. Normal nonrefundable guarantees against a percentage of box office receipts should be deferred and recognized as revenue on the date of the exhibition of the film.

Television exhibitions Exhibition contracts of film rights for television usually provide for more than one exhibition over a specific period. In addition, most television contracts include a package of several films. These type of contracts expire on the date of the last authorized telecast, or on a specific date, if it occurs sooner. Payment for the contract is usually made in installments over a period which is shorter than that of the licensing agreement. The Motion Picture Guide requires that all of the following conditions be met before revenue can be recognized on a television exhibition contract:

1. The sales price for each film is known.
2. The cost of each film can be reasonably determined.
3. Collection of the full contract is reasonably assured.
4. The licensee has accepted the film in accordance with the conditions of the license agreement.
5. Availability of the film exists. The licensor can deliver the right and the licensee can exercise the right. Availability of the film exists when a film may be shown for the first time under a licensing agreement (SOP 79-4).

Revenue recognition should be postponed if an option or any other condition creates a doubt as to the ability or obligation of both parties to perform.

> **OBSERVATION:** *If a receivable from the sale of film rights extends over a long period and is either noninterest bearing or an unreasonable rate of interest is stated, the provisions of*

APB-21 (Interest on Receivables and Payables) should be applied. Thus, the present value of the long-term receivable will be recorded as a sale and the difference between the present value and face amount of the receivable will be recorded as deferred interest income.

Costs and Expenses

The production costs of motion picture films usually consists of (1) acquisition of story rights, (2)pre-production, (3) principal photography, and (4) post-production costs. Production costs are generally accounted for on an individual film basis. Production costs include all items that are required and necessary to complete a film. Production overhead is part of completing a film and should be allocated on a systematic and rational basis in accordance with GAAP.

Motion picture film talent is sometimes compensated, in part or all, by participation in the revenues produced by the film. A percentage amount from all, or specific revenues or profits, is the usual arrangement. The total participation is estimated and then amortized in the same manner as the amortization of production costs (see below).

A film may have a primary and secondary market. The first market in which the film is exhibited is the primary market and probably the market for which the film was produced.

Amortization   Amortization of production costs and other amortizable amounts should commence with the release of the film for exhibition purposes. The Motion Picture Guide recommends the "Individual Film Forecast Computation Method" for amortizing film production costs. This method amortizes the costs in the same ratio that current revenues bear to total estimated gross revenues. The computation is similar to the percentage of completion method used in long-term construction-type contracts. The following formula does not appear in the Motion Picture Guide, but may be used:

$$\frac{\text{Total Revenue to Date}}{\text{Total Estimated Gross Revenues}} \times \frac{\text{Total Amortizable Amount}}{} \ \text{less} \ \frac{\text{Prior Period Amortization}}{} = \frac{\text{Current Amortization}}{}$$

Care must be exercised in determining the "total estimated gross revenues" because long-term noninterest bearing revenues can only be included to the extent of their present values (APB-21). Thus, the difference between the present value of the estimated long-term gross revenue and its face amount, is recorded as deferred interest income at the inception of the contract. The "total revenues to date" in the fraction (numerator) must also exclude any interest income collected to date. In other words, both the numerator and denominator of the fraction do not include an imputed interest.

Periodic reviews should be made of the total estimated gross revenue and appropriate revisions made when current information dictates. Revisions should be made prospectively as a change in accounting estimate (APB-20).

The Motion Picture Guide states that periodic table computations may be used to determine amortization providing that the results approximate those computed under the "Individual Film Forecast Computation Method".

Inventory adjustments The inventory of motion picture films consists of the unamortized production and other properly capitalized costs. A periodic review must also be made of each individual film to determine whether the total estimated gross revenues for the film are enough to recover the unamortized costs, talent participation percentages, and all direct distribution expenses. When total estimated gross revenues are insufficient, an inventory write-down, to net realizable value, is necessary.

The inventory of story costs (rights to books, stage plays, etc.) must be reviewed periodically to determine whether they will be used in the production of a motion picture film. Industry practices dictate that story costs held for more than three years, which have not been set for production of a film, should be charged off to current production overhead. After being charged off, story costs should not be reinstated even if they are set for production.

Loans and interest costs Loans, guarantees, and advances by motion picture companies to independent producers should be recorded to reflect the substance of the transaction. Thus, when appropriate, loans, guarantees, and advances should be recorded as liabilities.

Many motion picture films are produced with borrowed funds

which are called production loans. The Motion Picture Guide concludes that it is not appropriate to capitalize any interest costs as production costs, and expressly states that interest costs be expensed as incurred.

> *OBSERVATION:* *FASB-34 (Capitalization of Interest Costs) specifically allows the capitalization of interest costs for assets which require longer than one year to complete. The cost of assets to which capitalized interest may be allocated include the cost of both those assets acquired for a company's own use and those acquired for sale in the ordinary course of business.*
>
> *Thus, it appears that the Motion Picture Guide is not up to date on recent changes in GAAP and apparently under proper circumstances, interest costs may be capitalized in the production of motion picture films that take longer than one year to produce.*

Financial statements The Motion Picture Guide requires that motion picture companies segregate assets and liabilities between current and noncurrent classifications with specific treatment for the following:

1. Unamortized film inventory in release to a primary market; completed films not released, reduced by secondary market allocations, if any; and television films in production that are under contract for sale, should all be classified as current assets.
2. Secondary market allocations of films which will not be realized within 12 months and all related film production costs, should be classified as noncurrent.
3. Production costs which are allocated to secondary television markets should be classified as noncurrent. These costs should be amortized, as revenues are recorded from secondary television markets. (Note: This treatment of production costs allocated to secondary television markets is expected to avoid reclassification of items, back and forth, between current and noncurrent classifications).
4. Liabilities should be recorded in accordance with existing GAAP. Thus, current liabilities are obligations whose liquidation is reasonably expected to require the use of current assets or the creation of other current liabilities (ARB-43).

5. From the time of execution to the time of revenue recognition, license agreements for the sale of television film rights are to be considered as executory and should not be reported on the balance sheet until revenues are recognized. Amounts received on such agreements should be reported as advance payments and classified as current or noncurrent according to the circumstances.

6. A disclosure of all additions to and transfers from noncurrent inventory should appear in the Statement of Changes in Financial Position which should otherwise be prepared in accordance with GAAP.

Disclosures   The Motion Picture Guide expressly concludes that the following financial statement disclosures should be made for companies in the motion picture film industry:

1. Accounting policies peculiar to the industry (APB-22).
2. A breakdown of film inventories, including films, (1) released, (2) completed, but not released, and (3) in process. In addition, the amount of story rights should be disclosed.
3. A description of the amortization methods of film costs used by the company.

Comprehensive Illustration

The following is a comprehensive illustration of the preferable accounting principles contained in this chapter.

MOTION PICTURE COMPANY
STATEMENT OF FINANCIAL POSITION
As of June 30, 1980 and 1979

	(in thousands)	
	1980	*1979*
Assets		
Current assets		
Cash	$ 00,000	$ 00,000
Receivables, less allowances of $00,000—1980; $00,000—1979	000,000	000,000
Inventories (Note 3)	000,000	00,000
Prepaid expenses and other current assets	0,000	00,000
Total current assets	000,000	000,000
Long-term receivables	00,000	00,000
Inventories (Note 3)	00,000	00,000
Fixed assets, at cost		
Land	0,000	0,000
Buildings	00,000	0,000
Machinery and equipment	00,000	00,000
Leasehold improvements	0,000	0,000
	00,000	00,000
Less accumulated depreciation and amortization	00,000	00,000
Fixed assets, net	00,000	00,000
Broadcasting licenses	0,000	0,000
Excess of cost over net assets of acquired company	00,000	00,000
Other assets and deferred charges	00,000	00,000
	$000,000	$000,000

Liabilities and Stockholders' Equity

Current liabilities		
Loans payable (Note 5)	$ 0,000	$ 0,000
Accounts payable and accrued expenses	00,000	00,000
Contractual obligations and participants' shares	00,000	00,000
Accrued income taxes	0,000	00,000
Total current liabilities	000,000	000,000

Advance collections on contracts	00,000	00,000
Amounts due after one year		
Contractual obligations and participants' shares	00,000	00,000
Loans payable (Note 5)	00,000	00,000
Subordinated debentures (Note 6)	000,000	000,000
Stockholders' equity (Notes 5, 6 and 8)		
Preferred stock—$.00 par value; authorized		
0,000,000 shares; none issued	—	—
Common stock—$.00 par value; authorized		
00,000,000 shares; issued 0,000,000 and 0,000,000,		
respectively	000	000
Capital in excess of par value	00,000	00,000
Retained earnings	00,000	00,000
	000,000	000,000
Less treasury shares (00,000), at cost	00	00
Total stockholders' equity	000,000	000,000
Contingent liabilities and commitments (Note 9)		
	$000,000	$000,000

See Accompanying Notes to Financial Statements

MOTION PICTURE COMPANY
STATEMENT OF STOCKHOLDERS' EQUITY
Years Ended June 30, 1980 and June 30, 1979

(in thousands)

	Common Stock		Capital in Excess of Par Value	Retained Earnings (Deficit)	Treasury Stock	Total Stockholders' Equity
	No. of Shares	Amount				
Balance at June 25, 1978	0,000,000	$000	$00,000	$(00,000)	$(00)	$ 00,000
Exercise of stock options and warrants	000,000	00	0,000	—	—	0,000
Net income	—	—	—	00,000	—	00,000
Balance at June 30, 1979	0,000,000	000	00,000	00,000	(00)	000,000
Exercise of stock options, including tax benefit	000,000	00	0,000	—	—	0,000
Conversion of debentures	000,000	00	0,000	—	—	0,000
Dividends ($.00 per share)	—	—	—	(0,000)	—	(0,000)
Net income	—	—	—	00,000	—	00,000
Balance at June 30, 1980	0,000,000	$000	$00,000	$ 00,000	$(00)	$000,000

Accompanying Notes to Financial Statements

MOTION PICTURE COMPANY
STATEMENT OF CHANGES IN FINANCIAL POSITION
Years ended June 30, 1980 and June 30, 1979

	(in thousands)	
	1980	*1979*
Financial resources generated		
Income from operations	$ 00,000	$ 00,000
Add (deduct) items not affecting working capital:		
Amortization and depreciation:		
Non-current film costs	00,000	00,000
Fixed assets	0,000	0,000
Other	0,000	0,000
Gain on sale of leasehold interests	—	(0,000)
Charge in lieu of Federal income taxes	—	0,000
Working capital generated from operations	00,000	00,000
Non-current film production costs transferred to current	00,000	00,000
Increase in advance collections on contracts	00,000	0,000
Increase in contractual obligations and participants' shares	0,000	—
Increase in non-current loans payable	00,000	—
Issuance of common stock on exercise of stock options and warrants and on conversion of debentures	0,000	0,000
Sale of net assets of television station	—	00,000
Sale of leasehold interests	—	00,000
Non-current portion of mortgage assumed	—	(0,000)
Other, net	0,000	—
Total financial resources generated	000,000	000,000
Financial resources utilized		
Additions to non-current film costs	000,000	00,000
Purchase of fixed assets	00,000	0,000
Decrease in contractual obligations and participants' shares	—	0,000
Decrease in non-current loans payable	—	00,000
Decrease in subordinated debentures	0,000	000
Dividends	0,000	—
Other, net	—	0,000
Total financial resources utilized	000,000	000,000
Increase in working capital	$ 00,000	$ 0,000

Increases (decreases) in components of working capital

Cash	$ (0,000)	$ (0,000)
Receivables	00,000	00,000
Inventories	00,000	00,000
Prepaid expenses and other current assets	(0,000)	00,000
Loans payable	(000)	0,000
Accounts payable and accrued expenses	(00)	(00,000)
Contractual obligations and participants' shares	0,000	(00,000)
Accrued income taxes	00,000	(00,000)
Increase in working capital	$ 00,000	$ 00,000

See Accompanying Notes to Financial Statements

MOTION PICTURE COMPANY
STATEMENT OF INCOME
Years Ended June 30, 1980 and June 30, 1979

	(in thousands)	
	1980	*1979*
Revenues	$000,000	$000,000
Costs and expenses		
Costs relating to revenues	000,000	000,000
Selling, general and administrative expenses	00,000	00,000
Interest expense	00,000	00,000
	000,000	000,000
Income before non-recurring gain and income taxes	00,000	00,000
Gain on sale of leasehold interests (Note 2)	—	00,000
Income before income taxes	00,000	00,000
Income taxes (Note 4)	00,000	00,000
Income before extraordinary credit	00,000	00,000
Benefit of net operating loss carryforwards	—	0,000
Net income	$ 00,000	$ 00,000
Per share of common stock (Note 1)		
Income before extraordinary credit	$ 0.00	$ 0.00
Extraordinary credit	—	.00
Net income	$ 0.00	$ 0.00
Net income, assuming full dilution	$ 0.00	$ 0.00

See Accompanying Notes to Financial Statements

NOTES TO FINANCIAL STATEMENTS

Note 1—Summary of Significant Accounting Policies

Principles of Consolidation   The consolidated financial statements include the accounts of the Company and its subsidiaries operating in the United States and in foreign countries without exchange restrictions.

Foreign Currency   Foreign assets and liabilities are translated to their U.S. dollar equivalents based on rates of exchange prevailing at the end of each respective period except for film inventories and fixed assets, which are translated at rates prevailing at acquisition. Revenue and expense accounts are translated at weighted average exchange rates during the period except for amortization of film inventory and depreciation of fixed assets, which are based on the historical dollar equivalents of the related assets. Aggregate exchange gains and losses arising from the translation of foreign assets and liabilities and from foreign currency transactions are included in net income.

Recognition of Revenues   Revenues from theatrical exhibition of feature films are recognized on the dates of exhibition. Revenues from television licensing agreements are recognized when each film is available for telecasting by the licensee. Long-term receivables and the related liabilities to participants arising through such television licensing are recorded at their present value.

Revenues from the sale of amusement games, records and pre-recorded tapes (net of estimated returns) and other tangible merchandise are recognized upon shipment.

Accounting for Film Costs   Production, print and pre-release and national advertising costs are capitalized at inception. The individual film forecast method is used to amortize these costs based on the revenues realized in proportion to management's estimate of ultimate revenues to be received. Unamortized film costs are compared with net realizable values on a film-by-film basis and losses are provided when indicated. The costs of cooperative and other forms of local advertising are charged to expense as incurred.

Guarantees of loans and certain other financing arrangements with third parties, made in connection with the production of films, are accounted for as Company debt and the related unamortized amounts are included in inventory.

The costs of feature films in release, feature films completed but not released, and television films are classified as current assets to the extent such costs are expected to be recovered through the respective primary markets. All other costs relating to film production are classified as non-current assets.

Depreciation and Amortization of Fixed Assets Depreciation and amortization are based on the straight-line method at various rates related to the useful lives or, for leasehold improvements, over the term of the lease, if shorter. Maintenance, repairs and minor renewals are charged to expense.

Intangibles The excess of cost over net assets of an acquired company and the broadcasting licenses of radio stations are being amortized on a straight-line basis over forty years. The cost ($0,000,000) of the broadcasting license for a television station acquired prior to October 31, 1970 is considered to have continuing value and is not being amortized.

Income Per Share Income per share of common stock is computed by dividing net income by the weighted average number of common and common share equivalents (options and warrants) outstanding during the period (0,000,000 in fiscal 1980 and 0,000,000 in fiscal 1979). Income per share, assuming full dilution is computed as described above with the additional assumptions that common share equivalents are exercised at the higher of the average or ending market price and that the Company's convertible subordinated debentures are converted into common stock resulting in the elimination of the related interest expense, net of income tax. The number of shares of common and common share equivalents used in computing fully diluted income per share in fiscal 1980 and 1979 were 00,000,000 and 0,000,000, respectively.

Income Taxes Income taxes are computed on financial statement income with deferred taxes being recognized on items of income or expense which enter into a different fiscal period on a tax return basis. Investment tax credits are accounted for under the flow-through method.

Note 2—Sales of Assets

In 1978, the Company sold its leasehold interests in its home office building for a cash payment of approximately $0,000,000 (substantially all of which was used to reduce loans payable under the Revolving Credit Agreement) and the assumption by the purchaser of the then existing mortgage of approximately $0,000,000. The net gain realized, after taxes, by the Company on the transaction was $0,000,000 ($0.00 per share).

In August 1979, the Company sold substantially all of the net assets of one of its television stations for $00,000,000 in cash, which approximated the carrying value of the net assets sold. The proceeds were used to liquidate bank and certain secured debt. Revenues and operating profits for this station in 1980 were approximately $0,000,000 and $000,000, respectively.

Note 3—Inventories

Inventories as of June 30, 1980 and June 30, 1979 are comprised of the following:

(Dollars in thousands)	Current	Non-Current
June 30, 1980		
Unamortized film production costs:		
Released	$ 00,000	$00,000
Completed, not released	00,000	0,000
In process	00,000	00,000
	00,000	00,000
Recording costs and artists' advances	00,000	—
Merchandise and raw materials:		
Records, music and packaging materials	00,000	—
Amusement games	0,000	—
Other	0,000	—
	$000,000	$00,000
June 30, 1979		
Unamortized film production costs:		
Released	$ 00,000	$00,000
Completed, not released	00,000	0,000
In process	0,000	00,000
	00,000	00,000
Recording costs and artists' advances	00,000	—
Merchandise and raw materials:		
Records, music and packaging materials	0,000	—
Amusement games	0,000	—
Other	0,000	—
	$ 00,000	$00,000

See Accompanying Notes to Financial Statements

Note 4—Income Taxes

The provisions for income taxes are comprised of the following:

Fiscal Year (Dollars in thousands)	1980	1979
Federal:		
Current	$0,000	$00,000
Charge in lieu of income taxes	—	0,000
Deferred	0,000	(0,000)
	0,000	00,000
State	0,000	0,000
Foreign	0,000	0,000
	$00,000	$00,000

Deferred taxes are recognized principally for amortization of film production costs and television income, which enter into different fiscal periods for financial statement and tax return purposes.

The statutory Federal income tax rates of 00% in fiscal 1980 and 00% in fiscal 1979 are reconciled to the Company's effective Federal income tax rates as follows:

Fiscal Year	1980	1979
Statutory Federal income tax rate	00%	00%
Investment credits	(00)	(00)
Foreign taxes	(00)	(0)
State taxes	(0)	(0)
Capital gain rates	—	(0)
Other, net	—	(0)
Effective tax rate	00%	00%

Investment tax credit carryforwards for financial statement purposes aggregated approximately $00,000,000 at June 30, 1980. Carryforwards on a tax return basis aggregated approximately $00,000,000 and expire as follows: 1982—$0,000,000; 1983—$0,000,000; 1984—$0,000,000; 1985—$0,000,000; 1986—$0,000,000.

Note 5—Loans Payable

Loans payable at June 30, 1980 and June 30, 1979 are as follows:

Fiscal Year (Dollars in thousands)	1980	1979
Revolving Credit Agreement	$00,000	$00,000
Other (principally foreign)— 0%-00.0%	0,000	0,000
	00,000	00,000
Less: current maturities	0,000	0,000
	$00,000	$00,000

Under a Revolving Credit Agreement with a group of banks, as amended, the Company is permitted loans up to $000,000,000 until December 31, 1982, at which time any balance then becomes payable in equal quarterly installments commencing March 31, 1983 through December 31, 1985. Borrowings under the agreement bear interest at ¼ of 1% per annum above the prime rate and a commitment fee of ½ of 1% per annum is payable on any unused credit. Additional interest is payable if cash balances maintained with the banks do not equal 5% of the maximum credit plus 15% of outstanding loans. Security for performance under the agreement is limited to rights, property and receivables related to feature film and television product.

Average short-term foreign borrowings for fiscal 1980 and 1979 approximated $0,000,000 and $0,000,000, respectively. The highest month-end balance of such borrowings was $0,000,000 for fiscal 1980 and $0,000,000 for fiscal 1979. The approximate weighted average interest rate applicable to such borrowings computed on month-end balances for fiscal 1980 and 1979 was 00.0% and 00.0%, respectively.

At June 30, 1980, debt maturities under the above borrowing arrangements for the four fiscal years subsequent to fiscal 1981 are as follows: 1982—$00,000; 1983—$00,000,000; 1984—$00,000,000; 1985—$00,000,000.

Under the Revolving Credit Agreement and the indentures relating to the subordinated debentures, certain restrictions are placed on the Company with respect to working capital, stockholders' equity and cash dividends on common stock. Under the most restrictive provision, cash dividends subsequent to January 1, 1980 may be paid only from the aggregate of $00,000,000 and 00% of net income earned subsequent to June 30, 1979. At June 30, 1980, retained earnings of approximately $00,000,000 were unrestricted.

Note 6—Subordinated Debentures

Subordinated debentures at June 30, 1980 and June 30, 1979 are as follows:

Fiscal Year (Dollars in thousands)	1980	1979
00.0% due May 1, 1990	$00,000	$00,000
0.0% convertible due November 1, 1994	0,000	0,000
0.0% convertible due August 1, 1987	0,000	00,000
	000,000	000,000
Less: Sinking fund requirement included in current liabilities	000	000
	$00,000	$00,000

The 00.0% Debentures (presented net of unamortized debt discount—1980—$0,000,000; 1979—$0,000,000) must be retired through a sinking fund commencing on April 30, 1983 at the annual rate of 0% of the April 30, 1982 principal balance, which rate increases to 00% in 1985 and to 00% in 1988. The Company may call the debentures at any time at redemption prices which reduce from 000.0% to approximately par in 1989.

The 0.0% Debentures are convertible into common stock at $00.00 per share (an aggregate of 000,000 shares), subject to certain antidilution provisions. The debentures must be retired through a sinking fund at the annual rate of $000,000 from October 31, 1980, which obligation may be satisfied at the Company's option by application of converted or acquired debentures. The Company may call the debentures at any time at redemption prices which reduce from a current 000.0% to par in 1992.

The 0.0% Debentures are convertible into common stock at $00.00 per share (an aggregate of 00,000 shares), subject to certain antidilution provisions. The debentures must be retired through a sinking fund at the annual rate of $000,000 through 1981 and $000,000 from July 31, 1982 until fully retired, which obligation may be satisfied at the Company's option by application of converted or acquired debentures. The Company may call the debentures at any time at redemption prices which reduce from a current 000.0% to par in 1986.

Note 7—Pension and Incentive Compensation Plans

The Company has several pension plans covering substantially all of its employees not covered by union plans. During fiscal 1980, the Company made substantial improvements in the benefits provided under its principal pension plan and revised actuarial assumptions as to salary increases, asset valuation and turnover and retirement rates to reflect current experience. The annual contribution of $0,000,000 for fiscal 1980 ($000,000 for fiscal 1979) is sufficient to fund current costs and past service costs being amortized over 00 years.

As of the latest valuation date (June 30, 1980), unfunded past service costs amounted to approximately $0,000,000 and the estimated liability for vested benefits exceeded the assets of the pension funds by approximately $0,000,000.

Under the Company's incentive compensation plan for key employees, $0,000,000 and $0,000,000 have been provided based upon performance in fiscal 1980 and 1979, respectively.

Note 8—Stock Options and Warrants

Pursuant to the Company's Key Employees' Non-Qualified Stock Option Plan adopted in fiscal 1975 (as amended by the stockholders on November 18, 1976), options may be granted to purchase up to an aggregate of 0,000,000 shares of common stock at prices equal to the fair market value of the shares at the time the options are granted. Options are exercisable in cumulative annual installments of 00.00% (00% for options granted prior to November 18, 1977), commencing one year after the date of grant and expiring ten years after grant.

A "qualified" plan with similar provisions was terminated upon the adoption of the present plan, with the exception of the then outstanding options.

As provided for under the November amendments, options granted through December 15, 1977 could be granted at $00.0, the market price at June 28, 1977, the date on which the concept of a new plan was approved by the Board of Directors. Options for 000,000 shares were so granted.

The following schedule summarizes the changes in stock options for the two fiscal years ended June 30, 1980:

(Dollars in thousands, except per share amounts)	No. of Shares	Option Price Per Share	Total
Outstanding at June 25, 1978			
(000,000 exercisable)	000,000	$ 0.00	$0,000
Granted	000,000	00.00	0,000
Exercised	(000,000)	0.00	(000)
Cancelled	(00,000)	0.00	(000)
Outstanding at June 30, 1979			
(000,000 exercisable)	000,000	0.00	0,000
Granted	000,000	00.00	0,000
Exercised	(000,000)	0.00	(0,000)
Cancelled	(000,000)	0.00	(0,000)
Outstanding at June 30, 1980			
(000,000 exercisable)	000,000	$ 0.00	$0,000

Options covering 000,000 shares became exercisable during fiscal 1980 (000,000 during fiscal 1979). When options and warrants are exercised, the proceeds, including any applicable tax benefits, are credited to common stock and capital in excess of par value.

In fiscal 1979, 000,000 shares were issued upon exercise of warrants at a price ($0.00 per share) equal to 000% of the market value at date of issuance of the warrants. In October 1979, options for 000,000 shares issued in connection with an acquisition were exercised at an aggregate exercise price of approximately $000,000.

At June 30, 1980, options for 000,000 shares were available for grant and 000,000 shares were reserved for exercise of stock options.

Note 9—Contingent Liabilities and Commitments

The Company is involved in various lawsuits, claims and inquiries. Management believes that the resolution of these matters will not have a material adverse effect on the financial position or the results of operations of the Company.

The Company rents certain properties under non-cancellable, long-term operating leases which expire at various dates. At June 30, 1980, the minimum aggregate rental commitment under all non-cancellable leases was as follows: 1981—$0,000,000; 1982—$0,000,000; 1983—$0,000,000; 1984—$0,000,000; and $0,000,000 for future years. Certain of these leases provide for additional payments for taxes, insurance, and maintenance and, in most cases, renewal options. Non-capitalized financing leases are insignificant.

Total approximate rent expense under all leases was as follows: 1980—
$0,000,000; 1979—$0,000,000.

Note 10—Subsequent Event

In July 1980, the Company announced an agreement in principle for
the sale of its Record operations. Such sale is subject to approval by the
Boards of Directors of the Company and the purchaser and by the Company's lending banks and to the execution of a definitive agreement. If
the transaction is consummated, the Company will receive a net cash
payment of approximately $00,000,000 resulting in an after-tax profit early
in fiscal 1981. Revenues from the Record operations were $00,000,000 in
fiscal 1980 and its operating results were not significant to the Company's
consolidated results of operations.

RECORD AND MUSIC COMPANIES

Overview

Music publishers usually control the copyright on their music and are frequently owned by an artist-composer. On the other hand, record companies must usually depend on an artist who is employed under a personal service contract to produce the record master that is used in manufacturing the ultimate product. As a general rule, the caliber and reputation of the recording artist has a direct effect on the success of any album or individual record.

The more successful recording artists are paid a nonrefundable advance against future royalties. Lesser known recording artists are not paid any advance and frequently must bear some of the cost of producing the record master.

A record master is produced by an expert sound engineer. Each instrument and voice is first recorded separately on magnetic tape. The sound engineer then combines each instrument and voice, emphasizing and deemphasizing as he deems appropriate. This process is called "mixing" and is probably the most important phase of manufacturing a record. The mixing process produces a "record master" which is used to make acetate discs that are coated with metal. The metal coated disc is used to produce the mold that is eventually used to make the final product. Record masters are also utilized to produce tapes that are used to manufacture tape cartridges and cassettes. In order to produce a record master the following costs are usually incurred:

a. costs for the recording studio
b. costs for engineers, mixing experts, directors, and other technical talent
c. costs for musicians, arrangers, vocal background, and similar other talent
d. costs for producing the record master itself

Music publishers usually license others, on a royalty basis, to use their music. Other sources of income for music publishers include royalties from public performances, revenue from the music used in motion picture films, and revenue from the sale of sheet music.

Music publishers are usually members of ASCAP (American Society of Composers, Authors, and Publishers), or some other society or association. These organizations act as collection agencies for music publishers and composers by monitoring radio and TV stations, and live performances. Copyright laws provide that each time that music is played publicly, the publisher and/or composer are entitled to a minimum royalty. By monitoring radio and TV station and live performances, ASCAP collects the royalties due to various publishers and/or composers. After collecting the royalties, ASCAP makes periodic remittances to the publisher and/or composer.

One of the major accounting problems in the record and music industry is the timing of the recognition of a sale. This is because of the return privileges that manufacturers and distributors must make to their customers. In addition, some manufacturers create discounts by including a certain number of free records in proportion to the size of the order.

Preferable Accounting Principles

The preferable accounting principles for the record and music industry appear in Statement of Position 76-1 (Accounting Practices in the Record and Music Industry).

Revenue recognition The right to return merchandise may be unlimited or limited, and may be disguised by granting customers unlimited exchange privileges.

Statement of Position 75-1 contains the preferable accounting principles that should be followed in recognizing revenue in certain sales transactions in which the buyer has the right to return previously purchased property to the seller. SOP 75-1 applies to those situations in which personal property may be returned because of existing industry practice, or as a result of a contractual agreement. SOP 75-1 does not cover real estate or lease transactions and is silent on its coverage of regulated industries. However, in accordance with the Addendum to APB-2, companies in regulated industries should comply with SOP 75-1.

The realization principle requires that revenue be earned before it is recognized. Revenue is usually recognized when the earning process is complete and an exchange has taken place (APB Statement-4). The earning process is not complete until collection of the sales price is reasonably assured (APB-10).

It is common practice in some industries for dealers and distributors of personal property to have the right to return unsold merchandise. The right to return merchandise is usually an industry practice but also occurs as a result of a contractual agreement. The return period can last for a few days, as in the perishable food industry, or can last for several years, which is not infrequent for some types of publishers. The rate of return of some publishers may be as high as 60%, while in other industries such as perishable foods, the rate of return may be insignificant.

As long as a right to return exists and the returns can be significant, the seller is exposed to reacquiring the ownership of the property. In other words, the risks and rewards of ownership are not, in substance, passed on to the buyer.

Since the earning process is not complete until collection of the sales price is reasonably assured, certain accounting problems arise in recognizing revenue when the right to return exists.

SOP 75-1 contains the preferable accounting principles for recognizing revenue when the right of return exists. However, all of the ordinary tests for recognizing a sale under GAAP must be met before applying the preferable accounting principles.

In order to recognize a sale with a right of return, all of the following provisions must be met:

1. The price between the seller and buyer is substantially fixed.
2. The seller has received full payment, or the buyer is indebted to the seller and payment is not in any way excused until the merchandise is resold.
3. Physical destruction, damage, or theft of the merchandise would not change the buyer's obligation to the seller.
4. The buyer has economic substance, and is not a front, straw party, or conduit, existing for the benefit of the seller.
5. No significant obligations exist for the seller to help the buyer resell the merchandise.
6. A reasonable prediction can be made on the amount of future returns.

All of the above provisions must be met before revenue is recognized when a right of return exists. Also, a provision must be made for any costs or losses which may occur in connection with the return of any merchandise.

After the return privilege has substantially expired, the seller may recognize as revenue any remaining balance which was initially set aside for future returns.

Where merchandise returns are significant, financial statements should disclose the amount of gross sales and the accounting policies covering merchandise returns.

Inventory valuation   Inventories should be carried at the lower of cost or market. Scrapped or broken records should be valued at their expected salvage value.

Artist compensation   As with all other items of income and expense, royalties must be accounted for on the accrual basis of accounting.

Royalty advances should be recorded as prepaid royalties (an asset) when evidence is available that such advances will be recouped from future royalties.

Future royalty guarantees and commitments, if material, should be disclosed by footnotes to the financial statements.

Cost of record masters   Cost of record masters should be recorded as an asset if it is reasonably assured that such costs will be recovered from expected future revenue. The cost of a record master should be amortized to income in proportion to the net revenue that is expected to be realized.

Any portion of the cost of a record master which is recoverable from the artist should be accounted for appropriately.

Licensor income and licensee cost   Licenses are usually based on a minimum guarantee which is generally paid in advance by the licensee. The licensee should record this minimum payment as a deferred charge which should be expensed over the term of the license agreement. The licensor should record the receipt of a minimum license guarantee as deferred income which should be amortized over the terms of the license agreement.

An outright sale of certain rights must be distinguished from a minimum license guarantee. When a licensee receives from the licensor a noncancelable contract for a specified fee which grants certain rights to the licensee who may use these rights at any time without restriction, an outright sale has been consummated, and not a license. Under these circumstances the licensor recognizes revenue at the time of the sale.

Intangible assets Intangible assets acquired in a business combination should be accounted for in accordance with existing GAAP (APB-17).

Intangible assets should normally be amortized by the straight-line method. However, if the cost of the intangible asset can be reasonably related to the expected net revenues which are expected to be realized, then amortization should be based on this relationship.

PREFERABLE ACCOUNTING PRINCIPLES

CONTRACTORS

CONSTRUCTION CONTRACTORS

Overview

The *preferable accounting principles* and practices for construction contractors appear in the industry audit guide entitled "Audits of Construction Contractors" (hereinafter referred to as the Construction Contractors Guide).

Generally, existing promulgated GAAP are used in accounting for construction contractors. The Construction Contractors Guide contains a discussion on the applicability of the completed contract method and the percentage-of-completion method of accounting for long-term construction contracts. In addition, the Construction Contractors Guide contains a review of (1) the provision for possible losses, (2) renegotiation refunds, (3) cost-plus contracts, (4) terminated government contracts, (5) working capital, and (6) contractors' equipment. Most of these same topics are covered, in detail, in the industry audit guide entitled "Audits of Government Contractors".

In the case of long-term construction type contracts, revenue may be recognized either by the completed contract method, or the percentage-of-completion method. The percentage-of-completion method is *preferable* when the estimated cost to complete the contract and the extent of progress made on the contract are reasonably determinable. When estimates are unreliable, the completed contract method should be used.

Completed contract method The completed contract method recognizes income only on completion or substantial completion of the contract. A contract is regarded as substantially complete if the remaining costs are insignificant.

Excess of accumulated costs over related billings should be reflected in the balance sheet as a current asset, and excess of accumulated billings over related costs should usually be reflected as a current liability. The reason why these items are treated as a current asset or a current liability is because of the *normal operating cycle concept*, which is discussed later in this chapter under the caption "working capital."

In the case of more than one contract, the accumulated costs or liabilities should be separately stated on the balance sheet. The preferred terminology for the balance sheet presentation should be "(Costs)(Billings) of uncompleted contracts in excess of related (billings)(costs)."

In some cases, it is preferable to allocate general and administrative expenses to contract costs as opposed to period income. In years when no contracts are completed, a better matching of costs and revenues is achieved by carrying general expense as a charge to the contract. If a contractor has many jobs, however, it is more appropriate to charge these expenses to current periods.

In all cases, although income is not recognized until completion of the contract, a provision for an expected loss should be recognized when it becomes evident that a loss on the contract is apparent.

The primary advantage of the completed contract method is that it is based on final results rather than on estimates. The primary disadvantage of the completed contract method is that it does not reflect current performance when the period of the contract extends over more than one accounting period.

The following are important points to remember in accounting for contracts under the completed contract method:

1. Charge applicable overhead and direct costs to a construction in progress account (an asset).
2. Credit billing and/or cash received to advances on construction in progress account (a liability).
3. At completion of the contract, gross profit or loss is recognized, as follows:
   Contract price less total costs = gross profit or loss
4. At interim balance sheet dates, the excess of either the construction in progress account or the advances account over the other is classified as a current asset or a current liability. It is a current asset or a current liability because of the normal operating cycle concept.
5. An expected loss on the total contract is discovered by:
   a. adding estimated costs to complete to the recorded costs to date to arrive at total contract costs
   b. adding to advances any additional revenue expected to arrive at total contract revenue
   c. subtracting b from a to arrive at total estimated loss on the contract

Losses should be recognized in full in the year they are discovered.

Percentage-of-completion method Revenues are generally recognized when (1) the earning process is complete, or virtually complete and (2) an exchange has taken place. Accounting for long-term construction contracts on the percentage-of-completion method is an exception to the basic realization principle. This exception is allowed because usually the ultimate proceeds from the contract are available, and a better matching of periodic income results.

The principal advantages of the percentage-of-completion method are the reflection of the status of the uncompleted contracts and the periodic recognition of income currently rather than irregularly as contracts are completed.

The principal disadvantage of the percentage-of-completion method is the necessity of relying on estimates of the ultimate costs.

The percentage-of-completion method recognizes income as work progresses on the contract.

The recommended method for recognizing income is to determine the percentage of estimated total income either (1) that incurred costs to date bear to total estimated costs based on the most recent construction information, or (2) that may be indicated by such other measure of progress toward completion appropriate to the work performed.

During the early stages of a contract, all or a portion of items such as material and subcontract costs may be excluded, if it appears that the results would produce a more meaningful allocation of periodic income.

When current estimates of the total contract costs indicate a loss, a provision for the loss on the entire contract should be made. However, when a loss is indicated on a total contract that is part of a related group of contracts, the group may be treated as a unit in determining the necessity or providing for losses.

The following are important points to remember in accounting for contracts under the percentage-of-completion method:

1. Journal entries and interim balance sheet treatment are the same as the completed contract method, except that the amount of estimated gross profit earned in each period is recorded by charging the construction in progress account and crediting realized gross profit.
2. Gross profit or loss is recognized in each period by the following formula:

$$\frac{\text{total costs}}{\text{to date}} \times \begin{array}{c}\text{total estimated}\\\text{gross profit or}\\\text{loss}\end{array} - \begin{array}{c}\text{gross profit}\\\text{recognized}\\\text{to date}\end{array} = \begin{array}{c}\text{realized}\\\text{gross}\\\text{profit}\end{array}$$

3. An estimated loss on the total contract is recognized immediately in the year it is discovered. However, any previous gross profit or loss reported in prior years must be included in the computation.

Renegotiation   The Renegotiation Act of 1951 allows the federal government to recover from a government contractor, any profits considered to be excessive. Renegotiation applies to companies which have annual sales of one million dollars or more from contracts or subcontracts covered by the Renegotiation Act of 1951. Brokers and agents are covered if their annual commissions from contracts or subcontracts covered by the Renegotiation Act of 1951 are $25,000 or more.

Renegotiation involves the adjustment of the original selling price or contract. Since the government makes renegotiation adjustments an integral part of a contract, a provision for such probable adjustments is necessary. This provision for renegotiation should be based on the contractor's past experience, or on the general experience of the particular industry, and it is shown in the income statement as a reduction of the related sales or contract income. If a reasonable estimate cannot be made, disclosure of the inability to provide for a provision for renegotiation should be fully disclosed in the financial statements or footnotes thereto. The provision for renegotiation is reported as a current liability in the balance sheet.

In those unusual cases where collection from the government is not reasonably assured, it may be preferable to employ the installment sale or cost recovery method in accounting for a government contract.

When a provision for renegotiation is made in a particular year, and the subsequent final adjustment differs materially, the difference should be shown in the income statement of the year of final determination.

Cost-plus-fixed-fee contracts   Cost-plus-fixed-fee (CPFF) contracts generally provide that the customer pay a fixed fee in addition to all specified costs involved in fulfilling the contract. The contract may include the manufacture of a product or only the performance of services, and the customer may or may not withhold a specified percentage (retainer) of the interim payments until completion of the entire contract.

One of the main problems in accounting for CPFF contracts is when profits should be recognized. As a general rule, profits should not be recognized until the right to full payment becomes unconditional, which is usually when the product has been delivered and accepted, or the services fully rendered (completed-contract method). However, when CPFF contracts extend over several years, the completed contract method may be utilized or the percentage-of-completion method may be used, provided that costs and profits can be reasonably estimated and realization of the contract is reasonably assured.

Terminated government contracts A government contract usually contains a provision which allows the federal government to terminate a contract. Termination may be made for the convenience of the government, or in the event a contractor defaults on the contract. The termination settlement procedures and practices differ significantly between a termination for the convenience of the government and in the case of a default by the contractor.

The federal government will terminate a contract for its convenience when termination is deemed to be in the best interest of the government.

When a contract is terminated for the convenience of the government, the regulations require that the contractor be compensated for any work performed, including a reasonable profit, and any settlement expenses incurred by the contractor.

If a contract is terminated by the government because of default by the contractor, no payment is made for costs on undelivered, or unaccepted work, and settlement expenses cannot be recovered by the contractor. In addition, the contractor may be liable for "excess reprocurement costs" which the government may incur while replacing or acquiring the services or product that the contractor was supposed to supply.

The determination of profit or loss in a terminated government contract is made as of the effective date of termination. This is the date that the contractor accrues the right to receive payment on that portion of the contract which has been terminated.

Although most government contracts provide for a minimum

profit percentage formula in the event agreement cannot be reached, the amount of profit to be reported in the case of termination for the convenience of the government is the difference between all allowable costs incurred and the amount of the termination claim.

If it is impossible to determine a reasonable estimate of the termination claim for reporting purposes, full disclosure of this fact should be made by footnote to the financial statements, which should describe the uncertainties involved. In other words, those parts of the termination claim which can be reasonably ascertained should be reported, and those which cannot be reasonably ascertained should be disclosed in a footnote to the financial statements.

Termination claims should be classified as current assets. Prior to termination notice, advances received should be deducted from termination claims receivable for reporting purposes. Loans received on the security of the contract or termination claim should be separately shown as current liabilities.

The cost of items included in the termination claim that are subsequently reacquired by the contractor should be recorded as a new purchase, and the amount should be applied as a reduction of the termination claim. These types of reductions from the termination claim are generally referred to as *disposal credits*.

Working capital　In the ordinary course of business there is a continuing circulation of capital within the current assets. For example, with a manufacturer, cash is expended for materials, labor, and factory overhead that are converted into finished inventory. After being sold, the inventory is usually converted into a trade receivable and, on collection of the receivable, is converted back to cash. The average time elapsing between expending the cash originally and receiving the cash back from the trade receivable is called an operating cycle. One year is used as a basis for segregating current assets when the operating cycle occurs more frequently than once a year. When the operating cycle is longer than one year, as with the lumber, construction, tobacco and distillery businesses, then the longer period should be used as the operating cycle. In the event that a business clearly has no normal operating cycle, the one-year rule is used.

The classification of current assets and current liabilities for a specific company is directly related to the company's normal operating cycle. Some construction companies' operating cycles are shorter than one year and the one-year rule must be observed.

However, if the normal operating cycle of a construction company is longer than one year, the longer period should be used for determining whether an asset or liability is current or noncurrent.

Contractors' equipment   Construction equipment may be rented or owned. Owned equipment should be recorded at cost and depreciated in a systematic manner over the estimated useful lives of the individual assets.

Leased equipment may represent, in substance, a purchase and should be capitalized, if appropriate, under existing promulgated GAAP (FASB-13).

Contractors' equipment is usually classified as (1) machinery and equipment, (2) tools and equipment, and (3) trucks and autos. Many contractors establish an hourly rate for each piece of machinery. Thus, it is sometimes necessary to maintain a subsidiary ledger on the operating costs of each piece of machinery.

Disclosures   Generally, long-term construction-type contracts require no special disclosure, since they are, in fact, the nature of the contractor's business. However, unusual or extraordinary commitments should be fully disclosed in the financial statements or footnotes thereto.

When a significant part of a contractor's business is derived from government contracts, such disclosure should be made in the financial statements, indicating the uncertainties involved and the possibility of renegotiation in excess of any amount reflected on the financial statements. In addition, the basis of determining the provision for renegotiation should be also disclosed (prior experience, industry experience, etc.).

Material amounts of termination claims should be classified separately from other receivables in the financial statements. Termination claims should be stated at the amount estimated as collectible, and adequate provision or disclosure should be made for items of a controversial nature. Claims against the federal government, if material, should be segregated from other receivables.

Exposure Draft—Proposed SOP and Audit and Accounting Guide—Construction and Production-Type Contracts

On December 21, 1979 an Exposure Draft for a proposed Statement of Position (SOP), entitled "Accounting for Performance of Construction-Type and Certain Production-Type Contracts" was issued by the AICPA. In addition, on January 5, 1980 an Exposure Draft for a proposed new audit and accounting guide entitled "Audit and Accounting Guide for Construction Contractors" was also issued by the AICPA. The proposed audit and accounting guide, when promulgated, will supersede the old industry audit guide entitled "Audits of Construction Contractors" which was issued in May 1965.

The recommendations in the Exposure Draft for the proposed SOP take precedence over any existing accounting principles and practices that conflict with those appearing in the new proposed audit and accounting guide and also those appearing in the industry audit guide entitled "Audits of Government Contractors". "Audits of Government Contractors" is not superseded by either of the proposed publications, but is amended in one respect. The "Audits of Government Contractors" permits the use of either the "cumulative catch-up method", or the "reallocation method" for accounting for changes in estimates under the percentage-of-completion method of accounting. The proposed SOP amends the "Audits of Government Contractors" by stating a preference for the "cumulative catch-up method" in accounting for changes in estimates under the percentage-of-completion method.

Perhaps, one of the most important differences in the two proposed publications from existing literature on this subject is the coverage provided by the new publications. The new publications cover all industries in which construction-type and production-type contracts are used, whereas the existing literature covered only the construction industry. Thus, construction or production type contracts for ship building, electronics equipment, and architectural and engineering design are covered by the proposed SOP and proposed audit and accounting guide.

The preferable accounting principles that appear in the proposed SOP should be identical with those in the proposed audit and accounting guide. However, the proposed audit and accounting guide covers the auditing aspects for construction-type and certain production-type contracts.

The following is a brief summary of the proposed preferable accounting principles which appear in the new publications.

Determining accounting policy The percentage-of-completion method and the completed-contract method are both acceptable under GAAP, but not as alternatives. In other words, a contract should either qualify for the percentage-of-completion method or the completed-contract method, based on the specific circumstances. The percentage-of-completion method is preferred when the estimated cost to complete, the extent of construction progress and contract revenues and costs are reasonably determinable. The proposed SOP states that a presumption exists that reasonable estimates can be made by entities that have significant contracting operations.

In those circumstances where contract revenue and contract cost cannot be definitively determined, a range of contract revenue and contract cost should be used. When using a range for revenue and cost, the minimum revenue in the range should be used and the maximum cost in the range should be used. Thus, the most conservative gross profit or loss should be used until more accurate estimates can be made. In the event that a range cannot be determined, a zero estimate of profit should be used until more accurate estimates are available. In using a zero estimate of profit, contract revenue will be equal to contract costs. However, frequent periodic reviews should be made and when more reliable estimates are available they should replace the zero estimate. A change in estimates based on ranges or based on zero profit should be accounted for prospectively as a change in an accounting estimate.

The proposed SOP requires specific and documented evidence in those situations where the percentage-of-completion method is not utilized. Thus, the completed-contract method should only be used when the percentage-of-completion method cannot be used, or when the consequences are immaterial.

Profit centers The proposed SOP states that each individual contract represents a profit center for the recognition of revenue, the accumulation of costs, and the determination of profit or loss. However, groups of contracts may be so closely related that they constitute a single profit center.

Revised estimates Invariably, estimates are revised during the construction period. Estimates of revenue and costs may change at any time because of many factors. Revisions resulting from changes in estimates are accounted for as changes in accounting estimates. The two methods usually used to account for changes in estimates are (1) the cumulative catch-up method, and (2) the reallocation method.

Under the cumulative catch-up method the effect of revised estimates is recognized in the period of revision. In other words, the entire effect of any revised estimates is recognized in the current period.

Under the reallocation method the effects of any revision is spread prospectively over the current period and any remaining subsequent periods. In other words, the effect of any revision is recognized ratably in the period of revision and any remaining periods.

The proposed SOP requires that the cumulative catch-up method be used to account for the effects of any revised estimates.

Comprehensive Illustration

The following is a comprehensive illustration of the preferable accounting principles contained in this chapter.

CONSTRUCTION CONTRACTOR
STATEMENT OF POSITION
As of December 31, 1980 and 1979

	1980	1979
ASSETS		
Cash	$ 00,000,000	$00,000,000
Certificates of Deposit	0,000,000	
Accounts and Notes Receivable (Note 3)	00,000,000	00,000,000
Retentions Receivable Due Upon Completion of Construction Contracts (Note 3)	0,000,000	0,000,000
Inventories—at lower of cost (average or specific identification) or market (Note 4)	00,000,000	000,000
Costs and Estimated Earnings in Excess of Billings on Uncompleted Construction Contracts	0,000,000	000,000
Total	00,000,000	00,000,000
Assets of Subsidiaries (Notes 1 and 2):		
Land	00,000,000	0,000,000
Other—net	00,000,000	00,000,000
Property Held for Projects Under Development—at cost	0,000,000	0,000,000
Equipment—net (Note 5)	0,000,000	000,000
Other Assets (Note 1)	00,000,000	0,000,000
Total	$000,000,000	$00,000,000

LIABILITIES AND STOCKHOLDERS' EQUITY

Liabilities		
Payable Within One Year:		
Current portion of long-term debt	$ 0,000,000	$ 000,000
Notes payable to banks at 000% at December 31, 1980	000,000	0,000,000
Accounts payable	00,000,000	00,000,000
Billings in excess of costs and estimated earnings on uncompleted construction contracts	0,000,000	000,000
Other accrued liabilities	0,000,000	0,000,000
Total liabilities payable within one year	00,000,000	00,000,000

Deferred Taxes (Note 6)	0,000,000	00,000,000
Long-Term Debt, other than subordinated debt (Note 7)	00,000,000	00,000,000
Subordinated Indebtedness (Note 7)	00,000,000	0,000,000

Stockholders' Equity
(Notes 2, 7 and 10):
Preferred stock—par value, $0.00; authorized, 0,000,000 shares; issued—none
Common stock—par value, $0.00; authorized, 0,000,000 shares; issued; 0,000,000 shares in both years (after giving effect to the three-for-two stock split)

stock split)	0,000,000	0,000,000
Capital in excess of par value	0,000,000	0,000,000
Retained earnings	0,000,000	0,000,000

Less shares held in treasury—at cost; 00,000 shares in both years (after giving effect to the three-for-two stock split)

split)	(000,000)	(000,000)
Stockholders' equity	00,000,000	00,000,000
TOTAL	$000,000,000	$00,000,000

See Accompanying Notes to Financial Statements

CONSTRUCTION CONTRACTOR
STATEMENT OF STOCKHOLDERS' EQUITY
Years Ended December 31, 1980 and 1979

	Common Stock	Capital in Excess of Par Value	Retained Earnings	Shares Held in Treasury	Stockholders' Equity
Balance, December 31, 1978 (Note 2)	$0,000,000	$0,000,000	$0,000,000	$(000,000)	$00,000,000
Net loss			(000,000)		(000,000)
Cash dividends ($.00 a share)*			(000,000)		(000,000)
Issuance of 000,000* shares of common stock in a private placement	000,000	0,000,000			0,000,000
Balance, December 31,1979	0,000,000	0,000,000	0,000,000	(000,000)	00,000,000
Net income			0,000,000		0,000,000
Cash dividends ($.000 a share)			(000,000)		(000,000)
Issuance of 000,000 shares of common stock in three-for-two stock split (including $0,000 of cash paid in lieu of fractional shares—Note 10)	000,000	(000,000)			(0,000)
Balance, December 31, 1980	$0,000,000	$0,000,000	$0,000,000	$(000,000)	$00,000,000

See Accompanying Notes to Financial Statements

*After giving effect to the three-for-two stock split

CONSTRUCTION CONTRACTOR
STATEMENT OF CHANGES IN FINANCIAL POSITION
Years Ended December 31, 1980 and 1979

	1980	1979
Source of Funds		
Operations:		
Income (Loss) before extraordinary item	$ 0,000,000	$ (00,000)
Expenses not affecting cash:		
Depreciation	000,000	000,000
Amortization	(00,000)	00,000
Deferred income taxes	(0,000,000)	(000,000)
Total from operations before extraordinary item	0,000,000	(00,000)
Extraordinary item		000,000
Total from operations after extraordinary item	0,000,000	(000,000)
Increase in liabilities resulting from purchase of Subsidiary:		
Payable within one year	00,000,000	
Other	0,000,000	
Proceeds from borrowings and issuance of securities:		
Long-term debt	00,000,000	00,000,000
Subordinated debt	00,000,000	
Common stock issued		0,000,000
Increase in accounts payable	0,000,000	0,000,000
Increase in billings in excess of costs and estimated earnings on uncompleted contracts	0,000,000	
Increase in current portion of long-term debt	0,000,000	000,000
Decrease in retentions receivable due upon completion of construction contracts	000,000	00,000
Decrease in property held for projects under development	000,000	000,000
Decrease in accounts and notes receivable		000,000
Decrease in inventories		000,000
Decrease in costs and estimated earnings in excess of billings on uncompleted construction contracts		000,000
Other sources of funds	000,000	
Total	$00,000,000	$00,000,000

Application of Funds:

Increase in assets resulting from purchase of Subsidiary:		
Receivables	$ 0,000,000	
Inventories	00,000,000	
Property	000,000	
Other assets	0,000,000	
Increase in accounts and notes receivable	000,000	
Increase in inventories	000,000	
Increase in costs in excess of billings and estimated earnings on uncompleted construction contracts	000,000	
Increase in assets of subsidiaries:		
Land	0,000,000	$ 0,000,000
Other	0,000,000	0,000,000
Increase in property held for projects under development	000,000	
Increase in equipment		000,000
Increase in other assets	0,000,000	0,000,000
Decrease in current portion of long-term debt	00,000	
Decrease in notes payable to banks	000,000	000,000
Decrease in other accrued liabilities	0,000,000	000,000
Decrease in billings in excess of costs and estimated earnings on uncompleted construction contracts		00,000
Decrease in long-term debt	000,000	0,000,000
Decrease in subordinated indebtedness	0,000,000	
Other applications of funds		000,000
Cash dividends	000,000	000,000
Purchase of fractional shares in three-for-two stock split	0,000	
Total	00,000,000	00,000,000
Increase in Cash and Certificates of Deposit	00,000,000	000,000
Cash and Certificates of Deposit, Beginning of year	00,000,000	0,000,000
Cash and Certificates of Deposit, End of year	$00,000,000	$00,000,000

CONSTRUCTION CONTRACTOR
STATEMENT OF INCOME
Years Ended December 31, 1980 and 1979

	1980	1979
Revenues:		
Construction contracts and related revenues (Notes 1 and 2)	$ 000,000	$00,000,000
Other	0,000,000	0,000,000
Gross Revenues	000,000,000	00,000,000
Construction and Related Costs (Notes 1 and 2)	000,000,000	00,000,000
Income from Construction Contracts and Other Revenues (Notes 1 and 2)	00,000,000	0,000,000
Expenses:		
General and administrative	00,000,000.	0,000,000
Selling expense	0,000,000	
Mortgage and closing costs	0,000,000	
Interest on Loans	0,000,000	000,000
Total	00,000,000	0,000,000
Income (Loss) Before Income Taxes and Extraordinary Item	0,000,000	(000,000)
Income Tax Expense (Benefit) (Note 6)	0,000,000	(000,000)
Income (Loss) Before Extraordinary Item	0,000,000	(00,000)
Extraordinary Item—capital loss on sale of the Company's investment in a marketable equity security (net of deferred income tax benefits of $000,000)		(000,000)
Net Income (Loss)	$ 0,000,000	$ (000,000)

Earnings (Loss) per Common
and Common Equivalent
Share(Note 9):

Earnings (Loss) before extraordinary item	$0.00	$(.00)
Net income (Loss)	$0.00	$(.00)

Earnings (Loss per Share—
Assuming Full Dilution
(Note 9):

Earnings (Loss) before extraordinary item	$0.00	$(.00)
Net income (Loss)	$0.00	$(.00)

See Accompanying Notes to Financial Statements

NOTES TO FINANCIAL STATEMENTS

Note 1—Summary of Significant Accounting Policies

Principles of Consolidation   The consolidated financial statements include the accounts of the Company and all of its subsidiaries except the foreign subsidiaries (Note 2) and two domestic subsidiaries whose principal business activity is the rental of two high-rise apartment buildings. The investments in such subsidiaries are stated at equity in the underlying net assets in the consolidated balance sheets.

All intercompany accounts and transactions have been eliminated in the consolidated financial statements.

Recognition of Income   The Company recognizes income from sales of condominium apartments on the completed contract method of accounting (Note 2).

The Company follows the percentage-of-completion method of recording revenues and related costs from other construction contracts and provides currently for estimated losses on uncompleted contracts. The Company recognizes profits relating to sales of limited partnership interests and development fees on the percentage-of-completion method.

Joint Ventures   The Company's share of revenues, expenses and fees relating to construction joint ventures have been included in the appropriate accounts in the statements of consolidated income. Investments in joint ventures are carried at an amount equivalent to the Company's equity in the underlying net assets of such ventures.

Depreciation and Amortization   Depreciation on equipment is provided under the straight-line method at rates based upon estimated useful lives. Excess of cost of investments over related equities (after adjustment for tax benefits arising from the utilization of tax loss carryforwards of acquired companies) and excess of equity of investment over related cost is amortized over periods not in excess of forty years. Deferred debt issue expense is amortized over the life of the related debt applying the interest method. Properties held for projects under development are stated at the lower of cost or net realizable value.

Reclassification   Rental income and rental expense included in the 1979 statement of consolidated income have been reclassified to conform with the 1980 presentation.

Note 2—Subsidiaries—Changes in Accounting Policies

Certain foreign subsidiaries, some of which are 00%-owned, acquired land to develop, build and market condominium high-rise apartments. In years prior to 1980, the Company had consolidated the accounts and results of operations of such subsidiaries. Revenues and related costs on the sales of condominium apartments were recognized on the percentage-of-completion method of accounting. In 1980, because of the political and social unrest, the Company decided not to consolidate its foreign subsidiaries and to change its method of accounting for sales of condominium apartments to the completed contract method. Under the completed contract method, billings and costs are accumulated and income will only be recognized when construction is substantially complete and income is assured beyond a reasonable doubt. Recognition of income from a construction management contract has also been changed to a realization basis.

The 1979 financial statements have been restated to reflect the changes in consolidation policy and method of accounting for long-term contracts. The effects of adopting these changes for 1980 and 1979 are to decrease income before extraordinary item by $0,000,000 ($0.00 per share), and $0,000,000 ($0.00 per share), respectively. The change, in 1979, has the same effect on the net loss. The cumulative effect of these changes was to decrease retained earnings as of January 1, 1979 by $0,000,000.

Note 3—Accounts and Notes Receivable; Retentions Receivable

Receivables at December 31, 1980 and 1979 are classified as follows:

	1980	1979
Accounts receivable	$00,000,000	$00,000,000
Notes receivable	000,000	
Costs and estimated profits—not billed		00,000
Total accounts and notes receivable	00,000,000	00,000,000
Retentions receivable	0,000,000	0,000,000
Total	$00,000,000	$00,000,000

Note 4—Inventories

Inventories at December 31, 1980 and 1979 consist of the following:

	1980	1979
Land and land development costs	$00,000,000	
Construction costs—houses	00,000,000	
Other	000,000	$000,000
Total	$00,000,000	$000,000

Note 5—Equipment

Equipment, stated at cost, at December 31, 1980 and 1979 is as follows:

	1980	1979
Equipment and other	$0,000,000	$0,000,000
Accumulated depreciation	0,000,000	0,000,000
Equipment—net	$0,000,000	$ 000,000

Note 6—Income Taxes

There are no Federal income taxes currently payable for the years ended December 31, 1980 and 1979. Income tax expense (benefit) consists of the following:

	1980	1979
Federal income taxes:		
Current	$0,000,000	
Deferred	(000,000)	$(000,000)
State and local taxes:		
Current	000,000	
Deferred	(000,000)	(000,000)
Foreign:		
Current	0,000,000	00,000
Deferred		000,000
Total	$0,000,000	$(000,000)

Deferred tax expense (benefit) results from the recognition of income and expense in different periods for tax and financial statement purposes. The sources of these differences and the tax effect of each were as follows:

	1980	1979
Income from subsidiaries and joint ventures recognized on completed contract basis for income tax purposes and on percentage-of-completion basis for financial statement purposes	$ 000,000	$ 000,000
Offset of tax loss carryforwards against deferred tax credits	(0,000,000)	(0,000,000)
Income tax on unremitted earnings of foreign subsidiary	00,000	000,000
Other—net	000,000	000,000
Total	$(0,000,000)	$ (000,000)

Deferred taxes on the balance sheet will be reflected as a component of current tax expense in subsequent years as the above mentioned differences reverse. At December 31, 1980, the Company has a Federal tax loss carryforward of approximately $0,000,000, which may be applied against taxable income through 1985.

The effective tax rate was different from the normal United States Federal tax rate for the following reasons:

	1980	1979
Normal United States Federal tax rate	00.0%	00.0%
Increase (reduction) in taxes resulting from:		
State and local taxes net of Federal income tax	0.0	00.0
All other items	(0.0)	(0.0)
Actual effective tax rate	00.0%	00.0%

Note 7—Long-Term Debt

Long-term debt (less current maturities and sinking fund requirements) at December 31, 1980 and 1979 consists of the following:

	1980	1979
Mortgage payable of a subsidiary of the Company:		
Due June 1982	$ 0,000,000	$ 0,000,000
Notes payable of the Company to banks:		
Due January 1982	0,000,000	0,000,000
Due April 1982	0,000,000	0,000,000
Notes payable of a subsidiary of the Company to banks under a credit agreement	00,000,000	00,000,000
Long-term debt, other than subordinated	00,000,000	00,000,000
0% subordinated convertible debentures of the Company, due December 31, 1988 not convertible until 1982	00,000,000	0,000,000
Subordinated debt	00,000,000	0,000,000
Total	$00,000,000	$00,000,000

The mortgage payable, due June 1982, has a floating interest rate of 0% above prime (000% at December 31, 1980). The mortgages payable are collateralized by certain assets having a carrying value of $0,000,000 and $0,000,000 at December 31, 1980 and December 31, 1979, respectively.

The notes payable of the Company to banks at prime rate plus 0% are payable in twenty-four quarterly installments of varying amounts beginning on March 31, 1981, with the final payment due on December 31, 1986.

The 0% subordinated debentures of the Company, due December 31, 1988, are generally convertible on and after January 1, 1982 into 000,000 shares of the Company's common stock. Sinking fund requirements aggregate $0,000,000 annually from 1982 through 1985, with a balloon payment of $0,000,000 due at maturity. The debentures may be called by the Company on and after January 31, 1981. The principal amount of the debentures includes a loan origination fee due in semi-annual installments of $00,000 to June 30, 1987. The unamortized amount of the deferred debt issuance expense included in Other Assets is $000,000 at December 31, 1980.

Note 8—Pension Plan

The Company and its subsidiaries have a non-contributory pension plan covering employees not represented by a union. The total pension plan expense was $000,000 in 1980 and $000,000 in 1979. The Company's policy is to fund amounts equal to pension costs accrued. The pension fund's assets as of the most recent valuation date, July 1, 1980, exceeded the actuarially computed value of vested benefits.

Note 9—Earnings Per Share

Earnings per common and common equivalent share were computed by dividing net income by the sum of the weighted average number of shares of common stock and common stock equivalents outstanding during each year, after giving retroactive effect to the three-for-two stock split. Common stock equivalents are incremental shares arising from an appropriate adjustment for dilutive stock options.

Earnings per share—assuming full dilution were computed in 1980 with the appropriate adjustment for common stock equivalents mentioned above, after giving retroactive effect to the three-for-two stock split, and under the assumption that the convertible debentures were converted at the time of issuance and net income appropriately adjusted for interest, net of taxes. In 1979, the assumed conversion of the convertible debentures has not been included in the computation as the effect of such inclusion would be to decrease the per share loss.

Note 10—Common Stock

Stock split—on May 2, 1980 the Board of Directors approved a three-for-two stock split on the Company's common shares to stockholders of record as of May 20, 1980. The accompanying consolidated financial statements for 1980 give effect to the stock distribution applicable to the common shares issued on June 8, 1980, and accordingly, $000,000, the par value of the shares issued, has been transferred from capital in excess of par value to the common stock account. Cash of $0,000 was paid in lieu of fractional shares. Net income and dividends per share, as well as shares subject to option, shares reserved for conversion, and the related conversion prices have been adjusted to reflect the stock split.

Stock Options—on April 5, 1979 the Board of Directors of the Company authorized a new 1979 Key Employees Stock Option plan (the "Plan") for the granting of options to officers and key employees to purchase up to

Contractors

000,000 shares of the Company's common stock (restated to give effect to the three-for-two stock split) at 100% of the market price on the day the option is granted. Options under the Plan become exercisable at the rate of 00% of each year's grant beginning with the second year after the date of grant and are exercisable up to 0 years and 00 days after the date the option is granted.

The stock option activity during the years ended December 31, 1980 and 1979 was as follows:

	Number of Shares Under Option	
	1980	1979
Outstanding, January 1	000,000	
Granted	00,000	000,000
Outstanding, December 31	000,000	000,000
Available for grant December 31	00,000	00,000

Note 11—Segment Information

The Company's operations include the development, construction and management of real estate, and supplying contracting services to others. Although construction activities for others could represent a greater amount in future years, it accounted for less than 00% of revenues and income before extraordinary items in 1980 and 1979.

GOVERNMENT CONTRACTORS

Overview

The preferable accounting principles and practices for government contractors appear in the industry audit guide entitled, "Audits of Government Contractors" (hereinafter referred to as the Government Contractors Guide).

The United States Government has established regulations governing the procurement of services or property for its various agencies. These regulations, depending on the government agency, may be found in the Federal Procurement Regulations (FPR), the Armed Services Procurement Regulations (ASPR), the National Aeronautic and Space Administration Procurement Regulations, and the Atomic Energy Commission Procurement Regulations.

Government contracts may be for services, products, construction, or research and development. Contracts are obtained either by formal advertising or by negotiation. When the "negotiation" process is used, the government sends out requests for proposals (RFPs), or requests for quotations (RFQs), to certain individuals or companies that appear on the government's qualified bidder list.

Government contracts are usually classified as fixed-price contracts, or cost contracts. However, there are many different variations of these two broad types of contracts. For example, fixed-price contracts may also include an economic price adjustment or some sort of performance incentive. The most common type of cost contract is the cost plus fixed fee contract (CPFF). However, like fixed-price contracts, cost contracts may also include a provision for economic price adjustment or the payment of incentives.

The Assignment of Claims Act of 1940 permits a government contractor to assign all or part (not less than $1,000) of the proceeds of a government contract to a private lending institution. However, advances, progress payments, and loan guarantees by the federal government are available under certain conditions to government contractors. The most common method of payment used by the federal government for contracts is progress payments.

Government contractors must comply with the rules and procedures which appear in the procurement regulations. In most cases, the pronouncements of the Cost Accounting Standards Board (CASB) must be followed, and if the contract is subject to renegotiation, the rules and regulations of the Renegotiation Board must also be complied with. A government contractor can be required to disclose its cost accounting methods and practices and can be required to agree to consistently follow such cost accounting methods and practices. As a general rule, the federal government may terminate a contract for its convenience at any time.

Preferable Accounting Principles

Generally accepted accounting principles and practices that have been promulgated for commercial enterprises are generally applicable to government contractors. For reporting purposes, the accrual basis of accounting should be used. Revenue and expense recognition should be reported in accordance with existing GAAP. In the case of long-term contracts, revenue may be recognized either by the completed contract method, the percentage-of-completion method, or the unit-of-delivery method. The percentage-of-completion method is *preferred* when the estimated cost to complete the contract and the extent of progress are reasonably determinable. When estimates are unreliable, the unit-of-delivery method, or the completed contract method should be used.

Completed contract method The completed contract method recognizes income only on completion or substantial completion of the contract. A contract is regarded as substantially complete if the remaining costs are insignificant.

Excess of accumulated costs over related billings should be reflected in the balance sheet as a current asset, and excess of accumulated billings over related costs should usually be reflected as a current liability. In the case of more than one contract, the accumulated costs or liabilities should be separately stated on the balance sheet. The preferred terminology for the balance sheet presentation should be "(Costs)(Billings) of uncompleted contracts in excess of related (billings) (costs)".

In some cases, it is preferable to allocate general and administrative expenses to contract costs as opposed to period income. In years when no contracts are completed, a better matching of costs and revenues is achieved by carrying general expense as a charge to the contract. If a contractor has many jobs, however, it is more appropriate to charge these expenses to current periods.

In all cases, although income is not recognized until completion of the contract, a provision for an expected loss should be recognized when it becomes evident that a loss on the contract is apparent.

The primary advantage of the completed contract method is that it is based on final results rather than on estimates. The primary disadvantage of the completed contract method is that it does not reflect current performance when the period of the contract extends over more than one accounting period.

The following are important points to remember in accounting for contracts under the completed contract method:

1. Charge applicable overhead and direct costs to a construction in progress account (asset).
2. Credit billing and/or cash received to advances on construction in progress account (a liability).
3. At completion of the contract, gross profit or loss is recognized as follows:
   Contract price less total costs = gross profit or loss
4. At interim balance sheet dates, the excess of either the construction in progress account or the advances account over the other is classified as a current asset or a current liability. It is a current asset or a current liability because of the *normal operating cycle concept*.
5. An expected loss on the total contract is discovered by:
   a. adding estimated costs to complete to the recorded costs to date to arrive at total contract costs.
   b. adding to advances any additional revenue expected to arrive at total contract revenue.
   c. subtracting b from a to arrive at total estimated loss on contract.

Losses should be recognized in full in the year they are discovered.

Percentage-of-completion method   Revenues are generally recognized when (1) the earning process is complete, or virtually complete and (2) an exchange has taken place. Accounting for long-term contracts on the percentage-of-completion method is an exception to the basic realization principle. This exception is allowed because usually the ultimate proceeds are available and a better matching of periodic income results.

The principal advantages of the percentage-of-completion method are the reflection of the status of the uncompleted contracts and the periodic recognition of income currently rather than irregularly as contracts are completed.

The principal disadvantage of the percentage-of-completion method is the necessity of relying on estimates of the ultimate costs.

The percentage-of-completion method recognizes income as work progresses on the contract.

The recommended method for recognizing income is to determine the percentage of estimated total income either (1) that incurred costs to date bear to total estimated costs based on the most recent costs information, or (2) that may be indicated by such other measure of progress toward completion appropriate to the work performed.

During the early stages of a contract, all or a portion of items such as material and subcontract costs may be excluded if it appears that the results would produce a more meaningful allocation of periodic income.

When current estimates of the total contract costs indicate a loss, a provision for the loss on the entire contract should be made. However, when a loss is indicated on a total contract that is part of a related group of contracts, the group may be treated as a unit in determining the necessity of providing for losses.

The following are important points to remember in accounting for contracts under the percentage-of-completion method:

1. Journal entries and interim balance sheet treatment are the same as the completed contract method except that the amount of estimated gross profit earned in each period is recorded by charging the construction in progress account and crediting realized gross profit.

2. Gross profit or loss is recognized in each period by the following formula:

$$\frac{\text{total cost to date}}{\text{estimated total cost}} \times \begin{array}{c}\text{total estimated}\\\text{gross profit}\\\text{or loss}\end{array} - \begin{array}{c}\text{gross profit}\\\text{recognized}\\\text{to date}\end{array} = \begin{array}{c}\text{realized}\\\text{gross}\\\text{profit}\end{array}$$

3. An estimated loss on the total contract is recognized immediately in the year it is discovered. However, any previous

gross profit or loss reported in prior years must be included in the computation.

Unit-of-delivery method   Income recognition is made on the basis of units delivered. The sales value and cost of the units delivered are used to determine profit or loss. Cost of the units delivered may be based on actual cost or on the average cost per unit.

As with the completed contract method and the percentage-of-completion method, a provision for a loss on a contract, accounted for by the units-of-delivery method, should be recognized in the period in which it becomes evident that a loss on the contract is apparent.

Termination of a Government Contract

As mentioned previously, government contracts usually contain a provision which allows the federal government to terminate a contract. Termination may be made for the convenience of the federal government or in the event of a default by the contractor. The termination settlement procedures and practices differ significantly between a termination for the convenience of the government and in the case of default by the contractor.

The federal government will terminate a contract for its convenience when termination is deemed to be in the best interest of the government. When a contract is terminated for the convenience of the government, the regulations require that the contractor be compensated for any work performed, including a reasonable profit, and any settlement expenses incurred by the contractor.

If a contract is terminated by the government because of default of the contractor, no payment is made for costs on undelivered, or unacceptable work, and settlement expenses cannot be recovered by the contractor. In addition, the contractor may be liable for "excess reprocurement costs" which the government may incur while replacing or acquiring the services or product that the contractor was supposed to supply.

The determination of profit or loss on a terminated government contract is made as of the effective date of termination. This is the date that the contractor accrues the right to receive payment on that portion of the contract which has been terminated.

Although most government contracts provide for a minimum profit percentage formula in the event agreement cannot be reached, the amount of profit to be reported in the case of termination for the convenience of the government is the difference between all allowable costs incurred and the amount of the termination claim.

If it is impossible to determine a reasonable estimate of the termination claim for reporting purposes, full disclosure of this fact should be made by footnote to the financial statements, which should describe the uncertainties involved. In other words, those parts of the termination claim which can be reasonably ascertained should be reported, and those which cannot be reasonably ascertained should be disclosed in a footnote to the financial statements.

Termination claims should be classified as current assets. Prior to termination notice, advances received should be deducted from termination claims receivable for reporting purposes. Loans received on the security of the contract or termination claim should be separately shown as current liabilities.

The cost of items included in the termination claim that are subsequently reacquired by the contractor should be recorded as a new purchase, and the amount should be applied as a reduction of the termination claim. These types of reductions from the termination claim are generally referred to as *disposal credits*.

Renegotiation

The Renegotiation Act of 1951 allows the federal government to recover from a government contractor, any profits considered to be excessive. Renegotiation applies to companies which have annual sales of one million dollars or more from contracts or subcontracts covered by the Renegotiation Act of 1951. Brokers and agents are covered if their annual commissions from contracts or subcontracts covered by the Renegotiation Act of 1951 are $25,000 or more.

Renegotiation involves the adjustment of the original selling price or contract. Since the government makes renegotiation adjustments an integral part of a contract, a provision for such probable adjustments is necessary. This provision for renegotiation should be based on the contractor's past experience or on the general experience of the particular industry, and it is shown in the income statement as a reduction of the related sales or income. If a reasonable estimate cannot be made, disclosure of the inability to provide for renegotiation should be fully disclosed in the financial statements or footnotes thereto. The provision for renegotiation is reported as a current liability in the balance sheet.

In those unusual cases where collection from the federal government is not reasonably assured, it may be preferable to employ the installment sale or cost recovery method in accounting for a government contract.

When a provision for renegotiation is made in a particular year, and the subsequent final adjustment differs materially, the difference should be shown in the income statement of the year of final determination.

Disclosure

When a significant part of a company's business is derived from government contracts, such disclosure should be made in the financial statements or footnotes thereto, indicating the uncertainties involved and the possibility of renegotiation in excess of the amount provided. In addition, the basis of determining the provision for renegotiation should be disclosed (prior experience, industry experience, etc.).

Material amounts of termination claims should be classified separately from other receivables in the financial statements. Termination claims should be stated at the amount estimated as collectible, and adequate provision or disclosure should be made for items of a controversial nature. Claims against the government, if material, should be segregated from other receivables.

Generally, long-term contracts require no special disclosure, since they are, in fact, the nature of the contractor's business. However, unusual extraordinary commitments should be fully disclosed in the financial statements or footnotes thereto.

PREFERABLE ACCOUNTING PRINCIPLES

NONPROFIT ORGANIZATIONS

COLLEGES AND UNIVERSITIES

Overview

The preferable accounting principles for colleges and universities appear in the Industry Audit Guide entitled, "Audits of Colleges and Universities" (hereinafter referred to as the College and University Guide) and in SOP 74-8 (Financial Accounting and Reporting by Colleges and Universities).

Actually, SOP 74-8 supersedes a significant portion of the College and University Guide. The material superseded has been replaced by material appearing in "College and University Business Administration (1974)" published by the National Association of College and University Business Officers. Thus, the College and University Guide has been substantially revised from the original publication.

The primary objective in financial reporting for colleges and universities is accounting for the resources received by the institution and accounting for the uses made of these resources.

Preferable Accounting Principles

The main body of preferable accounting principles for nonprofit organizations appears in SOP 78-10 (Accounting Principles and Reporting Practices for Certain Nonprofit Organizations). However, the following industry audit guides which also contain preferable accounting principles for specific nonprofit organizations have been issued by the AICPA:

1. Hospital Audit Guide
2. Audits of Colleges and Universities
3. Audits of Voluntary Health and Welfare Organizations
4. Audits of State and Local Governmental Units (Excluded from FASB-32)

SOP 78-10 expressly applies to all nonprofit organizations not covered by the above listed industry audit guides. Thus, all nonprofit organizations are now covered by specialized accounting principles and reporting practices which are considered to be preferable for the purposes of APB-20 (Accounting Changes).

SOP 78-10 states that financial information prepared for internal use may be reported in any manner that management or the governing board of an institution deems appropriate under the circumstances. However, financial statements prepared for persons outside the management of the nonprofit organization must be prepared and presented in conformity with GAAP.

Both SOP 78-10 and the College and University Guide require that the financial statements of nonprofit entities be prepared and presented on the accrual basis of accounting and also recommend that nonprofit organizations utilize fund accounting to segregate restricted funds from unrestricted funds. The actual books and records of a nonprofit organization need not necessarily be kept on the accrual basis of accounting. However, financial statements which purport to be in conformity with GAAP must be prepared and reported on the accrual basis. In other words, financial statements for nonprofit organizations should generally be presented on the accrual basis in order to be in conformity with GAAP, but the underlying books need not be kept on the accrual basis of accounting.

Cash basis financial statements should ordinarily be considered special purpose reports and reported on by the independent auditor, as such. However, if cash basis financial statements are not materially different than the same statements would be on the accrual basis, the independent auditor may conclude that they are presented in conformity with GAAP.

In those situations, where a nonprofit organization has both restricted and unrestricted resources, fund accounting provides for the necessary segregation of the restricted resources and is considered desirable. Where restricted resources exist and fund accounting is not utilized to segregate resources, all significant restrictions on resources must be fully disclosed in the basic financial statements.

The more common fund accounts in colleges and universities are (1) current funds, (2) plant funds, (3) loan funds, (4) endowment funds, (5) annuity and life income funds, and (6) agency funds.

Current Funds

Current funds may be unrestricted or restricted. The distinction of a current fund, whether unrestricted or restricted, is that it can be used for current operating purposes in achieving the general goals of a particular institution. General goals for colleges and universities usually include costs expended for (1) instruction, (2) acquisition of capital assets, (3) research, and (4) acquisition of goods and services used in current operations.

A gift or bequest received by an institution may be restricted by the donor for a particular current operating purpose such as the addition of more faculty, or more books purchased for the library. In this event, the gift would appropriately be recorded in the restricted current fund. On the other hand, if a gift is received without any restrictions, it would be recorded in unrestricted current funds.

Unrestricted and restricted current funds must be used in the current near term. This is the definition of current funds which is analogous to current assets and current liabilities in a classified balance sheet. Thus, resources that will not be used for several years or which are restricted in the same manner, should not be classified as current funds. In addition, current funds must be used for general operating purposes of the institution.

The governing board of an institution may designate unrestricted funds for a particular purpose. In this event, the designated funds should appear as an appropriation of the unrestricted fund balance. However, the governing board also has the authority to rescind its actions and restore the designated funds to an unrestricted classification. Therefore, the term "restricted" should not be used for unrestricted funds which are designated by a governing board. Donor restricted funds and funds designated as restricted by a governing board should always be reported separately.

The assets and liabilities of a current fund may consist of similar assets and liabilities that appear on the balance sheet of a commercial enterprise. These assets and liabilities include cash, accounts and notes receivable, inventories, investments, and so forth. In addition, several accounts that are special to colleges and universities may appear on the current fund balance sheet. The two most common special accounts are "unbilled charges" and "unremitted appropriations" (also called undrawn appropriations). Unbilled charges are accounts receivable that for various reasons have not been properly billed and for which the revenue has been earned. Undrawn appropriations are accounts receivable, usually from federal, state or other governmental units, which have been earmarked for the institution but have not been received at the balance sheet date. From the standpoint of the users of financial statements of colleges and universities, the special terminology afforded these accounts receivable is somewhat questionable. However, the use of special terminology in financial statements for different types of industries is deeply ingrained in the specialized accounting principles and practices for these different types of industries.

Each current fund should have a fund balance account. In fund accounting the fund balance account is analogous to the stockholders' equity accounts on the balance sheet of a commercial enterprise. The term "restricted" should not be used for funds designated by the governing board because the governing board can rescind its own actions and reclassify designated funds as unrestricted. Donor restricted funds should always be reported separately from designated funds created by the governing board.

Unrestricted current funds are those which will be consumed over the near term for the general operating purposes of the institution. Restricted current funds are those which will be consumed over the near term for general operating purposes that have been specified by each donor of the restricted funds. A restricted current fund will usually consist only of liquid assets, such as cash, investments and receivables.

Current fund revenues consist of all resources earned or contributed during the period from unrestricted sources and all restricted resources that were actually expended or used during the period. Unexpended or unused restricted resources are not current fund revenues until they are actually expended or used for their restricted purpose. Until they are actually expended for the purpose designated by the donor, restricted resources are recorded as "additions" to the fund balance. "Additions" increase the fund balance and "deductions" decrease the fund balance. An "addition" is made by debiting a resource (asset) and crediting the fund balance. A "deduction" is just the opposite. Obviously, an "addition" to a fund balance is different than revenue or a transfer, and a "deduction" to a fund balance is different than an expenditure or a transfer. When an "addition" is actually deferred income, the credit is made to a deferred income account, such as "deferred support and revenue". This is usually true of unexpended resources that have been restricted for current operating purposes.

Until the restricted resources for current operating purposes have actually been expended, they should be accounted for as deferred income.

The more common sources of unrestricted and restricted current fund revenues of colleges and universities are (1) tuitions and other fees, (2) private contributions, (3) endowment income, and (4) public contributions (federal, state, and local). In addition, current fund revenues sometime arise from sales and services of various types of auxiliary activities and enterprises that are operated by an institution. The following is a brief summary of the more common sources of current fund revenues:

Tuitions and Other Fees

The gross amount of tuitions and other fees is recorded as current fund revenues. Scholarships, fellowships and other allowances for tuitions and fees should be recorded as expenditures. Thus, net tuitions and other fees is not usually shown on the statement of current fund revenues, expenditures, and other changes.

Tuitions and other fees which are, or must, be allocated to another fund should be recorded in their gross amounts in current fund revenues and a mandatory or nonmandatory, as the case may be, transfer made to the appropriate fund, or classification. For example, tuitions and other fees that are pledged under a contractual agreement, such as a bond debenture, are recorded as unrestricted current fund revenues and then accounted for as a mandatory transfer to the plant fund. However, fees charged for other than current operating purposes, such as a fee for renewal or replacements of plant equipment, are not recorded as current fund revenue, but as additions to the specific fund for which they are assessed.

Private Contributions

Gifts, grants, bequests, and all other types of unrestricted and restricted (when expended) contributions from private sources comprise this category of current fund revenues. Contributions from foreign governments are usually considered private contributions in accounting for colleges and universities in the U. S. and its possessions.

Endowment Income

Endowment, term endowment, and quasi-endowment funds are those in which the donor has usually dictated that the principal amount must be kept intact for perpetuity or for a specified period. However, the donor may or may not restrict the use of the income produced by the endowment principal. Thus, if the endowment income is unrestricted it should be recorded as current fund revenue. If the endowment income is restricted to current operating purposes and has been expended, it should also be recorded as current fund revenue. In the event the endowment income that is restricted to current operating purposes is not actually expended it should be recorded as an "addition" to the restricted current fund and accounted for as deferred income.

Endowment income or loss resulting from the sale of any part of the endowment principal is not considered income and must be added or deducted from or to the endowment principal.

Stabilization reserves which tend to spread or allocate current investment income over several periods are unacceptable for the purposes of GAAP. Thus, amounts included as unrestricted current fund revenues and additions to restricted current funds, from endowment investments for a particular period, must fairly equal the actual amount of such investment income and not be spread or allocated over several periods. (Further discussion of stabilization reserves appear in the section on Endowment Funds).

Public Contributions

Public contributions to colleges and universities are usually broken-down into (1) governmental appropriations, and (2) governmental grants and contracts. Government appropriations are funds that have been appropriated for an institution by the legislative act of a federal, state, or local governmental unit. In other words, the governmental unit has appropriated funds for a particular college or university. These governmental appropriations may be unrestricted or restricted. If the legislative act that created the appropriations specifically contains any restrictions on the use of the funds, such funds should be considered restricted and accounted for as such. However, if the funds are restricted and the governing board of the institution can change them to unrestricted without any additional legislative acts, such funds should be accounted for as unrestricted.

If a governmental appropriation is unrestricted, it should be recorded as current fund revenue. A governmental appropriation which is restricted to current operating purposes should also be recorded as current fund revenues, but only in the amount actually expended. Unexpended governmental appropriations that are restricted to current operating purposes should be accounted for as "additions" and not current fund revenues.

If the governing board has the power to change a restricted governmental appropriations, the funds should be accounted for as unrestricted.

Federal, state and local governmental appropriations should be identified separately for reporting purposes.

Governmental grants and contracts are usually the result of legislative appropriations but are not referred to as appropriations in accounting and reporting on colleges and universities. These appropriations should be identified as grant and contracts. Governmental grants and contracts include funds received in the form of grants and contracts for research, training, and other sponsored activities.

Grants and contracts that may be used for current operating purposes should be recorded as current fund revenues, as should expended amounts of grants and contracts that are restricted to current operating purposes. Unexpended amounts of grants and contracts which are restricted for current operating purposes should be accounted for as "additions."

Auxiliary Activities and Enterprises

Auxiliary activities and enterprises may generate significant amounts of revenue for a college or university.

Revenues may arise as part of the educational activities of an institution. For example, an institution may own a poultry or dairy farm for educational purposes. The poultry or dairy farm may produce goods which are sold and consumed by students, faculty and the general public. Thus, revenues are produced incidentally to providing education, research and instruction.

If the revenue from the sales and services of educational activities is significant, it should be accounted for separately. The selling educational department records its revenues and expenditures and the buying department records its purchases of goods or services in the same manner as those purchased from outsiders. Other sources of revenue from educational activities include publications, testing services, film rentals, and the sale of products or services.

Auxiliary enterprises are those which provide services or goods for students and faculty at fees which may or may not cover the cost of providing such services or goods. Residence halls, eating facilities, bookstores, barber shops, and movie theaters are examples of auxiliary enterprises. Only those revenues that are derived directly from the activities of the auxiliary enterprise are considered revenue.

Because of their size and significant revenues, hospitals operated by colleges or universities are always accounted for separately from other auxiliary enterprises. Resources from restricted contributions for hospitals, such as gifts, grants, contracts, or endowment funds are not considered resources or revenues from the hospital operations but are included in their respective restricted category and accounted for as such.

Unrestricted revenues of an auxiliary enterprise should be accounted for as current fund revenues. Restricted revenues of an auxiliary enterprise which may be used for current operating purposes are current fund revenues when expended for their restricted purpose.

Interdepartmental transactions between departments of an institution should not be reported as revenue but as reductions of expenditures of the department supplying the services or material. Thus, transactions of service departments or storerooms of an institution should not be reported as revenue but as a reduction of expenditures. The recipient department records the interdepartment services or materials as an expenditure in the amount billed by the supplying department.

Current fund expenditures are those that are expended for general current operating purposes of the college or university. Expenditures for the general current operating purposes of an institution include expenditures for (1) educational, (2) auxiliary activities and enterprises, (3) hospitals, and (4) other related activities.

Educational expenditures include all those that are expended for a college or university's educational programs. Educational expenditures are classified on a functional basis. The more common educational expenditures are for (1) instruction, (2) academic support, (3) research, (4) institutional support, (5) scholarships and fellowships, (6) operation of, and maintenance of plant facilities, and (7) public services.

Expenditures for auxiliary activities and enterprises are also made on a functional basis. All direct and indirect expenditures including an allocation of costs shared with other departments may be charged to the operation of auxiliary activities and enterprises.

As mentioned previously, revenues and expenditures for the operation of a college or university owned hospital are usually accounted for separately because of their financial significance. However, expenditures that are properly classified as instructional or research which take place within the hospital should be excluded from the operation of the hospital and appropriately accounted for as educational and research expenditures.

Mandatory transfers between funds are those which are required to be made because of contractual or legal agreements. Nonmandatory transfers between funds are those which are made by the governing board at its discretion. Deductions from a fund are not expenditures, but represent a required decrease in a fund balance. The more common deductions of a fund are (1) refunds of gifts from donors, and (2) return of unused or unexpended federal, state, or local governmental funds which may be required by law.

Plant Funds

As many as four or more separate related funds may comprise the plant funds. The most common four are (1) investment in plant, (2) retirement of indebtedness, (3) renewals and replacements, and (4) unexpended.

Investments in Plant

Cost is the basis for the valuation of purchased or constructed assets. Donated assets are valued at their appraised or fair market values at the date of the gift. Valuation of assets should be disclosed in the financial statements as required by existing GAAP.

Depreciation expense should be reported in the plant fund section of the statement of changes in fund balances. Allowance for depreciation may be disclosed in the balance sheet.

Existing indebtedness for plant fund assets should be recorded in the investment in plant fund. However, indebtedness incurred to finance asset acquisitions that have not been acquired or built, may be recorded in the unexpended plant fund until such assets are actually acquired or built, and at that time they should be transferred to the investment in plant fund.

On the sale or other disposition of plant fund assets, the asset and any related liabilities should be removed from the investment in plant fund. Any proceeds should be transferred to the unexpended plant funds, and a legal opinion should be obtained to determine whether the proceeds are restricted or unrestricted. Unrestricted proceeds that are not transferred to unrestricted current funds should be disclosed separately in the unexpended plant fund.

The investment in plant fund balance indicates the net investment in plant assets.

Retirement of Indebtedness

The net assets of the retirement of indebtedness fund represent resources that are available for the payment of indebtedness on plant assets. Assets of this fund are usually very liquid and consist of cash, short-term investments, and receivables.

Mandatory and nonmandatory transfers are made to the retirement of indebtedness fund to accumulate required sinking fund payments, interest on debt, and other principal payments which periodically become due on indebtedness of plant assets.

Renewals and Replacement Fund

The net assets of the renewals and replacement fund represent resources that are available for the renewal or replacement of plant assets.

Assets held in the renewal and replacement fund are usually liquid and consist of cash, short-term investments and receivables.

Unexpended Plant Funds

The net assets of the unexpended plant fund represent resources that are available for the acquisition or construction of plant assets.

Assets held in the unexpended plant fund are usually liquid and consist of cash, short-term investments and receivables.

Restricted and unrestricted funds   In all of the funds that comprise the total plant fund, the distinction between restricted and unrestricted fund balances must always be maintained.

If the assets and liabilities of all funds that make up the total plant funds are combined for reporting purposes, the fund balance of each fund should be separately disclosed. Funds designated by the governing board of the institution should be separately disclosed from donor restricted funds.

Loan Funds

Loan funds are usually created by gifts from donors with the stipulation that the gift be used for loans to students, faculty and other staff members of the institution. The gift is usually self-perpetuating, in that, the principal and interest received from one borrower is then loaned to the next borrower, and so forth. Assets of a loan fund are generally quite liquid.

The fund balance of a loan fund should be reduced by the amount of the provision for doubtful loans. Loan receivables should be reported at their face value. Interest on loans is generally not recorded until actually collected and is usually insignificant in relationship to the financial statements taken as a whole.

Endowment Funds

Endowment funds are usually established by gifts from private or public donors. The donor establishes the conditions of the gift and how the principal and income on the principal should be used. As a general rule, only the income from the endowment principal can be expended for either restricted purposes or unrestricted purposes, as stipulated by the donor. Thus, the endowment principal remains intact for a specified period or in perpetuity.

The more common classes of endowments are (1) pure endowments, (2) term endowments, and (3) quasi-endowments. The important requirement of an endowment fund is that its principal amount must be maintained intact.

A "pure endowment" is one in which the donor stipulates that the principal must be kept intact in perpetuity. The income produced by the principal may be designated for unrestricted or restricted purposes, or may have to be added back to the principal, in accordance with the donor's instructions.

A "term endowment" is the same as a pure endowment, except that a portion, or all of the principal may be used, after a specified period, or certain event has occurred.

A "quasi-endowment" fund is not created by an outside donor. It is created by the governing board of the institution and may be discontinued by the governing board. A "quasi-endowment" fund contains resources that the governing board desires to keep invested. Since "quasi-endowment" funds are basically used for the same purposes as other endowment funds, they are classified and accounted for in a similar manner. However, a "quasi-endowment" fund is a voluntary fund which may be discontinued by the governing board of the institution.

Annuity and life income funds are not endowments and should be reported in a separate fund. However, in practice, immaterial amounts of annuity and life income funds are frequently combined with endowment funds. In this event, the caption "Endowment and Similar Funds" is usually used instead of "Endowment Funds".

For balance sheet purposes, endowment funds are combined as one fund. However, for accounting purposes, each endowment is kept in a separate fund. Where restrictions on the type of investment that can be made are the same for several endowment funds, the principal of these funds may be pooled for investment purposes.

Educational institutions consider income yield, rents, interest, dividends, royalties and similar items as their "traditional yield". "Traditional yield" is usually accounted for as revenue which may be used for general institutional purposes. However, endowment fund gains or losses that result from the sale of part or all of the endowment principal are not considered revenue, and should be added or deducted from or to the endowment principal amount.

The "total return" approach to the management of investments of endowment and quasi-endowment funds has been utilized by some educational institutions. A "spending rate" is established by the governing board which is met by the "traditional yields". If the "traditional yields" are insufficient to meet the established "spending rate", then a portion of the realized net gains on endowment or quasi-endowment investments is made available by the governing board to make up part or all of the deficiency. Sometimes unrealized net gains are also made available by the governing board. Thus, net gains on endowment principal may be converted to revenue, by the governing board, under the "total return" concept. The College and University Guide specifically states that converting net gains on endowment principal to revenue is unacceptable. Any net gains from endowment investments which are used currently by the governing board of an institution should be accounted for as a transfer of endowment funds to other funds and not accounted for as revenue to other funds. In the event that net gains from endowment investments are transferred to a restricted fund as deferred support and revenue, the net gains from endowment investments should be transferred as deferred support and revenue of that restricted fund. A transfer does not occur when net gains from quasi-endowment investments are involved, because quasi-endowment funds are created by the governing board out of current funds and they do not have any legal restrictions.

Gain or loss should be recognized on the sale or transfer of an investment from one fund to another. The current market, or appraised value on the date of sale or transfer should be used to determine the amount of gain or loss.

Carrying value of investments   Purchased investments should be accounted for at cost and contributed or donated investments should be accounted for at the fair market value or appraised value at the date of the gift.

The College and University Guide permits another alternative valuation method for reporting investments, providing that all investments of all funds are reported by the alternative valuation method. The alternative valuation method for reporting all investments of an educational institution is current market value or fair value at the reporting date. Thus, the College and University Guide condones the reporting of investments at amounts which can significantly exceed original cost. However, SOP 78-10 (Accounting Principles and Reporting Practices for Certain Nonprofit Organizations) also permits the use of market value in excess of cost for reporting investments.

> *OBSERVATION: The availability of so many valuation methods for investments of nonprofit organizations appears to be confusing and certainly questionable.*

Annuity and Life Income Funds

As a general rule, an annuity issued by a college or university is controlled by some regulatory agency. An annuity is usually an agreement whereby the educational institution receives certain resources and agrees to pay a stipulated amount periodically to one or more beneficiaries. The resources (assets) are either income producing, or are invested to produce income. The income produced is then used to pay the periodic payments to the beneficiaries. At a specified time, the periodic payments cease and the resources become the property of the institution. At this time, the resources are transferred from the annuity fund to unrestricted current fund revenues, if the annuity agreement contained no restrictions on the use of the resources. However, if the resources are restricted, they are transferred to the fund specified by the agreement and accounted for in accordance with the restrictions.

Although the College and University Guide describes two different methods for accounting and reporting annuity funds, only one is considered acceptable for the purposes of GAAP. The acceptable method is called the "actuarial method". Under this method, the actuarial value of the periodic payments that must be made to the beneficiaries is determined and recorded as a liability in the annuity fund. The opening journal entry for an annuity fund under the actuarial method is, as follows:

Resources (assets)	$XX,XXX	
Annuity payable		$ X,XXX
Fund balance		XX,XXX

The annuity payable is a liability account which is reduced for each periodic payment that is made. However, the annuity payable account must be recomputed periodically and adjusted for actuarial gains or losses, particularly those caused by changes in the life expectancy of the beneficiaries.

The valuation methods for reporting investments held in annuity funds are the same as those for investments held in endowment and other funds.

The other method for accounting and reporting annuity funds appears in a manual entitled "College and University Business Administration (1974)" published by the National Association of College and Business Officers. This method does not provide for a liability in the amount of the present value of the annuity payable and is not considered acceptable for the purposes of GAAP.

Life income and annuity agreements are quite similar. Under

each type of agreement, the institution receives resources (assets), the institution makes periodic payments to designated beneficiaries, and after the last periodic payment is made the resources are transferred to the institution in accordance with the stipulations contained in the agreement. The difference between the two types of agreements is the periodic payment. In an annuity agreement the amount of periodic payment may be whatever is agreed upon. However, in a life income agreement the periodic payments consist only of the income actually earned on the resources.

Many nonprofit organizations maintain "pooled life income funds" which must be carefully planned and executed to insure a tax-exempt status.

Each life income agreement must be accounted for in a separate fund. For reporting purposes, all life income funds may be combined. In practice, when life income funds are immaterial they are usually included with endowment funds under the caption "Endowment and Similar Funds".

The valuation methods for reporting investments held in life income funds are the same as those for investments held in endowment and other funds.

At the termination of the life income agreement, the periodic payments of income cease and the resources become the property of the institution. At this time, the resources are transferred to the fund designated by the agreement and accounted for in accordance with any restrictions.

Agency and Other Funds

An institution may hold resources as custodian or agent for student and faculty organizations, individuals, and others. Agency fund resources are usually received on behalf of others and subsequently paid out in accordance with the agency agreement. Sometimes a small fee is charged by the institution for acting as custodian or agent.

Agency resources should be maintained in a separate fund. However, in practice, if the agency funds are insignificant they are reported as assets and liabilities of current funds. In addition, there is usually no need for unrestricted and restricted funds classification in accounting for agency funds.

Other funds used by colleges and universities are recorded and reported in a similar manner to the funds covered herein.

Financial Statements

Financial reports of colleges and universities are usually made up of a balance sheet, a statement of changes in fund balances, and a statement of activity which is usually called the statement of current fund revenues, expenditures, and other changes.

At all times, the financial statements of colleges and universities should clearly indicate those funds that are externally restricted (outside donors) and those funds that are internally restricted by the governing board of the institution.

Temporary loans between funds should be recorded as a receivable by the fund making the loan and as a payable by the fund receiving the loan. However, if the loan is not expected to be repaid in a reasonable time, the loan should be considered permanent and recorded as an interfund transfer.

Loans from externally restricted funds are sometimes authorized by the governing board of a college or university. Interest on such loans may also be authorized. If legal restrictions exist against lending or recording loans from externally restricted funds, appropriate disclosure should be made in the financial statements, or footnotes thereto.

If a college or university does not directly or indirectly control the principal of an endowment type fund held in trust by outside parties, the funds should not be included in the financial statements of the college or university. However, pertinent information concerning these type of funds should be disclosed in the financial statements of the college or university. Endowment income distributions from funds held in trust by outside parties should be recorded on the accrual basis. In addition, the right to any future endowment income should be disclosed in the financial statements, if appropriate.

On the other hand, if a college or university has the legal enforceable right to the income from endowment type funds held in trust by outside parties, it may be appropriate for the college or university to report the resources of such funds in its financial statements. In this event, the resources and all pertinent facts must be adequately disclosed in the financial statements or footnotes thereto.

If a religious order or group sponsors a college or university, the accounting records of the college or university must be kept separate from those of the religious order or group.

Services contributed by members of a religious order or group should be accounted for as a gift and a corresponding expenditure. The gift and corresponding expenditure should be recorded at the fair value of such services at the time they are performed.

It may be desirable to include detailed supplementary schedules with the basic financial statements of colleges and universities. These detailed supplementary schedules may include information as to (1) the source and purpose of gifts received, (2) the operations of auxiliary enterprises, (3) the types of investments held by the institution, (4) the details of long-term debt, and (5) the sources of current fund revenues.

The College and University Guide requires that a change in accounting method made to comply with the provisions of the Guide, should be reported as a prior period adjustment, and financial statements of prior periods should be restated.

> *OBSERVATION: FASB-16 defines a prior period adjustment as (1) a correction of an error in a prior period statement, or (2) an adjustment for the realization of the tax benefits of the preacquisition operating loss carryforwards of purchased subsidiaries. Thus, unless the College and University Guide has officially amended FASB-16, without due process, the change in accounting method cannot be treated as a prior period adjustment under existing GAAP.*

In addition, the College and University Guide prescribes that the provisions of APB-20 (Accounting Changes) apply to financial statements of colleges and universities, except for the following items which relate to the results of operations of a commercial enterprise:

a. The inclusion in net income of the prior years' cumulative effect on retained earnings caused by a change in an accounting principle.
b. Disclosure of the pro-forma information on net income that is required by APB-20 and all earnings per share data.

The following are recommended for reporting a change in accounting principle for a college or university:

a. Prior years' financial statements should be presented as previously reported.
b. The effect of the change in accounting principle for the current and prior years should be disclosed in the financial statements or footnotes thereto.
c. The statement of changes in fund balances should include the cumulative effect of the change in accounting principle.

Comprehensive Illustration

The following is a comprehensive illustration of the preferable accounting principles contained in this chapter.

COLLEGE AND UNIVERSITY
BALANCE SHEET
As of December 31, 1980, and 1979

	(In thousands)	
	1980	*1979*

ASSETS

Current Funds:

Unrestricted:

	1980	1979
Cash	$ 000	$ 000
Investments—approximates market value	0,000	000
Accounts receivable:		
Patient care (less $0,000 in 1980 and $0,000 in 1979 for doubtful accounts)	00,000	00,000
Other (less $000 in 1980 and $000 in 1979 for doubtful accounts)	0,000	0,000
Inventories and deferred charges	0,000	0,000
Due from plant funds	00,000	00,000
Total unrestricted	00,000	00,000
Restricted:		
Cash	0,000	0,000
Investments (market value, 1980, $00,000; 1979, $00,000)	00,000	00,000
Receivables	0,000	0,000
Due from current unrestricted funds	00,000	0,000
Total restricted	00,000	00,000
Total current funds	$ 00,000	$ 00,000

Student Loan Funds:

	1980	1979
Cash	$ 000	$ 000
Investments—approximates market value	000	000
Loans receivable (less $0,000 in 1980 for doubtful accounts)	00,000	00,000
Total student loan funds	$ 00,000	$ 00,000

Endowment and Similar Funds:

	1980	1979
Cash	$ 000	$ 000
Investments (market value, 1980, $000,000; 1979, $000,000)	000,000	000,000
Due from plant funds	00	00
Total endowment and similar funds	$000,000	$000,000

Plant Funds:

Cash	$ 00	$ 0,000
Deposits with trustees	00,000	0,000
Investments (market value, 1980, $00,000; 1979, $00,000)	00,000	00,000
Land, buildings, and equipment	000,000	000,000
Total plant funds	$000,000	$000,000

LIABILITIES AND FUND BALANCES

Current Funds:

Unrestricted:

Accounts payable and accrued expenses	$ 00,000	$ 00,000
Deferred revenues	00,000	00,000
Due to current restricted funds	00,000	0,000
Total unrestricted	00,000	00,000

Restricted:

Advances from governmental agencies	0,000	0,000
Medical malpractice self-insurance accrual	0,000	0,000
Fund balances	00,000	00,000
Total restricted	00,000	00,000
Total current funds	$ 00,000	$ 00,000

Student Loan Funds:

Fund balances:

Federal grants refundable	$000,000	$ 00,000
University funds—restricted	0,000	0,000
Total student loan funds	$ 00,000	$ 00,000

Endowment and Similar Funds:

Mortgage and note payable	$ 0,000	$ 0,000
Fund balances:		
Endowment	00,000	00,000
Quasi-endowment:		
Restricted	00,000	00,000
Unrestricted:		
Specific schools and departments	00,000	00,000
General support	00,000	00,000
Reinvested income ($0,000 unrestricted)	0,000	
Total endowment and similar funds	$000,000	$000,000

Plant Funds:

Accounts payable	$ 000	$ 0,000
Bonds, mortgages, and notes payable	000,000	00,000
Due to other funds	00,000	00,000
Fund balances (includes unrestricted unexpended funds, 1980, $0,000; 1979, $00,000)	000,000	000,000
Total plant funds	$000,000	$000,000

See Accompanying Notes to Financial Statements

COLLEGE AND UNIVERSITY
STATEMENT OF CHANGES IN FUND BALANCES
Years ended December 31, 1980, and 1979

	(In thousands)	
	1980	1979
Current Unrestricted Funds		
Balance at beginning of year	$ —	$ —
Add:		
Revenues	000,000	000,000
	000,000	000,000
Deduct:		
Expenditures and mandatory transfers	000,000	000,000
Appropriations to other funds—net:		
Plant funds for capital improvements	0,000	0,000
Quasi-endowment	0,000	0,000
Other funds	000	000
	000,000	000,000
Balance at end of year	$ —	$ —
Current Restricted Funds		
Balance at beginning of year	$ 00,000	$ 00,000
Add:		
Gifts and grants	00,000	00,000
Endowment income	0,000	0,000
Other	0,000	0,000
	00,000	00,000
Deduct—expenditures	00,000	00,000
Transfers and appropriations from (to) other funds—net	(0,000)	000
Balance at end of year	$ 00,000	$ 00,000
Student Loan Funds		
Balance at beginning of year	$ 00,000	$ 00,000
Add:		
Gifts and grants	0,000	0,000
Interest income	000	000
	0,000	0,000
Deduct:		
Loans canceled or written off	000	000
Allowance for administrative costs	000	000
Provision for uncollectible loans	0,000	
Other	000	000
	0,000	000

Transfers from other funds:		
Mandatory transfers from current		
unrestricted funds for matching grants	000	000
Appropriation from current unrestricted		
funds	000	
Other funds—net	000	00
	000	000
Balance at end of year	$ 00,000	$ 00,000

Endowment and Similar Funds

Balance at beginning of year	$000,000	$000,000
Add (deduct):		
Gifts	0,000	0,000
Endowment income added to principal	000	000
Net gain (loss) on sales of investments	(0,000)	(0,000)
Other	000	00
	000	(000)
Transfers from (to) other funds:		
Current funds:		
Reinvested income	0,000	
Other unrestricted funds		
appropriations—net	0,000	0,000
Plant funds—net	0,000	0,000
Other funds—net	000	(000)
	0,000	00,000
Balance at end of year	$000,000	$000,000

Plant Funds

Balance at beginning of year	$000,000	$000,000
Add:		
Gifts and grants	00,000	0,000
Investment income	0,000	0,000
Expired life income agreements		0,000
Other	000	000
	00,000	00,000
Deduct:		
Interest on indebtedness	0,000	0,000
Net loss on sale or retirement of fixed assets	0,000	000
Replacement of hospital units' equipment		
(not capitalized)	0,000	0,000
	0,000	0,000

Transfers from (to) other funds:
  Current unrestricted funds:
    Mandatory transfers for:

Debt service	0,000	0,000
Replacement of hospital units' fixed assets	0,000	0,000
Appropriations	0,000	0,000
Endowment and similar funds—net	(0,000)	(0,000)
Other funds—net	0,000	000
	00,000	0,000
Balance at end of year	$000,000	$000,000

See Accompanying Notes to Financial Statements

COLLEGE AND UNIVERSITY
STATEMENT OF CURRENT FUNDS REVENUES, EXPENDITURES, AND TRANSFERS
Years ended December 31, 1980 and 1979

	(In thousands) 1980			1979
	Unrestricted	*Restricted*	*Total*	
Revenues:				
Tuition and fees	$000,000		$000,000	$ 00,000
Governmental appropriations	00,000		00,000	00,000
Gifts and grants	0,000	$00,000	00,000	00,000
Endowment income	00,000	0,000	00,000	00,000
Hospitals and clinics	00,000		00,000	00,000
Indirect cost recovery on research and sponsored programs	00,000		00,000	00,000
Auxiliary enterprises	00,000		00,000	00,000
Real estate properties	00,000		00,000	00,000
Other	0,000	0,000	00,000	00,000
Total revenues	$000,000	$00,000	$000,000	$000,000
Expenditures and Transfers:				
Instruction and other academic programs	$ 00,000	$ 0,000	$ 00,000	$ 00,000
Patient care services	00,000	0,000	00,000	00,000
Research and other sponsored programs		00,000	00,000	00,000
Libraries	0,000	000	0,000	0,000
Student services	0,000		0,000	0,000
Student aid	0,000	0,000	00,000	0,000
Operation of plant	00,000		00,000	00,000
Institutional services	00,000		00,000	00,000
General expenses	00,000		00,000	0,000
Mandatory transfers for:				
Debt service	0,000		0,000	0,000
Replacement of hospital units' fixed assets	0,000		0,000	0,000
Student loan fund matching grants	000		000	000
Total educational and general	000,000	00,000	000,000	000,000

Auxiliary enterprises:				
Operating costs	00,000		00,000	00,000
Mandatory transfers for debt service	0,000		0,000	0,000
Real estate properties:				
Operating costs	0,000		0,000	0,000
Mandatory transfers for debt service	0,000		0,000	0,000
Total expenditures and mandatory transfers	000,000	00,000	000,000	000,000
Appropriations to other funds— net:				
Plant funds for capital improvements	0,000		0,000	0,000
Quasi-endowment:				
Reinvested endowment income	0,000		0,000	
Other	0,000		0,000	0,000
Other funds	000		000	000
Total expenditures and net transfers	$000,000	$00,000	$000,000	$000,000

See Accompanying Notes to Financial Statements

SUMMARY OF SIGNIFICANT ACCOUNTING POLICIES

1. The University follows fund accounting policies as are customary for colleges and universities.

2. Funds classified as unrestricted represent funds available for any University use as distinguished from funds restricted externally for specific purposes. Unrestricted funds classified as other than current funds represent funds appropriated by the Board of Trustees for certain specific purposes. Endowment funds are subject to donor restrictions requiring that the principal be invested in perpetuity and that only the income be utilized. Quasi-endowment funds are administered in a manner similar to endowment funds; however, the principal may be expended by action of the Board of Trustees.

3. Required debt service payments relating to plant funds debt are provided from current unrestricted funds. The amounts provided are reported as mandatory transfers to plant funds in the accompanying financial statements.

4. Expenditures for normal replacement of equipment are not capitalized but are charged to the funds incurring the costs. All other expenditures for fixed assets are charged to plant funds and are capitalized. Depreciation of fixed assets is not recorded.

5. In accordance with the requirements of certain third-party payers for patient care services, the University transfers cash equivalent to an annual provision for depreciation of its hospital units' fixed assets from current unrestricted funds to provide for the replacement of its hospital units' fixed assets. The amounts transferred are reported as mandatory transfers to plant funds in the accompanying financial statements.

6. Investments and land, buildings, and equipment are carried at cost.

7. Other significant accounting policies are set forth in the notes to financial statements.

NOTES TO FINANCIAL STATEMENTS

1. The market value of unrestricted quasi-endowment funds at December 31, 1980, was $00,000,000 for specific schools and departments and $00,000,000 for general support.

2. Securities held in the University's consolidated investment pool (in which unrestricted quasi-endowment participates), with a market value of approximately $00,000,000, were pledged at December 31, 1980, as collateral under indentures and other debt instruments covering certain plant funds mortgages and bonds payable.

3. Expenditures for capitalized fixed assets totaled approximately $00,000,000 and $00,000,000 for the years ended December 31, 1980 and 1979, respectively.

4. The University records gifts when received. At December 31, 1980, unrecorded pledges of gifts amounted to $00,000,000 principally for restricted purposes.

5. In December 1979, the University received $0,000,000 representing the principal of an irrevocable life income trust that had been held and administered by a trustee. The University's benefactor, under the terms of a pledge agreement, had stipulated that the proceeds be used by the University to construct and equip a library; accordingly, the receipt of the trust principal was reported as an addition to plant funds. The University subsequently transferred this amount to quasi-endowment funds as reimbursement for amounts previously provided in connection with the construction of the library.

6. The University is self-insured for medical malpractice claims. In connection therewith, expenditures for the years ended December 31, 1980 and 1979, include provisions of approximately $0,000,000 and $000,000, respectively, representing actuarially determined estimates of costs relating to both asserted and unasserted claims resulting from incidents that occurred during the periods. The provisions have been funded in accordance with the requirements of certain third party payers and are included in current restricted funds in the accompanying balance sheet.

7. University employees are covered principally by defined contribution pension plans, both contributory and noncontributory. Pension costs are funded as accrued. The University's contributions to the plans (totaling approximately $00,000,000 and $00,000,000 for the years ended December 31, 1980 and 1979, respectively) are charged to current funds expenditures as made.

8. The University is defendant in various legal actions arising out of the normal course of its operations. Although the final outcome of such actions cannot presently be determined, the University's administration is of the opinion that eventual liability, if any, will not have a material effect on the University's financial position.

9. For purposes of comparison, certain 1979 amounts, as previously reported, have been reclassified in the accompanying financial statements.

HOSPITALS

Overview

The preferable accounting principles for hospitals appear in the Industry Audit Guide entitled "Hospital Audit Guide". In addition, the Hospital Audit Guide has been amended by the following Statements of Position (SOP):

SOP (Note) – Clarification of Accounting, Auditing, and Reporting Practices Relating to Hospital Malpractice Loss Contingencies (Note: This SOP does not have an identification number).

SOP 78-1 – Accounting by Hospitals for Certain Marketable Equity Securities

SOP 78-7 – Financial Accounting and Reporting by Hospitals Operated by a Governmental Unit

Generally accepted accounting principles (GAAP) should be followed in accounting for hospitals except when they are clearly inappropriate. It is unacceptable to value long-term security investments at current market value and assets at current replacement cost with depreciation calculated thereon. These procedures have sometimes been recommended by healthcare associations.

The accrual basis of accounting should be used by hospitals and net income should be determined and reported on for the entire organization. In those situations where a hospital has both restricted and unrestricted resources, fund accounting provides for the necessary segregation of the restricted resources and is considered desirable. Where restricted resources exist and fund accounting is not utilized to segregate resources, all significant restrictions on resources must be fully disclosed in the basic financial statements.

The financial statements for a hospital should include (1) a balance sheet, (2) a statement of changes in financial position, (3) a statement of changes in fund balances, and (4) a statement of revenue and expenses. The balance sheet should reflect the assets, liabilities, and fund balances of the hospital. Assets and liabilities should be clearly classified as current or noncurrent in accordance with the normal operating cycle of the hospital. Restricted and unrestricted fund balances should be adequately labeled and appropriately segregated. The total amounts of restricted and unrestricted funds should be separately set forth on the balance sheet except for those plant funds which are not susceptible to segregation. The sources of funds used to acquire plant assets are often a combination of unrestricted and restricted funds which cannot be clearly segregated. Thus, plant funds are usually reported separately, or segregated into restricted and unrestricted funds and combined with other restricted and unrestricted funds. Restricted resources should be separately reported in the balance sheet as part of their related fund balance, or reported in the balance sheet as deferred revenue until the restrictions are compiled with. The statement of changes in financial position summarizes all of the financing and investing activities of the hospital and reflects the amount of working capital generated from or used in operations for the period. The statement of revenue and expenses should present the results of operations for the period, and should reflect the principal sources of support and revenue. The statement of changes in fund balances should include a reconciliation of the beginning and ending fund balances. The statement of revenue and expenses may be combined with the statement of changes in fund balances.

A hospital should have no more than one of each of the following types of funds, although a fund may have other funds within it:

Operating fund   is used to account for all unrestricted resources and corresponding liabilities. Most everyday operating transactions are recorded and accounted for in this fund.

Specific purpose fund   is similar to an unrestricted trust fund in a governmental unit. Accounts for resources that are restricted to a specific purpose of use.

Endowment fund   accounts for gifts and endowments where the principal and income may be restricted to a specific purpose.

Plant fund   accounts for the physical plant and other fixed assets, accumulated depreciation and related long-term debt.

The following points are important to remember in the determination of net income for a hospital:

1. Revenue is recognized at standard rates on the accrual basis.
2. Uncollectible accounts, employee discounts, charity write-offs, and similar items are deductions from revenue.
3. Initial inventories of minor equipment are capitalized and charged to operating expense over a period of three years or less.
4. Replacements of minor equipment should be charged directly to operating expense in the year incurred.

Preferable Accounting Principles

The preferable accounting principles for hospitals which appear in the Hospital Audit Guide and its three related statements of position are as follows:

Property plant and equipment The preferable accounting principles for hospitals states that property, plant and equipment should be accounted for as part of unrestricted funds. In addition, liabilities that are related to property, plant and equipment should also be accounted for as part of unrestricted funds. Limitations, if any, on the use of proceeds from the disposition of property, plant and equipment should be appropriately disclosed in the financial statements or footnotes thereto.

Depreciation expense should be periodically recognized in the financial statements of hospitals in the same manner as that for commercial enterprises. Reimbursement by third parties for depreciation should be "matched" to the related expense in the financial statements. However, the reimbursement may be shown in the statement of changes in fund balances as a transfer to a restricted fund, from an unrestricted fund. When the reimbursement is actually expended by the hospital, a transfer is made back to unrestricted funds.

Provisions for replacement or expansion of a hospital's facilities should not appear as an expense on the statement of revenues and expenses. Such a provision should appear on the balance sheet as an appropriation of unrestricted funds.

Cost reimbursement which includes an amount for accelerated depreciation will create a timing difference if a different depreciation method is used for financial statement purposes. The deferred revenue from cost reimbursement will be equal to the difference between the two depreciation methods. When the timing difference reverses in subsequent periods, the deferred revenue should be recognized.

Timing differences   The effect of any timing difference should be reflected in the financial statements of hospitals in the same manner as that for a commercial enterprise.

Patient service revenue   Patient service revenue should be accounted for on the accrual basis at established rates, even if the full amount is not expected to be collected. In other words, patient service revenue is accounted for on a gross basis and deductions are made separately from gross revenue, or disclosed in some other manner.

Patient Service Revenue	$85,000
Deductions:	
Charity allowances	$ 7,500
Indigent patients	12,500
Provision for uncollectibles	5,000
	$25,000
Net Patient Service	
Revenue	$60,000

> **OBSERVATION:**   *Other methods of recognizing revenue, other than on the accrual basis reflecting gross revenue, is unacceptable for GAAP. In particular, the "discharge method", which recognizes revenue only at the time the patient is discharged, is definitely not permitted.*

Any difference between the actual payment received for cost reimbursement and amounts accrued at the end of a prior reporting period, should be accounted for in the statement of revenues and expenses as an adjustment to the related allowance account. However, if a difference qualifies as a correction of an error of a prior period, it may be treated as a prior period adjustment in accordance with FASB-16.

> **OBSERVATION:** *The Hospital Audit Guide states that, "Differences should not be treated as prior period adjustments unless they meet the criteria set forth in paragraph 23 of APB-9 (Reporting the Results of Operations), or are deemed to result from an error as indicated in APB-20 (Accounting Changes)."*
>
> *The Hospital Audit Guide's reference to paragraph 23 of APB-9 is apparently incorrect because paragraph 23 of APB-9 was superseded by FASB-16 in June 1977. The Hospital Audit Guide (second edition) was published about a year later in 1978.*

Hospitals operated by a governmental unit   Statement of Position 78-7 requires that government operated hospitals, like all other hospitals, be accounted for as enterprise funds. SOP 78-7 was issued to create more comparability in financial statements of the hospital industry and to rectify the practice of accounting for hospitals by governmental units as special revenue funds.

Donated services and supplies   Hospitals are likely to receive donated services, particularly hospitals operated by religious groups. Full and partial donated services should be recorded at fair value by a hospital if an employer-employee relationship, or its equivalent exists and there is an objective basis for placing a value on the services donated. The donated services should be recorded as nonoperating revenue with a corresponding debit to the appropriate expense account.

The fair market value of donated drugs, medicines, linens, supplies and other material which is usually purchased by the hospital should be recorded as other operating revenue.

Gifts, grants and other contributions   Gifts, grants and other contributions by donors may be restricted as to their use or may be unrestricted. Gifts, grants and other contributions should not usually be credited directly to fund balances, but should be reported in the statement of revenues and expenses. Unrestricted contributions are recorded at fair market value at the date of contribution and are reported as nonoperating revenue in the statement of revenues and expenses.

Gifts, grants and other contributions which are restricted as to their use, usually fall into three categories, as follows:

1. restricted for specific operating purposes
2. restricted to be used for additions to property, plant and equipment
3. restricted as endowment funds

Endowment funds may be classified as either term endowments or pure endowments and both should be accounted for as restricted funds. Usually, the principal of a term endowment may be expended by the governing board of the hospital upon the occurrence of a specific event or passage of time. The principal of a pure endowment may not be expended by the governing board. Pertinent information concerning the term of the endowment and what the funds may be used for, should be disclosed in a footnote to the financial statements. When term endowment funds become available for unrestricted use they should be reported as nonoperating revenue. However, if the term endowment funds remain restricted for a particular purpose, they should continue to be accounted for as restricted funds.

Funds which are restricted for specific operating uses should be accounted for either in a restricted fund or as deferred revenue in an unrestricted fund. When the expenditures are actually made for specific operating uses in accordance with the restrictions, the funds should be reported as other operating revenue.

Donor-restricted funds which must be used for additions to property, plant and equipment are considered as contributions to the hospital's permanent capital and are accounted for as restricted funds. However, when the expenditure is actually made for additions to property, plant and equipment, a transfer should be made from restricted funds to unrestricted funds.

Unrestricted funds A total of all unrestricted funds should appear on the balance sheet clearly designated as unrestricted. The governing board of a hospital may designate unrestricted funds for a particular purpose. In this event, the designated funds should appear as an appropriation of the unrestricted funds. However, the governing board also has the authority to rescind its actions and restore the designated funds to an unrestricted classification. Therefore, the term restricted should not be used for unrestricted funds which are designated by the governing board. Donor-restricted funds and funds designated by the governing board should always be reported separately.

If a hospital does not directly or indirectly control the principal of an endowment-type fund held in trust by outside parties, the funds should not be included in the hospital's financial statements. However, pertinent information concerning these type funds should be disclosed in the hospital's financial statements. Endowment income distributions from funds held in trust by outside parties should be recorded on the accrual basis by a hospital. In addition, the right to any future endowment income should be disclosed on the hospital's financial statements, if appropriate.

Pledges   Pledges may be unrestricted or restricted and should be classified as such in a hospital's financial statements. Restricted pledges must be recorded and reported as restricted funds. Revenue from unrestricted pledges, less an allowance for uncollectibles, should be recorded as nonoperating revenue in the period in which the pledge is made. Pledges received for a future period should be recorded as deferred nonoperating revenue, or included in restricted funds.

Malpractice loss contingencies   Hospital malpractice loss contingencies must be recorded and reported on, in conformity with GAAP (FASB-5 and FASB Interpretation 14). If a malpractice loss contingency is probable as at the date of the financial statements and the loss can be reasonably estimated, an accrual should be made by a charge against revenue.

If it is probable that an unasserted claim will be asserted and there is reasonable possibility of an unfavorable outcome, disclosure of the unasserted claim should be made in the financial statements.

> **OBSERVATION:**   *Because of the significance of malpractice exposure to a hospital, the Hospital Audit Guide recommends that unasserted claims which do not require disclosure under FASB-5 also be fully disclosed in the financial statements.*

Should a hospital become uninsured for malpractice because of deductible provisions or no insurance, all of the pertinent facts should be fully disclosed in the financial statements or footnotes thereto.

> **OBSERVATION:** *An unnumbered Statement of Position, issued March 1, 1978, by the Auditing Standards Division of the AICPA, contains the preferable accounting principles, which are discussed above, for recording and reporting hospital malpractice loss contingencies.*

Marketable equity securities Statement of Position 78-1 covers the *preferable accounting principles* on accounting by hospitals for certain marketable equity securities. SOP 78-1 requires that hospitals comply with existing promulgated GAAP (FASB-12) in accounting for certain marketable equity securities. SOP 78-1 also reaffirms that FASB-12 expressly excludes nonprofit organizations. Thus, hospitals which are operated for profit should comply with the promulgated GAAP (FASB-12) on accounting for certain marketable securities while not-for-profit hospitals are expressly excluded by the same GAAP (FASB-12). However, the Hospital Audit Guide subsequently states that not-for-profit hospitals should also comply with FASB-12.

> **OBSERVATION:** *Requiring that not-for-profit hospitals comply with FASB-12, the Hospital Audit Guide, without formal action of the FASB, apparently amends FASB-12 as far as it affects not-for-profit hospitals.*

Therefore, all hospitals, profit or nonprofit, should comply with the provisions of FASB-12 and cost should no longer be used as a valuation method for marketable securities. Marketable equity securities of all hospitals should be carried at the lower of aggregate cost or market, determined at the balance sheet date. In addition, all of the provisions of FASB-12, including disclosure requirements must be complied with.

> **OBSERVATION:** *Care should be exercised in using the illustrative financial statements which appear in the Hospital Audit Guide. Note 1 to the sample financial statements, which appears on page 48 of the Guide, incorrectly states that the marketable equity securities are stated at "cost".*

Accounting changes   The Hospital Audit Guide requires that adjustments resulting from compliance with its provisions be treated as adjustments of prior periods, and that all financial statements presented be restated to reflect such compliance.

> *OBSERVATION:*   *A change in, or a new, promulgated GAAP, or the issuance of an industry audit guide by the AICPA constitutes sufficient support for a change in an accounting principle (FASB Interpretation-20). However, the correction of an error in previously issued financial statements is not an accounting change (APB-20).*
>
> *Corrections of errors in previously issued financial statements may be made as a prior period adjustment (FASB-16). However, a change in an accounting principle is usually accounted for by reflecting the "cumulative effects" of the change in the income statement of the year the change is made. Thus, it is doubtful whether adjustments resulting from compliance to the Hospital Audit Guide can appropriately be made as prior period adjustments under existing promulgated GAAP.*

Comprehensive Illustration

The following is a comprehensive illustration of the preferable accounting principles contained in this chapter.

NON-PROFIT HOSPITAL
BALANCE SHEET
As of June 30, 1980 and 1979

	1980	1979
ASSETS		
Cash (Note 1)	$ 0,000,000	$00,000,000
Investments (Note 2)	0,000,000	0,000,000
Research grants receivable	0,000,000	0,000,000
Construction grant receivable (Note 3)	0,000,000	—
Contributions receivable	000,000	000,000
Inventories (Note 4)	000,000	000,000
Property and equipment, less accumulated depreciation of $0,000,000 and $0,000,000 (Note 5)	00,000,000	00,000,000
Other assets	000,000	000,000
	$00,000,000	$00,000,000

LIABILITIES AND FUND BALANCE		
Checks issued against future deposits	$ 000,000	$ 000,000
Accounts payable	000,000	000,000
Accrued expenses (Notes 6 and 7)	000,000	000,000
Other liabilities	000,000	00,000
Deferred income (Note 7)	0,000,000	0,000,000
	0,000,000	0,000,000
Commitments and contingencies (Notes 3, 8 and 9)		
Fund balance (Includes $00,000,000 and $00,000,000 Property and Equipment Fund)	00,000,000	00,000,000
	$00,000,000	$00,000,000

See Accompanying Notes to Financial Statements

NON-PROFIT HOSPITAL
STATEMENT OF SUPPORT, REVENUES AND EXPENSES AND CHANGES IN FUND BALANCE
Years Ended June 30, 1980 and 1979

	1980	*1979*
Public support and revenues:		
Public support:		
Contributions	$00,000,000	$00,000,000
Special events (net of direct expenses of $000,000 and $000,000)	000,000	000,000
Total public support	00,000,000	00,000,000
Revenues:		
Research and construction grants	0,000,000	0,000,000
Health insurance	0,000,000	0,000,000
Investment income	000,000	000,000
Cafeteria income	000,000	000,000
Miscellaneous	00,000	000,000
Total revenues	0,000,000	0,000,000
Total public support and revenues	00,000,000	00,000,000
Functional expenses:		
Program services	00,000,000	00,000,000
Supporting services:		
Fund raising	0,000,000	0,000,000
General and administrative	0,000,000	0,000,000
Total supporting services	0,000,000	0,000,000
Total expenses	00,000,000	00,000,000
Public support and revenues		
Over expenses	0,000,000	0,000,000
Fund balance, beginning of year	00,000,000	00,000,000
Fund balance, end of year	$00,000,000	$00,000,000

See Accompanying Notes to Financial Statements

SUMMARY OF ACCOUNTING POLICIES

/Combination

The combined financial statements include the accounts of the Non-Profit Hospital, Associated Charities (AC), and Non-Profit Hospital Foundation. These organizations are commonly controlled and operate under the name and for the exclusive benefit of Non-Profit Hospital. Balances and transaction between the organizations are eliminated.

Investments

Investments are stated at market value. Donated investments are recorded at estimated value at date of receipt.

Inventories

Inventories are valued at the lower of cost (first-in, first-out) or market and consist of drugs, medical, surgical and other general hospital supplies. Donated supplies are recorded at replacement cost at date of receipt.

Property Equipment and Depreciation

Assets purchased are stated at cost and assets donated are recorded at estimated fair market value on the date of receipt. Depreciation is computed over the estimated useful lives of the assets on the straight-line method.

Donated Materials and Services

Donated materials are reflected as contributions in the accompanying financial statements at their estimated values at date of receipt. No amounts have been recorded for donated services as no objective basis is available to measure the value of such services.

Public Support and Revenues

All contributions are considered to be available for unrestricted use unless specifically restricted by the donor. Pledges for contributions are recorded as received and allowances are provided, when necessary, for amounts estimated to be uncollectible. Research grants are recognized as the revenues are earned, which generally is when designated costs are incurred.

Fund Balance

The fund balance of Non-Profit Hospital and affiliated organizations is designated for the future operating and capital expenditure needs of the Hospital.

Federal Tax Status

The Internal Revenue Service has classified Non-Profit Hospital, Associated Charities, and the Non-Profit Hospital Foundation, Inc. as exempt from federal income taxes under Section 501(c)(3) of the United States Internal Revenue Code; as an organization, contributions to which are deductible under Section 170(c) of the Code; and as an organization that is not a private foundation as defined in Section 509(a) of the Code.

NOTES TO FINANCIAL STATEMENTS

Note 1—Cash

Cash accounts are summarized as follows:

	June 30,	
	1980	*1979*
Certificates of deposit	$0,000,000	$ 0,000,000
Savings accounts	0,000,000	0,000,000
Checking accounts	0,000,000	0,000,000
Totals	$0,000,000	$00,000,000

Note 2—Investments

Investments, carried at market value, are summarized as follows:

	June 30,	
	1980	*1979*
Commercial paper	$0,000,000	—
U.S. Government obligations:		
Treasury bills	000,000	0,000,000
Treasury bonds and notes	000,000	000,000
Other government agencies	0,000,000	—
Land	000,000	000,000
Bankers' acceptance notes	000,000	—
Stocks	000,000	000,000
Corporate and municipal bonds	000,000	0,000,000
Totals	$0,000,000	$0,000,000

At June 30, 1980 and 1979, cost of investments exceeded market value (cumulative depreciation) by $00,000 and $00,000, respectively. Included in investment income for the years ended June 30, 1980 and 1979 are $0,000 of unrealized appreciation and $00,000 of unrealized depreciation, respectively.

Note 3—Construction Grants Receivable

The construction grant receivable of $0,000,000 and $0,000,000 at June 30, 1980 and 1979 represents an approved grant to be received from the National Cancer Institute for partial funding of an animal research facility which is estimated to cost approximately $0,000,000. As of June 30, 1980, $00,000 had been spent on construction of the facility.

Note 4—Inventories

Inventories consist of the following:

	June 30,	
	1980	1979
Drugs	$000,000	$000,000
Medical and surgical supplies	000,000	000,000
General supplies	000,000	000,000
Totals	$000,000	$000,000

Note 5—Property and Equipment

Major classes of property and equipment are summarized as follows:

	June 30,	
	1980	1979
Land and improvements	$ 000,000	$ 000,000
Building and improvements	00,000,000	00,000,000
Equipment	0,000,000	0,000,000
Totals	00,000,000	00,000,000
Less accumulated depreciation	0,000,000	0,000,000
Net property and equipment	$00,000,000	$00,000,000

Note 6—Accrued Expenses

Accrued expenses are summarized as follows:

| | June 30, | |
	1980	1979
Vacation pay	$000,000	$000,000
Pension plan contribu-		
tion (Note 8)	00,000	000,000
Salaries	000,000	000,000
Miscellaneous	0,000	0,000
Totals	$000,000	$000,000

Note 7—Deferred Income

Deferred income represents unearned revenues and is summarized as follows:

| | June 30, | |
	1980	1979
Research grants	$0,000,000	$0,000,000
Construction grant	000,000	—
Contributions for spe-		
cific purposes	000,000	00,000
Totals	$0,000,000	$0,000,000

Note 8—Pension Plans

The Hospital maintains a trusteed noncontributory pension plan for substantially all employees over 00 years of age who have completed one year of service. The Hospital's general policy is to fund pension costs accrued. Amounts charged to operations under the plan include normal cost and amortization of past service costs over a 00-year period. At June 30, 1980, the assets of the pension plan exceeded the actuarially computed value of vested benefits. The costs of this plan for the years ended June 30, 1980 and 1979, were $000,000 and $000,000, respectively.

Members of the Hospital's professional staff not covered by this pension plan are covered by a Hospital-sponsored retirement annuity program, which is administered by a medical/academic professional group plan. The costs of this retirement annuity program charged against operations were $000,000 in 1980 and $000,000 in 1979.

AC has a defined contribution retirement plan for all its employees who have one year of service with the organization. The plan was funded by annual contributions to a trust based on a percentage of earnings and years of service with the organization. On January 26, 1980, the Board of Directors agreed to fund its retirement plan through the purchase of a group annuity rather than through its retirement trust, and the assets of the trust were transferred to the insurance carrier for the purchase of the annuity. The contributions to the plan for the years ended June 30, 1980 and 1979 were $00,000 and $00,000, respectively.

Note 9—Leases

The Hospital leases certain equipment and office facilities under noncancellable operating leases which expire at various dates to 1984.

Management expects that in the normal course of operations, leases that expire will be renewed or replaced by other leases. Total rent expense for the year ended June 30, 1980 and 1979, was $000,000 and $000,000, respectively.

At June 30, 1980, the remaining minimum annual rental commitments were as follows:

Year ending June 30	Office facilities	Equipment	Total
1981	$00,000	$000,000	$000,000
1982	00,000	000,000	000,000
1983	00,000	00,000	00,000
1984	—	0,000	0,000
Total minimum lease payments	$00,000	$000,000	$000,000

VOLUNTARY HEALTH AND WELFARE ORGANIZATIONS

Overview

The preferable accounting principles and practices for voluntary health and welfare organizations appear in the industry audit guide entitled "Audits of Voluntary Health and Welfare Organizations", (hereinafter referred to as the Voluntary H&W Guide).

Voluntary health and welfare entities are non-profit organizations which obtain most of their operating funds from donations by the general public. The majority of these organizations use their resources to improve the overall health and welfare of a specific segment of society. Many of these voluntary groups focus their efforts on problems involving the health and welfare of indigent individuals.

Most of the resources of a voluntary health and welfare organization are derived from cash contributions, pledges, and donated services and material. These resources may be restricted or unrestricted. A contribution or pledge may be restricted by the donor for a specific purpose, such as a building fund. Restricted gifts may only be used for the purpose specified by the donee. Obviously, unrestricted gifts may be used for any purpose that the governing board of the voluntary health and welfare organization sees fit. Restricted gifts must be accounted for separately from unrestricted gifts.

A voluntary health and welfare organization may keep its books on the cash basis, accrual basis, or the modified accrual basis, of accounting. However, when financial statements are reported on in conformity with GAAP, the accrual basis of accounting is required.

Because of the necessity to account for restricted gifts separately from unrestricted resources, most organizations use the concept of fund accounting. The following are the more common fund accounts used by voluntary health and welfare organizations:

Current Unrestricted Funds All resources which are unrestricted are accounted for in this fund. The governing board may use these funds to carry out the general operating objectives of the organization. However, the governing board has the power to appropriate unrestricted funds for a designated purpose. In this event, the portion of the fund balance so designated should be appropriately captioned as "appropriated" in the current unrestricted fund section. In other words, the designated portion remains in the current unrestricted fund but is clearly marked as appropriated. Current unrestricted funds designated for a specific purpose should not be transferred to a restricted fund.

Current Restricted Funds These resources are available currently for operating purposes, but may only be used for the purpose specified by the donor.

Plant and Equipment Fund Fixed assets are generally accounted for in this fund. Also, the unexpended portion of gifts made for the purpose of acquiring, replacing or repairing fixed assets, are accounted for in this fund. In addition, any mortgage or liability related to the fixed assets are accounted for in the plant and equipment fund.

Frequently, current unrestricted funds are used to acquire fixed assets. When this occurs, a transfer from the current unrestricted fund to the plant and equipment fund should be made.

When a fixed asset is sold or otherwise disposed of, the gain or loss should be accounted for as income or loss of the plant and equipment fund. The proceeds on the sale of the fixed asset may have to be reinvested in another fixed asset according to the original terms of the gift. However, if the resources to purchase the fixed asset were transferred to the plant and equipment fund from the current unrestricted fund, the proceeds should be transferred back to the unrestricted fund.

Endowment Funds Resources may be donated to an organization for a specific period or in perpetuity, with instructions on how the earnings of the principal may be expended, and what the principal may be used for, if any, after the specific period ends. For example, a $100,000 cash gift may be made by a donor with instructions that the earnings be used for unrestricted purposes, and after the specified period ends, the principal must be returned to the donor. In this case, the earnings on the $100,000 should be periodically transferred to current unrestricted funds and at the end of the specified period the $100,000 is returned to the donor.

The different types of endowments that donors can create are almost endless. However, in accounting for endowment funds, the restrictions of the donor must be clearly followed.

Other Funds   Other funds may be established by a voluntary health and welfare organization to serve specific purposes. For example, an agency fund may be necessary to account for assets which are merely held by the organization with specific instructions on how and when the assets are to be disbursed. Agency funds are sometimes called "custodian funds".

Since the assets received in an agency fund are not the property of the organization, they should not be included in the financial statements. However, agency fees received by the organization for acting as a custodian is income to the organization and should be accounted for as such.

Investments   Investments held by a voluntary health and welfare organization may be unrestricted or restricted. Unrestricted investments are accounted for in an unrestricted fund and income from these investments usually is used for current unrestricted purposes. Restricted investments are accounted for in restricted funds such as an endowment fund, and income from these investments are used in the manner specified by the donor.

Investments may be purchased by the voluntary health and welfare organization or they may be donated to the organization. If the investment is donated to the organization it may be unrestricted or restricted. The receipt of the investment from the donor is accounted for in the appropriate fund (unrestricted or restricted) as income (contribution). Donated investments are recorded and accounted for at their fair value at the date of the donation.

The basis of all investments should be fully disclosed in the financial statements and such basis should be used consistently for each type of investment in each fund of the organization. It is preferable that both the cost and market value for all investments be disclosed in the financial statements or footnotes thereto. Investments or assets transferred from one fund to another fund should be recorded at market value on the date of transfer. Gain or loss should be recorded by the fund making the transfer and the recipient fund should account for the investment or asset at market value.

The Voluntary H&W Guide states that the prevalent method of accounting for purchased investments is cost and for donated investments fair market value at the date of gift. However, the Voluntary H&W Guide also states that purchased investments may be carried at market value.

Income and Gains and Losses   Income from investments and gains and losses on investments are accounted for differently in each fund, as follows:

Unrestricted Funds   Income and gains and losses from investments in unrestricted funds are accounted for as unrestricted revenue. Income and gains and losses from investments in restricted funds which are legally available for unrestricted purposes are accounted for as unrestricted revenue.

Restricted Funds   The Voluntary H&W Guide states that income and gains and losses from investments in restricted funds should be included in the revenue of the restricted funds.

The Voluntary H&W Guide states that investment income of endowment funds which is restricted by the donor should be included in the revenue of the appropriate restricted fund.

Plant Fund and Depreciation   As mentioned previously, most voluntary health and welfare organizations maintain a separate fund to account for fixed assets used in the organization's program.

Fixed assets may be acquired by purchase or by donation. Purchased fixed assets should be accounted for at cost, and donated fixed assets at market value on the date of donation. Donated fixed assets are recorded as income (contribution) in the plant fund upon their receipt. However, if donor-imposed restrictions prevent the use or disposal of the donated fixed asset, then their receipt should be recorded as income (contribution) to a donor restricted fund.

Unrestricted donations of fixed assets which will be converted to cash or used for the production of income should not be recorded in the plant fund. Instead, these unrestricted donated fixed assets should be recorded as income (contribution) to the current unrestricted fund and appear on the balance sheet of the current unrestricted funds.

The Voluntary H&W Guide requires that depreciation on fixed assets is usually appropriate. Depreciation expense should appear in the statement of activity of the fund in which the fixed assets are recorded.

Cash Contributions and Pledges To a large extent, voluntary health and welfare organizations depend upon contributions and pledges from the general public to support the activities of the organization. Contributions may be in cash or pledges, and also may be unrestricted or restricted. A contribution or pledge may be restricted for operating purposes, restricted for the acquisition of fixed assets, or a restricted endowment. The restrictions may also provide for current or future use. All contributions restricted for future use are recorded as deferred income and appear as a deferred credit on the balance sheet of the appropriate fund.

A provision for uncollectible pledges should be provided based on prior experience and an aging of the receivables. The allowance for uncollectible pledges and the net pledges receivable should be appropriately disclosed in the financial statements of the voluntary health and welfare organization.

A voluntary health and welfare organization may use one or more of the following methods to solicit support for its activities:

1. direct-mail
2. radio and television
3. special events
4. door-to-door solicitation
5. from other agencies or organizations

Contributions collected by other organizations and earmarked for a voluntary health and welfare organization should be accounted for as receivables.

Donated Material and Services If significant in amount, donated materials should be recorded at their fair value on the date of receipt. However, donated materials must have a fair value that can be objectively determined. Donated materials which merely pass through the organization to an ultimate beneficiary, such as used clothing, should not be recorded, unless the amounts involved are substantial. In that event, the donated materials should be recorded as a contribution with an offsetting entry to expenditures, and such substantial amounts should be appropriately disclosed in the financial statements.

Donated and contributed services should not be recorded as revenue and an offsetting expense, unless all of the following conditions exist:

1. The services are significant and represent recurring normal activities of the nonprofit entity which would ordinarily be performed by salaried personnel if the donated services were not available.
2. The nonprofit entity controls the donated services in the same manner as an employer-employee relationship, including control over time, location, nature and performance of the donated services.
3. The amount to be recorded as donated or contributed services can be clearly determined by the nonprofit entity.
4. The services of the nonprofit entity are not primarily for the benefit of its members. Thus, religious, professional, trade, labor, and political organizations would not record donated or contributed services.

The treatment of recording or not recording donated or contributed services should be fully disclosed by footnote to the financial statements.

If the fair value of significant amounts of material and facilities can be reasonably determined, they should be recorded by a nonprofit entity. Material and facilities of insignificant value should not be recorded, as well as materials and facilities which pass through the nonprofit organization to charitable beneficiaries.

Functional Classification of Expenses Expenses should be classified and grouped by the functions of the particular organization. The most common groups of functional classifications for a voluntary health and welfare organization are (1) program support services, (2) fund raising and (3) management and general. The total amount of each functional expense should be clearly disclosed in the financial statements.

Program support expenses are expenditures which are directly related to the organizations program. For example, if an organization's program was cancer research then only those expenditures directly related to the actual research on cancer should be classified as program support expenses. Expenditures for fund raising or general and administrative expenses should not be classified as program support expenses.

Fund raising expenditures should be also classified functionally and separately disclosed in the financial statements. Costs of mailing lists, postage, direct mail, personnel salaries, and advertisements for funds, are properly classified as fund raising expenses and should be functionally classified and separately disclosed in the financial statements.

The management and general expense classification includes overhead expenses, such as general bookkeeping, budgeting, and the general expense of the governing board of the organization. Management and general expenses should be functionally classified and separately disclosed in the financial statements.

Obviously, no two organizations are likely to have the exact same expenses and functional classification. Large organizations may have many more functional classifications if they have many different programs. The important point to remember is that voluntary health and welfare organizations and most nonprofit entities should report their expenses on a functional basis.

> **OBSERVATION:** *For a more detailed discussion on the functional classification of expenses see SOP 78-10 (Principles and Reporting Practices for Certain Nonprofit Organizations) which appears elsewhere in this publication.*

Financial Statements The actual books and records of a nonprofit organization need not necessarily be kept on the accrual basis of accounting. However, financial statements which purport to be in conformity with GAAP must be prepared and reported on the accrual basis. In other words, financial statements for nonprofit organizations should generally be presented on the accrual basis to be in conformity with GAAP, but the underlying books need not be kept on the accrual basis of accounting.

Cash basis financial statements should ordinarily be considered special purpose reports and reported on by the independent auditor, as such. However, if cash basis financial statements are not materially different than the same statements would be on the accrual basis, the independent auditor may conclude that they are presented in conformity with GAAP.

In those situations, where a nonprofit organization has both restricted and unrestricted resources, fund accounting provides for the necessary segregation of the restricted resources and is considered desirable. Where restricted resources exist and fund accounting is not utilized to segregate resources, all significant restrictions on resources must be fully disclosed in the basic financial statements.

The basic financial statements for a nonprofit organization should include a balance sheet, statement of changes in financial position, statement of activity, and all necessary related footnotes.

The balance sheet should reflect the assets, liabilities, and fund balances of the nonprofit organization. Assets and liabilities should be clearly classified as current or noncurrent in accordance with the normal operating cycle of the enterprise. Restricted and unrestricted fund balances should be adequately labeled and appropriately segregated. The total amounts of restricted and unrestricted funds should be separately set forth on the balance sheet except for those plant funds which are not susceptible to segregation. The sources of funds used to acquire plant assets are often a combination of unrestricted and restricted funds which cannot be clearly segregated. Thus, plant funds are usually reported separately, or segregated into restricted and unrestricted funds and combined with other restricted and unrestricted funds.

Restricted resources should be separately reported in the balance sheet as part of their related fund balance, or reported in the balance sheet as deferred revenue until the restrictions are complied with.

The statement of changes in financial position summarizes all of the financing and investing activities of the nonprofit organization and reflects the amount of working capital generated from or used in operations for the period (APB-19).

The statement of activity should present the results of operations and changes in fund balances for the period and also includes a reconciliation of the beginning and ending fund balances. The statement of activity should reflect the principal sources of support and revenue, and additions to endowment, plant, and capital funds.

A separate statement of activity and separate statement of

changes in fund balances may be utilized instead of one statement of activity depicting both activities.

The statement of activity should clearly indicate the excess or deficiency of support and revenue, over expenses, before capital additions and after capital additions, if any.

> **OBSERVATION:** *For a more complete discussion on financial statements for nonprofit organizations see SOP 78-10 (Accounting Principles and Practices for Certain Nonprofit Organizations) elsewhere in this publication.*

Comprehensive Illustration

The following is a comprehensive illustration of the preferable accounting principles contained in this chapter.

VOLUNTARY HEALTH AND WELFARE ORGANIZATION BALANCE SHEET
As of December 31, 1980 and 1979

	1980	1979
Current Funds—Unrestricted		
Assets		
Cash, including $00,000 in 1980 and $000,000 in 1979 in interest-bearing accounts	$ 00,000	$ 000,000
Marketable securities, at cost (approximates market)	000,000	000,000
Accounts receivable from sales of promotional materials, less allowance for doubtful accounts of $00,000 in 1980 and $00,000 in 1979	000,000	000,000
Membership support receivable	0,000,000	0,000,000
Other accounts receivable	00,000	00,000
Travel and miscellaneous advances	00,000	00,000
Prepaid pension costs (Note 4)	000,000	000,000
Prepaid expenses and other assets	00,000	00,000
	$0,000,000	$0,000,000
Liabilities and Fund Balances		
Accounts payable	$ 000,000	$ 000,000
Deposits on promotional materials	00,000	0,000
Deferred revenue (Note 2)		
Membership support	0,000,000	0,000,000
Training programs	00,000	00,000
Total liabilities	0,000,000	0,000,000
Fund balances (Exhibit):		
Designated by the Board of Governors for special purposes	000,000	000,000
Undesignated, available for general activities	000,000	000,000
	000,000	000,000
	$0,000,000	$0,000,000

Current funds—Restricted

Assets

Cash in interest-bearing accounts	$ 000,000	$ 000,000
Marketable securities, at cost (approximates market)	00,000	000,000
Personnel development program pledges receivable due through 1981 (Note 2)	000,000	0,000,000
Grants and other receivables:		
National Corporate Development	000,000	000,000
Other	00,000	—
	$0,000,000	$0,000,000

Liabilities and Fund Balances

Accounts payable	$ 00,000	$ 0,000
Deferred revenues (Note 2)	000,000	0,000,000
Fund balances	000,000	0,000,000
	$0,000,000	$0,000,000

Land, Building and Equipment Fund

Assets

Pledges receivable due through 1981	$ 0,000	$ 00,000
Fixed assets (Notes 2 and 3)		
Land	000,000	000,000
Improvements other than building	00,000	00,000
Building	0,000,000	0,000,000
Leasehold improvements	00,000	00,000
Furniture and equipment	000,000	000,000
Less—Accumulated depreciation	(000,000)	(000,000)
	0,000,000	0,000,000
	$0,000,000	$0,000,000

Liabilities and Fund Balances

Mortgage note payable (Note 3)	$0,000,000	$0,000,000
Fund balances:		
Expended	000,000	000,000
Unexpended—Restricted	0,000	00,000
	000,000	000,000
	$0,000,000	$0,000,000

VOLUNTARY HEALTH AND WELFARE ORGANIZATION
STATEMENT OF SUPPORT, REVENUE, AND EXPENSES AND CHANGES IN FUND BALANCES

Year Ended December 31, 1980, With Comparative Totals for 1979

	Current Funds		1980 Land, Building and Equipment Fund	Total All Funds	
	Unrestricted	Restricted		1980	1979
Public Support and Revenue (Note 2):					
Public support—					
Membership support	$0,000,000	—	$ —	$0,000,000	$0,000,000
Contributions	00,000	000,000	0,000	0,000,000	0,000,000
Total public support	0,000,000	000,000	0,000	0,000,000	0,000,000
Grants from governmental agencies	—	00,000	—	00,000	00,000
Other revenues—					
Service memberships	00,000	—	—	00,000	00,000
Sale of supplies and services (Note 2)	00,000	—	(00,000)	(0,000)	000,000
Program service fees	000,000	000,000	—	0,000,000	0,000,000
Rental income	00,000	—	—	00,000	00,000
Investment income	000,000	—	—	000,000	000,000
Gain on sale of fixed assets	0,000	—	—	0,000	0,000
Miscellaneous	00,000	—	—	00,000	0,000
Total other revenue	0,000,000	000,000	(00,000)	0,000,000	0,000,000
Total public support and revenue	0,000,000	0,000,000	(00,000)	$0,000,000	$0,000,000

Expenses:

Program services (Note 1)—					
Planning	000,000	000,000	00,000	$0,000,000	$0,000,000
Campaign support	0,000,000	000,000	00,000	0,000,000	0,000,000
Allocations	00,000	—	000	00,000	000,000
Communications	000,000	—	00,000	000,000	000,000
Management improvement services	0,000,000	000,000	00,000	000,000	000,000
Total program services	0,000,000	0,000,000	000,000	0,000,000	0,000,000
Supporting Services—					
Management and general	0,000,000	—	00,000	0,000,000	000,000
Fund raising	00,000	—	0,000	00,000	00,000
Total supporting services	0,000,000	—	00,000	0,000,000	000,000
Total expenses	0,000,000	0,000,000	000,000	$0,000,000	$0,000,000
Excess (deficiency) of public support and revenue over expenses	000,000	(000,000)	(000,000)		(000,000)
Other Changes In Fund Balances:					
Property and equipment acquisitions and mortgage payments from unrestricted funds	(000,000)	—	000,000		000,000
Fund transfers	000,000	(000,000)	—		—
Return to donor, unexpended grant funds	—	(0,000)	—		—
FUND BALANCES, beginning of year	000,000	0,000,000	000,000		000,000
FUND BALANCES, end of year	$ 000,000	$ 000,000	$000,000		$000,000

VOLUNTARY HEALTH AND WELFARE ORGANIZATION
STATEMENT OF FUNCTIONAL EXPENSES
Year Ended December 31, 1980, With Comparative Totals For 1979

	Program Services						Supporting Services				
	Planning	Campaign Support	Allocations	Communications	Management Improvement Services	Total	Management and General	Fund Raising	Total	Total 1980	Total 1979
Salaries	$ 000,000	$ 000,000	$ 0,000	$ 000,000	$0,000,000	$0,000,000	$ 000,000	$ 00,000	$ 000,000	$0,000,000	$0,000,000
Employee benefits (Note 4)	00,000	000,000	000	00,000	000,000	000,000	000,000	0,000	000,000	000,000	000,000
Payroll taxes, etc.	00,000	00,000	00	00,000	00,000	000,000	00,000	000	00,000	000,000	000,000
Total employee compensation	000,000	0,000,000	00,000	000,000	0,000,000	0,000,000	000,000	00,000	000,000	0,000,000	0,000,000
Professional fees and contract service payments	000,000	000,000	0,000	00,000	000,000	000,000	00,000	0,000	000,000	000,000	000,000
Supplied	0,000	00,000	(0.000)	0,000	00,000	00,000	00,000	0,000	00,000	00,000	00,000
Telephone	00,000	00,000	000	00,000	00,000	000,000	00,000	0,000	00,000	000,000	000,000
Postage and Shipping	00,000	00,000	0,000	00,000	00,000	000,000	0,000	000	0,000	000,000	000,000
Occupancy	00,000	00,000	000	00,000	00,000	000,000	000,000	0,000	000,000	000,000	000,000
Printing, artwork, etc.	000,000	000,000	00,000	00,000	000,000	000,000	000,000	0,000	000,000	000,000	000,000
Conferences, conventions, meetings and major trips	000,000	000,000	00,000	00,000	000,000	000,000	00,000	000	00,000	000,000	000,000
Subscriptions and reference publications	0,000	0,000	00	000	0,000	00,000	0,000	00	0,000	00,000	00,000
Membership dues	00,000	000	000	000	0,000	00,000	0,000	00	0,000	00,000	00,000
Scholarship awards	00,000	00,000	000	000	000,000	000,000	0,000	0	0,000	000,000	000,000
Rental and maintenance of equipment	0,000	0,000	00	00,000	00,000	00,000	00,000	000	00,000	00,000	00,000
Personnel acquisitions and other expenses	0,000	0,000	00	000	0,000	0,000	000,000	0,000	000,000	000,000	00,000
Total before depreciation	0,000,000	0,000,000	00,000	000,000	0,000,000	0,000,000	0,000,000	00,000	0,000,000	0,000,000	0,000,000
Depreciation of buildings and equipment (Note 2)	00,000	00,000	000	00,000	00,000	000,000	00,000	0,000	00,000	000,000	000,000
Total expenses	$0,000,000	$0,000,000	$ 00,000	$ 000,000	$0,000,000	$0,000,000	$0,000,000	$ 00,000	$0,000,000	$0,000,000	$0,000,000

VOLUNTARY HEALTH AND WELFARE ORGANIZATION
SUPPLEMENTARY STATEMENT OF CHANGES IN CURRENT UNRESTRICTED FUND BALANCES
Year Ended December 31, 1980 (Exhibit)

	Designated by the Board of Governors for Special Purposes					Undesignated, Available for General Activities	Total
	Film Revolving	Consulting Service and International	Program Development	Pension Plan Prepayment Note 4	Total		
Total public support and revenue	$ —	$ —	$ —	$ —	$ —	$0,000,000	$0,000,000
Total expenses	—	—	—	00,000	00,000	0,000,000	0,000,000
Excess (deficiency) of support and revenue over expenses	—	—	—	(00,000)	(00,000)	000,000	000,000
Property and equipment acquisitions and mortgage payments from unrestricted funds	—	—	—	—	—	(000,000)	(000,000)
Transfers	—	0,000	00,000	000,000	000,000	000,000	000,000
Fund balance, beginning of year	000,000	0,000	00,000	000,000	000,000	000,000	000,000
Fund balance, end of year	$000,000	$0,000	$00,000	$000,000	$000,000	$ 000,000	$ 000,000

See Accompanying Notes to Financial Statements

NOTES TO FINANCIAL STATEMENTS

Note 1—Voluntary Health and Welfare Organization

Voluntary Health and Welfare Organization ("the Company") is a national association supported primarily by member organizations, receives annual membership support based upon an allocation of the members' contributions from the public.

Note 2—Summary of Significant Accounting Policies

The accompanying financial statements were prepared to conform with the Industry Audit Guide for Voluntary Health and Welfare Organizations of the American Institute of Certified Public Accountants and the book, *Accounting and Financial Reporting*, published by the Company.

Expenditures for land, building and equipment in excess of $000 are capitalized. Depreciation is calculated using the straight-line method over the following useful lives.

Improvements other than building	10 years
Building	35 years
Furniture and equipment	3-5 years

Membership support is net of members' related fund-raising expenses.

Contributions received directly, pledges for the personnel development program, and grants from corporations and foundations for special programs are recognized as receivables in the year in which the pledges or grants are received. The related revenue is deferred until the year specified for use by the donor.

Certain member pledges for the personnel development program entitle the professional staff of those members to participate in training programs at no additional cost. Costs of such training are reflected as expenses of the program when incurred.

Deferred membership support revenue represents pledges and payments received from local member organizations for 1981 support.

Sales of supplies are recognized upon passage of title to the purchaser. Fees for services are recognized at the time the service is rendered. Sales of supplies and services are reported net of directly related expenses of $0,000,000 in 1980 and $0,000,000 in 1979, including allocated depreciation of $00,000 in 1980 and $00,000 in 1979.

Note 3—Mortgage Note Payable

The mortgage note payable bears annual interest of 00% and is secured by the building, land and related improvements. Principal and interest payments of $00,000 are due monthly through September 1999.

Note 4—Employee Benefits

The Company has a noncontributory pension plan covering substantially all employees. Pension expense was $000,000 in 1980 and $000,000 in 1979. Prior service costs are being amortized over 40 years, for the basic plan, and over 30 years for amendments. Pension cost is funded as accrued. During 1978, the Company made a prepayment of its accrued pension liability of $000,000. This amount is being amortized over 10 years. As of January 1, 1980, the actuarially computed value of vested benefits exceeded fund assets, including the prepayment, by approximately $000,000.

Employees accrue vacation during each vacation year ending June 30. Vacation earned during a vacation year must be taken within six months after the end of such year and may be paid only upon termination. In addition, employees involuntarily terminated are allowed severance pay at varying amounts depending upon classification and length of service. As of December 31, 1980 and 1979, the Company had established a liability of $000,000 and $00,000, respectively, for accrued vacation and termination benefits.

Note 5—Custodian Fund

As of December 31, 1980, the Company held $0,000 in an interest-bearing account relating to a custodian fund for labor staff conferences.

CERTAIN NONPROFIT ORGANIZATIONS

Overview

The following industry audit guides have been issued by the AICPA covering certain types of nonprofit organizations:

1. Hospital Audit Guide
2. Audits of Colleges and Universities
3. Audits of Voluntary Health and Welfare Organizations
4. Audits of State and Local Governmental Units (Excluded from FASB-32)

SOP 78-10 expressly applies to all nonprofit organizations not covered by the above listed industry audit guides. Thus, all nonprofit organizations are now covered by specialized accounting principles and reporting practices which are considered to be preferable for the purposes of APB-20 (Accounting Changes).

Preferable Accounting Principles

SOP 78-10 states that financial information prepared for internal use may be reported in any manner that management or the governing board of an institution deems appropriate under the circumstances. However, financial statements prepared for persons outside the management of the nonprofit organization must comply with the provisions of SOP 78-10.

Accrual basis and fund accounting The actual books and records of a nonprofit organization need not necessarily be kept on the accrual basis of accounting. However, financial statements which purport to be in conformity with GAAP must be prepared and reported on the accrual basis. In other words, financial statements for nonprofit organizations should generally be presented on the accrual basis to be in conformity with GAAP, but the underlying books need not be kept on the accrual basis of accounting.

Cash basis financial statements should ordinarily be considered special purpose reports and reported on by the independent auditor, as such. However, if cash basis financial statements are not materially different than the same statements would be on the accrual basis, the independent auditor may conclude that they are presented in conformity with GAAP.

In those situations, where a nonprofit organization has both restricted and unrestricted resources, fund accounting provides for the necessary segregation of the restricted resources and is considered desirable. Where restricted resources exist and fund accounting is not utilized to segregate resources, all significant restrictions on resources must be fully disclosed in the basic financial statements.

The basic financial statements for a nonprofit organization should include a balance sheet, statement of changes in financial position, statement of activity, and all necessary related footnotes.

The balance sheet should reflect the assets, liabilities, and fund balances of the nonprofit organization. Assets and liabilities should be clearly classified as current or noncurrent in accordance with the normal operating cycle of the enterprise. Restricted and unrestricted fund balances should be adequately labeled and appropriately segregated. The total amounts of restricted and unrestricted funds should be separately set forth on the balance sheet except for those plant funds which are not susceptible to segregation. The sources of funds used to acquire plant assets are often a combination of unrestricted and restricted funds which cannot be clearly segregated. Thus, plant funds are usually reported separately, or segregated into restricted and unrestricted funds and combined with other restricted and unrestricted funds.

Restricted resources should be separately reported in the balance sheet as part of their related fund balance, or reported in the balance sheet as deferred revenue until the restrictions are complied with.

The statement of changes in financial position summarizes all of the financing and investing activities of the nonprofit organization and reflects the amount of working capital generated from or used in operations for the period (APB-19).

The statement of activity should present the results of operations and changes in fund balances for the period and also includes a reconciliation of the beginning and ending fund balances. The statement of activity should reflect the principal sources of support and revenue, and additions to endowment, plant, and capital funds.

A separate statement of activity and separate statement of changes in fund balances may be utilized instead of one statement of activity depicting both activities.

The statement of activity should clearly indicate the excess or deficiency of support and revenue, over expenses, before capital additions and after capital additions, if any.

Comparative financial statements for nonprofit organizations are desirable but not required by SOP 78-10.

Combined financial statements   SOP 78-10 defines control as the direct or indirect ability of one nonprofit enterprise to influence the direction of the management and policies of another nonprofit enterprise by ownership, contract, or otherwise. Combined financial statements are required if one or more of the following conditions is met:

1. Control of one nonprofit enterprise over another enterprise.
2. A reporting entity allows other separate entities to solicit funds in its name and substantially all solicited funds are transferred to, or otherwise used by the reporting entity.
3. Resources are transferred to another separate entity by a reporting entity and such resources are held for the benefit of the reporting entity.
4. A controlled entity which performs assigned functions for a reporting entity and whose funds are from sources other than public contributions.

Combined financial statements of nonprofit enterprises should disclose the relationship between all combined entities.

Loosely affiliated local entities need not be combined with a parent or national entity where resources are substantially collected and expended in the local area. However, local affiliates and affiliates of entities which do not meet the criteria for combined financial statements should be fully disclosed in the separate financial statements of all affiliated entities.

The provisions of SOP 78-10 concerning combined financial statements do not apply to religious organizations if the combined statements would result in meaningless financial information.

Disclosure of contributions to a nonprofit entity by its board members, employees, or officers, is not required, providing no reciprocal economic benefits flow to these individuals as a result of their contributions.

Support, revenue, and capital additions   The statement of activity for nonprofit organizations is sometimes called the "Statement of Support, Revenue, Expenses, Capital Additions, and Changes in Fund Balances", or sometimes just the "Statement of Changes in Fund Balances". A reconciliation of the beginning and ending fund balances which shows the activity for the period should be included as part of the statement of activity.

Revenues for a nonprofit entity may come from dues, services, ticket sales, and investment income. However, in most instances, revenues do not produce enough funds to cover regular operating costs and nonprofit organizations must seek support from individuals, corporations, foundations, governmental units, and others. Thus, support funds are different from revenues and should be appropriately segregated in the statement of activity. Revenue and support funds may be unrestricted or restricted to a particular use by the donor or because of legal restrictions.

Restricted funds may be classified as capital additions or as current restricted resources. Capital additions include resources which have been restricted by the donor, or otherwise, to be used for endowment, plant, or loan funds, for an extended period, or permanently. Investment income and gains or losses on investments held in capital funds may also be restricted to become part of the principal of the restricted capital fund. Thus, this type of investment income and gains or losses are also properly classified as capital additions.

Until actually used for their restricted purpose, resources restricted for the acquisition of plant assets, should be classified on the balance sheet as deferred capital support. Only when these resources are actually used for their restricted purpose, should they be reported in the statement of activity as capital additions.

As mentioned previously, the statement of activity should clearly indicate the excess or deficiency of support and revenue, over expenses, before capital additions, if any, and after capital additions.

Capital additions do not include restricted resources that must be used for current or future program activities or supporting services. These types of restricted resources are recorded as revenue in the statement of activity when economic compliance with the donor's restrictions are made by the nonprofit entity. If economic compliance has not been made, the restricted resources should be accounted for on the balance sheet as deferred revenue. Economic compliance is made when the nonprofit entity incurs expenses for the particular restriction in the manner specified by the donor. Only expenses incurred after the receipt of the restricted contribution can be considered unless the donor has agreed otherwise. Thus, if an appeal is made by a nonprofit entity for a specific program and contributions are received, then economic compliance will occur when and to the extent that subsequent expenses are incurred for the specific program. In other words, revenue or support may be recognized to the extent that expenses are incurred which comply with the donor's restrictions. Any amounts that can not be recognized should be accounted for as deferred revenue or support in the balance sheet.

Legally enforceable pledges should be recorded as assets and reported on the balance sheet at their estimated realizable values. Pledges may be unrestricted or restricted. If restricted, they may be capital additions, or for support and revenue, and should be accounted for accordingly.

Donated and contributed services   Donated and contributed services should not be recorded as revenue and an offsetting expense, unless all of the following conditions exist:

1. The services are significant and represent recurring normal activities of the nonprofit entity which would ordinarily be performed by salaried personnel if the donated services were not available.
2. The nonprofit entity controls the donated services in the same manner as an employer-employee relationship, including control over time, location, nature and performance of the donated services.
3. The amount to be recorded as donated or contributed services can be clearly determined by the nonprofit entity.
4. The services of the nonprofit entity are not primarily for the benefit of its members. Thus, religious, professional, trade, labor, and political organizations would not record donated or contributed services.

The treatment of recording or not recording donated or contributed services should be fully disclosed by footnote to the financial statements.

If the fair value of significant amounts of material and facilities can be reasonably determined, they should be recorded by a nonprofit entity. Material and facilities of insignificant value should not be recorded, as well as materials and facilities which pass through the nonprofit organization to charitable beneficiaries.

Transfer of endowment funds   The "total return" approach to the management of investments of endowment and quasi-endowment funds has been utilized by some nonprofit organizations. A "spending rate" is established by the governing board which is met by traditional yields (dividends and interest). If the traditional yields are insufficient to meet the "spending rate" then a portion of the realized net gains on endowment or quasi-endowment investments is made available by the governing board to make up part or all of the deficiency. Sometimes unrealized net gains are also made available by the governing board. SOP 78-10 requires that any net gains (realized or unrealized) from endowment investments which are used currently, should be accounted for as a transfer of endowment funds to other funds. In the event that net gains from endowment investments are transferred to a restricted fund which is reported as deferred support and revenue, the net gains from endowment investments should be transferred as deferred support and revenue of that restricted fund. A transfer does not occur when net gains from quasi-endowment investments are involved because quasi-endowment funds are already supposed to be accounted for as part of current funds.

Marketable securities and other investments   SOP 78-10 requires that marketable securities and other investments be reported in the financial statements of nonprofit entities, as follows:

Marketable Debt Securities   where there is the intention and ability to hold debt securities to their maturity, they should be reported at amortized cost, market value, or the lower of amortized cost or market value.

Marketable Debt and Equity Securities   where these securities are not expected to be held to maturity, they should be reported at either market value, or the lower of cost or market value.

Other Investments   should be reported at either fair value or the lower of cost or fair value.

All investments in each of the three groups above should be consistently valued by the same method. If market value is not used as a basis of valuation for a particular group, then market value for the particular group should be disclosed in the financial statements. Increases or decreases in market value for investments carried at market value, should be recognized in the period in which they occur.

Declines in investments carried at the lower of amortized cost or market value should be recognized when the aggregate market value of a particular group of investments is less than the aggregate amortized cost of the group. Subsequent recoveries of aggregate market value should be recorded in the period of recovery, but in no event exceed the original cost of the group. Adjustments in valuation of noncurrent investments should be recognized by increasing or decreasing the related fund balance. Adjustments in valuation of current investments are reported in the statement of activity in the same manner as realized gains or losses. Investments held in current restricted funds should be treated as current investments for the purposes of adjusting valuations.

If a restricted fund is a party to an interfund sale or exchange of an investment the following applies:

1. The buying fund records the purchase at fair value.
2. The selling fund should recognize a gain or loss equal to the difference between the carrying amount of the investment and the fair value at the date of sale or exchange.

With the exception of life, income, and custodial funds, the notes to the financial statements should disclose the following for all funds:

1. Total investment income for the period.
2. A summary of the total realized and unrealized gains and losses from investments for the period.

> **OBSERVATION:** *The provisions of SOP 78-10 concerning marketable equity securities conflict with those of SOP 78-1 (see Hospital Audit Guide). SOP 78-10 permits the use of market value in excess of cost as a valuation method where SOP 78-1 closely follows the provisions of FASB-12 (Marketable Securities).*
>
> *Both SOP 78-10 and SOP 78-1 constitute an amendment to FASB-12 insofar as FASB-12 expressly excludes nonprofit entities from its provisions. SOP 78-1 expressly applies the promulgated GAAP of FASB-12 to nonprofit entities, while FASB-12 expressly excludes nonprofit entities. SOP 78-10 contains most of the promulgated GAAP of FASB-12, but also establishes market value in excess of cost as a valuation method.*
>
> *A reasonable solution for the inconsistencies between SOP 78-10, SOP 78-1 and FASB-12, would be to amend FASB-12 to include nonprofit entities, and amend SOP 78-10 to eliminate the use of market value in excess of cost as a valuation method.*

Functional expense classification The cost of providing services or activities of a nonprofit entity which receives substantial contributions from the general public should be reported on a functional basis in the statement of activity. If contributions from the general public are insignificant, a nonprofit entity may use another basis to report its services or activities, but the functional basis is still preferred. In the event that the functional basis of reporting services or activities is not used, notes to the financial statements should contain a description of the basic services and programs of the nonprofit entity. The costs of each significant program and supporting activity should be presented separately on a functional basis in the statement of activity.

SOP 78-10 requires that nonprofit entities record purchased fixed assets at cost and donated fixed assets at fair value at the date of receipt. SOP 78-10 requires retroactive adjustments to capitalize fixed assets which previously have not been capitalized. In addition, the amount of any assets pledged as collateral and the basis of their valuation should be disclosed in the financial statements.

Recognition of depreciation expense as a cost is required by SOP 78-10. Depreciation expense should be systematic and rational and allocate the cost of a fixed asset over its estimated useful life. The amount of depreciation expense for historical cost assets and other than historical cost assets should be separately disclosed in the financial statements.

Assets that are not exhaustible and structures used primarily as houses of worship need not be depreciated.

Inexhaustible collections owned by museums, art galleries, botanical gardens, and libraries, should be capitalized at cost, if purchased, or at fair value, if donated. However, they should not be depreciated unless they are clearly exhaustible. Alternative methods of valuing these collections should be used if historical cost is not available. However, if it is clearly impractical to determine a value for such collections they need not be capitalized. In this event, the word "collection" should appear on the balance sheet with no dollar amount, and a footnote to the financial statements should fully disclose and describe the collection.

Interfund loans Loans from restricted, endowment or plant funds may sometimes be authorized by the governing board of a nonprofit entity. Interest on such loans may or may not be authorized by the governing board. If legal restrictions exist against lending or recording such loans, appropriate disclosure should be made in the financial statements. When the intended sources for repayment of interfund loans are not readily available, the loan should be considered permanent and recorded as an interfund transfer.

Significant amounts of interfund loans of restricted funds should be fully disclosed in the financial statements, or footnotes thereto.

Unrestricted funds A total of all unrestricted funds should appear on the balance sheet clearly designated as unrestricted. The governing board of a nonprofit entity may designate unrestricted funds for a particular purpose. In this event, the designated funds should appear as an appropriation of the unrestricted funds. However, the governing board also has the authority to rescind its actions and restore the designated funds to an unrestricted classification. Therefore, the term restricted should not be used for unrestricted funds which are designated by the governing board. Donor restricted funds and funds designated as restricted by the governing board should always be reported separately.

If a nonprofit entity does not directly or indirectly control the principal of an endowment-type fund held in trust by outside parties, the funds should not be included in the nonprofit entity's financial statement. However, pertinent information concerning these type funds should be disclosed in the nonprofit entity's financial statements. Endowment income distributions from funds held in trust by outside parties should be recorded on the accrual basis by a nonprofit entity. In addition, the right to any future endowment income should be disclosed in the nonprofit entity's financial statements, if appropriate.

Transition The FASB presently has on its agenda a project entitled "Objectives of Financial Reporting by Nonbusiness Organizations", which may contain conflicting conclusions than those of SOP 78-10. Thus, SOP 78-10 expressly concludes that the principles and practices it contains, should not be adopted until after the FASB completes its project. An announcement will be made as to the specific date that SOP 78-10 will be adopted, after the FASB concludes its similar project. However, nonprofit entities may voluntarily adopt the preferable accounting principles appearing in SOP 78-10 at an earlier date, if they desire.

> *OBSERVATION: FASB-32 includes SOP 78-10 as one of the publications containing preferable accounting principles. The effective date for FASB-32 is October 31, 1979. Thus, one may conclude that the preferable accounting principles in SOP 78-10 are effective as of October 31, 1979 and nonprofit entities making a change in an accounting principle must change to those in SOP 78-10.*

PREFERABLE ACCOUNTING PRINCIPLES

MISCELLANEOUS

SECURITIES BROKERS AND DEALERS

Overview

Brokers and dealers in securities may provide many different types of service. The major business of most brokers and dealers is buying and selling securities and commodities for customers and also buying and selling securities and commodities for their own account. Other business activities of brokers and dealers are (1) underwriting the issuance of securities, (2) private placement of securities, (3) investment advisory services and (4) marketing all types of tax shelters.

When a broker and dealer buys or sells securities and commodities for customers, it may act as an agent (broker) or as a principal (dealer). When acting in the capacity of an agent, the broker charges its customers a commission for executing buy and sell orders on various markets. When acting in the capacity of a principal, the dealer makes a profit or loss by buying or selling for its own account. A broker and dealer in securities and commodities must disclose, in each transaction with its customers, whether it is acting in the capacity of an agent or as a principal.

An investor can purchase securities and commodities on a "long" basis or on a "short" basis. A "long" position in a stock or commodity means that the investor owns the stock or commodity and has acquired the investment with the expectation that its market value will increase. A "short" position means that the investor has borrowed the stock or commodity from the broker and sold it with the expectations that its market value will decrease, at which time the investor purchases the stock or commodity to replace the stock or commodity borrowed from the broker. The profit on a "short" position is the difference between the funds received from the sale of the borrowed stock or commodity and the price paid for the purchase of the stock or commodity which was borrowed from the broker.

An investor can purchase stocks and commodities for cash or on "margin". In a cash transaction, the full purchase price of the stock or commodity must be paid by the investor on the settlement date of the transaction. In a "margin" transaction only a percentage of the full purchase price must be made by the investor on the settlement date. The broker extends credit to the investor for the balance of the purchase price, but retains as collateral the securities or commodities purchased by the investor. The "margin" percentage for securities is regulated by the Board of Governors of the Federal Reserve System and, at the end of 1979, the "margin" percentage was 50%. Thus, an investor with $100,000 could purchase up to $200,000 of securities on margin. As discussed later, "margin" rates on commodities are usually much less than that for securities, and the rates on commodities are set by the various commodity exchanges.

Obviously, brokers must charge interest on the funds they lend on "margin" accounts. The interest rate charged to investors by brokers is usually the prime rate plus ½ to 4 percentage points. The percentage points above the prime rate are charged in accordance with the size of the investor's investment portfolio, the activity of the account, and the prior experience with the investor.

Federal regulations on margin accounts are quite complex and require that margin requirements be periodically determined. Generally, the required margin, at any given time, is a percentage of the market value of the margined securities. However, the investor's equity in a margin account is the difference between the market value of the margined securities and the amount of funds borrowed from the broker. Thus, if an investor purchases $100,000 of securities when the margin requirement is 50%, the amount of the investor's equity must be $50,000. The investor's equity can be paid in cash, securities, or commodity contracts. If securities or commodity contracts are used for the investor's equity, they are valued at their market values on the settlement date. Now, lets assume that the market value of the $100,000 worth of securities purchased by this investor decreases to $90,000. The margin requirement on $90,000 at the 50% rate would be $45,000. However, the investor's equity in the margin account has decreased to $40,000 ($90,000 market value, less $50,000 owed to the broker). Thus, the broker must issue a "margin call" to the investor in the amount of $5,000. Margin calls must be paid promptly or the broker can automatically sell some or all of the margined securities to raise the money to pay the "margin call". Now, lets assume that the market value of the $100,000 worth of securities purchased by this investor, instead of decreasing, increases to $120,000. The margin requirement on $120,000 at the 50% rate would be $60,000. However, the investor's equity in the margin account has increased to $70,000 ($120,000 market value, less $50,000 owed to the broker).

Thus, the $10,000 of excess investor's equity ($70,000) over the margin requirement ($60,000) may be used by the investor to purchase additional securities, or withdrawn in cash. However, with the $10,000 of excess equity the investor may purchase up to $20,000 of securities at market value. Assuming that the investor does purchase the additional $20,000 of securities, the market value of the margin account would increase from $120,000 to $140,000. The 50% margin requirement would increase from $50,000 to $70,000 which means that the investor can borrow an additional $20,000 from the broker to pay for the additional securities purchased. The investor's equity of $70,000 would remain unchanged.

Detailed records of customers' margin accounts must be kept by brokers and dealers in securities. These records will usually reflect (1) the name of the margin customer, (2) the market value of the securities in the margin account, (3) the customer's equity in the account, (4) the excess or deficiency in the amount of margin, (5) the miscellaneous account balance required by Regulation T, and (6) other pertinent customer instructions and information.

The margin department of a broker and dealer in a securities is usually responsible for approving margin accounts, extensions of credit, and the issuance of margin calls for deficiencies in customer margin accounts. Both securities and commodities can be purchased on margin. However, the margin requirements for commodities are significantly less than that for securities. Margin requirements for commodities are usually regulated by the commodity exchange on which the commodity is traded. It is not unusual for customers to purchase commodities for as little as 15% equity and 85% margined. However, commodity margin requirements are computed daily and customers are immediately notified of any deficiency in their margin accounts. If the deficiency is not paid by the customer in a few days, the broker has the right to liquidate all or part of the customer's margin account to make up the deficiency.

Many types of commodities are traded on various commodity exchanges. Grains, such as wheat, barley, corn, oats, etc., metals, such as gold, silver, platinum, copper, lead, zinc, etc., meats, such as cattle, pork bellies, turkeys, etc., and miscellaneous items such as cotton, plywood, eggs, soybean, etc., are examples of some of the many types of commodities traded. Commodities, like securities, may be purchased long or sold short. Each commodity contract consists of a specified quantity of the commodity.

A commodity may be traded in the form of a spot contract or future contract. A spot contract is for the current month and usually involves paying cash and taking physical delivery of the commodity. The current month is called the "spot month". However, the great majority of commodity transactions involve future contracts. This is because most investors do not want the actual delivery of the commodity and they "cover" their positions before the spot month, or before the commodity contract expires. Future contracts are traded on the basis that an investor agrees to buy or sell a certain quantity of a specific commodity in a future month other than the current month in which the trade is made. Thus, in June 1980 an investor can agree to buy 100 ounces of gold in June 1981, based on a price that is established in June 1980. If the price of gold rises six months later, the price of the June 1981 gold contract will also increase proportionately. The investor can then sell a commodity contract for 100 ounces of June 1981 gold. Thus, the long position for the purchase of 100 ounces of June 1981 gold, is offset by the short position for the sale of 100 ounces of June 1981 gold, resulting in a profit. If the investor had thought that the price of gold was going to decrease over the next year, then a contract for 100 ounces of June 1981 gold should be first sold. Subsequently, if the price of gold declines, the price of the June 1981 gold contract would also decline. Thus, the investor could purchase a June 1981 gold contract for less than the sales price of the June 1981 gold contract that was originally sold. The difference, less brokerage commissions, is the investor's profit. If commodities are purchased or sold on margin, an investor's profit would be decreased by the amount of interest paid on the margin account.

The price of most commodities can fluctuate considerably. Most commodity exchanges have established limitations on the daily price movement of many commodities. For example, silver has a daily price limitation of ten cents an ounce. Thus, the price of silver cannot increase or decrease more than ten cents per ounce from the previous days closing. Up-the-limit and down-the-limit are terms frequently used by commodity traders.

The commodity markets play an important role in the economy of a country. Farmers, food processors, metal manufacturers, millers, and others who must store large quantities of commodities as inventory can minimize their exposure to price fluctuation by a process called "hedging". Thus, if a farmer believes that the price of his crop of corn is going to be substantially less in the future, he can sell corn futures today and make actual delivery of the corn when his crop is ready for harvest. Alternatively, the farmer can close out his short position by purchasing spot contracts of corn in the month he is ready to sell his crop. The profit made on the commodity contracts will offset his actual losses. The process of "hedging" is an integral part of many businesses and would not be possible without the existing commodity futures markets.

Some commodities are not federally regulated but some commodities are regulated by the Commodities Exchange Act. Most regulated commodities are in the agriculture industries, such as grains, eggs, potatoes, cotton, and soybean. The most important federal regulations require that commodity exchange members submit daily reports of their commodity trading activity and also limits the number of future contracts that any one person can acquire and own in any one commodity for speculation purposes.

Transactions on commodity exchanges are cleared and settled by a clearing association appointed by the exchange. Thus, all buy and sell transactions in future commodity contracts are handled by a clearing association. A settlement price for all open commodity contracts is established at the close of business each day by all commodity exchanges. This process is referred to as "marking-to-market". Each broker must settle his net difference on all open contracts in cash each day with the clearing association. On the brokers books the daily settlement is posted to a contract difference account which is eventually reposted to each customer's account to reflect any gain or loss. However, those brokers located long distances from cities in which commodity exchanges are located must usually deal with a correspondent broker. Thus, instead of a contract difference account, an account with the correspondent broker is utilized.

Securities are generally traded in round lots of 100 shares. Transactions involving less than 100 shares are called "odd lots". The commission charged by brokers for handling an odd lot transaction is much higher than the commission charged for round lot transactions. In addition, securities may be "listed" or "unlisted". A "listed" security is one which is traded on a stock exchange. An "unlisted" security is one that is not listed on a stock exchange but may be traded through a network of securities brokers and dealers, the largest of which is the National Association of Securities Dealers (NASD). Unlisted securities are frequently referred to as "over-the-counter" stocks.

In buying or selling an unlisted or over-the-counter security, a customer places an order with a stockbroker. The order may specify a certain price or it may be a market order. If a price is specified by the customer, the stockbroker must execute the order at the specified price. However, since most securities are traded in eighths of a point ($1/8$), a customer may specify a price and also give the stockbroker an eighth or a quarter of a point discretion. Under no circumstances can the broker execute the order in violation of the customer's instructions. A market order, on the other hand, is executed by the stockbroker at whatever the market price is at the time the order is executed.

When a stockbroker receives an order for an unlisted security he may refer to the pink sheets to determine what brokers deal in the security in the customer's order. Another method for locating a dealer in a particular security is an EDP system that is kept and supported by various interested parties. The stockbroker merely inserts the symbols for the particular security and the bid and ask price of the security appear on a little TV screen, along with other pertinent information concerning that particular security. After locating a broker or dealer in the particular security, the order is either consummated in accordance with the customer's instructions, or the order is not executed. Then, the stockbroker usually informs the customer by telephone of the results. If an order was consummated the stockbroker sends the customer a written confirmation that details the transaction, commissions, and taxes due on the order, and the total amount due the stockbroker. Since unlisted securities are not marginable, the customer usually must pay the full amount due the stockbroker. The brokers or dealers involved in the execution of the order settle their accounts between them directly or through the National Clearing Corporation. If the customer was purchasing stock, the stockbroker would have to deliver a check in the agreed amount to the other party (broker, dealer or clearing association) and the other party would, in turn, be obligated to deliver executed stock certificates, properly endorsed to the stockbroker for eventual delivery to the customer.

Transactions in listed securities differ in some respects from transactions in unlisted securities. Let's assume that a customer contacts his stockbroker and wants to buy 1,000 shares of Singer Manufacturing Corporation. As the stockbroker is talking to the customer on the telephone he looks up the symbol for Singer and finds out that the symbol is SMF. The stockbroker pushes the buttons SMF on his stock information machine and all of the pertinent data for SMF appears on a little TV screen. Some of the data available on the TV screen is the amount of dividend that the company pays, the date of the last dividend payment, the total shares of SMF traded so far on that particular day, the highest price and lowest price that SMF has traded for on that particular day, and last but not least, the present bid and ask price for SMF which was $10.00 bid and $10.50 ask. The bid and ask prices are established by the specialist on the floor of the New York Stock Exchange who handles SMF securities. A specialist frequently handles more than one security and usually three or four. The specialist is charged with the responsibility of maintaining an orderly market in those securities in which he specializes. The bid price represents the price a seller would receive for the next 100 shares. The ask price represents the price a buyer would have to pay for the next 100 shares. However, there may be more shares available at the same bid and ask prices. The bid and ask prices are established by the specialist when there are no other specific offers to buy or sell. When specific offers are available the specialist will use them to establish a bid and ask price. Thus, the spread between the bid and ask will fluctuate from an eighth to possibly a full point. At this juncture in the stock transaction, the stockbroker tells the customer that the ask price for SMF is 10½. The customer tells the stockbroker to buy 1,000 shares of SMF at 10½. The stockbroker fills out an order ticket and asks the customer how long the order is good for. The customer reaffirms that his offer to buy 1,000 shares of SMF at 10½ is good till the end of the day. The stockbroker marks "day order" on the form, delivers it to a person in the teletype room where the order is teletyped to the stockbroker's representative at the New York Stock Exchange.

At the stock exchange the representative for the stockbroker goes to the SMF specialist's booth to place the customer's order. If the order is eventually filled that day, a teletype is sent back to the broker confirming the purchase. The broker notifies the customer and subsequently the customer is sent a written confirmation detailing the entire transaction and indicating the amount due to the stockbroker.

Each stock exchange usually has its own clearing organization where members of the exchange can settle their transactions. Transactions between members are offset by the clearing organization so that only net differences need be settled. By netting the transactions, the amount of movement of cash and documents is minimized.

Option trading has been around for many years but has only recently become popular among traders and investors. Options are called "puts" and "calls". A "put" is an option to sell stock to a designated buyer at a stated price during a specific period. A "call" is an option to buy stock from a designated seller at a stated price during a specified period. The specified option period varies from one month to as long as a year. Many options on listed securities are traded on some stock exchanges. The price of an option depends on the market price of the underlying security on the date the option is purchased and the length of the exercise period. To the price of the option there must be added the broker's commission for handling the transaction. If the option is not exercised by the last day of the stated exercise period, the price paid for the option plus commissions becomes a total loss. Thus, an option must increase in value before it is worth exercising. For example, General Motors is selling for $50.00 per share and you want to purchase a "put" to sell 100 shares of GM for $50.00 per share anytime within the subsequent 90 days. Options are usually sold in round lots (100 shares), the same as other securities. You call your stockbroker who obtains a quote of $250.00 for the option you want. If you purchase the option for $250.00 to sell 100 shares of GM in the next 90 days at $50.00 per share, you are gambling that the price of GM will fall in the next three months. Lets say that GM falls to $40.00 per share within the three month option period. That means that you can purchase 100 shares of GM at the $40.00 per share market price and deliver the same shares to the designated person in your option who must pay you $50.00 per share. Alternatively, you may be able to just sell the option outright, providing there is an established market or that your broker can find a buyer.

There are various types of option combinations, such as a "straddle", a "spread", and "strips" and "straps". The following is a brief description of these types of options:

"Straddle"   is the purchase or sale of one put and one call on the stock, same number of shares, same exercise period, and the same exercise price.

"Spread"   is exactly the same as a "straddle" except for the exercise price. In a "spread" the exercise price for the put is slightly less than current market, and the exercise price for the call is slightly more than current market.

"Strip"   is two puts and one call for the same stock.

"Strap"   is two calls and one put for the same stock.

Options which are traded on a stock exchange are handled the same way that stock orders are handled. However, options which are not listed on an exchange are normally handled by the Put and Call Brokers and Dealers Association, Inc. This Association usually maintains a market for options on most traded securities. However, as long as a buyer and seller agree, any two individuals can create an option.

Since stock options are not marginable under existing regulations, a customer must pay the full amount due to the broker on or before the settlement date.

Arbitrage transactions usually involve a particular security and the attempt to make profits from price differentials. International arbitrage is the buying and selling of securities in various foreign markets in an attempt to make profits from price differentials. For example, a security may be selling at $50.00 per share in one country and in another country the same security may be selling for $49.50 per share. An arbitrager would attempt to buy the security at $49.50 in one country and simultaneously sell the security in the other country for $50.00 per share.

Another example of arbitrage has to do with the price disparity between a convertible security and the stock in which it is convertible. Suppose that a preferred security was selling for $95.00 per share and was convertible into 10 shares of common stock which were selling for $10.00 per share. In this situation, an arbitrager would simultaneously sell the common stock short at $10.00 per share and purchase enough convertible stock at $95.00 per share which would be exactly convertible into the number of common stock sold short. In other words, for every ten shares of common sold short at $10.00 per share, the arbitrager would purchase one share of the convertible stock at $95.00 per share, which is convertible into ten shares of common. The net result is that the arbitrager is selling ten shares of common for $100.00 (10 × $10.00) and is buying the convertible preferred for $95.00 which is convertible into ten shares of common at a cost of $9.50 per share. The arbitrager winds up owning no securities but making a fifty cent per share profit on each share involved in the arbitrage transaction.

Stock rights and warrants may be used in arbitrage transactions along with the securities of merging companies or companies in the process of reorganization. Most arbitraging is done by highly competent individuals who are specialists in arbitrage transactions.

The underwriting function that is performed by securities brokers and dealers plays an important role in the formation of capital for both government and industry. When a local, state, or federal agency is raising funds by the issuance of debt securities, underwriters individually or as groups purchase the entire issue at a price established by a bidding process. Thus, the governmental unit receives all of its funds and the securities brokers and dealers resell the purchased securities to the public, usually at a profit.

However, some private issues may be handled by the securities brokers and dealers on a "best effort basis". This means that the securities are not purchased outright by the brokers and dealers but are sold by them on a "best efforts basis". The same process is used when a company wishes to issue new or additional securities. For example, ABC Corporation wishes to raise capital by the sale of one million shares of its common stock. If a market is already established for ABC stock, the underwriter will probably purchase all of the million shares at a price slightly less than the existing market. The price below market is determined by many factors, including past experience and the prestige of the issuer. If ABC Corporation was unknown and raising capital publicly for the first time, the underwriter might insist on a "best effort" deal.

Frequently, in connection with an offering for the sale of securities registered with the SEC, the accountant is requested to issue a "comfort letter" to the underwriter handling the offering. Comfort letters are not required by the SEC, but underwriters, as a defense against possible claims arising from the offering, usually insist on them.

A comfort letter usually covers a time period that commences on the date of the auditor's report and ends (cutoff date) about five business days before the issuer or selling security holder delivers the securities to the underwriter (closing date). The letter is ordinarily dated, by the accountant, on or shortly before the closing date.

The main content of the comfort letter, from the underwriter's point of view, is a negative assurance that nothing has come to the attention of the accountants as a result of certain specified procedures that would cause them to believe that certain enumerated items are not true. The enumerated procedures which are applied during the comfort letter period, are as follows:

1. We have read the unaudited statements (specify).
2. We have read the minutes of the stockholders', board of directors', and other appropriate committees.
3. We have made inquiries of management responsible for financial and accounting matters as to whether the unaudited financial statements present fairly in all material respects and comply with the SEC Act.
4. The foregoing procedures do not constitute an examination in accordance with GAAP, and we make no representations as to the sufficiency of the foregoing procedures.
5. Nothing came to our attention as a result of the foregoing

procedures that causes us to believe that the unaudited statements are not presented fairly; that there was any change in the capital or debt structure of the company.

Securities brokers and dealers also handle the private placement of funds for companies and investors. Private placements are usually exempt from registration with the SEC. A private placement is where a company wants to raise capital and does not want to get involved in a public offering. In a private placement of funds, a securities broker or dealer acts as a middleman and raises the required funds from a small group of private investors. For its services, the broker and dealer receives a fee based on the amount of money involved.

As mentioned earlier, most securities brokers and dealers also trade and invest for their own account. This means that they actually buy and sell for themselves with the intent of making a profit. Securities which are being traded by the broker/dealer are accounted for as inventory. However, securities being held for investment must be clearly marked as such before the 31st day after their purchase in order to qualify for capital gains treatment under existing federal tax regulations.

SECURITIES EXCHANGE ACT OF 1934

The Securities Exchange Act of 1934 provides for the regulation of securities exchanges and of over-the-counter-markets, operating in interstate and foreign commerce, and through the mails, to prevent inequitable and unfair practices on such exchanges and markets. The following is a brief summary of the Act:

Securities and Exchange Commission The 1934 Act establishes a Securities and Exchange Commission composed of five Commissioners that are appointed by the President, with the advice and consent of the Senate.

Unregistered exchanges   It is unlawful for any broker, dealer, or exchange to use the mails or interstate commerce, directly or indirectly, for the purposes of transacting any securities business of any nature with any other exchanges, unless such exchanges (1) are registered under the 1934 Act, or (2) are exempt from registration under the 1934 Act.

Margin requirements   For the purpose of preventing excessive use of credit for the purchase of securities, the Board of Governors of the Federal Reserve System shall from time to time prescribe rules and regulations as to margin requirements. The present margin requirement is 50%. The margin rate is the amount of credit permitted to be extended on the purchase of securities from a registered dealer or broker.

It is unlawful for any broker, dealer, or exchange to extend credit on securities in contravention of that prescribed by the Board of Governors of the Federal Reserve System.

Restriction on borrowings—brokers and dealers   It is unlawful for brokers and dealers to borrow in the ordinary course of business a total indebtedness of more than 2,000% of their net capital, or a lower amount that may from time to time be prescribed by the Commission.

Manipulation of security prices   It is unlawful for any person, directly or indirectly, by the use of the mails or interstate commerce, or any facility of a national securities exchange, or member thereof:

1. to create a false or misleading appearance of active trading or market in any security, registered on a national securities exchange
2. to effect a series of transactions in any security on a national securities exchange, creating actual or apparent active trading in a security or raising or depressing the price of such security
3. to induce the purchase or sale, as a broker or dealer, to effect the rise or fall of any security
4. to make false or misleading statements with respect to any material fact, as a broker, dealer, or any other person, in selling or offering for sale any security

Regulation of Manipulative and Deceptive Devices Section 10:
It is unlawful for any person, directly or indirectly, by use of the
mails or interstate commerce, or of any facility of a national securities exchange,
1. to effect a short sale or employ a stop-loss order in contravention of the rules of the Commission
2. to use or employ, in connection with the purchase or sale of
   any security, any manipulative or deceptive devices or con-
   trivances in contravention of the rules of the Commission

Registration Requirements for Securities It is unlawful for any
member, broker, or dealer to effect any transaction in any security
(other than an exempted security) on a national securities exchange, unless a registration is effective for the security in accordance with rules of the Commission.

Periodical and Other Reports Every issuer of a security registered with the Commission shall file, in accordance with rules of
the Commission:

1. such information and documents as the Commission may
   require to keep its registration statement current
2. annual reports, certified if required, by rules of the Commission, by independent certified public accountants

Proxies It shall be unlawful for any person, by use of the mails
or in interstate commerce, or any facility of a national securities
exchange, to solicit a proxy for any security (except exempted securities) in contravention of the rules of the Commission.

Over-The-Counter Markets No broker or dealer shall use the
mails or interstate commerce to induce the purchase or sale of any
security (other than exempted securities), otherwise than on a national exchange, unless such broker or dealer is registered in accordance with the rules of the Commission.

Directors, Officers, and Principal Stockholders Any person who
directly or indirectly is the beneficial owner of more than 10% of
any one class of equity security (other than exempted securities),

or is an officer or director of the issuer, shall file at the time of the registration of such security a statement of the amount of equity securities owned beneficially and quarterly thereafter a statement of any changes.

Insider Trading Section 16(b): For the purpose of preventing unfair use of insider information that may have been obtained by any beneficial owner, director, or officer, by reason of his relationship to the issuer, any profit realized by such person from any purchase and sale, or any sale and purchase, of any equity security of such issuer (other than exempted securities) *within a period of less than six months* shall inure and be recoverable by the issuer. Suit for recovery may be instituted by the issuer, or any owner of any security of the issuer, if the issuer shall fail or refuse to bring suit within 60 days after request.

This section of the Act is commonly referred to as the insiders short-swing profit provision, and the leading case in this area was the *SEC v. Texas Gulf Sulphur.*

Accounts, Records, and Examination Every national securities exchange member, broker, and dealer shall make, keep, and preserve for such periods such accounts and other records as the Commission shall prescribe.

Any broker or dealer or other person extending credit who is subject to the rules and regulations prescribed by the Board of Governors of the Federal Reserve System shall make such reports as the Board may from time to time require.

Liability for Misleading Statements Any person who shall make or cause to be made any statement under this Act that at the time and in light of the circumstances under which it was made was false or misleading with respect to any material fact shall be liable to any person (not knowing that such statement was false or misleading) who, in reliance on such statement, shall have purchased or sold a security at a price that was affected by such statement, for damages caused by such reliance, unless the person sued shall prove that he acted in good faith and had no knowledge that such statement was false or misleading.

Commission's Powers The Commission is authorized to take such action that is necessary to protect investors, including (1) suspending any registered security and (2) withdrawing the registration of any exchange or security.

Penalties Any person found guilty under this Act is punishable by a fine of $10,000 ($500,000 in case of an Exchange) or imprisonment for not more than two years, *or both*.

Any issuer who fails to file required information may be fined $100 for each day such failure continues.

One of the most important rules that has been promulgated by the SEC is Rule 10 (b)-5 which states:

It shall be unlawful for any person, directly or indirectly, by the use of any means or instrumentality of interstate commerce, or of the mails, or of any facility of any national securities exchange,

a. to employ any device, scheme, or artifice to defraud,
b. to make any untrue statement of a material fact or to omit to state a material fact necessary in order to make the statement made, in the light of the circumstances under which they were made, not misleading, or
c. to engage in any act, practice, or course of business that operates or would operate as a fraud or deceit on any person, in connection with the purchase or sale of any security.

Preferable Accounting Principles

The Preferable Accounting Principles for securities brokers and dealers appear in the industry audit guide entitled "Audits of Brokers and Dealers in Securities" (hereinafter referred to as the Securities Guide).

The Securities Guide points out that the usual practice in the securities industry is to record transactions on the "settlement date", instead of the "trade date", which is the date used by most other industries. The Securities Guide considers the use of the "settlement date" to be a departure from GAAP, but its effect are not usually material and thus is permitted.

> **OBSERVATION:** *The "settlement date" usually occurs five days after the "trade date". This five day period is necessary because written confirmations are mailed out and received by customers during this five day period. The written confirmations are absolutely necessary because most transactions are handled over the telephone and frequent mistakes occur. In addition, a customer could deny that an order was even placed, or placed by an unauthorized person. Thus, it appears that the five days are necessary for the earning process to be completed and the realization of revenue recognized.*
>
> *Perhaps, the Securities Guide is incorrect in its assertion that recording transactions in the securities industry on the "settlement date", instead of the "trade date", is a departure from GAAP.*

All of the disclosures normally required by GAAP, must be included in financial statements prepared for securities brokers and dealers. This includes, but is not limited to, (1) accounting policies, (2) depreciation and amortization policies, (3) unrealized gain and losses on marketable securities, (4) unconsolidated investments, (5) intangible assets, (6) deferred income taxes, (7) lease obligations, (8) contingent liabilities, (9) stock option plans, and, (10) capital changes.

Other preferable accounting principles which are widely dispersed and not appropriately labeled in the Securities Guide, are described below.

Unclassified balance sheet   The Securities Guide does not require a classified balance sheet for brokers and dealers of securities. However, descriptive captions should be utilized. Marketable investments should be reported separately from those investments not readily marketable. Not readily marketable investments include those for which no independent public market exists and those which must be registered with the SEC before they can be publicly offered for sale.

If amounts due to or from correspondent brokers are significant they should be reported under a separate caption and not included in an "omnibus account".

Statement of changes in financial position   This is a mandatory statement when reporting in conformity with GAAP. Thus, brokers and dealers in securities must include a statement of changes in financial position in their financial reports. A statement of changes in subordinated liabilities is required by the SEC from securities dealers and brokers. In addition, the auditor must include the statement of changes in subordinated liabilities in his audit report when reporting to the SEC.

Results of operations   The statement of income should reflect the different sources of revenue. Expenses should be functionally reported. Brokers and dealers that are public companies must disclose their operating results because of existing law. However, nonpublic brokers and dealers are not required to disclose their operating results. The Securities Guide states that it is preferable for both public and nonpublic companies to disclose their operating results in conformity with GAAP.

Customers' receivables   Customers' receivables usually appear on the balance sheet under the caption "Customers' Partly Secured and Unsecured Accounts". An allowance for uncollectible amounts that can be reasonably anticipated should be provided for and reported on the balance sheet.

Valuation of investments   Trading investments held as inventory and investments held for capital gain should be reported on the financial statements, as follows:

1. Marketable securities should be reported at their current market value at the date of the balance sheet.
2. Long-term investments in joint ventures and common stock should be accounted and reported for using the Equity Method (APB-18).
3. Not readily marketable securities and other similar investments at fair value as determined by management at the date of the balance sheet. In addition, the cost of these securities and investments should be parenthetically disclosed in the financial statements.

4. Both unrealized and realized gains and losses are included in the determination of net income for the reporting period. If unrealized gains and losses are material they should be disclosed in the financial statements along with their aggregate effect on net income. Unrealized gains and losses result from the increase or decrease in current market value or fair value from one reporting date to the next. Realized gains and losses result from the actual sale or other disposition of the securities or investments during the reporting period.

5. Deferred taxes should be provided for as a result of timing differences created by the unrealized gains and losses for the reporting period. Care should be exercised where capital gain tax rates apply.

Securities sold under a repurchase agreement should be included, at their current market value, in trading investments or investments held for capital gain whichever is appropriate, and the cost of their repurchase should appear as a liability. Thus, securities sold under a repurchase agreement appear as an asset and a liability on the balance sheet.

Call options that have been sold against securities and investments held for trading or capital gains, should be separately reported, if significant, as "Securities for Endorsed Outstanding Calls". These securities should be valued at their contract price or current market, whichever is lower.

When a brokerage firm sells an option through the National Put and Call Association, the brokerage firm must guarantee its performance on the option. These guarantees represent a contingent liability and if significant should be reported in the financial statements.

Commitments Underwriting contracts, when issued contracts, and delayed delivery contracts, if significant, should be disclosed in the financial statements.

Membership in exchanges Membership in exchanges that are used for operating purposes, should be valued for reporting purposes at cost, unless there has been a permanent impairment of the asset, in which case the membership should be valued at net realizable value.

Contributed exchange memberships used for operating purposes that are subordinated to claims of the general creditors should be reported at market value and the offsetting credit should appear as "liabilities subordinated to the claims of the general creditors".

Option premiums The money received for an option should be amortized to income over the life of the option. This is necessary to match revenue with the related costs as required by GAAP.

Comprehensive Illustration

The following is a comprehensive illustration of the preferable accounting principles contained in this chapter.

SECURITIES BROKER AND DEALER
STATEMENT OF FINANCIAL CONDITION
As of June 30, 1980 and 1979

	1980	*1979*
Assets:		
Cash	S 00,000,000	S 0,000,000
Cash and U.S. Treasury bills segregated under the Commodity Futures Trading Act	000,000,000	000,000,000
Deposits with exchange clearing associations and good faith deposits (including U.S. Treasury bills of $0,-000,000 in 1980 and $0,000,000 in 1979, at market value)	0,000,000	00,000,000
Receivables:		
Customers	000,000,000	000,000,000
Brokers and dealers	000,000,000	00,000,000
Others	0,000,000	0,000,000
Mortgage and construction loans	00,000,000	
Securities purchased under agreements to resell (including $0,000,000 in 1980 and $000,000,000 in 1979, financed by matched repurchase agreements)	0,000,000	000,000,000
Securities owned, at market value (Note 3)	000,000,000	000,000,000
Spot commodities owned, at market value		000,000
Secured demand notes receivable subject to preferred stock agreements (Note 6)	0,000,000	0,000,000
Secured demand notes receivable (Note 7)	000,000	0,000,000
Memberships in exchanges, at cost (market value $0,000,000 in 1980 and $0,-000,000 in 1979)	0,000,000	0,000,000
Deferred expenses and other assets	0,000,000	0,000,000
Office equipment and installations (net of accumulated depreciation and amortization of S0,000,000 in 1980 and S0,000,000 in 1979)	00,000,000	0,000,000
Purchased mortgage service contracts	0,000,000	
Excess of cost over fair value of net assets acquired	0,000,000	0,000,000
	S0,000,000,000	S0,000,000,000

Liabilities and Stockholders' Equity:

Short-term bank loans (Note 4)	$ 000,000,000	$ 000,000,000
Payables:		
Customers	000,000,000	000,000,000
Brokers and dealers	000,000,000	000,000,000
Banks	000,000,000	000,000,000
Accrued federal, state and local income taxes	00,000,000	0,000,000
Other accrued liabilities and payables	00,000,000	00,000,000
Securities sold under agreements to repurchase (including $0,000,000 in 1980 and $000,000,000 in 1979 matched by securities purchased under agreements to resell)	0,000,000	000,000,000
Securities sold but not yet purchased, at market value (including $00,000,000 in 1980 and $000,000,000 in 1979 of market value offset by exchangeable and arbitrage securities owned) (Note 3)	000,000,000	000,000,000
Deferred income taxes	000,000	000,000
	000,000,000	000,000,000
Term notes (Note 5)	00,000,000	0,000,000
Subordinated indebtedness (Note 7)	00,000,000	00,000,000
Secured demand obligations subject to preferred stock agreements and stockholders' equity:		
Secured demand obligations subject to preferred stock agreements (Notes 6 and 8)	0,000,000	0,000,000
Stockholders' Equity (Notes 8, 9, 10 and 12):		
Preferred stock, $.00 par value, 0,000,000 shares authorized, 00,000 shares (1980) and 00,000 shares (1979) issued and outstanding; stated at mandatory redemption and liquidation value $0,-000,000 (1980) and $0,000,000 (1979) less unamortized excess of such value over fair value at issuance	0,000,000	0,000,000
Common stock, $.00 par value, 00,000,000 shares authorized, 0,000,-000 shares (1980) and 0,000,000 shares (1979) issued	000,000	000,000
Additional paid-in capital	00,000,000	00,000,000
Retained earnings	00,000,000	00,000,000
Stockholders' equity	00,000,000	00,000,000
Total secured demand obligations subject to preferred stock agreements and stockholders' equity	00,000,000	00,000,000
	$0,000,000,000	$0,000,000,000

SECURITIES BROKER AND DEALER
STATEMENT OF OPERATIONS
Years Ended June 30, 1980 and 1979

	1980	1979
Revenues:		
Commissions	$000,000,000	$000,000,000
Investment banking	00,000,000	00,000,000
Market making and principal		
transactions	00,000,000	00,000,000
Interest	00,000,000	00,000,000
Mortgage banking	0,000,000	
Other	00,000,000	0,000,000
	000,000,000	000,000,000
Expenses:		
Compensation and benefits	000,000,000	000,000,000
Brokerage, commissions and		
clearance fees	00,000,000	00,000,000
Communications	00,000,000	00,000,000
Office and equipment	00,000,000	00,000,000
Promotion	0,000,000	0,000,000
Interest	00,000,000	00,000,000
Other	00,000,000	00,000,000
	000,000,000	000,000,000
Income before taxes on income	00,000,000	00,000,000
Provision for taxes on income (Note 13)	00,000,000	0,000,000
Net Income	$ 00,000,000	$00,000,000
Net Income per share (Note 14):		
Primary	$0.00	$0.00
Fully diluted	$0.00	$0.00
Cash dividends per common share	$ .00	$ .00
Weighted average number of common and		
common equivalent shares (Note 14)	0,000,000	0,000,000

See Accompanying Notes to Financial Statements

STATEMENT OF STOCKHOLDERS' EQUITY
Years ended June 30, 1980 and 1979

	Preferred Stock, $.10 Par Value	*Common Stock, $.00 Par Value*	*Additional Paid-in Capital*	*Retained Earnings*
Balance, June 30, 1978	$ 000,000	$000,000	$00,000,000	$00,000,000
Conversions of preferred stock into common stock	(0,000,000)	00,000	0,000,000	
Conversions of secured demand obligations subject to preferred stock agreements	0,000,000			
Conversion of subordinated notes		000	00,000	
Capital stock issued in connection with:				
XYZ acquisition		00,000	0,000,000	
ABC purchase agreement		0,000	0,000,000	
Employee stock purchase plan		00,000	0,000,000	
Stock options exercised		0,000	000,000	
Amortization of excess of mandatory redemption value over fair value of preferred stock at issuance	00,000			(00,000)
Net income				00,000,000
Dividends:				
Preferred stock				(000,000)
Common stock				(0,000,000)
Balance, June 30, 1979	000,000	000,000	00,000,000	00,000,000

Conversions of preferred stock into common stock		0,000	000,000	
Conversion of subordinated notes		0,000	000,000	
Capital stock issued in connection with:				
Employee stock purchase plan		0,000	0,000,000	
Stock options exercised		00,000	0,000,000	
Amortization of excess of mandatory redemption value over fair value of preferred stock at issuance	00,000			
Net income				00,000,000
Dividends:				
Preferred stock				(00,000)
Common stock				(000,000)
Balance, June 30, 1980	$ 000,000	$000,000	$00,000,000	$00,000,000

In addition, the Company purchased $0,000,000 of its common stock in fiscal 1980.

There were no treasury stock transactions in fiscal 1979.

STATEMENT OF CHANGES IN FINANCIAL POSITION
Years Ended June 30, 1980 and 1979

	1980	1979
Source:		
Net income	$ 00,000,000	$00,000,000
Items included in net income not requiring or generating funds:		
Depreciation and amortization	0,000,000	0,000,000
Provision (credit) for deferred taxes on income	(00,000)	0,000,000
Funds provided by operations	00,000,000	00,000,000
Increase in short-term bank loans and payables to banks	00,000,000	00,000,000
Decrease (increase) in net receivables from customers	00,000,000	(00,000,000)
Increase in other payables	00,000,000	0,000,000
Increase in term notes	00,000,000	0,000,000
Increase in subordinated indebtedness	00,000,000	0,000,000
Decrease (increase) in spot commodities owned	000,000	(000,000)
Increase in income taxes payable	0,000,000	0,000,000
Decrease (increase) in net securities owned	0,000,000	(0,000,000)
Other	000,000	000,000
Issuance of common and preferred stock in connection with the following:		
Stock purchase plan	0,000,000	0,000,000
Exercise of stock options	0,000,000	000,000
Conversion of subordinated indebtedness	000,000	
Conversion of secured demand obligations subject to preferred stock agreements		0,000,000
XYZ acquisition		0,000,000
	$000,000,000	$00,000,000
Application:		
Increase in cash and securities on deposit	$ 00,000,000	$00,000,000
Decrease in net payables to brokers	0,000,000	00,000,000
Decrease (increase) in securities sold under repurchase agreements, net	00,000,000	(00,000,000)
Increase in mortgage and construction loans	00,000,000	
Increase in purchased mortgage service contracts	0,000,000	
Increase in excess of cost over fair value of net assets acquired	000,000	000,000
Increase in exchange memberships	0,000	000,000
Repayments and conversions of subordinated indebtedness	0,000,000	0,000,000
Dividends on capital stock	0,000,000	0,000,000
Repurchase of common stock	0,000,000	
	$000,000,000	$00,000,000

NOTES TO FINANCIAL STATEMENTS

Note 1—Summary of Accounting Policies

The consolidated financial statements include the accounts of the Company and its subsidiaries, all of which are wholly owned.

Securities owned are maintained on a settlement-date basis and are valued at market with appreciation or depreciation reflected in the consolidated statements of operations.

Security transactions and the related commission revenues and expenses are recorded on settlement date. Commission revenues and related commission expenses on commodity futures transactions are recorded at the time the position is closed.

Securities purchased under agreements to resell and securities sold under agreements to repurchase are financing transactions which are adequately collateralized by negotiable securities and are carried at the amounts at which the securities will be subsequently resold or repurchased.

Mortgage loans ($00,000,000) which are held for sale are stated at the lower of cost or aggregate market, with market generally based upon outstanding commitments that the Company has acquired from investors for the purchase of such mortgages. The cost and related market value of certain Government National Mortgage Association Mortgage-Backed Securities (GNMA securities) that the Company is committed to acquire and/or sell are also utilized in the lower of cost or aggregate market determination. Substantially all the mortgage loans held for sale are insured or guaranteed by either Federal Government agencies or private mortgage insurance.

Mortgage banking revenues consist principally of the following:

loan origination fees, recorded as revenues upon the funding of residential loans and over the period of construction loans,

loan servicing revenues, based generally on a percentage of the outstanding principal balances of serviced mortgages, recorded as the installment collections on the mortgages are received,

gains and losses on sales of mortgage loans and related GNMA securities, including net commitment fees, recorded at the time of sale.

Depreciation and amortization of office equipment and installations are provided on the straight-line method. Office equipment is depreciated over useful lives of 0 to 00 years, while installations are amortized over the lesser of the economic useful life of the improvement or the term of the lease.

Excess of cost over fair value of net assets acquired is being amortized on a straight-line basis over 00 years. Such excess has been increased in 1980 and 1979 to reflect additional costs incurred, principally settlement of income tax assessments and litigation related to acquired companies.

Costs incurred in connection with the acquisition of contractual rights to service mortgage loans (not exceeding the present value of the future net servicing income) and in connection with the formation of certain GNMA securities for which the Company retains loan servicing rights are deferred and amortized by the sum-of-the-years digits method over the estimated average life of the related mortgages. Accumulated amortization relative to these deferred costs at June 30, 1980 amounted to $000,000.

Note 2—Acquisitions:

As of March 31, 1980, a wholly owned subsidiary of the Company agreed to acquire all the outstanding common stock of Mortgage Corporation (MC), a mortgage banker, for $00,000,000 in cash and the following Subordinated notes:

0% Senior Subordinated Convertible Notes ($000,000 matures on December 31, 1985 and $0,000,000 on June 30, 1986)	$0,000,000
0% Subordinated Note due January 31, 1981	0,000,000
	0,000,000

For accounting purposes, the acquisition, completed as of June 30, 1980 has been treated as a purchase, and accordingly, operating results of MC are included in the consolidated results of operations of the Company from the date of acquisition. The purchase cost was allocated to the fair value of the net assets acquired.

Had the acquisition occurred on July 1, 1978, pro forma results of operations of the Company for the years ended June 30, 1980 and 1979 would have been as follows:

	1980	1979
Revenues	$000,000,000	$000,000,000
Income before taxes on income	$ 00,000,000	$ 00,000,000
Net income	$ 00,000,000	$ 00,000,000
Earnings per share:		
Primary	$0.00	$0.00
Fully diluted	$0.00	$0.00

On August 26, 1978, the Company acquired the business and net assets of XYZ for the following shares of common and preferred stock:

	Number of Shares	Estimated Fair Value
Common stock	000,000	$0,000,000
Preferred stock, 0% cumulative convertible series	00,000	0,000,000
		$0,000,000

For accounting purposes, the acquisition has been treated as a purchase. Accordingly, the results of operations of XYZ are included in the consolidated results of the Company from the date of acquisition. The excess of the fair value of net assets acquired over cost (approximately $000,000 at June 30, 1980) has been allocated to XYZ office equipment and installations.

Note 3—Marketable Securities

Securities owned and securities sold but not yet purchased consist of the Company's firm trading and investment securities at quoted market values. These securities are summarized as follows:

	1980	1979
Owned:		
Certificates of Deposit	$ 00,000,000	$ 00,000,000
United States Government,		
State and Municipal Obligations	00,000,000	00,000,000
Corporate Bonds	00,000,000	0,000,000
Corporate Stocks and Options	00,000,000	00,000,000
	$000,000,000	$000,000,000
Sold but not yet purchased:		
United States Government,		
State and Municipal Obligations	$ 0,000,000	$ 00,000,000
Corporate Bonds	00,000,000	0,000,000
Corporate Stocks and Options	000,000,000	00,000,000
	$000,000,000	$000,000,000

Note 4—Short-Term Bank Loans

At June 30, 1980, short-term bank loans aggregating $00,000,000 are collateralized by securities owned by the Company or pledged by issuers of secured demand notes, and $00,000,000 is collateralized generally by mortgage loans held for sale and construction loans receivable. Additionally, $00,000,000 of the short-term bank loans are collateralized by customers' securities. The average interest rate was 00.0% at June 30, 1980 and 0.0% at June 30, 1979.

Note 5—Term Notes

Term notes at June 30, 1980 are summarized as follows:

Collateral	Amount	Maturity Date	Interest Rate
Common stock of MC	$00,000,000	1981-1987	00%*
Office equipment	0,000,000	1979-1983	0%
Office equipment and installations	0,000,000	1979-1983	**
Other	000,000	1980-2003	0%-0%
	$00,000,000		

*At 000.0% of the bank's prime rate after July 1, 1983.
**Bank prime rate plus 0% to 0%.

The notes mature as follows (fiscal year basis):

1981	$ 0,000,000
1982	0,000,000
1983	0,000,000
1984	0,000,000
1985 to 2003	0,000,000
	$00,000,000

Note 6—Secured Demand Obligations Subject to Preferred Stock Agreements

These obligations bear interest at 0% per annum, mature in 1985 and may be converted at the option of either the holder or the Company into shares of 0% Senior Preferred stock. Conversion would be effected by a cash payment by the holder of $000 for each share with a concomitant reduction in the obligation.

Note 7—Subordinated Indebtedness

Subordinated indebtedness outstanding consists of the following:

	Amount	Maturity Date	Interest Rate
Senior Subordinated Debt: (a)			
Term notes (b)	$00,000,000	1981-1985	*
Subordinated debentures	00,000,000	1988-2003	00%
Subordinated debentures	0,000,000	1981-1983	00% above prime
0% Convertible subordinated notes	0,000,000	1985-1986	0%

Subordinated Debt: (a)

Capital notes	000,000	1982	00%
Secured demand notes	000,000	1981-1983	0%
Junior subordinated debentures	0,000,000	1981-1983	00% above prime
Junior convertible subordinated notes	000,000	1985	0%
	$00,000,000		

*0% above prime on $00,000,000 and at 000% of the greater of prime or commercial paper rate but not less than 00% over such rates on $0,000,000.

(a) Holders of subordinated debt in the aggregate principal amount of $00,000,000 have the right to require prepayment of all or a portion of the indebtedness under certain circumstances.

(b) Among the covenants of the Senior subordinated term notes, the Company is required to maintain net capital at least equal to 0% of the customer-related assets as defined by the Uniform Net Capital Rule. (See Note 15.)

The Company must also make prepayments of future maturities of term notes in any year in which net income exceeds scheduled term note payments plus preferred stock dividends paid. The prepayment for fiscal 1980 ($0,000,000) is due September 30, 1980.

Note 8—Preferred and Common Stock

The Company is authorized to issue Senior Preferred stock (0,000,000 shares), Preferred stock (0,000,000 shares) and Junior Preferred stock (0,000,000 shares), each with a par value of $.00 per share.

Note 9—Stock Options and Warrants

Under the qualified stock option plans, certain officers and key employees may be granted options to purchase an aggregate of 000,000 shares of common stock at not less than the fair market value on the date of grant. Options become exercisable in cumulative increments of 00% of the total number of shares subject to the option beginning one year from the date of grant and expire five years thereafter. During fiscal 1979, options for 00,000 shares were granted at $00.00 per share and options for 00,000 shares were granted at $00.00 per share. In 1980 options to purchase 000,000 shares were exercised at prices ranging from $0.00 to $00.00 per share. Options to purchase an aggregate of 000,000 shares of common stock were outstanding at June 30, 1980 at prices ranging from $0.00 to

$00.00 per share. At June 30, 1980, options for 000,000 shares were exercisable and 000,000 shares were reserved for future grants.

Warrants to purchase 0,000 shares of common stock at $00.00 per share, expiring in 1982, were outstanding at June 30, 1980.

Note 10—Stock Purchase Plan

The Company established an Employee-Stock Purchase Plan under which 000,000 shares of common stock may be purchased by employees at 00% of the fair market value on designated quarterly investment dates. During 1980, 00,000 common shares were sold to employees.

Note 11—Retirement Plan

The company has adopted a noncontributory retirement plan to cover substantially all its employees exclusive of employees of MC. Pension expense was approximately $0,000,000 in 1980 and $0,000,000 in 1979. It is the policy of the Company to fund accrued pension costs. At January 1, 1980, the most recent actuarial valuation date, pension plan assets exceeded the actuarially computed value of vested benefits. There are no past service costs under the plan at June 30, 1980.

MC has a profit-sharing plan in which all its employees having at least one year's continuous service participate. Voluntary contributions are made at the sole discretion of its Board of Directors. Employee benefits vest at the rate of 00% at the end of the first full year of an employee's participation and at 00% per year thereafter.

Note 12—Dividend Restrictions

The Company's subordinated and long-term note agreements restrict the payment of dividends on the Company's stock. Dividends may be paid on common stock up to an amount equal to 00% of the average net income for the two previous fiscal years, provided that after such payments, the Company's net worth, as defined, would exceed specified minimums. At June 30, 1980, $0,000,000 of retained earnings is available for common stock dividends during the fiscal year 1981.

Note 13—Provision for Taxes on Income

The provision for taxes on income consists of federal, state and local taxes as follows:

	1980	1979
Federal:		
Currently payable	$00,000,000	$0,000,000
Deferred	(00,000)	0,000,000
State and local	0,000,000	0,000,000
Reduction in excess of cost over fair value of assets acquired		000,000
	$00,000,000	$0,000,000

The Company and its subsidiaries file a consolidated federal income tax return. The effective income tax rate differs from the normal federal income tax rate for the reasons shown below:

	1980	1979
Federal income tax at normal rate	00%	00%
State and local	0	0
Investment credit	(0)	(0)
Other, principally tax exempt interest and dividends taxed at an effective rate of 0%	(0)	(0)
Effective income tax rate	00%	00%

The principal items comprising the deferred tax provision (credit) are:

	1980	1979
Payment (provision) for settlement of litigation		$ 000,000
Unrealized trading and investment income	$000,000	000,000
Rental payments accrued prior to 1979	00,000	000,000
Deferred compensation reserves	(000,000)	(000,000)
Reserve for bad debts	(000,000)	
Pension deductions	00,000	000,000
Accelerated depreciation on computer	00,000	000,000
Other	(000,000)	000,000
	$(00,000)	$0,000,000

Note 14—Net Income per Share

Net income per share of common stock is based upon the weighted average number of common and common equivalent shares outstanding during each year.

Fully diluted earnings per share assumes conversion into common stock of convertible subordinated debt, secured demand obligations subject to preferred stock agreements and Senior and Junior Preferred stocks.

Note 15—Net Capital Requirements

As a broker-dealer and member of the Stock Exchange, the Company is subject to the Uniform Net Capital Rule adopted and administered by the Exchange and the Securities and Exchange Commission. The Company has elected to compute its net capital under the alternative method of the rule which requires the maintenance of minimum net capital equal to 0% of aggregate debit balances arising from customer transactions, as defined. The Exchange may also require a member firm to reduce its business if net capital is less than 0% of aggregate debit balances and may prohibit a member firm from expanding its business and declaring cash dividends if net capital is less than 0% of aggregate debit balances. In addition, the Company may not allow withdrawal of subordinated capital if its net capital is less than 0% of such debit balances.

Under the terms of subordinated debt agreements, the Company is also required to maintain net capital, as defined therein.

At June 30, 1980, the Company's net capital, as defined, including secured demand obligations subject to preferred stock agreements and subordinated debt, aggregated $00,000,000 and was $00,000,000 in excess of minimum net capital and $00,000,000 in excess of net capital required by the most restrictive debt agreement.

Note 16—Commitments

The Company leases office space under leases expiring at various dates to 2000. Rent expense for 1980 and 1979 was $00,000,000 and $00,000,000, respectively. Minimum future rental commitments under such leases, which are operating leases, are as follows (fiscal year basis):

1981	$ 0,000,000
1982	0,000,000
1983	0,000,000
1984	0,000,000
1985-1989	00,000,000
1990-1994	00,000,000
1995-1999	00,000,000

Certain leases on office space contain escalation clauses providing for increased rentals based upon maintenance, utility and tax increases.

Note 17—Outstanding Letters of Credit

At June 30, 1980, the Company is contingently liable for letters of credit aggregating $000,000,000 used to satisfy margin deposits at option and commodity exchanges.

Note 18—Litigation

In the normal course of its business, the Company has been named a defendant in a number of lawsuits. After considering all relevant facts and the opinions of outside counsel, in the opinion of the Company and its General Counsel, such litigation will not in the aggregate have a material adverse effect on the Company's financial condition.

Note 19—Segment Reporting

The Company is engaged primarily in providing investment services. Other businesses in which the Company is engaged represent less than 00% of consolidated assets, revenues and pretax income. Revenues and assets of foreign operations are also less than 00% of the related consolidated amounts.

PERSONAL FINANCIAL STATEMENTS

Overview

The generally accepted accounting principles (GAAP) and practices which have been promulgated for commercial enterprises are also used in reporting on personal financial statements. Personal financial statements may be presented for a single individual, a husband and wife, a family, or a group of related individuals.

The preferable accounting principles and practices for personal financial statements appear in the industry audit guide entitled "Audits of Personal Financial Statements" (hereinafter referred to as Personal Statement Guide.)

Preferable Accounting Principles

The Personal Statement Guide recommends that a personal financial report should contain a (1) statement of assets and liabilities, (2) statement of changes in net assets, and (3) informative disclosure notes to the financial statements.

All of the personal financial statements mentioned above should be presented with two columns, one reflecting cost basis and the other reflecting estimated value basis. Comparative statements are encouraged and should definitely contain a statement of changes in net assets for the latest two years.

The concept of working capital is not readily applicable to personal financial statements. Thus, assets and liabilities should not usually be classified into current and noncurrent. However, it may be desirable to list assets and liabilities in the order of their liquidity and/or maturity.

Cost basis column   This column should display the net carrying amount of an asset at the date of the financial statements.

> *OBSERVATION: The Personal Statement Guide is apparently incorrect in the case of marketable equity securities which*

should not be reported on a cost basis. FASB Interpretation-10 requires that personal financial statements prepared in conformity with GAAP must comply with FASB-12 (Accounting for Certain Marketable Equity Securities). Thus, marketable equity securities appearing on personal financial statements should be reported at the lower of cost or market. The current and noncurrent groupings are not required because a balance sheet is unclassified for personal financial statement purposes.

Estimated value basis column This column should display the estimated fair value of the assets and liabilities at the date of the financial statements.

Quoted market prices, appraisals, and reasonable estimates may be used to determine estimated fair values. However, large blocks of securities may significantly affect the quoted market price if sold or liquidated all at one time and this factor should be given consideration when determining estimated fair values. In addition, difficulties may be encountered in determining fair value of closely-held businesses. In those cases where an investment in a closely-held business represents a substantial portion of the total assets, supplementary information regarding assets, liabilities, and operating results of the closely-held business should be disclosed by footnote to the personal financial statements.

Income taxes The current income tax liability to the date of the financial statements should be disclosed in the cost basis column of the statement of assets and liabilities. Deferred income taxes, if applicable, should also be provided for in the cost basis column in accordance with existing promulgated GAAP (APB-11).

Accrued income taxes on the net unrealized appreciation of assets should be provided for in the estimated value basis column on the statement of assets and liabilities. Net unrealized appreciation is usually the difference between the tax basis and the estimated value basis of the assets.

The method and basis for computing each type of income tax liability should be appropriately disclosed in the personal financial statements.

The Personal Statement Guide recommends that estimated values not be presented in personal financial statements without the related cost basis information.

Personal effects   Personal effects, if material, are properly included in personal financial statements. Thus, jewelry, art, and other personal effects, if material, should be included in both the cost basis column and the estimated value basis column on the statement of assets and liabilities.

Future interests   The present value of future interest in pension plans, trusts, annuities, profit-sharing plans, and other future interests or rights should be included as an asset in the estimated value basis column in the statement of assets and liabilities. If no immediate or future right exists in the future interest, or if fair value is indeterminable, disclosure should be made by footnote of all of the pertinent facts of the future interest.

Statement of assets and liabilities   As mentioned previously, this statement should be presented with two columns to reflect both cost basis and estimated value basis. There should be no segregation of current and noncurrent assets or liabilities.

The Personal Statement Guide recommends that the caption "Excess of assets over liabilities" be used to reflect the equity in the net assets.

Statement of changes in net assets   This statement should be presented to reflect the increases and decreases in assets and liabilities and also include income and expense items. The two column presentation depicting both the cost basis and estimated value basis should also be used for the statement of changes in net assets. The statement should start with the net assets at the beginning of the year, and end with the amount of net assets at the end of the year, for both the cost basis and the estimated value basis.

Footnote disclosures   Footnote disclosures should be made for both the cost basis and estimated value basis. Cost basis footnote disclosure should be presented separately from the estimated value basis footnote disclosures.

Supplementary information and schedules should be used generously to detail or explain information appearing in the financial statements.

Comprehensive Illustration

The following is a comprehensive illustration of personal financial statements presented in accordance with the recommendations of the Personal Statement Guide.

Mr. & Mrs. American
Statement of Assets and Liabilities
December 31, 1979

ASSETS		*Cost Basis*	*Estimated Value Basis*
Cash		$ 25,000	$ 25,000
Marketable securities	(Note 1)	7,000	7,000
Cash value of family life insurance		5,000	5,000
Interest in net assets of USA Partnership	(Note 2)	80,500	136,167
Residence, pledged on mortgage note	(Note 3)	90,000	160,000
Automobile, pledged on note payable	(Note 3)	5,000	5,000
Investment in gold	(Note 3)	3,000	5,000
Contingent asset	(Note 5)	—	—
Total assets		$215,500	$343,167
LIABILITIES			
Accounts payable and accrued expenses		$ 500	$ 500
18% Note payable, secured by automobile (due June 1, 1981)		3,000	3,000
8¼ Mortgage, maturing in 1998 secured by residence. (annual amortization and interest $8,268)		68,305	68,305
Accrued income taxes payable, net of prepayment		10,000	10,000
Accrued income taxes on unrealized asset appreciation	(Note 4)	—	31,917
Total Liabilities		$ 81,805	$113,722
EXCESS OF ASSETS OVER LIABILITIES		$133,695	$229,445

The Notes to this Personal Financial Statement are an integral part of the statement.

Mr. & Mrs. American
Statement of Changes in Net Assets
For the Year Ended December 31, 1979

	Cost Basis	Estimated Value Basis
NET ASSETS, January 1, 1979	$131,995	$185,495
Add—Income and Other Increases in Net Assets:		
Dividends on Stock	500	500
Interest Income	2,000	2,000
Salary from USA Partnership	20,000	20,000
Drawing from USA Partnership	20,000	20,000
Income from Mrs. American part time job	3,000	3,000
Increase in Value Since January 1, 1979:		
Interest in net assets of USA Partnership	—	25,000
Residence	—	30,000
Investment in gold	—	2,000
TOTAL	$ 45,500	$102,500
Deduct—Expenses and Other Decreases in Net Assets:		
Interest Expense	$ 6,300	$ 6,300
Decrease in the value of the automobile	1,000	1,000
Income taxes	15,000	15,000
Real estate taxes	1,500	1,500
Personal expenditures	20,000	20,000
Provision for income taxes on unrealized asset appreciation	—	14,250
Decrease in value since January 1, 1979:		
Marketable Securities	—	500
TOTAL	$ 43,800	$ 58,550
NET ASSETS, December 31, 1979	$133,695	$229,445

The Notes to this Personal Financial Statement are an integral part of the statement.

NOTES TO PERSONAL FINANCIAL STATEMENTS

Note 1   Marketable Securities

Market Value Dec. 31, 1979
Stocks—Quoted Closing or Latest Bid Prices

Stock	Shares	Cost	Market	Unrealized Gain or loss
Marketable Securities Portfolio				
Security A	100	$1,000	$1,500	$ 500
Security B	200	4,000	3,500	(500)
Security C	150	3,000	2,000	(1,000)
Totals		$8,000	$7,000	$(1,000)

For the purposes of Personal Financial Statements, marketable equity securities must be carried at the lower of aggregate cost or aggregate market in the cost basis column. (FASB Interpretation 10). Since the Statement of Assets and Liabilities is unclassified, all marketable securities should be classified as noncurrent (FASB 12).

Note 2   Interest In Net Assets of USA Partnership

A summary statement of the net assets of the partnership as of December 3, 1979.

Current Assets	$ 45,000
Land, Building and Equipment	400,000
Other Assets	5,000
Total Assets	$450,000
Current Liabilities	$ 6,000
Deferred Items	2,500
Long Term Debt	200,000
Total Liabilities	$208,500
NET ASSETS	$241,500

One third Interest in Partnership $80,500

Income for the year ended December 31, 1979 amounted to $60,000. Drawings by Mr. American were $20,000.

A Certified Public Accountant has performed Compilation and Review Services for the USA Partnership.

Estimated Value of USA Partnership

According to the USA Partnership Agreement, a withdrawing partner is to be paid an amount equal to the average of three estimates (one by each partner) multiplied by his percentage share.

Estimates

$600,000
$650,000   Avg. $650,000 − 241,500 = $408,500
$700,000   408,500 × ⅓ = $136,166.67

Note 3   Valuation of Other Assets

   a) Residence estimated value based upon recent sales of similar assets in the same area—$160,000
   b) Automobile value based upon dealers book value—$5,000
   c) Gold value is based upon December 31, 1979 market price—$5,000

Note 4   Accrued Income Taxes for Unrealized Appreciation

Accrual is made according to 1979 Federal Income Tax Capital Gain rates.

Note 5   Contingent Asset

Mr. American has a future interest of 5% of the net income over $100,000 in the XYZ Partnership in 1980. At the present time, this value is not determinable.

EMPLOYEE HEALTH AND WELFARE BENEFIT FUNDS

Overview

The preferable accounting principles and practices for employee health and welfare benefit funds appear in the industry audit guide entitled "Audits of Employee Health and Welfare Benefit Funds" (hereinafter referred to as the Employee H&W Guide).

Generally accepted accounting principles (GAAP) and practices that have been promulgated for commercial enterprises are also used in reporting on employee health and welfare benefit funds. The Employee H&W Guide discusses the application of GAAP as they apply to employee health and welfare benefit funds.

Employee health and welfare benefit funds are generally exempt from federal income taxes. However, such funds are required to file an annual information return with the Internal Revenue. In addition, employee health and welfare benefit funds are required by the 1958 Welfare and Pension Plans Disclosure Act to file certain information with the U.S. Department of Labor. The information that is required to be filed is:

1. a description of the initial plan
2. a description of any subsequent plan amendment
3. annual financial and nonfinancial information covering the plan's activities for the year

An employee health and welfare benefit fund can be established for many purposes. The most common types of plans are:

1. Health plans including medical expenses, dental expenses, medicines, major medical insurance, life insurance and accidental death insurance.
2. All types of disability plans which provide for benefits during periods of disability.

3. Vacation plans which accumulate vacation pay for its members.
4. Education plans which provide for payments for seminars, classes and other types of educational benefits.

Great care must be exercised in drafting the various provisions of an employee health and welfare benefit plan. The type of plan and its benefits must be clearly stated, as well as the amount and qualifications necessary to receive benefits.

A contributory plan is one in which the employee is required to pay certain amounts, while a noncontributory plan is usually funded entirely by the employer. A plan may be comprised of employees from one or more employers. Contributions may be required under collective bargaining contracts or may be entirely voluntary. Benefits may be paid out of the fund itself, a trust fund, or provided for by insurance policies purchased by the fund. Each employee health and welfare benefit fund is usually a separate legal and tax entity governed by a board of trustees.

An equal number of union and employer representatives usually make up the board of trustees of an employee health and welfare benefit fund which is established by a collective bargaining contract.

The board of trustees may set up operational guidelines for the fund based on the trust indenture, collective bargaining contract, or other legal document which has established the fund. The board has the responsibilities for the operation of the fund, but frequently retains a professional administrator to handle the day-to-day operations. However, insurance carriers, financial institutions or independent administrators under contract are sometimes engaged to run the every day affairs of the employee health and welfare benefit fund. It is appropriate for the board of trustees to expressly authorize any administrative fees. Administrative fees are usually based on a percentage of the average amount in the fund, on fees collected, or claims paid, or on a specified fee per member. Although the basic accounting principles and practices of an employee health and welfare benefit fund are the same as those used for commercial enterprises, certain special records must be maintained. The most important of these special records are as follows:

Contribution Records of Employers   Records of the contributions paid by employers must be separately maintained to detect correct payments and delinquencies. In addition, these records are necessary to prepare periodic contribution reports.

Contributions Records of Employees Records must be kept of the contributions paid by employees in contributory plans. These records are necessary to locate delinquencies and to determine whether correct payments have been made. If a self-payment plan is in effect for unemployed employees, records must be separately maintained to control such payments.

Eligibility Records for Plan Members Records must be maintained to indicate eligible and ineligible plan members in accordance with the specific eligibility requirements of the plan. Separate records must be kept for each plan member.

Claim Payment Records Records for claims paid must be kept for the current period and also on a cumulative basis. Cumulative records are necessary to determine whether any benefit limits have been reached.

Preferable Accounting Principles

The Employee H&W Guide expressly recommends the application of certain specialized accounting principles which are discussed in this section.

Accrual basis accounting Employee health and welfare benefit funds are required by the Employee H&W Guide to present financial statements on the accrual basis of accounting. The cash or modified cash basis of accounting are considered unacceptable for the presentation of financial statements that purport to be in conformity with GAAP.

Accounting changes As a result of its mandate of the accrual basis of accounting, the Employee H&W Guide recommends that this change in accounting principle be recognized by retroactively applying the accrual method and to restate the financial statements of prior periods which are presented. The Employee H&W Guide states that reference to paragraphs 27 and 28 of APB-20 should be made for a description of how to report an accounting change by retroactively restating the financial statements of prior periods.

In addition, the Employee H&W Guide states that revisions of estimates which are required in subsequent periods should be accounted for prospectively in accordance with APB-20 (Accounting Changes).

> *OBSERVATION:* *The Employee H&W Guide is apparently incorrect in its reference to paragraphs 27 and 28 of APB-20. These paragraphs refer to three of the four exceptions to the general rule that financial statements should not be restated for a change in accounting principle. The general rule is that a change in accounting principle should be accounted for by including the "cumulative effects" of the change in net income of the period of the change and not by restating financial statements of prior periods. The four exceptions to this general rule which require restatement of prior period financial statements are:*
>
> *a.   change from LIFO method of inventory pricing to another method*
>
> *b.   change in accounting for long-term construction-type contracts*
>
> *c.   change to or from the "full cost" method of accounting in the extractive industries*
>
> *d.   one-time change for closely held corporations in connection with a public offering of its securities or when such a company first issues financial statements (1) for obtaining additional equity capital from investors, (2) for effecting a business combination, or (3) for registering securities.*

Investments   Cost should be the basis of all investments except marketable securities. Gain or loss on an investment should be accounted for in the year of sale or exchange.

The Employee H&W Guide states that accounting for marketable securities is currently under study by the Accounting Principles Board, and future pronouncements may have an affect on the accounting of marketable securities by employee health and welfare benefit funds.

> *OBSERVATION:* *The 49 page "Audit of Employee Health and Welfare Benefit Funds" was published by the AICPA in 1972, and apparently has not been updated or revised since that date.*

In December 1975, the FASB promulgated FASB-12 (Accounting for Certain Marketable Securities). FASB-12 expressly does not cover nonprofit organizations, but does apply to profit making enterprises. However, SOP 78-1 (Hospital Audit Guide) generally requires that nonprofit hospitals comply with FASB-12, in spite of the fact that FASB-12 expressly does not cover nonprofit organizations. To add further confusion to this situation, SOP 78-10 (Accounting Principles and Reporting Practices for Certain Nonprofit Organizations) recommends still another method to value a portfolio of marketable equity securities. That method is market value even if market value exceeds cost!

Contributions receivable At any given balance sheet date, an employee health and welfare benefit fund may have contributions due from employers. Contributions due should be appropriately reported on the financial statements as receivables. If exact amounts are unknown, reasonable estimates should be used. In addition, an allowance for uncollectibles should also be set up, if appropriate.

Premium deposits Until applied against future premiums or refunded, premium deposits to insurance companies are assets of the employee health and welfare benefit fund, and should be reported as such on the financial statements.

Experience rating adjustments Some insurance group contracts provide for a refund or a deficiency based upon the excess of premiums collected over claims paid. These experience rating adjustments are not completed until after the end of the policy year. Thus, it becomes necessary for an employee health and welfare benefit fund to estimate the amount of the experience rating adjustment for reporting purposes at the balance sheet date. If the amount of an experience rating adjustment is unknown, reasonable estimates must be made based upon available information.

Property and equipment Property and equipment should be recorded at cost and depreciated or amortized in a systematic and rational manner, over the estimated useful lives of the assets.

GAAP should be used in disclosing information about property and equipment in the financial statements. Thus, the following minimum disclosures should be made:

1. depreciation expense for the period
2. balances of major classes of depreciable assets by nature or function
3. accumulated depreciation allowances by classes or in total
4. the methods used, by major classes, in computing depreciation

> **OBSERVATION:** *Promulgated GAAP (APB-12) requires that the above disclosures be made in the financial statements or in footnotes. In addition, the effect of a change from one depreciation method to another must be disclosed (APB-20).*

Claims   In a self-insured employee health and welfare benefit fund, any liability for claims reported but not paid, and an estimate of claims incurred but not reported, should be included in the financial statements. However, an insured employee health and welfare benefit fund does not have to report such claims as liabilities because they are usually the liability of, and paid by, the insurance company.

Insurance premiums   Insured employee health and welfare benefit funds usually contract with an insurance company to provide the necessary coverage for employee benefits. Group insurance contracts which provide specific employee benefits are generally written for a period of one year. The insurance contract should disclose the type of benefits covered, rules for eligibility, and a schedule of the benefits payable. Premiums due to insurance carriers which are unpaid at the balance sheet date should be accrued as a liability and reported as such in the financial statements.

Accumulated eligibility credits   Some employee health and welfare benefit funds have eligibility rules which provide for continual coverage in the event a participant becomes unemployed or if an employer's contributions are insufficient. Eligibility credits are accumulated over a specified period of time for each participant. In the event a participant becomes unemployed, or the employer's contributions are insufficient, the employee health and welfare benefit fund makes the payment for insurance coverage, or pays the benefits to the employee. Thus, an eligible participant does not lose his or her insurance coverage or benefits during periods of unemployment or when the employer's contributions are inadequate. Accumulated eligibility credits are based on prior employer's contributions and thus represent a liability of the employee health and welfare benefit fund. The liability for accumulated eligibility credits should be determined under current eligibility rules and should be reflected in the financial statements. The Employee H&W Guide states that accumulated eligibility credits are a liability and should not be reported as a segregation of the fund equity balance. Changes in the amounts of accumulated eligibility credits from one period to another should be charged or credited to operations.

Fund balance   The difference between the assets and liabilities of a fund is the fund equity balance. If the liabilities exceed the assets, a deficit fund balance exists. Restrictions on fund balances should be fully disclosed in the financial statements. Changes in a fund balance should consist only of results of operations for the current period and prior period adjustments.

Other financial statement disclosures   Besides the disclosures discussed in this chapter, the following additional disclosures should be made for an employee health and welfare benefit fund:

1. A footnote describing the activities of the fund and any significant changes.
2. A footnote disclosing the income tax status of the fund.
3. All other significant matters should be disclosed in accordance with existing GAAP.

EMPLOYEE STOCK OWNERSHIP PLANS (ESOP)

Overview

The preferable accounting principles and practices relating to certain employee stock ownership plans (ESOP) appears in SOP 76-3, entitled "Accounting Practices for Certain Employer Stock Ownership Plans".

An ESOP is usually a qualified stock bonus plan as defined by the Employee Retirement Income Security Act of 1974 (ERISA). A qualified stock bonus plan and money purchase pension plan are established to purchase the "qualifying employer's securities" as defined by ERISA. In most instances, existing law permits an ESOP to incur debt in order to acquire the "qualifying employer's securities." In addition, the qualifying employer may be allowed to increase its maximum investment tax credit up to one and a half percent more, providing the amount is contributed to an ESOP. Thus, an ESOP may incur liabilities to acquire the employer's stock and the employer will usually be allowed an extra 1½% of investment tax credit if the 1½% is contributed to the ESOP.

An ESOP usually borrows funds from a bank to acquire the qualifying employer's stock, and the bank loan is usually guaranteed by the employer, or the employer contractually agrees that future contributions to the ESOP will be enough to cover the obligation to the bank. In addition, the bank usually holds as collateral for the loan, a pledge from the employer to issue the stock to the ESOP.

Preferable Accounting Principles

Subject to certain limitations by the Internal Revenue Code, the employer's annual contributions to the ESOP are deductible. The ESOP uses the annual cash contributions and cash dividends, if any, on the employer's stock to pay the principle and interest on the bank loan and to pay its operating expenses. If excess funds are available, the ESOP will usually either invest in short-term investments or purchase additional shares of the employer's stock.

SOP 76-3 requires that the employer report a liability in its financial statements for the obligation of the ESOP when the obligation is guaranteed in any manner by the employer company. The journal entry required by SOP 76-3 is similar to the one required for unearned compensation in employee stock options (APB-25) as follows:

Stockholder's equity	$X,XXX	
Liability		$X,XXX

Thus, stockholder's equity is reduced by the amount of the obligation of the ESOP. The employer company then increases stockholder's equity and decreases the liability when the obligation is paid by the ESOP. Thus, the ESOP's liability reported on the financial statements of the employer company is only reduced as the ESOP pays the obligation.

The employer's compensation expense for a period is the amount paid or committed to be paid to the ESOP during that period. However, SOP 76-3 requires that this compensation expense for the period, be broken-down into compensation expense and interest expense incurred on the ESOP's obligation. Thus, the employer must report separately the compensation portion and the interest portion of the annual contribution paid or committed to be paid for the period. The terms of the ESOP's obligation, including interest rates, must be disclosed in the employer's financial statements or footnotes thereto.

SOP 76-13 requires that all shares of the employer which are held by the ESOP should be treated as outstanding shares of the employer company. Thus, the determination of EPS of the employer company must include all outstanding shares held by the ESOP. Under no circumstances, should dividends on the shares held by the ESOP be treated as compensation expense by the employer company.

The additional 1½% of investment tax credit should be treated by the employer company as a reduction of income tax expense in the same period in which the 1½% is contributed to the ESOP.

As defined by the Internal Revenue Code, excess contributions by an employer company to an ESOP may be carried forward for tax purposes. Thus, a timing difference may arise which should be accounted for in accordance with existing GAAP (APB-11).

PREFERABLE ACCOUNTING PRINCIPLES

TOPICAL INDEX